A HISTORY OF
Kane County

A HISTORY OF

Kane
County

Martha Sonntag Bradley

1999
Utah State Historical Society
Kane County Commission

ISBN 0-913738-40-9
Library of Congress Catalog Card Number 98-61327
Map by Automated Geographic Reference Center—State of Utah
Printed in the United States of America

Utah State Historical Society
300 Rio Grande
Salt Lake City, Utah 84101-1182

Contents

Acknowledgments

I grew up with tales of John Mangum and his plural wives Martha and Elizabeth and the rough terrain and huge brilliant skies of Kane County. My grandmother wove stories far more entrancing than fairy-tales of the Mormon pioneers—of traveling bundled under heavy piles of quilts in winter storms in the wagon bed of a buckboard, of learning to midwife babies from her mother and aunts, and of how to be strong, pragmatic, and brave. How could I not be a historian, with years of Kane County's stories woven into my head like ribbons in my braids?

When the county history project was first announced, I was greedy for it. What better way to know a place well than to research and write of it? In many ways, this process has been like completing a degree in Utah history; the state's history becomes local in Kane County. The Depression, the Spanish Flu epidemic, shifts in economic trends impacted real people with faces I now recognize. Many have become friends. I acknowledge their part in this project.

Numerous pioneer and other historical narratives illumine this book, as do issues of the *Kane County Standard*. The oral history project of Kane County High School under the direction of Carol

Sullivan was important in bringing present voices into the story. Members of the Kane County History Society, in particular Beth Martin, Jo Smith, Deanne Glover, Dennis Judd, Anna Johnson, and Kane County Clerk Karla Johnson, extended vital assistance, providing materials, names, and encouragement. Allan Kent Powell and Craig Fuller of the Utah State Historical Society have been the most patient men imaginable, untiring in their encouragement and invaluable in their expertise. I have appreciated their help more than they know. The excellent and tireless research of David Hampshire and others helped me complete this manuscript.

My six children are my own Vermilion Cliffs—they kept my course steady and true, as the cliffs did for early travelers. Jason, Elizabeth, Rachael, Emily, Katelyn, and Patrick, and now grandchildren Mark and Aspen seem to believe in me, and that trust carries me to a higher plane. I am a better person for my association with them.

I owe a debt of gratitude to five other individuals who made particular contributions to the project. Elizabeth Bradley's and Mark Wilson's beautiful writing and sensitivity to the subtleties of the desert landscape strengthened the chapter on the land. Allen D. Roberts's knowledge of rural Utah's buildings helped create a richer sense of the backdrop of this story. Michael W. Homer's sharing of European travel accounts to Kane County provided a unique twist to the exploration tales of this history. Fred Esplin, whose families helped settle this area, provided colorful photographs that gave real faces to the players in this narrative. I thank Richard Firmage for his work in editing, ordering, and amplifying the material I collected.

The county commissioners are men and women who have introduced me to the county's grand scenery and have tied me to it. The Paria, the Vermilion Cliffs, Zion Canyon form the backdrop for this story and in many ways my dreams of my own people—of raspy John Mangum and my splendid grandmother Vinnie Mae Mangum Graff. She loved this place and now so do I.

Finally, during the writing of this book I lost both my parents—Luonna Graff and George Tadje Sonntag—as well as two of my mentors and friends, Delmont Oswald and Lowell Durham. Each expected much of me, and I hope they would be satisfied with the results of my efforts. I celebrate their valuable contributions to my life.

General Introduction

When Utah was granted statehood on 4 January 1896, twenty-seven counties comprised the nation's new forty-fifth state. Subsequently two counties, Duchesne in 1914 and Daggett in 1917, were created. These twenty-nine counties have been the stage on which much of the history of Utah has been played.

Recognizing the importance of Utah's counties, the Utah State Legislature established in 1991 a Centennial History Project to write and publish county histories as part of Utah's statehood centennial commemoration. The Division of State History was given the assignment to administer the project. The county commissioners, or their designees, were responsible for selecting the author or authors for their individual histories, and funds were provided by the state legislature to cover most research and writing costs as well as to provide each public school and library with a copy of each history. Writers worked under general guidelines provided by the Division of State History and in cooperation with county history committees. The counties also established a Utah Centennial County History Council to help develop policies for distribution of state-appropriated funds and plans for publication.

Each volume in the series reflects the scholarship and interpretation of the individual author. The general guidelines provided by the Utah State Legislature included coverage of five broad themes encompassing the economic, religious, educational, social, and political history of the county. Authors were encouraged to cover a vast period of time stretching from geologic and prehistoric times to the present. Since Utah's statehood centennial celebration falls just four years before the arrival of the twenty-first century, authors were encouraged to give particular attention to the history of their respective counties during the twentieth century.

Still, each history is at best a brief synopsis of what has transpired within the political boundaries of each county. No history can do justice to every theme or event or individual that is part of an area's past. Readers are asked to consider these volumes as an introduction to the history of the county, for it is expected that other researchers and writers will extend beyond the limits of time, space, and detail imposed on this volume to add to the wealth of knowledge about the county and its people. In understanding the history of our counties, we come to understand better the history of our state, our nation, our world, and ourselves.

In addition to the authors, local history committee members, and county commissioners, who deserve praise for their outstanding efforts and important contributions, special recognition is given to Joseph Francis, chairman of the Morgan County Historical Society, for his role in conceiving the idea of the centennial county history project and for his energetic efforts in working with the Utah State Legislature and State of Utah officials to make the project a reality. Mr. Francis is proof that one person does make a difference.

ALLAN KENT POWELL
CRAIG FULLER
GENERAL EDITORS

KANE COUNTY

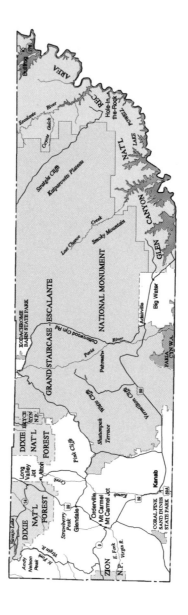

INDEX MAP

CHAPTER 1

Introduction

KANE COUNTY
AND A SENSE OF PLACE

Kane County is part of the great Colorado Plateau and is located on the southern boundary of the state of Utah between San Juan and Washington Counties, separated to the east from San Juan County by the Colorado River. To the north, the county is bordered by Garfield and Iron Counties. To the south is the Arizona Strip country of northern Arizona. One of the largest counties in the state, with some 3,904 square miles, or approximately 2.5 million acres, Kane County's boundaries have varied over time, influenced by the ruggedness of the land and the general sparse population of the region.[1]

While on a visit to Kane County in 1942, Wallace Stegner voiced his response to the area's beauty:

> The tiny oases huddle in their pockets in the rock, surrounded on all sides by as terrible and beautiful wasteland as the world can show, colored every color of the spectrum even to blue and green, sculptured by sandblast winds, fretted by meandering lines of cliffs hundreds of miles long and often several thousand feet high, carved and broken and split by canyons so deep and narrow that

1

the rivers run in sunless depths and cannot be approached for
miles. Man is an interloper in that country.[2]

Levi Savage, one of the first settlers to visit the area, first came to
future Kane County in 1860 with a flock of sheep. There he found
grass knee high stretching across the valley to Kanab Creek and moving like waves with the wind. It seemed that everywhere the valley
was carpeted with a sea of grass. A small stream of water ran from the
canyon north of the future townsite of Kanab to the southern side of
the valley. It ran through a thick growth of grass and willows,
although during the hot summer months it dried up altogether.

Three themes dominate the story of the settlement of Kane
County—the interaction of human beings with the landscape, the
interaction of human beings with each other, and the interaction of
greater manmade institutions. Here everything seems to appear in
extremes, especially the rugged plateaus of canyon country—raw,
exposed, thirsty land that seemingly defied settlement. Bands of
Navajo Indians threatened the security of more peaceful Paiutes, who
for security even lodged for a short period in forts with the settlers.
White settlement of the land was interrupted by its earlier inhabitants, forces beyond the control of the determined first generation of
pioneers. Later, the land itself and discouragement provided continual deterrents to settlement.

Human interaction with the land is always expressive of a certain
attitude or point of view. Here, the land is clearly in charge. The land
is forbidding, the weather sometimes violent and extreme. The environment and surroundings speak to centuries of changing geological conditions, climate, and history. The story of settlers who
struggled to survive in such a harsh region is often dramatic, but it is
always a story of fighters—those unwilling to leave and go to an eas-
ier place to survive.

The multicolored striations of the rock faces of Kane County's
canyon walls provide an apt image of the historical experience of this
place, layered with traces of previous generations' lives, and their
struggles to earn livings, raise families, build businesses, and participate in community life. It is what might be called the vernacular
landscape. The vernacular landscape is formed through the interplay

of natural places, cultural geography, and the manmade "built" environment. At its best, it is social history, or "history from the bottom up"—the history of common people interacting with the environment around them. At the intersection of these three elements lies the history of the cultural landscape—the production of spaces for shelter, for business, for recreation—human patterns impressed on the contours of the natural environment.

In some ways, the imprint of Kane County's inhabitants on the land around them is like a faint fingerprint on a window. It is a testimony to the strength and endurance of the pioneers, independent and hardy individuals. The county's history is in important ways the story of how this place was planned, designed, built, inhabited, appropriated, celebrated, and, sometimes, abused. Cultural identity, social history, and the building tradition are woven together here. The story of how different people lived in and used the natural world is fundamental to this narrative.

The earliest pioneer settlers of Kane County were called to the task by Brigham Young, leader of the Church of Jesus Christ of Latter-day Saints, more commonly known as the LDS or Mormon church. They were a hardy bunch—frontiersmen and missionaries, families usually with several children and sometimes several wives. In the late 1860s they began to build a fort where Kanab would eventually be located but were discouraged in their efforts at settlement by attacks from local Indians. In the 1870s the returning settlers were joined by a small group of farmers who earlier had made their homes in the Cottonwood area of the Salt Lake Valley. A third group soon joined them. The members of this last group had already lived in a difficult place—the LDS Muddy Mission in Nevada's Moapa Valley. They left Nevada because of what they considered excessive taxation and were advised by Brigham Young to resettle in Kane County. Primarily a group of farmers, because of their difficult experience in the Muddy Mission, they were up to the challenges the area presented.

Patterning their efforts on Mormon models throughout the settlement corridor, particularly in neighboring Washington County, the settlers attempted to organize field agriculture by planting hay, grain, row crops, and orchards. One Kanab woman, Rebecca Howell

Mace, put it this way, "These southern settlements were a sort of an experiment station, planted by Pres. B. Young with people from the southern states to demonstrate whether cotton, tobacco and other products of the south could be produced in southern Utah."[3]

The settlers were quick to find that farming was very difficult in the desert lands, where water was scarce and unpredictable. Some left, discouraged by repeated failures and privations; however, those who stayed and adapted to the environment found other ways of making a living. This adaptability became a common theme in the county's history.

A sense of place was formed by the native inhabitants as well as by colonizers, by housewives as well as mayors, by cowboys and by waitresses in restaurants. Each helped shape the landscape, both cultural and physical. Change over time can be traced in the ways that the sense of place and the space was modified over time. A sense of place is the way individuals and groups of individuals perceive the place they inhabit. It is, in a way, the personality a place takes on—the way it functions for people as the backdrop of their lives. Common phrases like "knowing one's place" or a "woman's place" imply political and even hierarchical meanings. We become attached to the places in which we live, our places become critical to our well being. Attachment to place takes on social, material, and ideological dimensions as people form ties to kin and community, as they purchase property or invest in land, as they devote time to community service.

An important theme of this history of Kane County is the attempt to identify the essential character of this place and how it has been formed by individuals engaged in economic production and social reproduction. In some places towns grew, inhabited by waves of settlers. These towns began with farming, ranching, lumber, or trading activities, rather than with manufacturing. Farm laborers, miners, cattlemen, or small business owners became the earliest builders of the economic enterprises that defined the place. The area was shaped for both economic and social purposes. The ways towns were laid out in regular grid patterns and the settlement of towns rather than isolated farmsteads reflected the traditional Mormon village settlement pattern and illuminated the settlers' ideological

On top of the East Rim Trail—Zion National Park. (Utah State Historical Society)

makeup, what they valued and of what they dreamed. As the country grew, configurations of streets and lots formalized the earliest uses of the land. This pattern of settlement evolved into an infrastructure of paved roads, bridges, water systems, and towns—all of which had substantial environmental effects.

Each technological and economic development brought with it a social and technological history. People promoted roads or campaigned against land-use polices as the development of the physical environment impacted their lives. An important part of the county's history is the examination of power struggles as they appear in the public record and as they are exhibited in the planning, design, construction, and use of the environment and natural resources. Each situation can be understood in terms of power and authority—as efforts to assume, extend, resist, accommodate, or even conquer. The intensity and scale of this exchange has increased during the second half of the twentieth century and represents for the people of Kane

County a classic confrontation between quintessential American values—individualism versus cooperation, federal power versus local power, private versus public.

Another useful concept in the examination of Kane County's history over time is the notion of "place memory," defined by one sociologist "the stabilizing persistence of place as a container of experiences that contributes so powerfully to its intrinsic memorability. An alert and alive memory connects spontaneously with place, finding in it features that favor and parallel its own activities. We might even say that memory is naturally place-oriented or at least place-supported."[4] Place memory suggests that human beings connect the built and natural environments, and entwine them into the cultural landscape. This explains in part the power of historic places to help citizens define their public pasts; places trigger memories for insiders, define the line between those inside and those out, who shares a common past and who does not. At the same time, places often can represent a sense of the past that draws outsiders in.

In Kane County a sense of the past is present. Besides the numerous historic buildings that line Kanab's streets or that are found in Long Valley, for example, it would be impossible for most people to spend any length of time in the county without pondering the significance of the efforts of the initial generation who first worked the fields, diverted the water, and endured the summer heat in makeshift shelters. The landscape stimulates such thoughts.

Much of Kane County is not readily accessible. Isolated from the more populated sections of the state, off railroad or major transportation and shipping routes, it is a place apart, defined in part by its beautiful rugged landscape. In some ways, the area's isolation and the way the canyons contain the valleys created ideal situations for stock raising, which has always been important to the cultural and economic life of the area. One article written in 1935 described it this way:

> Shut in on the north by the great continental divide of the Rocky
> mountains where snow fell so deep during most winters that vehi-
> cles could not pass over its summit, bordered on the south by the
> Kaibab plateau and the great Colorado river gorge, with the only

A traveler on his way from Panguitch to Kanab in 1907. (Utah State Historical Society)

crossing at Lees Ferry, 97 miles distant, it is easily the most inaccessible place in the United States.[5]

Kane County has always been on the periphery of the main areas of settlement. Isolated geographically, this remote region has had to provide different answers to questions of survival. This has been a place apart, which has become an important part of the way place here is defined. This distinctiveness is part of the area's attraction to outsiders—the county's canyons and river gorges invite those seeking adventure and relief from the chaotic pace of the modern world.

The seven towns and other areas of Kane County are presently served by one primary roadway, U.S. Highway 89, and a few state roads: Utah Highway 9, which runs westerly from Mount Carmel to Interstate 15; Utah 11, which heads south from Kanab into Arizona; and Utah 14, which traverses a westerly course from Long Valley Junction to Cedar City in Iron County. Kane County also features many miles of graded but unpaved roads and trails; but there are relatively few paved roads due to the sparseness of the population. In addition to those mentioned, paved roads include the road north of U.S. 89 into Johnson Canyon; a road into Yellowstone Canyon leading to Coral Pink Sand Dunes State Park; a short stretch of road to Alton and beyond toward the Alton Amphitheater, and another short stretch around the recreation area at Navajo Lake and Duck Creek.

Some of the important graded roads include an old route that goes from Hole-in-the-Rock on upper Lake Powell northwesterly to Escalante; a jeep trail that is north of U.S. 89 accessing Cottonwood Canyon, Grosvenor Arch, Kodachrome Basin, and eventually Cannonville; the extensions of the Johnson Canyon Road, which splits near Black Rock Peak, with the west fork leading to Glendale and the east fork traversing the Pink Cliffs and up to Cannonville. There is also a partly paved roadway connecting Scenic Byway 9 on the south to Utah 14 on the north, providing access to hiking and camping destinations in the area.

U.S. Highway 89 itself runs the length of the state, proceeding through every town in Kane County except Alton, which lies about three miles to its east, including Big Water near Lake Powell. As one travels along it moving south-southwesterly past the northern Kane County line, it takes a southeasterly turn just south of Mount Carmel and continues until it reaches Kanab. Highway 89 exits the county seat in an easterly direction past Johnson Canyon and Crescent Butte before veering northeasterly across Telegraph Flat and the Paria River Valley. The road then heads southward through Five Mile Valley and then runs in an easterly direction past the former Adairville, across East Clark Bench, and into Big Water. From there Highway 89 heads southeasterly past the western end of Wahweep Bay at Lake Powell before crossing over into Arizona. Thus Highway 89 is important for its role both in intrastate and interstate travel and commerce and as the county's primary transportation link between communities.

Today, the area's economy is based on tourism, trade, services, and government. What manufacturing is done locally has been based on the extraction of natural resources: timber from the Kaibab Forest, coal from the Kaiparowits Plateau fields, various minerals

Glen Canyon. (Utah State Historical Society)

from small mines in the area. For a period in the 1920s, debate raged over the future of Arizona Strip land south of Kane County, and it was uncertain if it would be best served by Arizona or Utah government. This controversy highlighted the relative isolation of the region.

International visitors to Kane County speak of this place as a hub of some of the world's most beautiful and scenic natural wonders—the Grand Canyon, Kaibab National Forest, Zion National Park, and Bryce Canyon National Park, among others. Writers have found their inspiration for stories here; for example, *The Last of the Plainsman* and *Riders of the Purple Sage* by western writer Zane Grey featured the enchanting landscape and folklore of the pioneer settlers.

In 1967 a Bureau of Land Management publication described Kane County as a virtual wonderland for outdoor adventure:

> Vermillion Cliffs . . . Coral Pink Sand Dunes . . . Kodachrome Flats . . . White Cliffs . . . Pink Cliffs—these names of geologic features in south central Utah give a clue to the area's principal characteristic: color. This is "red rock" country, with a spectacular view of eroded, highly colored landscape at almost every bend in the road. This is wilderness—not densely forested and green, but stark, expansive and uninhabited.[6]

In 1993 a group of Kanab High School students asked area old-timers what they thought had changed most about Kane County. Many of those interviewed had seen incredible technological changes in their lifetimes, changes that for the most part had impacted the county fairly dramatically. According to one resident: "The good changes have been paved roads, reliable cars for transportation, television, electricity, and refrigeration. When I was young, travel was mostly with horses and wagons. There were few cars. Today it's a whole different story."[7]

Lester Y. Johnson watched with wonder as the county changed. He remembered the first curbs and gutters, the motels and cafes that were built to service the motion picture industry, and the number of tourists increasing from hundreds to thousands. Calvin Johnson remembered a time when everyone knew everyone else in town and people were willing to help when others were in need. "If you had to harvest your wheat, you didn't have to hire someone you had the guys there to help," he claimed.[8] Emma Swapp Mulliner said that the biggest change for her was "opening up the dead end street on her block."[9] This final comment is particularly telling. For most of us, history—the story of change—is local. What impacts our own lives or the lives of our families is what is most important and most significant to us. Emma Mulliner felt the impact of local growth and development in a very personal way. The place in which her history played out was defined by neighborhood, by a network of family and friends, and by her town. Her sense of belonging to a place started at home and ended not very far from there.

There is a rich community history that comes from the people who inhabited this place, dozens of diaries, journals, and other sources are excerpted in the two Daughter of Utah Pioneers histories of Kane County. Others, handed down through the generations, have remained in family hands and speak to the heritage of resourcefulness and hard work.

It is telling how differently institutions, individuals and communities describe their sense of the place they inhabit. But it is a sense that is forged over time and space through the interaction of people, organizations, and agencies. It is as elusive as a rainbow, but there right in front of us begging to be understood.

I hope this history will continue the process of pulling back the layers of the past, revealing a sense of place both past and future. It is well to consider the words of Frederick Jackson Turner: "Each age writes the history of the past anew with references to the conditions uppermost in its own time. . . . The aim of history, then, is to know the elements of the present by understanding what came into the present from the past. For the present is simply the undeveloping past, the past the undeveloped present."[10] The basic purpose of history, it seems, is not to arrest time but to mediate sensitively with the forces of change. It is to understand the present as a product of the past and a modifier of the future, an understanding of the dynamic, continuous flow of human experience.

Endnotes

1. Allan Kent Powell, ed., *Utah History Encyclopedia* (Salt Lake City: University of Utah Press, 1994), 296.

2. Wallace Stegner, *Mormon Country* (New York: Hawthorne Books, 1942), 45.

3. Rebecca Howell Mace, journal, 70, Archives of the Chruch of Jesus Christ of Latter-day Saints, Salt Lake City; hereafter cited as LDS Archives.

4. Edward S. Casey, *Remembering: A Phenomenological Study* (Bloomington: University of Indiana Press, 1987), 186–87.

5. *Deseret News,* 19 December 1935.

6. "South Central Utah," U.S. Bureau of Land Management, 1967, 36.

7. Allen M. Cox, interview with Jennifer Barnhurst, 29 April 1993, Kanab, Utah.

8. Calvin Johnson, interview with Martha Bradley, 13 July 1995, Kanab, Utah.

9. Emma Swapp Mulliner, interview with Chablis McDonald, 9 May 1993, Kanab, Utah.

10. Frederick Jackson Turner, "The Significance of History," in *Early Writings of Frederick Jackson Turner,* edited by Everett E. Edwards (Madison: University of Wisconsin Press, 1938), 52–53.

CHAPTER 2

THE LAND

The topography of Kane County is made up largely of mountainous peaks and plateaus, deep canyons, and stretches of unbroken land, some surfaced with sand so deep that traveling over it can be very difficult. The mountains are composed chiefly of red and white sandstone. The coloring, together with the beautiful configuration of some of the canyons and cliffs, helps make the county outstanding for its scenic beauty. The chief mountainous areas are the Vermilion Cliffs near Kanab, the Pink Cliffs in the northwestern corner of the county, the White, Pink and Gray Cliffs in the central part of the county, and the Red Bluffs of the southwestern corner. The chief plateaus are the Markagunt and Paunsaugunt to the north and the Kaiparowits and the Kaibab (Buckskin) Plateaus to the south. Other interesting natural features include a number of volcanic craters in the mountain ranges and plateaus.

Red rock canyons and undulating valleys decorate Kane County. Wooded highlands are incised by deep canyons and contained by high cliffs. Wildlife roams amid vegetation adapted to the generally dry climate. Rivers are fronted by towering cliff walls. Layer upon layer of rock tells the story of the land, and the story of this mainly uninhabited county continues with the landscape. A sparse population generally utilizes the canyons, mesas, and plateaus for undeveloped grazing land. Here geography, climate, and geology are all done on a grand scale—high plateaus, deep dramatic canyon walls, and brillantly contrasting colors of rock and sand. Here the silence of the surroundings can engulf one. In the words of one report: "Terraced plateaus, cliff-bounded mesas, monoclinal ridges, and straight-sided canyons—all impressive for magnitude and ruggedness"—are found in the Glen Canyon National Recreation Area in the eastern portion of the county.[1]

That area found in the neighborhood of Lake Powell includes a maze of brilliant red-walled canyons cutting through the turquoise water. Side canyons at the edge of the lake offer natural marvels. This lake backs up into about 100 major side canyons. Natural arches and bridges, including Stevens Arch and LaGorce Arch, decorate the Escalante canyons. The Orange Cliffs and Romana Mesa are other attractions found at Lake Powell.

Lake Powell, which was formed by Glen Canyon Dam in nearby Arizona after its completion in the mid-1960s, contains some 1,960 miles of shoreline, equivalent to the length of the west coast of the continental United States. The lake, named after early Colorado River explorer John Wesley Powell, has a capacity of 26 million acre-feet of water. Extending for miles up the former channels of the Colorado River and the San Juan River, Lake Powell provides access to scenery previously considered by many to be inaccessible in Kane and San Juan Counties. However, the lake also covered many historic and archaeological sites with water.

Shaped like a triangle, with Lake Powell at its base, is the Kaiparowits Plateau. This plateau, in the eastern region of Kane County, is the county's highest landform; its westward-tilted top has an altitude of more than 7,000 feet for a distance of fifty miles. The vast plateau remains largely uninhabited and undeveloped except for relics of coal exploration, an oil field, and some use for cattle grazing. Much of it is included in the newly created Grand Staircase-Escalante National Monument.

The eastern portion of the Kaiparowits Plateau is called Fiftymile

Mountain for the distance it stretches from south of Escalante to the Colorado River.[2] The escarpment of the Straight Cliffs, rising about 1,000 feet, creates the eastern boundary of the Kaiparowits Plateau. Fiftymile Mountain contains at least two natural arches, as well as fossils, dinosaur tracks, and numerous archaeological sites, including pictographs, petroglyphs, cliff dwellings, and rock shelters. Vegetation is sparse. Rising from the arid landscape of the canyon, this plateau is the largest mesa still roadless in southwestern Utah.[3]

The Hole-in-the-Rock Road lies at the foot of the Straight Cliffs, another natural feature of Kane County. This route was established by a group of Mormon pioneers in 1879–80 on their way to establish a settlement in future San Juan County. They blasted and chipped a portion of the road out of the massive sandstone cliffs and then drove and lowered their wagons down through it. An almost unbelievable feat of imaginative construction and labor, the trail now is impassable by either animal or vehicle, making it hard to imagine the wagon train traveling through it. The other portion of this road in San Juan County was also difficult to construct and travel.

Lying some twelve miles from the eastern rim of the Kaiparowits Plateau, the Escalante River flows in a channel bed lower than 4,000 feet.[4] The region of the Escalante River Canyon, the lower section of which is in Kane County, is a labyrinth of narrow and deep-sided canyons. The canyon country is characterized by different layers of sandstone, mudstone, siltstone, gypsum, and reddish shales. Wind and water have worked on these rock layers to produce a varied collection of fins, domes, buttes, cliffs, arches, bridges, and deep canyons.[5] Canyon walls tower over the floor between them. The 100-mile-long main Escalante River Canyon can at times prove to be dangerous to the unwary due to flash floods racing through the narrow passages, sweeping up everything in their path. The river is generally shallow, however, with the deeper water near the lower end and Lake Powell.

The deeply entrenched Hackberry Canyon lies between the Upper Paria River Gorge and Cottonwood Canyon. Several smaller canyons branch off the larger canyons. The colorful layers of the "ascending staircase" of cliffs in southwestern Utah expose millions

The Lower Escalante River and its junction with the Colorado River. (Utah State Historical Society)

of years of geological history as a result of the cliff-and-terrace type of physiography.

The Kaibab Plateau extends into Utah across the Arizona Strip area of northern Arizona north of the Grand Canyon, rising from 2,000–4,000 feet above the plateaus to the east and west. Covered with rich forest land, it spreads for miles at a height of more than 8,000 feet. The northern edge of what has been called Grand Canyon country is a series of terraces, separated by lines of cliffs oriented east-west, formations called "Terrace Plateaus" by John Wesley Powell. In the distance, between St. George and Lees Ferry, they rise vertically, forming a rainbow of colors and strata of rock. Although this land generally faces south, it tilts to the north, ascending from the Shinarump, to the Vermilion, to the White, and finally to the Pink Cliffs, like the steps of a giant staircase—and, in fact, the name "Grand Staircase" has been applied to the whole expanse.

In many ways, the key to these canyons is the movement of water.

Four principal waterways carved out the region's main canyons over millions of years: the Virgin River draining the southeastern face of the Markagunt Plateau; Kanab Creek moving through both narrow canyons and open valleys of the White, Vermilion, and Shinarump Cliffs regions; the Paria River, which heads through the Pink Cliffs on the eastern rim of the Paunsaugunt Plateau, for the most part through Bryce Canyon; and the Escalante River, with its headwaters also north in Garfield County in the region of Boulder Mountain. In the Markagunt and Paunsaugunt Plateaus 152,559 acres of the Dixie National Forest extend into the county.

The Virgin River and its tributaries have carved through many layers of strata, eroding the land into deep and narrow canyons towered over by mesas and other dramatic sandstone formations. The main flow, moving through the Parunuweap, impedes all but the most daring travelers. Below Zion National Park, the Virgin River flows through the Hurricane Cliffs and leaves behind the Colorado Plateau. Kanab Creek, however, flows entirely within the Colorado Plateau. Just a few miles below Kanab and Fredonia, Arizona, Kanab Creek enters a canyon before it joins the Colorado River in the Grand Canyon toward the middle of its length.

Located toward the center of Kane County, running north to south, is the Paria River. Named with a Paiute Indian word meaning "muddy water," the Paria River lives up to its name, racing through vast canyons and past enormous cliffs collecting sediment. The river's headwaters begin in the Table Cliffs Plateau of the Dixie National Forest and the Pink Cliff formations of Bryce Canyon National Park. It flows into the Colorado River at Lees Ferry. Along the Paria River, in the heart of Paria Canyon, is a 200-foot-long natural arch, Indian ruins, abandoned ranch sites, and canyons as much as 1,500 feet deep and only twelve feet wide. Historian C. Gregory Crampton described the Paria River's movement in his book *Land of Living Rock*: "Through a succession of narrow, straight-walled canyons, lined with cottonwoods, the Paria makes its fantastic way through the White and Vermilion cliffs and through a tortuous fifty-mile-long gorge across the back of the Paria Plateau. It breaks out into the open for a few miles and then at Lee's Ferry its waters join those of the Colorado to begin the long run through Grand Canyon."[6]

The Paria River near Paria townsite. (Allan Kent Powell)

The Paria Canyon Primitive Area in Kane County and in Arizona was designated in 1969 and includes thirty-five miles of magnificent canyon. It features a popular backpacking trek, although frequent flash floods are a lingering danger and at times make the narrows impassable. A journey through the rugged area usually begins or ends at Lees Ferry, just south of the border in Arizona.[7]

Spectacular rock formations full of saturated color gave Kodachrome Basin State Park its name. Great lithic spires jut up from the valley floor—different in rock composition and color from the rock bases that support them. The slender stone columns, or "chimney rocks," are made of a hard, gray, stratified limestone. Some geologists believe "the unusual stone formations are actually petrified geysers, or sandpipes, and that Kodachrome Basin once was somewhat similar to Yellowstone National Park today with its geothermic activity. The ancient springs and geysers are thought by those scientists to have filled with sediment and then solidified. Unlike the delicate, red sandstone formations of nearby Bryce Canyon National Park, Kodachrome's structures are made of calcite and sandstone, resulting in a hard, cementlike composition. Bryce was formed by the continual freezing and thawing of the seasons, explain park rangers, while Kodachrome's slickrock structures were formed by water and wind.[8] Forces of erosion formed and continue to mold peculiar-shaped pinnacles and rocks called "hoodoos," especially at areas like Kodachrome Basin.

Layers of soft pink and white siltstone, sandstone, dolomite, and limestone were deposited in a Paleocene lake system, creating the layers of the rock formations of Bryce Canyon. Geologists think these deposits were laid down some 60 million years ago, when lime-rich sand and mud carried along by streams and rivers was deposited into shallow lakes, with the lighter silt and clay particles settling to the lake bottoms farther from shore. Through millions of years, wet and dry cycles created limestone rock layers of different hardness that are known today as the Claron Formation.[9]

Bryce Canyon is a series of amphitheaters carved into the Paunsaugunt Plateau and spreading from north to south more than twenty miles. The otherworldly formations of Bryce Canyon are the result of erosion that has occurred over millions of years. A fabulous assemblage of rock spires and temples make up Bryce Canyon National Park. The southern part of Bryce Canyon lies in Kane County. Visitors to Bryce Canyon find it unlike any place they have ever been before and some scramble to find apt images or allusions to depict its beauty. Its formations have been described as sentinels on castle walls, as monks and priests in their robes, and as cathedrals and congregations. Onlookers have seen motifs reminiscent of windows, minarets, gables, pagodas, pedestals, and temples. Many nineteenth-century references are to the medieval, the supernatural, or the exotic in building and art, including grotesque beasts, gargoyles, lions, dragons, idols, and heathen gods, nave and architrave, pagoda, pantheon, and mosque. Early pioneer Ebenezer Bryce (after whom the park was named) was more prosaic in describing the canyon when he said, "It's a hell of a place to lose a cow."[10] Bryce, a Mormon immigrant from Scotland, established his homestead near the little town of Tropic in 1875 at the base of the canyon, where he grazed livestock and tried to survive.

A Paiute Indian, called by local whites "Indian Dick," in 1936 told a National Park Service naturalist the Paiute tradition of how Bryce

Canyon was formed. He explained how the most ancient peoples, known to the Paiutes as the Legend People, had the capability to take on the forms of birds, mammals, and lizards. "For some reason the Legend People in that place were bad; they did something that was not good, perhaps a fight, perhaps some stole something. . . . Because they were bad, Coyote turned them all into rocks. You can see them in that place now, all turned into rocks; some standing in rows, some sitting down, some holding onto others. You can see their faces, with paint on them just as they were before they became rocks," he related.[11]

Navajo myths recounted in the book *Grand Canyon Country* tell of the creation of the Grand Canyon. According to one legend, during the time of an extensive rainfall the sea rose to great heights and finally made an outlet for itself by carving the gigantic chasm into the depths of the earth. Another legend tells of a brave chief who married a beautiful young girl whom he loved very much but who died soon after their marriage ceremony. The gods loved this chief because he revered them and because he was a wise and generous leader. He was so sad over the loss of his wife that the hearts of the gods were touched and they decided to make a special concession and let him visit the spirit world. The one thing they required of him was that when he returned he never tell anyone of his route. The gods then turned the route into the Grand Canyon and filled the lower part with water—the Colorado River.[12]

As a gateway to the North Rim of the Grand Canyon, Kanab in particular and Kane County in general share to some extent the romance of the Grand Canyon, particularly the Kaibab Forest and Plateau of the North Rim. In 1927, M.R. Tillotson, superintendent of Grand Canyon National Park, Frank J. Taylor of the National Park Service, and Horace M. Albright, director of the National Park Service collaborated on an account of their time spent in the Grand Canyon region. The book, *Grand Canyon Country,* recounts the history of the park, describes the geology and terrain, and identifies the wildlife that inhabits the area. The authors described the trail along the North Rim, called the "Kaibab Trail," as being particularly rich in animal and bird life:

The Kaibab Forest—an important source of timber and grazing area for Kane County residents. (Utah State Historical Society)

To the traveler approaching the North Rim of the Grand Canyon from Zion and Bryce Canyon National Parks, and from southern Utah, the limitless Kaibab Forest is a welcome transition from the tropic climate of the desert and the Prismatic Plains, crossed in the vicinity of Kanab and Fredonia, or Pipe Spring National Monument. The high, dry, bracing, pine-laden air, the dim forest aisles, and the frequent glimpses of wild deer and white-tailed squirrels make the road to the North Rim a fitting prelude to the silent symphony of the Grand Canyon itself. Kaibab is a Piute Indian word meaning "mountain-lying-down," a description that fits it well. It is a vast plateau, some 50 miles long and 35 miles wide, containing approximately 500 square miles of Yellow Pine, White and Douglas Fir, Engelmann and Colorado Blue Spruce— one of the most beautiful virgin forests in the United States.

The picturesque charm of this dense forest of dark evergreens is greatly enhanced by an understory of quaking aspen, with its white, birch-like bark and light green leaves attached to the twigs in such a manner that even the slightest breeze sets them all to "quaking," or trembling. This picture is even more beautiful in the early fall after the first frosts have touched the quaking aspens, turning these leaves to every shade, from a bright golden yellow to a deep burnt orange. A strip of the Kaibab Forest extending northward from the rim of the Canyon for a distance of from ten to twelve miles is within Grand Canyon, but is actually part of the National Forest.[13]

The area we now call the Colorado Plateau was created more than 10 million years ago. Pressures within the earth later fractured the plateau and erosive forces then separated it into a series of lesser plateaus, including the Paunsaugunt Plateau where Bryce Canyon is located. From desert to high alpine meadows, deep and colorful canyons separate the plateaus and mountains in the Dixie National Forest, and parts of this national forest lie along the northern border of Kane County. Predominantly a series of plateaus, the forest area is better supplied with moisture than is most of southern Utah.[14]

Navajo Lake lies in the northwest corner of the county in the Dixie National Forest atop the Markagunt Plateau, which reaches 10,000–11,000 feet in elevation. This natural lake is home to four types of trout—cutthroat, rainbow, brook, and German brown.[15]

At the easternmost extension of the White Cliffs (composed of Navajo Sandstone) is the Paria River. The white and yellow sandstone cliffs were created as the river flowing down the eastern side of the Paunsaugunt Plateau sliced through the rock layers, helping scoop out an area that eventually resembled an amphitheater. The Paria also helped created the unique beauty of Bryce Canyon by eroding weak rock layers while leaving more enduring rock formations.[16] At the base of the Vermilion Cliffs is Kanab. The landscape includes the cliffs, benches, moderately entrenched canyons, and badlands beneath the cliffs, as well as Long Valley—the valley of the East Fork of the Virgin River.

Two thousand acres of pink sand sweep across the basin floor of Coral Pink Sand Dunes State Park. The sand has blown in from nearby rock formations over the millenia. Cactus and an occasional cedar tree decorate the dunes. After rain, ephemeral ponds collect in the area, which was formed in a sheltered depression along the 200-mile-long Sevier Fault. The dunes rise to heights of twenty feet or more.[17] Adjacent to the sand dunes is Moquith Mountain, near the

Arizona border. Ponderosa pine, pinyon, juniper, and Gambel oak cover the slopes of this small mountain. The canyons located in the eastern part of the area also contain some cottonwood and box elder trees.

Vegetation

Twisted juniper trees and pinyon pine, the source of pine nuts, an important food resource of early people in the area, dominate the vegetation in Kane County. The semiarid mountains and plateaus are ideal for the pinyon-juniper forests. Some ponderosa pine trees can be found in suitable habitats, including canyon rims in the Paria River Valley, Hackberry Canyon, and Zion National Park. Sagebrush, bunchgrass, and ephedra (Mormon tea) all thrive in much of the county.

In the Glen Canyon area, plant life has been divided by many botanists into five principal associations. (1) *Streamside.* Common species include sandbar willow, tamarisk, arrowweed, common reed, and saltgrass, and may include Gambel oak, hackberry, Fremont cottonwood, cheatgrass, and cattail. (2) *Terrace.* Common species include greasewood, rabbitbrush, sand sagebrush, dropseed grass, and Indian ricegrass, and may include arrowweed, shadscale, hackberry, blackbrush, and snakeweed. (3) *Hillside:* This association consists mainly of widely spaced low shrubs. Species include snakeweed, shadscale, hackberry, and blackbrush, and may include Indian ricegrass, prickly pear, and hedgehog cactus, serviceberry, silver buffaloberry, and cliff rose. Flowers include sego and mariposa lilies, eriogonium, prickly poppy, prince's plume, gaillardia, lupine, locoweed, euphorbia, globemallow, blazing star, evening primrose, gilia, penstemon, Indian paintbrush, and golden aster. (4) *Hanging gardens.* These are areas where moisture seeps from canyon walls. Common species include maidenhair fern, columbine, red monkeyflower, cardinal flower, false Solomon's seal, and evening primrose. (5) *Plateau.* The pinyon-juniper association, which includes bitterbrush, cliff rose, galleta, blue grama grass, and Indian ricegrass.[18]

Hackberry Canyon plant life includes pinyon, juniper, ponderosa pine, sagebrush, bunch-grass, and Mormon tea. The Paria River Valley vegetation is typical of semi-desert regions. Pinyon and juniper with occasional ponderosa pine dominate canyon rims. Heavy clay soils support sparse stands of dropseed, shadscale, and prickly pear. Looser sandy soils support fair stands of Indian ricegrass as well as buckwheat, rabbitbrush, and saltbrush. Riparian tree species include cottonwood, willow, and box elder.[19]

In Kodachrome Basin, common plants include those of the pinyon-juniper association. Plants associated with the upper Sonoran life zone include yucca, prickly pear, sagebrush, snakeweed, evening primrose, and beeplant. In Bryce Canyon, plant life includes big sagebrush on the valley floor and pinyon and juniper below the rim. A ponderosa forest surrounds the campground and visitor center; it includes greenleaf manzanita, Rocky Mountain juniper, and antelope bitterbrush. South toward Rainbow Point, species include spruce, fir, and bristlecone pine. At Moquith Mountain, plant life include ponderosa pine, pinyon, juniper, and Gambel oak. The canyons hold cottonwood and box elder. Stands of Douglas-fir may be found on south-facing canyon walls. Ponderosa pine can grow near the local sand dunes.[20]

Wildflowers in the county include sego lily, star lily, ceanothus, antelope bitterbrush, arrowleaf balsamroot, yarrow, bush cinquefoil, wax currant, yellow evening primrose, wild iris, Indian paintbrush, penstemon, wallflower, twinpod, Oregon grape, wild rose, blue columbine, Arizona thistle, scarlet gilia, aster, clematis, blue flax, rabbitbrush, goldenrod, gumweed, and senecio.[21]

Geology

A vast amount of Kane County's landscape is dominated by layered rocks. The layers come in many different colors and arrangements, being formed from as much as 2 billion years ago to sediment being laid down today. From the sheer cliffs of pastel Navajo Sandstone rising more than 2,000 feet in Zion National Park to the pink hoodoos of Bryce Canyon, these rock formations inspire the imagination. Kane County's landscape has been variously laid down, uplifted, and shaped by wind and water erosion for the past hundreds of millions of years.

The county's topographical features developed in sedimentary rocks on surface slopes extending from the high plateaus southeast to the Colorado River. Water is carried down these slopes into the canyons. Streams, typical of the region, run intermittently, flowing for short distances for most of the year; but during seasonal rains and local showers they flow more constantly. Despite the fact that there are few beaches or large areas of sand in dunes, sand piles are located between steam channels and at various places along the rivers' courses. Although the area feels like desert land, there actually are no stretches of salt and alkali except for the lower Escalante Valley, called the Escalante Desert by locals. The stretch of land between Wahweap and Rock Creeks has no water and only sparse, highly specialized types of vegetation that have adjusted over time to low rainfall levels and thin soil.

In Glen Canyon, according to one study, soil, in the true sense of the word, is rare in the area. On flat-topped mesas and plateaus the soil, weathered from the underlying rock, forms a thin mantle, but even here the soil cover is not continuous. On the plateau edges the areas of disintegrated shale and sandstone have no agricultural value. In general the conditions are unfavorable for making and retaining soils. Scanty vegetation, absence of sod, sudden showers, and rapid runoff favor removal of the soil as rapidly as it is formed. Large areas of bare rock are exposed. Most of the soil that is present in this region is transported soil. It has been brought to its present position by streams and wind. Some depressions on the surface and some rock cracks have been filled with debris washed from nearby places. A number of former canyons and tributary valleys are flanked with soil deposited at high-water stages. Similar soil is displayed here and there at the bases of cliffs, on open flats, and within canyons.[22]

Like Bryce Canyon and other area canyons, Glen Canyon was carved out of sedimentary rock by a river—here the Colorado River wound its way over millenia through Navajo Sandstone and other rock deposited scores of millions of years before. Much of Glen Canyon and its side canyons are now submerged by the waters of Lake Powell, a loss bitterly lamented by many. The Glen Canyon region is actually a series of canyons of various sizes—deep, steep-walled, and separated by narrow ridges or broad mesas. The elevation generally varies from the level of Lake Powell at about 3,700 feet to mesas of more than 6,000 feet in elevation. The highest local elevation is 7,451 feet.

The walls of the canyons, the mesas and buttes, and the rock that runs for miles and miles all feature only sparse vegetation. Wind sweeps across such areas, further stripping them of the plant covering that exists along creek beds or on the tops of plateaus. The colors of this land in great part are those of the rocks and canyons themselves—reds and browns, with occasional bursts of gold or orange against darker walls of greys.

Climate

Kane County's aridity has impacted the land and its people in dramatic ways, making it difficult to farm and limiting sites for settlement. Hard local showers are characteristic of rainstorms, and the summer months of July, August, and September are the season of maximum precipitation. Rainshowers can drop large quantities of water on the ground, causing flat surfaces to become lakes and dry washes to run torrents. Plants, however, obtain only a small portion of this moisture due to subsequent rapid evaporation. Clear skies are normal more than 80 percent of the time.

Snow may fall on the Kaiparowits Plateau any time between the middle of September to the middle of May and may stay on the ground for weeks or months. Snow rarely remains long enough to interfere with grazing on the lower lands drained by the Escalante River, Wahweap Creek, Warm Creek, Kanab Creek, and other streams near the Colorado River, however.

Wildlife

The Glen Canyon region and other riparian areas of the county abound in wildlife. Seasonal birds include western, eared, and pied-billed grebes; American white pelican; great blue heron; snowy egret; Canada goose; mallard; green-winged and cinnamon teals; shoveler; ring-necked duck; common goldeneye; turkey vulture; red-tailed and Swainson's hawks; northern harrier; prairie falcon; American kestrel; American coot; American avocet; black-necked stilt; killdeer; long-billed curlew; spotted, least, and Wilson's sandpipers; California, ring-billed, Franklin's, and Bonaparte's gulls; mourning and rock doves; black-throated, gray, and MacGillivary's warblers; red-winged blackbird; Cassin's finch; house, vesper, sage, and chipping sparrows; gray-headed junco; great horned and long-eared owls; black-chinned, broad-tailed, and rufous hummingbirds; downy woodpecker; western and Cassin's kingbirds; Say's phoebe; dusky flycatcher; western wood-pewee; horned lark; violet-green and cliff swallows; American crow; mountain chickadee; pygmy nuthatch; and mockingbird.

Mammals include pika, whitetail and blacktail jackrabbits, and mountain and desert cottontails. Abert, red, and rock squirrels are found in various areas. Spotted, antelope, and golden-mantled ground squirrels can also be found in the county. Whitetail prairie dog; least, Uinta, Colorado, and cliff chipmunks; northern and valley pocket gophers; five species of wood rats; muskrat; heather and Mexican voles; and porcupine are among the county's mammals. Coyote, red and gray foxes, black bear, ringtail, longtail and shorttail weasels, badger, striped and spotted skunks, river otter, bobcat, and mountain lion are among the area's carnivores and omnivores. Mule deer, pronghorn, and elk are larger game animals.

Reptiles include striped whipsnake, western patch-nosed snake, gopher snake, common kingsnake, and western diamondback rattlesnake. Lizards include chuckwalla, collared, leopard, lesser earless, side-blotched, eastern fence, desert spiny, western whiptail, plateau striped whiptail, and desert horned.[23]

In the Paria River Valley no official inventory has been made of wildlife, but observed bird species include eagles, raven, hawks, dove, killdeer, white-throated swift, and cliff swallow. Mammals include raccoon, fox, beaver, bobcat, and mule deer.

In Kodachrome Basin, observed birds include the golden eagle, raven, pinyon jay, mourning dove, robin, loggerhead shrike, mountain and western bluebirds, blue grosbeak, and lazuli bunting. Mammals include mule deer, mountain lion, coyote, spotted skunk, gray fox, bobcat, kit fox, kangaroo rat, and antelope ground squirrel.

Bryce Canyon seasonal birds include the common nighthawk; white-throated swift; black-chinned, broad-tailed, and rufous hummingbirds; northern flicker; western wood pewee; horned lark; violet-green swallow; Steller's jay; common raven; mountain chickadee; white-breasted, red-breasted, and pygmy nuthatches; robin; Brewer's blackbird; and vesper and chipping sparrows. Mammals include long-legged and small-footed myotis, big brown bat, striped skunk, badger, gray fox, mountain lion, bobcat, yellowbelly marmot, golden-mantled ground squirrel, red and rock squirrels, Colorado chipmunk, northern pocket gopher, beaver, deer mouse, Utah whitetail prairie dog, coyote, mule deer. Reptiles and amphibians include tiger salamander; northern sagebrush, side-blotched, tree, and mountain short-horned lizards; striped whipsnake, Great Basin rattlesnake, Rocky Mountain toad, Great Basin spadefoot toad, and leopard frog.[24]

One might travel through the seemingly desolate, isolated, and dry county and miss the incredible diversity which lies hidden or just beneath the surface. This is an area which speaks richly to the shifting currents of time and earth—its history is written on canyon walls and in river gorges. Nature here needs to be understood and appreciated for its great beauty and the lessons it can teach about strength and endurance. One of the most sensitive historians who has written about the area in his description of the Grand Canyon captures this essence:

> The unity and oneness, the wholeness of the Grand Canyon country is not apparent to the casual observer; it is fragmented by a profusion of manmade boundaries: state, county, national park, national monument, national forest, national game preserve, national recreation area, Indian reservation, to say nothing of township, and range. . . . The political boundaries that cut up the Grand Canyon tend to cause people to consider it politically rather than in terms of its history or its natural regions. . . . Man-made boundaries serve the purpose for which they were intended, but in the Grand Canyon country they never define or entirely encompass the natural geographical or physiographical unities, and they have little to do with the larger chapters of history.[25]

The "larger chapters of history" span millions of years of change, leaving traces, which speak to the cycles and rhythms of the natural world that human beings are powerless to change.

ENDNOTES

1. "The Glen Canyon Survey in 1957," *Anthropological Papers*, University of Utah, No. 30.1, March 1958, 3.

2. Allan Kent Powell, *The Utah Guide* (Golden, CO: Fulcrum Publishing, 1995), 302.

3. John Perry and Jane Greverus Perry, *The Sierra Club Guide to the Natural Areas of Colorado and Utah* (San Francisco: Sierra Club Books, 1985), 285.

4. "The Glen Canyon Survey in 1957," 4.

5. Powell, *Utah Guide*, 303.

6. C. Gregory Crampton, *Land of Living Rock* (New York: Alfred A. Knopf, 1972), 38.

7. Perry and Perry, *Sierra Club Guide*, 296.

8. Ibid.

9. Powell, *Utah Guide*, 374.

10. Perry and Perry, *Sierra Club Guide*, 247.

11. Powell, *Utah Guide*, 374.

12. See M.R. Tillotson, Frank Taylor, and Horace Albright, *Grand Canyon Country* (Palo Alto, CA: Stanford University Press, 1929).

13. Ibid., 85.

14. Powell, *Utah Guide*, 266.

15. Ibid., 320.

16. Ibid., 375.

17. Ibid., 366.

18. Perry and Perry, *Sierra Club Guide*, 276–77.

19. Ibid., 277.

20. Ibid., 292.

21. Ibid., 248–49.

22. "The Glen Canyon Survey in 1957," 5.

23. Perry and Perry, *Sierra Club Guide*, 276.

24. Ibid., 247.

25. Crampton, *Land of Living Rock*, 6.

CHAPTER 3

EARLY INHABITANTS
AND FIRST WHITE
EXPLORATION

Ancient Cultures

Long before the Mormons or any other persons of European descent settled southern Utah different Native American peoples lived there. Anthropologists, archaeologists, and historians have identified ancient desert cultures living in southern Utah dating back as early as 11,000 years ago. Archaeologists have divided prehistoric people into various cultures and groups based upon factors such as their location, practices of subsistence, use of tools, types of shelter, and household items. It is believed by many researchers that those now known as Paleo-Indians inhabited the region first, spreading throughout western North America after their ancestors crossed the Bering Straits during the great Ice Ages of the Pleistocene epoch some 25,000 to 15,000 years ago. These people were hunter-gatherers, hunting for food and clothing the great megafauna of the glacial period, animals that include the now-extinct mammoth, mastodon, cave bear, giant sloth, and sabre-toothed cat.

The chronology of the hunter-gatherer Paleo-Indian and Archaic cultures dates from about 10000–1500 B.C. The Paleo-Indian people roamed the wilderness in Kane County in Glen Canyon 9,000 to 11,000 years ago. Paleo-Indians were supplanted by or developed into what is now called the Archaic Culture, people characterized by their use of different projectile points and other cultural artifacts as well as by their strategies for adapting to the generally drying and warming climate. The Archaic people have been divided into subcultures by anthropologists, one being the Desert Archaic Culture of the greater Southwest, including future Kane County, Utah. People of the Desert Archaic Culture learned how to live on the land, respecting it. With the wildlife and plant life being a vital part of their community, these hunting and gathering people knew where to find and how to make use of the plants and animals around them. They used these natural resources for shelter, food, clothing, and medicinal purposes. The Desert Culture people were hunter-gatherers but were more dependent on edible seeds, plants, berries, and small game than were their predecessors on the land.

Life was difficult in this harsh desert environment, and the early inhabitants of the land developed incredibly resourceful means of survival—hunting, foraging, and eventually even engaging in rudimentary farming for food. The availability of water, as has always been true in the history of the region, would largely determine their ability to survive and develop culturally. In southern Utah, precipitation generally varies dramatically with altitude. The early Native American peoples were sensitive to these variations and were familiar with the variety of plants and animals that lived in the various locales. For example, deer could be hunted in the higher elevations, while desert sheep and rabbits flourished in the lowlands. Besides hunting, wild plants offered the people some diversity in their menu—pine nuts, cactus fruit, and various seeds and berries were gathered and many were carefully preserved and saved for the long winter months. Near dependable sources of water, later inhabitants—from both the Fremont and Anasazi cultures—grew corn, beans, and squash with primitive irrigation techniques. Like the white settlers of the region a thousand years later, they learned ways to bring water to serve their needs, adapting for survival to the conditions dictated by the land.

The Fremont peoples generally settled in the Great Basin and northern portion of the Colorado Plateau, while the unrelated Anasazi flourished in the region generally south of the Colorado River but including extreme southern Utah and the Arizona Strip area. The Anasazi, named with a Navajo word meaning the ancient ones or ancient enemies, were the dominant culture in the future Kane County region from about the beginning of the Christian era. Their well-known culture was distinguished for its horticulture, artifacts, and dwellings. The culture has been divided into two main periods by some archaeologists: the earlier, known as the Basketmaker Period (to about A.D. 700), and the later, known as the Pueblo Period (from A.D. 700–1300). The Basketmaker Anasazi lived off the land, hunting and gathering, but they also began to practice corn horticulture and were well known for their intricate basket weaving, pottery, rock art, and masonry structures.[1]

The Basketmaker Anasazi probably lived in caves or temporary shelters early on and eventually began to build more permanent structures—what were known as pithouses. These pithouses were shallow, circular lodges dug halfway into the earth and then walled and roofed with a combination of rocks, logs, and mud using post-and-beam construction techniques and masonry for the base. People entered through a passageway leading from the ground outside. The entranceways were built in a T-shape configuration, with the top half being slightly larger than the bottom. While by far the most typical shape of the pithouse was a circle with an antechamber, other configurations included a keyhole shape and a "D" shape. Pithouses were originally used as shelters; some eventually evolved into areas of ritual and religious activity.

During the Pueblo period, the ground entrance to pithouses became a small ventilation shaft, and people entered from the roof through a small hole and descended down a ladder into the room. This later Anasazi culture reached a pinnacle in the development of their pueblo shelters, mastering dry-masonry techniques. Some Anasazi people built their houses in cliff caves and sheltered box canyons for greater protection. Village complexes developed in many places (generally outside Utah), such as Mesa Verde in Colorado and Chaco Canyon in New Mexico. Smaller structures of fine workmanship were built in cliff walls and niches in many parts of southern Utah, including Kane County. The pithouse evolved into the more sophisticated form of the ceremonial kiva, which was usually lined internally with masonry or masonry covered with plaster.

The Anasazi sometimes decorated the masonry walls of their houses with murals, pegs for hanging their clothes and tools, and dug-out shelves and seats. They also produced fine pottery. The craftsmanship of these "ancient ones" is reflected in their discovered artifacts including jewelry, feathered robes, and pottery.

The Anasazi disappeared from their Southwestern settlements by about the year 1250. The reason for their disappearance is not known, although there are two possibilities favorably considered by many researchers. It is possible that a prolonged period of drought either starved them or forced them to relocate elsewhere, or it is also thought that perhaps they were driven out or absorbed by newcomers to the land, ancestors of the Navajo or of the Numic-language-speaking tribes to the north—the Ute, Shoshoni, and Paiute peoples. The modern Pueblo villages in New Mexico are believed by some to be populated by descendants of the Anasazi.

Anasazi ruins still stand in Kane County among other places in the Four Corners area. Numerous sites are found on the Kaiparowits Plateau and in Cottonwood Canyon, for example. The largest site is in Kitchen Corral Canyon. Glen Canyon housed numerous Anasazi sites that are now flooded and submerged by Lake Powell. Fortunately, before completion of Glen Canyon Dam, archaeological teams from the University of Utah and the Museum of Northern Arizona worked to inventory, salvage, and photograph ancient Native American sites in the canyon.[2] In Forgotten Canyon, located in the Glen Canyon region, elaborate cliff dwelling structures have been found. One site is named Defiance House after a pictograph there of three warriors carrying shields. Other art panels are located along the back wall of the alcove. Eleven separate structures, a retaining wall, storage structures for food, and a ceremonial room are found there.[3] Other structures and artifacts have been found in numerous places in Kane County, indicating that for centuries these ancient people roamed the area's valley floors and canyons foraging for foodstuffs, locating dependable water supplies, and trying to live harmoniously with the forces of nature.

From the fourteenth century to the time of white settlement, the land was inhabited by the ancestors of the Native Americans who lived in the area at the time of the coming of Euro-Americans. In particular, the Paiutes were able to adapt to the harsh, semiarid land, although there was doubtless some incursions by Ute Indians to the northeast and Navajos from the east and southeast. The new inhabitants did not generally practice horticulture and reverted to a hunting-gathering lifestyle, best suited to the limited resources of the semiarid land. The size of groups was also limited, most likely to families of just a few individuals.

The Paiutes did not generally have horses or the material resources of their more powerful and more warlike neighbors, and thus they often became victimized by Utes, Navajos, the later Spanish explorers and traders (all of whom captured Paiute women and children and sold them into slavery), and they were eventually victimized too by the Mormon and other white settlers who appropriated the best resources and areas to themselves.

Navajos generally lived in the areas south and east of the Colorado River, where they successfully developed a somewhat nomadic ranching existence and were noted for their cultural artifacts, including finely woven blankets. They did have some interest in the lands north of the river, however, as was later evidenced in the 1860s and 1870s by hostilities that erupted between white settlers of Kane County and the Arizona Strip with Native Americans including Navajo Indians.

Little is known of the period before the coming of the whites, as the artifacts of those who displaced the Anasazi are few and inferior in quality to those of their predecessors. Still, it can be asumed that Kane County was the home and hunting grounds for generations of Native Americans, who doubtless loved the land that has later come to be appreciated by so many others.

Explorers and Missionaries

Early travelers through the region thought of it as a passage— Kane County's canyons and rivers were routes to someplace else, usually a place less extreme in climate and remote in geography. The Colorado River, for instance, was for a time considered a possible transportation route from the interior of the continent to the ocean. Many of the first explorers of Kane County also were looking for passages for railroad or other transportation routes, or for places with more water, more arable land, and more vegetation. Other explorers, scientists, and surveyors came to chart the land and identify its resources. They found a place that was scientifically intriguing and also extraordinarily beautiful. Others later came as tourists and adventurers to Kane County because of its geographical wonders, drawn by the unique physical character of the place and (in a few instances) because of the continuing presence of an Indian population.

The earliest known white exploration of Kane County was by members of the Domínguez-Escalante party of 1776. Sponsored by the Spanish government of the Province of New Mexico, the party's leaders were men of God—Franciscan monks—who saw the land as the setting for missionary and settlement efforts. The principal objective of the small group of about a dozen men (including Indian guides) of the expedition was to discover an overland route from Santa Fe, New Mexico, through Utah to the San Francisco area of California. A secondary objective of the officials who sent them was to bring glory to the king of Spain and perhaps to open a trade route that would be of commercial and economic benefit. The two Franciscan friars were hopeful of preaching the gospel to the Native Americans who inhabited the regions through which they traveled.

To accompany the expedition's leader, Fray Francisco Atanasio Domínguez, and his second in command, Fray Silvestre Vélez de Escalante, the governor of New Mexico sent a small group including Don Bernardo de Miera y Pacheco, who became the company's cartographer.[4] Escalante had already spent a year among the Hopi Indians in New Mexico hoping to learn what he could about lands to the west. He heard about the dangers and difficulties of traveling through the country—high sierras to cross, rivers that were impossible to traverse, and other mysteries little understood.

The names the party gave the places they saw reflected their culture. They traveled northwest from Santa Fe, crossing into present-

The Crossing of the Fathers. The location where the 1776 Dominguez/ Escalante expedition crossed the Colorado River on the way back to New Mexico. (Utah State Historical Society)

day Utah near the Uinta Basin and continuing west to the area of Utah Lake. They then turned south-southwest, finally deciding because of the lateness of the season to abandon their hope of continuing to California, deciding instead to return to Santa Fe. They spent some time in Kane County during their return. Traveling south from future Cedar City and passing through the Toquerville region, they traveled just south of the present town of La Verkin.

From mid-October to early November, the party members wound their way north of the Grand Canyon, seeking a passage across the Colorado River. The group spent much of that time in what is now Arizona, as they first moved along the base of the Hurricane Cliffs, relieved at the more moderate weather. From there they turned in a southeasterly direction toward Pipe Spring, traveling across the Kaibab Plateau. Traveling through the region south of Kanab they went northeasterly, perhaps entering future Kane County on 22 October in the region near Coyote Spring. They then traveled in a south-southeasterly direction to the House Rock Valley area near Lees Ferry. When they reached the Colorado River they followed the river upstream, crossing the Paria River and the Sentinel Rock River while experiencing considerable difficulty manuvering around the cliffs alongside the Colorado River. One later historian described their discouragement as they wound their way north, entering into Kane County in their search for a passsage across the river:

> Suffering greatly from thirst and hunger and nearly exhausted, trying in vain to find a crossing place amid the high, steep walls along the great river until they attained a point a short distance west of where the Rio de Nabajos (present San Juan River) enters it, and here, at last, they found a crossing at the Colorado River which had been used by the Indians from time immemorial, and which is today celebrated as the "Crossing of the Fathers."[5]

Crossing the river on 7 November, they exited future Kane County with joyful hearts. A few days later they reached the Hopi pueblos. From there their route was better defined and more easily traversed. They arrived in Santa Fe in early January 1777, after a journey of five months and some 1,600 miles.

In addition to the careful notes they took about the most favorable route through the country, they also observed the habits of the various groups of Native Americans they confronted—including Utes, Paiutes, and others. They described the Paiutes as gentle people who lived in small groups and foraged for survival. They dressed poorly and inadequately (according to European standards) covered their bodies with clothing. From these Indians, however, they received excellent insight into methods of survival in the desert, the best routes to take, and information about other Native Americans.

Both prior to and after the Domínguez-Escalante expedition, other Spanish explorers, soldiers, and merchants from New Mexico entered Utah, in the process helping develop the Old Spanish Trail between New Mexico and California that crossed central Utah, exiting the future state on the west near present-day St. George and on the east in the Moab region. By 1830 the trade route was well developed, and in the next two decades it was used by hundreds of travelers and traders. Future Kane County was just outside of the route area, however, and, although it is quite likely that some people ventured into the region, history does not record the event. It is likely that few Euro-Americans entered the region due to the barrier of the Grand Canyon to the south and the difficulties reported by Domínguez and Escalante in their attempt to return to Santa Fe through the region. Trappers may have traversed the region in their search for beaver in the 1830s and early 1840s, but since much of the future county was not prime beaver habitat, it is probable that any such incursion into the area was limited. The coming of the Mormons to the Great Basin in 1847 would soon change the situation, however.

Early Government and Mormon Explorers

Before the Mormons reached the Great Basin they had received information about its geography from a variety of different sources, but the great bulk of the information concerned the northern part of the future state of Utah. Government reports of the 1840s, including those of U.S. Army explorer John Charles Frémont, were important in the settlement of the general region, although the region of Kane County was little explored until the 1860s and 1870s by government explorers. In 1847, when the Mormons first entered the Great Basin, Utah was actually part of Mexican territory, but the Mexican War and subsequent treaty of Guadalupe Hidalgo in 1848 brought the entire region of the West from California to New Mexico under the control of the United States.

Reports first had reached Mormon church leader Brigham Young about the Colorado River area from men traveling in the Mormon Battalion en route to California in 1846 as soldiers fighting in the Mexican War. When Young later was planning his proposed State of Deseret, he foresaw the importance of trade routes and roads moving out of the center of the Mormon kingdom in every direction. Control over the southern portion of the Mormon territory was a key to maintaining theological and temporal control over the area. For a period of time, Young even reportedly contemplated bringing immigrants across Panama, then north by sea and up the Colorado River.[6] Government surveys of the area facilitated his evaluation of the territory for settlement efforts as well as the development of transportation routes. The series of towns that were founded subsequently created what has been called the "Mormon Corridor" and were key to this expansion. Kane County was not part of this "corridor," but its eventual settlement by Mormons was related to the earlier settlements, from which settlers branched out throughout the region.

Late in 1849, Brigham Young sent an exploration party to southern Utah headed by Mormon apostle Parley P. Pratt. Their mission was to identify land for settlement along the southern route to California, which approximated the present routh of Interstate 15 in the state. Of prime importance was the proximity of land to available sources of water and other key natural resources, its location along the transportation corridor of the Wasatch Front and Wasatch Plateau, and its distance from other settlements. Pratt and his party traveled as far south as the Virgin River Valley; but it is likely that in contrast to some of the more verdant and inviting lands to the north, Pratt found the far southern country desolate and uninviting. He described it as a region "thrown together in dreadful confusion . . . a country in ruins."[7] Unconcerned about geological formations, he measured the land's value in terms of its potential for agricultural settlement.

Despite this report, Brigham Young's plan for a regionwide kingdom (proposed to Congress as the state of Deseret) required that a passage to California be established in order to ensure regional control by the Mormons. Therefore, once the Iron Mission had been established near Parowan, Young named two Mormon apostles—Amasa M. Lyman and Charles C. Rich—to establish a colony in southern California to extend the influence of the church. A colony of approximately 520 Mormon pioneers settled San Bernardino, California, under their direction. Mormons began to solidify their settlements in southern Utah, but the Kane County region lay outside their sphere of influence for the first few years of settlement.

Not long after the Mormons claimed much of the Intermountain West for their own, with settlements that spread into Idaho and as far south as southern California, government surveyors came to Utah to explore the area and to establish the possibility of future transportation routes. Especially after the Civil War, the United States government was able to turn its attention to surveying and better understanding the public domain, and it sponsored a number of scientific expeditions to the West, some of which traversed the land that would become Kane County.

The California gold rush that began in 1849 brought a new focus to routes into and through the West, and new interest was shown in the Old Spanish Trail north and west of future Kane County. Exploration of the area by non-Mormons supplemented Mormon efforts to identify locations for settlement. Lieutenant A.M. Whipple explored westward along the 35th parallel through northern Arizona in 1853 searching for a possible transcontinental railroad route. In 1855, U.S. Army Captain T.J. Cram requested $10,000 to survey the Colorado River for its potential as a shipping route.[8] In 1856 the army assigned such a survey to Lieutenant Joseph C. Ives.

Much of the work of mapping, surveying, and identifying new routes throughout the West came under the direction of the U.S. Army Corps of Topographical Engineers. The corps' studies were straightforward, technical, and scientific, in contrast to the sometimes romantic and poetic accounts of travelers or missionaries. Railroad surveys sponsored by the government or other interested parties were also important for the information they provided about southern Utah. By the time the transcontinental railroad was completed in 1869, an important web of roads had spread throughout the region. There were important northern and southern routes for transcontinental travelers as well as roads linking the ever-expanding number of Mormon settlements, including some in Kane County.

Lieutenant Joseph C. Ives produced his *Report Upon the Colorado River of the West* in 1861, and the government produced 11,000 copies. It was concise, readable, and informative, and it included lithographs by Ives himself and two other artists on his expedition in 1857–58 from the mouth of the Colorado River to the Grand Canyon, a mission in part to determine the feasibility of moving troops into Utah by way of the Colorado and Vigin Rivers as part of the Utah War of 1857–58. Such troop movement was not feasible; in fact, Ives was soon forced from the Colorado River as he learned it was not navigable by steamboat in the Grand Canyon.[9]

Important to the Mormon colonization effort was the organization of an Indian mission in Harmony in early 1854. The mission was soon reestablished at Santa Clara Creek in Washington County. Based

Jacob Hamblin, an early explorer and settler of Kane County. (Utah State Historical Society)

on the Mormon idea that the Indians were the descendants of ancient Book of Mormon peoples, as well as the need to pacify the Native Americans as white Mormon settlers intruded on their ancestral lands, the Indian mission involved gathering information about Native American lifestyles and behaviors, including the location of settlements and nomadic patterns of movement through the area, and, most importantly, the establishment of harmonious relationships with key Indian leaders. Much of this effort in Kane County occurred under the leadership of Jacob Hamblin. While his role was in part to keep peace with the Indians, he also became adept at guiding visitors through Indian territory and was successful in some ways in convincing his new Indian friends that the Mormons meant them no harm. He found, however, that the idea of actual "conversion" or baptism into Mormonism was more difficult for many of the Indians to understand.[10]

Jacob Hamblin's knowledge of the area facilitated government exploration. As a guide, Hamblin led or assisted a series of men through the region–including John Wesley Powell.[11] Powell made one of a series of efforts to chart and scientifically explore the West beyond the hundredth meridian. Each successive effort produced reports on the geology, geography, biology, and ethnology of the area and helped to publicize the western region to the rest of the United States.

John Wesley Powell was a Union soldier in the Civil War who lost his right forearm at the Battle of Shiloh. Discharged with the rank of major, Powell began teaching geology at Illinois Wesleyan University. It was this work that was the impetus behind his scientific explorations of the Colorado River region. Before his travels, no one had made a systematic study of the river's path and canyons, as no one was known to have traveled the length of the river. The region rightly had been considered dangerous, and few attempted to travel it. Fur trapper James Ohio Pattie had described the geography of the Grand Canyon region in 1826 as "these horrid mountains."[12] In his 1869 journey down the river, Powell and his small group of men left Green River, Wyoming, and traveled down the Green and Colorado Rivers through the Grand Canyon on their historic voyage of discovery. They gave names to various features, including the Dirty Devil River and Desolation, Cataract, Glen, and Marble Canyons.

Powell initiated a second river voyage in 1871 and saw the advantage of having Jacob Hamblin help supply the expedition. Hamblin also provided valuable guide service in the region for Powell and his men. The survey of the general Colorado Plateau region by Powell and his subordinates would be completed in 1879, and for much of that time Kanab was one of the major centers of operations of the researchers.[13]

Powell's reports established his general reaction to the region's landscape. His writings are marked by a sense of respect at nature's power. As a scientist he documented available water supplies and climatic conditions as well as his observations about the ways the inhabitants of the land–Native Americans, Mormon settlers, and Spanish-Americans—utilized the region's natural resources. He identified aridity as one of the most distinctive features of the region and emphasized the extreme geographic difference between America's east and west, which he believed ought to lead to reforms in federal land policy. An excerpt from his book *The Exploration of the Colorado River and its Canyons* detailing his journeys captures his writing style and describes a bit of Glen Canyon in Kane County.

> August 4–To-day the walls grow higher and the canyon much narrower. Monuments are still seen on either side; beautiful glens and alcoves and gorges and side canyons are yet found. After dinner we find the river making a sudden turn to the northwest and the whole character of the canyon changed. The walls are hundreds of feet higher, and the rocks are chiefly variegated shades of beautiful colors–creamy orange above, then bright vermilion, and below, purple and chocolate beds, with green and yellow sands. We run four miles through this, in a direction a little to the west of north, wheel again to the west, and pass into a portion of the canyon where the characteristics are more like those above the bend. At night we stop at the mouth of a creek coming in from the right, and suppose it to be the paria, which was described to me last year by a Mormon missionary. Here the canyon terminates abruptly in a line of cliffs, which stretches from either side across the river.[14]

Perhaps most importantly, Powell established the fact that the Colorado River was navigable but that it was highly unlikely that it could become a commercial transportation route.

Frederick S. Dellenbaugh's wrote of his experience with Powell's exploration of the Colorado River as part of the second expedition of 1871–72. Dellenbaugh was only twenty-two years of age when he

Jacob Hamblin and John Wesley Powell meet with a group of Paiute Indians on the Kaibab Plateau in the early 1870s. (Utah State Historical Society)

accompanied the exploration party. He recounted the experience in his books *A Canyon Voyage* and *The Romance of the Colorado River*. In September 1871 Powell's party was at the mouth of the Paria River. Their plan was to leave their boats there for the winter while they proceeded their land survey work of "triangulation."[15] Some members of the group camped in a valley between the Kaibab Plateau and the Paria Plateau, alongside a spring in a gulch of the Vermilion Cliffs. The campsite was located along the old Mormon trail between the Mormon settlements in Iron, Washington, and Kane Counties and what was called the "Moki country," often traveled by Jacob Hamblin and other parties on trade expeditions.

When the party reached sight of Kanab, Dellenbaugh, like so many other explorers and travelers through the area, was awestruck by the magnificent backdrop formed by the Vermilion Cliffs. He wrote, "At length, we were ordered across the Kaibab to the vicinity of Kanab, and I shall never fail to see distinctly the wonderful view from the summit we had of the bewildering cliffland leading away northward to the Pink Cliffs. The lines of cliffs rose up like some giant stairway, while to the south-eastward the apparently level plain was separated by the dark line of Marble Canyon."[16] At the top of the plateau they came upon a suitable campground eight miles from Kanab in a shallow, open valley bordered by tall pine trees. There was no visible spring, but there was a thin layer of snow on the ground which the adventurers melted for water. Dellenbaugh was aware of how infrequently the area had been traveled through, and he speculated that, "The Kaibab, still frequently called Buckskin Mountain, must have received this first name from its resemblance to a buckskin stretched out on the ground."[17]

The government party under the general direction of Powell's brother-in-law Almon Thompson began their work of surveying the area on a baseline located just below Kanab, beginning their triangulation of the area at that point. Kanab resident Brigham L. Young accompanied Dellenbaugh and others as a surveyor on a journey into the Grand Canyon. He drew maps of the area which are housed in the Library of Congress. The maps were also used in preliminary work for Glen Canyon Dam some three-quarters of a century later.

Yet another survey conducted under the auspices of the United States Geographic Surveys of the West program was directed from 1869 to 1872 by Captain George M. Wheeler. The intention was to create a detailed topographical survey west of the one hundredth meridian of the United States. The ambitious project included detailed mapping, evaluation of natural resources, and a careful

analysis and description of the geology, botany, and zoology in an
area of some 1,443,360 square miles.[18]

Wheeler traveled to Kane County in 1871 and again in 1872. His
party mapped the lower Virgin River Valley in 1871. The party consisted of twenty-five scientists and engineers, twenty-five officers, fifty
privates, two guides, and a group of packers, herders, and laborers.
The following is a portion of the report—a panoramic view of parts
of Washington, Iron, and Kane Counties.

> Skirting the rim of the plateau a break in the wall is finally found,
> and the train taken down into box canyon along a descent having
> an angle of fully 55 degrees at the head of La Verken Creek. The
> summit of the southern rim [of the Markagunt Plateau], at an alti-
> tude of over 10,000 feet, affords one of the finest panoramic views
> then witnessed—the Virgin River lying at our feet, the Colorado
> Canyon in the distance, plateaus, canyons, and mountains to the
> east, mountains high and frowning to the north, and the mountains
> and desert to the west and southwest, the ranges bordering the
> Colorado, especially the Virgin. Below us lay the brown and black
> bristling ridges of the eroded mesas that for grandure of beauty and
> desolation of appearance far surpass all that words can express.[19]

According to one historian of the area, the government scientists
also gave names to the places they explored—for example, naming
the cliffs for their dominant colors,

> Pink, White, and Vermillion—and the most predominant strata in
> Grand Canyon was called the Redwall Limestone. They chose Indian
> names for the massive plateaus—Markagunt, Paunsaugunt,
> Shivwits, Uinkaret, Kanab, Kaibab, and Coconino. For variety they
> gave names like these to lesser features: Bright Angel Creek, Witches'
> Water Pocket, Sockdolager Rapids, Marble Canyon, Smithsonian
> Butte, House Rock Spring, Wild Band Pocket, Thousand Wells,
> Iceberg Canyon, Vulcan's Throne, and Vishnu Temple.[20]

Native Americans also had given names to local rock formations
and locations. Kanab was a Paiute word for "Place of the Willows,"
because of the willows that lined Kanab Creek. To the Paiute, the
word Kaibab means "Mountain-lying-down," which is the way the
Kaibab Plateau can be seen to appear from a distance. After the

Mormon settlement of the area, family names—including Johnson, Bryce, and Lee—identified certain locations. Though govenment explorers furnished useful information about the area, most of it was not of much practical value to Mormon settlers and gentile (non-Mormon) cattlemen who had begun to settle the area earlier based on their simple observations of where they might establish themselves and their families. It was with the Mormons that white settlement of the area that was soon to be known as Kane County began in the 1860s.

ENDNOTES

1. See Robert H. Lister and Florence C. Lister, *Those Who Came Before* (Globe, AZ: Southwest Parks and Monuments Association, 1983.

2. See, for example, Jesse D. Jennings, *Glen Canyon: A Summary,* University of Utah Anthropological Paper No. 81 (Salt Lake City: University of Utah, 1966) as well as other publications in the series.

3. "Lake Powell Pamphlet," n.d., 37, Utah State Historical Society Library.

4. 1 See Ted J. Warner, ed., *The Domínguez-Escalante Journal* (Provo: Brigham Young University Press, 1976), and Herbert S. Auerbach, "Father Escalante's Route," *Utah Historical Quarterly* 9 (April 1941): 73–80.

5. Ibid., 79.

6. Journal History, 9 March 1849, LDS Archives.

7. See Juanita Brooks, "The Southern Indian Mission," in Under the Dixie Sun, ed. by Hazel Bradshaw (N.p.: Washington County Daughters of Utah Pioneers, 1950).

8. Andrew L. Neff, *History of Utah* (Salt Lake City: Deseret News Press, 1940), 805–6.

9. See Allan Kent Powell, ed., *Utah History Encyclopedia* (Salt Lake City: University of Utah Press, 1994), 179.

10. See Juanita Brooks, *Mountain Meadows Massacre* (Norman: University of Oklahoma Press, 1962); Thomas D. Brown, "Journal of the Southern Indian Mission," Dixie College, St. George, Utah; and Richard Lloyd Dewey, ed., *Jacob Hamblin: His Life in His Own Words* (New York: Paramount Books, 1995).

11. Melvin T. Smith, "Colorado River Exploration and the Mormon War," *Utah Historical Quarterly* 38 (Summer 1970): 207–23.

12. C. Gregory Crampton, *Land of Living Rock,* 10.

13. Numerous accounts have been published detailing the events.

Among them are John Wesley Powell, *Report on the Explorations of the Colorado River of the West* (1875); John Wesley Powell, *Report on the Lands of the Arid Regions of the United States With a More Detailed Account of the Land of Utah* (1878); Grove Karl Gilbert, *Geology of the Henry Mountains* (1890); Grove Karl Gilbert, *Lake Bonneville* (1890); Clarence E. Dutton, *Geology of the High Plateaus of Utah* (1880); and Clarence E. Dutton, Tertiary History of the Grand Canyon District (1882).

14. John Wesley Powell, *Exploration of the Colorado River and its Canyons* (Reprint. New York: Dover Publications, 1895), 233–34.

15. Frederick S. Dellenbaugh, *The Romance of the Colorado River* (New York: Knickerbocker Press, 1909), 304. See also Ellsworth L. Kolb and Emery Kolb, *Through the Grand Canyon from Wyoming to Mexico* (Reprint. New York: Macmillan, 1946).

16. Dellenbaugh, *Romance of the Colorado River,* 305.

17. Ibid.

18. The fifty published sheets of the Wheeler topographic atlas cover 326,891 square miles and the manuscript sheets an additional 31,174 square miles—some 46 percent of which was in Utah. The overall study also produced nine annual progress reports, eighteen special reports, and a final comprehensive report in 1886.

19. Quoted in Herbert E. Gregory, "Scientific Exploration in Southern Utah," *American Journal of Science* 248 (October 1945): 535.

20. Crampton, *Land of the Living Rock,* 7.

CHAPTER 4

FIRST SETTLEMENT OF KANE COUNTY AND INDIAN TROUBLES

When the United States government acquired the land that would become Utah Territory in 1848 with the Treaty of Guadalupe Hidalgo ending the Mexican War, the way was paved for settlement of the Kane County area. The Compromise of 1850 formally organized Utah Territory while admitting California as a state and defining other territory formerly claimed by Mexico. In organizing Utah Territory on 9 September 1850 Congress rejected the application for the State of Deseret petitioned by Mormons on 2 March 1850. The territorial legislature was not granted authority over land distribution, water regulation, or timber use.

Mormon church president Brigham Young played a direct role in the establishment and development of more than 300 settlements founded in the thirty-year period between the pioneers' arrival in the Great Basin in 1847 and his death in 1877. More than one hundred other towns were settled after the pattern he established from 1877 until the end of the nineteenth century.

While the story of Mormon settlement of the Great Basin is considered by many to be an epic of significant dimensions, the Mormon colonization efforts of the arid region of southwestern Utah along the tributaries to the Colorado River were even more than usually heroic. The lower regions around the canyons of the Colorado are generally desertlike, virtually dry except for occasional springs and the rivers that traverse the land. The land itself is generally forbidding—few plants or trees dot the terrain, the earth is sandy and easily eroded. The area was only marginally habitable for whites after considerable effort to tame the land. Local Native Americans had used and valued the land, resisting white encroachment on their ancestral lands and the resulting competition for scarce resources.

Kane County was somewhat isolated due to its difficult terrain and geographic location. South of Kanab the Kaibab Plateau and the great Colorado River gorge created a formidable obstacle to travel through the region. Though harsh, the area was not without its attractions. The Mormons were drawn to the region because of the possible potential the Colorado River held for navigation through the area, the mild climate and potential for agriculture, the timber resources of the plateau areas, and the possibility that the hills were rich with mineral wealth. Settlements also could serve as a buffer betwen the more settled areas of Iron and Washington Counties and hostile Ute and Navajo Indians to the east. Because of the area's proximity to the emigrant route to southern California, settlements in the area also could serve as supply towns.

As soon as the initial companies of Mormon immigrants had platted Salt Lake City, planted their crops, and started home building, they turned their sights toward expansion throughout the territory. After first exploring the canyons and land of the Salt Lake Valley itself, Brigham Young focused his attention on the exploration of the region. The Latter-day Saints spent their first two years in the Great Basin struggling to survive. But, by the fall of 1849, Young was ready to embark upon the most ambitious colonization effort in the country's history. Wilford Woodruff recorded in his journal Young's intention to "have every hole and corner from the Bay of San Francisco known to us." On 9 March 1849, Brigham Young himself wrote: "We hope soon to explore the valleys three hundred miles south and also the country as far as the Gulf of California with a view to settlement and to acquiring a seaport." The vast territory included in the proposed State of Deseret of 1849 confirmed the Mormon church's plan to solidify its control over an extensive area as a place where "scores of thousands will join us in our secluded retreat."[1]

When the proposed State of Deseret was first delineated in March 1849, it included practically all of present-day Utah, Nevada, and Arizona, and large portions of present-day Oregon, Wyoming, Colorado, New Mexico, Idaho, and California. Brigham Young envisioned the expansion necessary to fill this Mormon empire through colonization efforts centered in Utah. An integral part of this plan was a proposed "Mormon Corridor" to the Pacific, ocean travel to a Pacific Coast seaport being considered by many to be a more convenient way for overseas immigrants to travel to the Great Basin.

Brigham Young looked to the lower Colorado River area soon after initial settlement in Salt Lake City was underway. By 1849 the southern California trail had been established to the south due in part to the efforts of Jefferson Hunt and others who had led gold-seekers to California along a southern route that in part anticipated the later corridor of Mormon settlements at the foot of the Wasatch Front and Wasatch Plateau. Mormon leaders were looking to establish southwestern communities even before the establishment of the Territory of Utah by Congress in 1850.[2]

Like other Mormon settlement efforts, Mormon colonization of the area was directed from church headquarters in Salt Lake City. Centralized control and direction governed almost all colonization efforts. Church leaders attempted to obtain a familiarity with local resources, the situation in terms of potential confrontations with Native Americans, and the general suitability of the areas for settlement, sending out advance exploratory or missionary parties. Locations for new settlements also were carefully considered for ways they could benefit the church. Sites close to natural resources, on the edge of transportation routes or corridors, and locations critical to defense or security reflected the concerns of Brigham Young and his vision of a Mormon stronghold.

Despite the careful planning and far-reaching vision of church leaders, however, the Mormon Corridor as planned did not fully materialize, although it did extend into southern Utah, facilitating the settlement of Kane County. Settlements of the church helped to appropriate the best agricultural lands of various areas as they were situated to occupy strategic points at entrances to the Intermountain region. The settlement of Kane County was part of this effort.

Settlement in the Kane County area was driven by three motives: the extension of the Mormon empire into the Arizona Strip area, the need to obtain grazing land for the ranchers of Washington County, and the hoped-for conversion of Native Americans to the Mormon church. When the first Mormons came to the area, they looked at the region's potential for settlement with a critical eye. The climate was very dry, with an average annual rainfall of only about fourteen inches. Vegetation spoke to the dry conditions. The lowlands were covered with juniper, cacti, sagebrush, and rabbitbrush—flora that could survive with limited water. The highlands to both the north and south had more varied species, including larger trees and undergrowth—spruce, pines, and quaking aspens—which could provide lumber for building.

Because water was so crucial to the survival of settlers, the creeks, lakes, and rivers were vital to settlement efforts. Several rivers traversed Kane County and offered varied opportunities for irrigation and culinary uses. Much of the landscape is defined by its proximity to the Colorado River, the dominant river system. Besides the Colorado, locations along the Paria River, the Escalante River, Kanab Creek, and the Virgin River all became areas of settlement. Duck Lake in the Pink Cliffs area, Hidden Lake located near Long Valley, and other smaller sources of water made water available, even if some of it was limited or difficult to divert.

Leaders and many in the initial parties of the Mormon colonization companies were specifically called to the work; some men received their calls directly from the church president himself. In other situations, colonization leaders called men to join them in the effort. These calls were considered to be the will of God and were in some cases designated as church missions. Settlers for any given group often were chosen because of their expertise and skills they could bring to the enterprise. Usually, each group included some newcomers along with older, more experienced pioneers. Some, in fact, were called repeatedly to start new towns. In the settlement of the towns of Kane County, the names of Mangum, Johnson, Judd,

Meeks, Hamblin, Esplin, Chamberlain, and Stewart, among others, figure prominently and appear repeatedly. Some settlements had special missions; for example, the Cotton Mission and various Indian missions had from the first specific agendas to perform. For the most part, however, colonies were established to provide places to live for new immigrants and to expand and solidify the hold of the Mormon church throughout the region.

Important to settlement of the Kane County area was the organization of the Southern Indian Mission, for it was the Mormon missionaries assigned to proselytize among the Native Americans who first more thoroughly explored the area and established initial contact with the local Indians. John D. Lee led various groups that explored much of the southern Utah country in 1852, including the area around Duck Creek, various parts of the Virgin River, and Long Valley Canyon, befriending local Indians in the process. Lee then helped establish Fort Harmony in 1852 and moved there himself. In the Mormon church's April 1853 general conference, Brigham Young further developed the idea of the Southern Indian Mission. Jacob Hamblin and others were at Santa Clara by the spring of 1854 befriending the area's Native Americans.[3]

When outsiders came through the area, some of the Mormon missionaries served as scouts and ambassadors to the Native Americans, and they also gathered information for Brigham Young about the government's designs on the area. Exploration of the area was driven by the desire for conversions and the search for freight and transportation routes, defensive positions, and sites for future settlements.

Relations between the Mormon church and the government had an effect on local affairs, although Kane County was not settled at the time of the so-called Utah War of 1857–58, when federal troops under Colonel Albert Sidney Johnston installed newly appointed territorial governor Alfred Cumming after hearing false reports of a Mormon rebellion. At the time of Kane County's creation and settlement, the Mormon church and territorial officials were often at odds, particularly over the Mormon practice of polygamy, but outright hostilities were avoided. Still, the two groups did not really cooperate in dealing with the Black Hawk War and other Indian troubles of the late 1860s, which did profoundly affect Kane County. One effect of the Utah War on Kane County was that the name of the county comes from a non-Mormon friend of the Mormons, Colonel Thomas L. Kane, who helped negotiate peace in 1858 between the Mormons and the federal troops without blood being shed in battle.

When Johnston's Army threatened Utah on the north, future Kane County was considered among other areas as a stronghold for Mormons to retreat to. Mormon fear and hostility were evidenced in the Mountain Meadows Massacre in Washington County in September 1857, in which more than 120 California-bound emigrants were killed by Mormons and Indians in a treacherous massacre. Brigham Young sent Jacob Hamblin to explore the possibilities of retreating to the region. In fact, Young's belief that it might be necessary to move the Mormons to another locale was one impetus behind Hamblin's contacts with area Native Americans. This helped to establish the Mormons' Southern Indian Mission and eventually led to the settlement of Kane County.

The missionaries of the Southern Indian Mission were well suited for the work. They were dedicated, brave men attracted to the area and the challenge of the work, and their exploratory and missionary efforts in 1854 and after were most important to settlement of the region. Jacob Hamblin had felt the call to work among the Native Americans a few years earlier when he had the impression "that if he took not the blood of this remnant of Israel, by them he would not die."[4] A longtime member of the church, ordained to the Mormon priesthood by Joseph Smith, Hamblin was appointed president over the Santa Clara Indian Mission on 4 August 1857. On his first journey across the Arizona Strip he took along as guides Chief Naraguts of the Kaibab band of Southern Paiutes and some of his men. They traversed the southward-facing escarpment of the Vermilion Cliffs and on the second night of their journey reached a well-known watering hole for local Indians moving through the area, later known to whites as Pipe Spring. For Hamblin it was a welcome surprise.

Following essentially the same route east as the earlier Domínguez-Escalante expedition, the Mormons crossed the Colorado River at the Crossing of the Fathers and proceeded to

On numerous occasions Navajo Indians crossed the Colorado River and entered Kane County. (Utah State Historical Society)

Oraibi. There, the Hopi Indians welcomed them with a feast of meat, piki bread, beans, and peaches. Hamblin's group visited other Hopi villages and the men recorded in their journals all the novel and exotic things they saw.

Jacob Hamblin was a Mormon who came to know Kane County well. He became familiar with its canyons, rivers, and valleys as he served as a missionary to the area's Native Americans for the Mormon church. Thales H. Haskell accompanied Jacob Hamblin and other missionaries on the second trip made by the Mormon missionaries to Indians who resided along the border area between Kane County and northern Arizona. When he made the journey Haskell was twenty-five years old and had lived most of his life in what was considered the Indian frontier. He kept a journal detailing his experience on this trip in the winter of 1857–58. One entry shows his sense of adventure and the privations of what he considered the "work of the Lord."

Friday 21st—Got up at daylight, packed up, and started, following an Indian horse track, the Indians having told us that it
would lead us to water. We traveled on till we came to a place
where the track turned to the right down a steep ledge of rocks
where it was almost impossible for our animals to go. We counseled together a few minutes whether it was best to take a straight
course to where we supposed the water would be or to follow the
track. Finally, concluded to follow the track. We had the luck to
get down the rocks safe. Continued to track the horse in search of
water. In vain. Got off our course and rather bewildered. As it was
very hot some of us began to get very thirsty. Others got to quoting
Shakespeare when one of the boys remarked that he wished
Shakespeare was in hell and he was with him if they had such a
commodity as water there. I write this to show how savage men
feel traveling without water. At length we got scattered out one or
two in a place hunting for water. Finally came together at the
mouth of a kanion which headed in the Buckskin Mountains
[Kaibab Plateau]. . . . We soon arrived at the springs—watered—
took supper and all felt well.[5]

When Hamblin made another expedition across the Colorado
River in October 1859, he brought a large supply of goods to trade
and made plans to build a boat to ferry the Colorado River near the
mouth of the Paria River in present-day Arizona. Instead, however,
his group again crossed at the Crossing of the Fathers in Utah. On a
third trip, which Hamblin made in the fall of 1860, hostile Navajos
killed George Albert Smith, Jr., son of a Mormon apostle, after he
became separated from the others in the party, the first death in an
increasingly tense relationship between white settlers and local native
inhabitants of the area. Navajos had been engaged in hostilities with
the United States cavalry outside of Utah and saw the Mormon party
as more white invaders of their land.

Jacob Hamblin made notable efforts to avoid war with the
Indians and to sincerely understand their culture throughout the settlement period. Also important as a pathmaker, he helped map the
network of trails that connected Utah and Arizona, and the Mormon
Virgin River settlements and the Hopi villages, as well as numerous
paths that led through river gorges and into hitherto unfamiliar

canyons. Despite the efforts of Hamblin and others to understand and placate the Indians, Mormon appropriation of Indian lands and resources led to conflicts, including the Walker War of the mid-1850s, which hindered the settlement of southern Utah.

From its earliest years, Utah's territorial legislature realized the importance of financing road and bridge building projects along the Mormon Corridor—the settlement region extending basically north-south at the western base of the Wasatch Mountains in the north and the high plateaus in central and southern Utah. From settlements along this corridor, subsequent settlements developed, including those in Kane County. Road laws were enacted in the 1850s and appropriations were made annually to each county in response to the road-building needs of a burgeoning population. During the decade from 1860 to 1870, the legislature was especially active in approving funding that would substantially expand Utah's road system. Land was obtained and roads and bridges were constructed, including a "road to connect Washington and Piute counties through Kane County" approved 20 January 1865, soon after the creation of Kane County. This project was assisted by a $2,000 appropriation from the legislature. An additional $1,200 was authorized in 1866 "to make roads in Kane County, to be expended under the direction of the county clerk."[6]

The Creation of Kane County

Despite Brigham Young's grand dream of a Mormon empire that stretched from California to the Rocky Mountains with his proposed State of Deseret, the Territory of Utah as created by Congress was much smaller, although still huge, embracing most of present-day Utah and Nevada as well as substantial portions of Wyoming and Colorado. However, by the time Utah became a state in 1896 the original boundaries of the territory had been substantially reduced. Before he died in 1877, Brigham Young saw the territorial boundaries reduced upon five separate occasions.

Regardless of this reduction in physical size, Mormon colonization of the territory was uniquely effective. As each new area was settled, local government was organized and defined new boundaries, usually those of counties. As the territory itself was reduced in size, the number of counties increased. By the time of statehood there were a total of twenty-seven counties. Two others would be formed in the twentieth century after statehood. Between 1850 the designation of the original counties—Utah, Great Salt Lake, Sanpete, Tuilla (Tooele), Weber, and Little Salt Lake (Iron)—in early 1850 and statehood in 1896, county boundaries changed some ninety times due to local politics, settlement patterns, and available resources. The legislature created new counties as settlement proceeded to the point that an area needed local government.[7]

Originally, the territory that would eventually comprise Kane County was included in Washington County when it was created in March 1852. At this time, Washington County stretched horizontally across the entire southern edge of Utah territory, a distance of some 600 miles. Iron County to the north was redefined to also stretch across the territory, the border between the two counties being somewhat ill-defined as a latitudinal line marked from the southern edge of the Great Basin, which was designated in 1856 as a point four miles north of the northeast corner of Fort Harmony.[8] The southern edge of Washington (and later Kane) County would be clarified in print as the boundary of the territory but not precisely determined until the labors of the John Wesley Powell-directed surveys of the early 1870s of the rugged Arizona Strip country north of the Grand Canyon.

As late as the 1860s, Short Creek and Pipe Spring in Arizona were considered by some to be part of the county, and the individuals who played a key role in settling these areas moved easily over county lines. The entire region of southern Utah and northern Arizona was first settled by groups of Mormons, either sent on colonizing missions by church leaders or exploring the area from neighboring settlements in search of other settlement areas. During this period, new settlements were continually being started, but many were soon abandoned or dwindled due to problems with Native Americans or the movement of settlers to more promising sites. Boundaries and jurisdictions of authorities also frequently changed. Kane County, in fact, in its early days had three different county seats, none of which are part of the county today.

On 16 January 1864, the Utah Territorial Legislature approved an act that officially created Kane County. Its boundaries were defined on the west to include the upper Virgin River area, including Virgin City, the principal town in the new county at the time. It extended east across the remainder of the territory, thus occupying the great part of what had been Washington County, which now only included the remaining territory on the west, which was rapidly diminishing as Congress periodically assigned former territory in Utah to what was first the territory and then the new state of Nevada (created in October 1864). Kane County, as mentioned, was named for Colonel Thomas L. Kane, a non-Mormon friend of the Mormons who had been instrumental in negotiating a peaceful settlement to the so-called Utah War of 1857–58. Washington and Iron Counties also were greatly reduced in 1861 as a result of congressional action creating the territory of Colorado, reducing Utah Territory by some three degrees of longitude on the east to its later statehood boundary.

In January 1866 the territorial legislature redefined all the county boundaries, and Grafton was named the county seat of Kane County. On 12 January 1867 the legislature again defined county boundaries and named Rockville the county seat. In 1869, on 19 February, boundaries were again redefined in the area and Toquerville was named the county seat.[9] At that time, Harmony to the north was considered part of Kane County, as was also Kanarraville, which had been part of Iron County (and would be returned to that county within a few years). This brought Kane County to its greatest size, including virtually all of present-day Zion National Park, although much smaller Washington County had a population that was far greater due to flourishing St. George and surrounding towns. From this point, Kane County suffered various reductions in size until it reached its present dimensions in the 1880s.

Kanab

One of Brigham Young's earliest priorities was the building of forts, which he counseled every settlement to do after early difficulties and hostilities between the intruding Mormons and local Native Americans. When his instructions were not followed, he publicly chastised the Latter-day Saints. In an address in the Salt Lake Tabernacle on 31 July 1853, for example, he chided the people in

Sanpete County for not "forting up" as he had advised them to do. He criticized small and poorly built forts, always encouraging his people to choose the best locations and erect the most functional, highest-quality, well-designed structures possible.

Young's fellow leaders in the Mormon church echoed his teachings. On the strength of this churchwide direction, one or more forts went up in almost every community settled in from 1847 through the late 1860s, including Kanab in Kane County. The earliest forts were quickly built stockades, generally made of walls of vertical logs or squares of four walls of side-by-side log cabins, facing interior courtyards. Some forts were made of rocks and adobe mud poured into board forms to create thick, tapered walls. More labor-intensive and costly but also more sturdy were fort walls built of adobe bricks. A few forts, such as the extant Cove Creek Fort built in 1867 in Millard County, were made entirely of rock.

Kanab is Kane County's oldest and most populous city. Its settlement began humbly with the digging of crude dugouts by Jacob Hamblin and others starting in 1858. As small parties of settlers moved to the outpost in 1859 and later as part of the Mormon church's effort to extend its domain, the most experienced pioneers led their fellows in the tasks of settlement. A primitive fort was built in stages from 1865–69. It has been described as being two rows of between five and seven crude log cabins constructed on the west and on the east. On the north, one or two more cabins were built with doors facing into the 112-foot-square enclosure. Running along the south and probably partway along the north, large cedar posts, set vertically, tied tightly with rawhide strips, formed a relatively secure fence.

The earliest settlement parties included several experienced builders. Moses Farnsworth, a good mason, helped build many area pioneer homes. Edward Pugh, a builder from England, came to Utah in 1852, living first at Mill Creek. On his way to the West, he bought a threshing machine in Chicago, the first ever brought to Utah. John Rider, who helped build the Kanab fort, also worked on numerous early houses. From Ireland, Rider also had resided previously at Mill Creek. Allen Frost and James Lewis were brickmakers, a technology available in Utah after 1865. Kanab had two designer-builders who served effectively as architects—Reuben Broadbent and Charles Cram. Cram had practiced architecture in Salt Lake City, where he was a close acquaintance of Brigham Young, and became a successful builder in Kane County. Both he and Broadbent also labored as carpenters, as did Wandle and George Mace and John Stanford. The Maces and Broadbent also made cabinets and furniture. The Averett brothers were stonecutters and masons who had earlier helped construct substantial rock buildings at Manti and Ephraim in Sanpete County. Most of the early structures in Kanab were small and primitive. As family size and means grew, lean-tos and other additions were attached to the original buildings.

After the initial settlement of Kanab, explorers moved throughout the area in search of suitable land for settlement and as rangeland for cattle. Settlers first began running cattle in the Arizona Strip country as early as 1863. Ranches were established by W.B. Maxwell at Short Creek, by James M. Whitmore at Pipe Spring and Moccasin, and by Ezra Strong of Rockville on the Virgin River. Much of the land in the long valley north of Kanab was fertile and surrounded on both sides by high mountain walls. Abundant grass bordered the river that ran through the valley. Families at Berryville and Priddy Meeks at the south end of the valley all attempted to raise and graze stock in the area. Soon a number of settlements were located in the valley—now known as Long Valley—including Berryville (Glendale), 1864; Orderville; Winsor (Mt. Carmel), 1864; and Pahreah (Paria), 1865.

Although Kanab has always been the focal point of county activities and the principal settlement in Kane County, small towns in Long Valley were also important centers of agricultural and stock-raising activities. Long Valley features dramatic rock cliffs, mountainous land covered with pine trees and other vegetation, and a river running through the valley. In 1862 a team of ranchers led by John and William Berry of Kanarraville first examined Long Valley for possible rangeland for their cattle. Priddy Meeks was one of those on the journey. Meeks had come to Long Valley in 1852 from Parowan, sent by Brigham Young to locate new land for possible settlements and for grazing.[10] Even though the valley was narrow and surrounded by high mountain walls, the land in the valley was fertile and had a ready source of water, and the valley was quite long—hence the name

it came to be given. Tall and ample grass for feed lined the banks of
the river.

Berryville (Glendale)

Actual first settlement of the valley probably occurred in 1864.
John and William Berry settled in the area and then were joined by
their two older brothers, Robert and Joseph. William and Robert
Berry brought their wives—sisters Dena and Isabelle Hales. They
named their new home Berryville. The permanent settlement later
would be renamed Glendale. The valley was first called Berry Valley.
The first shelters were arranged together in a square fort. The simple
log cabins with dirt roofs and floors had doors that led into the center of the fort, which quickly became the playground for the children.
Logs taken from nearby forests were used in the construction. The
fort contained two gates, the central open space, and a log stockade
for domestic animals. A barn was built for milk cows and other animals, and the settlers eventually ran a diary at the facility.

The next year, an influx of new settlers led to the building of new
structures. The fort was expanded with heavy timbers and by 1866
included twenty-five dirt-roofed log cabins. The roofs leaked and the
dirt floors were often muddy, however, creating an unhealthy environment. Sickness was common at the fort during the early years.
The first baby born there was Sarah Meeks, the daughter of Priddy
Meeks and his wife Mary Jane Meeks, on 9 September 1864.

While the small group lived in the fort they held church meetings and gathered to sing songs and tell stories around a campfire at
night. Despite their efforts to create a normal life, they were always
aware of the potential danger that Indians posed. Everything seemed
to be going well until 1865, when trouble arose between the white
settlers of the area and the native Paiutes, perhaps as part of general
Indian discontent in central and southern Utah, exacerbated by starvation faced by many the previous winter. The area the Berrys chose
for settlement was home to about one hundred Indians. This group
of Paiutes had historically been friendly to the white intruders and
lived in temporary villages, roaming across the country to hunt and
forage for food. In addition to the Paiutes, Navajos also frequented
the region. Their main camps were farther to the south and east,

where they lived in permanent dwellings and maintained large herds of sheep and some cattle. Known for their crafts—beautifully woven baskets and woolen blankets, Navajos traveled during the summertime to hunt and fish in the mountains of southern Utah. The whites intruded upon their set patterns of existence and competed with them for resources. This caused inevitable friction between the two groups, and a series of raids and violent confrontations resulted.

As a result of the conflicts that broke out farther north in 1865, Brigham Young encouraged the families who had settled outside Kanab to gather together in Kanab and in Berryville for safety until some resolution of the conflict—known generally as the Black Hawk War—was reached. In addition, Young initially called new settlers to go south and join the fledgling settlements there to bolster them and create a more substantial population base. Joseph and Ann Hopkins came to the Kane County area from Virgin, Moses and John Harris and their families came from Harrisburg, James Maxwell from Eagle Valley, George Spencer and his family from St. George, Hosea Stout from Dixie, and numerous others from the surrounding region. In autumn 1865, residents from Mt. Carmel and other outlying settlements retreated to Berryville for safety, although they returned in the spring to plant crops at their farms.

The next year, Joseph and Robert Berry and their families traveled to Salt Lake City with others from the area to visit the Mormon church's Endowment House. On their return, they stopped at their former home of Kanarraville, where the two-year-old daughter of Robert and Isabella became sick. Joseph Berry remained with the parents while the others continued on; however, within a few days, the child died. On their return trip, the Berrys, following the normal but lengthy route that went from Washington County settlements into northern Arizona, were attacked by Indians outside of Short Creek and Cane Beds and killed, probably on about 2 April 1866. Their bodies later were discovered by a freight team traveling along the road. The location of this tragedy has since that time been known as "Berry Knoll." The killings created fear among the region's white settlers. Martial law was declared in the region on 2 May, residents were urged to congregate in the larger towns and were instructed not to travel in small groups.

In June, Erastus Snow decided to order the settlers to abandon Long Valley for the greater safety of Utah's Dixie settlements. In the evacuation, one young child was killed when he was run over by a wagon. The settlers were guarded by a militia detachment and proceeded to Washington County by way of the now also abandoned town of Kanab.

Mt. Carmel (Winsor, or Windsor)

John D. Lee was one of the first Anglo-Americans to travel through the area of future Mt. Carmel. With John C.L. Smith, John Steel, John Dart, Soloman Chamberlain, Priddy Meeks, and F.F. Whitney he traveled through Long Valley in 1852. Priddy Meeks remembered the beautiful Long Valley with its lush and plentiful vegetation and decided it would be where he and his family would settle. In 1864, when settlers first came to the area they called it Winsor (often spelled Windsor) in honor of Anson P. Winsor, LDS bishop of Grafton and a religious leader of the area. Reuben Carter arrived in the area with a herd of sheep in the fall of 1864. He built a dugout in what is now the southwest end of town near where U.S. Highway 89 crosses Muddy Creek. The next year, they were joined by other families. H.B. Jolley brought with him a large herd of livestock, dug the area's first irrigation ditch, and began plowing fields for planting.

Silas Hoyt, Henry Gardner, and William Jolley were among the early settlers who arrived with their families. They built simple dugouts at first but eventually constructed log houses. Regional church leader Erastus Snow visited the fledgling settlement, traveling from St. George in the fall of 1865, and directed the settlers to survey a townsite, distribute lots, and make the area their permanent home. By the fall of 1865, a small townsite had been surveyed.

The first baby born in Winsor—Louisa Stevens—was born in a dugout. The settlers began their settlement efforts peacefully, but soon, as was true of other Long Valley towns, they were threatened by the local Indians, who increasingly objected to the white intrusion into their ancestral lands. For security, the group moved to the Berryville fort in the fall of 1865. There they barely survived on spartan rations during the winter of 1865–66. They had no wheat or flour; cornmeal made into crackers served in place of bread. While they were there, Indians raided their homes and drove off some of their cattle, destroying property and threatening their safety. In May 1866, to protect them, Erastus Snow, the Mormon general authority in charge of the region, sent ten militiamen from St. George led by Captain John Pierce. After a failed effort by Augustus P. Hardy, a militiaman who spoke the Navajo language, to negotiate a peace treaty with the Navajos the settlers decided to flee in June 1866.

They hurriedly hitched their oxen to all available wagons, pulled together what scant provisions they had left, and loaded their wagons with bedding and other goods. Many of the women and children rode in the wagons, but some had to walk alongside. Militiamen mounted on horseback rode guard alongside the caravan out of town. Along the way, some Navajos reportedly tried to provoke the settlers, throwing sand into the oxen's eyes, trying to get the settlers to react and begin some kind of confrontation. But, perhaps because of the presence of the women and children, the settlers continued patiently toward their destination in Washington County through canyons and over difficult terrain. At night they camped and waited fearfully for morning to arrive so they could continue their journey. One child died after being run over by a wagon and another was born during that difficult journey.

After traveling past Kanab, the refugees were sent to settlements throughout southern Utah. Some of them later returned to Long Valley.

Alton (Upper Kanab)

Alton developed from Upper Kanab and then continued in existence long after the older community failed. Lorenzo Wesley Roundy, who had come with the first group of Mormon pioneers to the Salt Lake Valley in 1847, came to the valley of upper Kanab Creek in 1865 with several other families seeking land for settlement. There they found tall grass, good fodder for their animals, streams of clear water, abundant wildlife in the nearby mountains, berries and other wild fruit for picking, and timber for their homes and fences. It seemed a perfect place to make a settlement.

Lorenzo Roundy's first wife, Susanna Wallace, and her children came to the site, which was first called Roundy's Station, and the family built two log cabins that first summer.[11] Only limited evidence remains of the location of other homes; piles of logs or rocks suggest that other settlers were there but it is unclear exactly where. That fall, Roundy left Susanna and traveled with his plural wife Priscilla Parrish and her family to Salem in Utah County. During his absence, Paiute Indians caused some trouble for settlers in the area. Susanna, who had only her fourteen-year-old son, Napolean, to protect the family, was scared. Other families left the fledgling community; however, Susanna Roundy stayed and waited for her husband, who eventually returned for her.

In 1865 the settlers of Upper Kanab, along with most of those in various other locations in the area, were ordered by Mormon church authorities to go to Kanab for protection and to help strengthen the fortifications located there. Others later were sent to Dixie or other locations. Lorenzo Roundy went to Kanarraville; he drowned in the Colorado River in 1876 at the age of fifty-seven in the process of ferrying supplies across the river, leaving his plural wives widows and their many children fatherless.

The Black Hawk War

During the 1860s, sporadic raids on white settlers on farms or ranches continued; but they increased dramatically between 1865 and 1867, perhaps as part of the general Native American anger and discontent that resulted in the Black Hawk War in central and southern Utah. Each fledgling white settlement had to make accommodations to the continued threat of attack. At the site of Kanab, the settlers raised their log fort during the winter of 1865–66. Inside the stockade, a twenty-by-thirty-foot stone structure provided additional security. The fort was vacated in 1866. Hostilities and conflict in southern Utah continued to 1872. Throughout southern Utah families vacated their homes and moved into forts. Eventually entire communities were abandoned for various lengths of time during the conflict.

In January 1866 stockmen Robert McIntyre and Dr. James M. Whitmore were killed by Native Americans near Pipe Spring.[12] This was the first of many attacks that signaled the beginning of the Black Hawk War in extreme southern Utah. Militia troops from St. George sent to investigate were hindered by severe weather but eventually came upon a small group of Indians. The accused Paiutes themselves were near starvation and were murdered by some of the militiamen in revenge for the deaths of Whitmore and McIntyre.

Jacob Hamblin made several peace expeditions to the Hopi (also known at the time as Moqui, or Moki) Indians, traveling on the trail that passed by Kanab over the north end of the Buckskin Mountain to the Hopi villages across the Colorado River. Despite successful negotiations between the Mormons and the area's Paiute and Hopi Indians, the Navajos continued to threaten the white settlers. Hamblin later wrote, "Many of the pioneers did not realize the situation the friendly Indians were made to suffer. Those that were unfriendly raided the settlements and drove off hundreds of head of cattle, horses, and mules. Many of the Indians who had at first been friendly went back to the old ways of raiding and stealing. This caused our people also to manifest hostility towards the red man."[13]

Though many Paiutes remained peaceful and even shared the Kanab fort with whites, some aggressive Navajos posed a significant and continuing threat to the security of local pioneers. Mormon church leaders ordered the evacuation of the area, and Pipe Spring and the Long Valley settlements were abandoned in the summer of 1866 after the settlers had planted their crops. The crops were left in the care of friendly Paiutes. Even as white settlers retreated to Washington County, attacks continued, and a number were killed. By the end of 1866 virtually all the settlements in the Kane County area had been deserted.

Early in 1867, a company including Jacob Hamblin, John R. Young, Ira Hatch, Thales Haskell, and forty-seven other men traveled to Native American villages across the Colorado River seeking peace. Considering the violence of the past two years, this took considerable courage, but peace was critical to the future of their settlements. Hamblin subsequently made other visits to area Native Americans and gradually established a position as a trusted advocate of peace. Hamblin centered his activities in the fort at Kanab, and it has been estimated that eventually as many as 350 Native Americans lived in the area with the pioneers, some planting and tending crops, helping guard the settlement, and clearing land. According to Benjamin

A Paiute Indian photographed in the early 1870s. (Utah State Historical Society)

Hamblin, a son of Jacob who lived at the fort, "eight or ten of these Indians grubbed brush from the land on the west side of the creek so that it could be planted for the white settlers when they came back from their forced evacuation. These Indians received their food from the church. The rations were issued by John Mangum. The other Indians hunted rabbits and wild game. At this time these friendly

Indians lived in the fort for protection and so they could render assistance to the men on guard in case of a raid from Navajos."[14]

By 1867 Black Hawk and most of his followers and sympathizers had made peace; however, hostilities continued with the Navajos in southern Utah, and there were also a few raids by hostile Ute Indians and others farther north that continued into the early 1870s. Settlers thus were apprehensive as they attempted to resettle the many communities abandoned in the mid-1860s during the hostilities. Kanab's fort was refurbished to accommodate Paiutes and Anglos alike. Navajos continued to raid and drove off about 2,500 head of stock in the area. The militia aided locals in pursuing the raiders but rarely took any prisoners. Hostile Navajos posed a serious threat to the security of white settlers, raiding throughout the greater Four Corners region, including Kane County. No one was exempt from attack.

When some Long Valley settlers attempted to return to their homes, they were attacked nine miles south of Mt. Carmel, their livestock were scattered, and many wagons partially destroyed. Jacob Hamblin, John Mangum, George Ross, and James Wilkins moved their families back to Kanab in 1869. Navajo raids continued throughout 1869 despite repeated efforts at negotiation. In September 1869 Jacob Hamblin moved from Santa Clara in Washington County to Kanab, where he could better manage his efforts to maintain peace with local Indians. The next year, Brigham Young traveled to Kanab with Major John Wesley Powell.

In 1869 Powell made his first exploration of the Colorado River, returning from the river by way of southern Utah settlements. Earlier, in September 1869, three men of his expedition—brothers Seneca and O.G. Howland and William Dunn—had left the exploring party at Separation Rapid in the Grand Canyon and hiked out to the north from there, being subsequently killed north of the Grand Canyon (perhaps in Kane County, but more likely in northern Arizona), reportedly by Shivwits Indians, who mistook them for some prospectors who had violated an Indian woman. Their bodies were never found, however, and some controversy still exists to the present time, including speculation that they could have been killed by Mormons of the Kane County region who mistook them for investigators of the

Mountain Meadows Massacre that had occurred to the west some twelve years earlier.[15]

In December 1869 Jacob Hamblin organized a farm for Native Americans on the Paria River, and efforts were made to help the Indians become self sufficient.[16] The following letter to Mormon leader Erastus Snow on 27 March 1870 indicates Hamblin's sincere devotion to the idea of helping to improve the standard of living for the Paiutes.

> I have just returned from Pahreah. All well there. Business prospering finely under the Presidency of William Meeks. There is a safe Guard House and small corral there where men can cook and lodge safely with 20 or 25 horses; one outside gate only for horses and corral. We have finished there one mile and a half of water ditch. I consider it permanent, as we need no dam. We have put in 6 acres of wheat and some garden seeds. We have eight laboring native men there, two women and six children. I took them in on condition that they subsist on half rations depending on roots and their former diet for the balance. They have a large bredth of land ready for the plow and were still clearing off, when I came away, at the rate of one acre and a half a day. There is no lack of water or the very best of land on the stream.
>
> We have not been able to discern any sign of Navajos since Bro. Miller came there. We have 800 yards of good fence newly put up at Kanab, we expect to finish the fencing this week. . . . [17]

Hamblin made ten crossings of the Colorado River between 1858 and 1871 under Brigham Young's instructions. On a trip in 1869 he first used the crossing near the mouth of the Paria River later called Lees Ferry. Lees Ferry marks the end of Glen Canyon at the place where the Colorado River enters Marble Canyon on its path to the Grand Canyon. It was the only location for some 275 miles along the Colorado River where a vehicle could somewhat conveniently be brought to the water's edge. In 1870, with wood from the Kaibab Forest, Jacob Hamblin built the first ferry at the location to haul settlers and supplies across the river. By 1872 John D. Lee had come to run the ferry and to hide from federal officials investigating the Mountain Meadows Massacre in 1857, in which more than 120 California-bound immigrants were killed by Mormons and Indians in Washington County. Lee moved to the area in December 1871 with one of his plural wives, Emma. She called the place "Lonely Dell." Eventually Lee established regular ferry service across the river. Although it was a natural crossing point of the river, the crossing was still extremely difficult and dangerous. As one historian described it: "The approach to the right bank from the west was easy enough, but on the left bank a ridge dipping sharply upstream rose almost vertically from the river's edge. The first ferry crossing was upstream from the base of the ridge, forcing travelers to cross the barrier, which soon acquired the name 'Lee's Backbone.'"[18] John D. Lee was captured by federal authorities, and was tried, convicted, and executed in 1877. His ferry continued to be used as an important crossing point of the Colorado River, however, and the area became known as Lees Ferry, a name it has continued to have ever since.

Endnotes

1. Ray M. Reeder, "The Mormon Trail: A History of the Salt Lake to Los Angeles Route" (Ph.D. diss., Brigham Young University, 1966), 240.

2. Ibid., 240–50.

3. See Angus M. Woodbury, "A History of Southern Utah and Its National Parks," *Utah Historical Quarterly* 12 (July–Oct. 1944): 144 n. 36, for a list of the original missionaries to the area's Native Americans.

4. Adonis Findlay Robinson, *History of Kane County*, 2.

5. Juanita Brooks, "Journal of Thales H. Haskell," *Utah Historical Quarterly* 12 (1944): 74.

6. "Territorial Appropriation Bill," in Appendix 3, Ezra C. Knowlton, *History of Highway Development in Utah* (Salt Lake City: Utah State Department of Highways, n.d.), 759, 765.

7. See James B. Allen, "The Evolution of County Boundaries in Utah," *Utah Historical Quarterly* 23 (July 1955): 261–78.

8. Ibid., 268.

9. Wilbur E. Dodson, "Historical Sketch of Kane County" (1937), 4–5, Utah State Historical Society Library.

10. See Woodbury, "A History of Southern Utah and Its National Parks," 142–43.

11. John W. Van Cott, *Utah Place Names* (Salt Lake City: University of Utah Press, 1990), 5.

12. An extended account of this attack is found in Robinson, *History of Kane County*, 8.

13. Richard L. Dewey, ed., *Jacob Hamblin: His Life in His Own Words*, 121.

14. Robinson, *History of Kane County*, 12.

15. See, for example, Wesley P. Larsen, "The 'Letter' Or Were the Powell Men Really Killed by Indians?" *Canyon Legacy* 17 (1993): 12–19.

16. Erastus Snow to Brigham Young, 7 December 1869, LDS Church Archives.

17. Quoted in James G. Bleak, "Annals of the Southern Utah Mission," Book B, 41–42, Dixie College Library, St. George, Utah.

18. C. Gregory Crampton, *Land of Living Rock*, 143.

CHAPTER 5

THE RESETTLEMENT OF KANE COUNTY, 1870–1880

Initial Resettlement of Kanab

Serious efforts at resettling Kane County began in 1870 with the arrival of a company of immigrants from the Cottonwood area of the Salt Lake Valley. In the 1870s the town of Kanab grew in spurts as companies of settlers were sent there from other settlements. Three waves of settlers recolonized the area. First, were those from the initial group of the 1860s who returned with Jacob Hamblin and a few others to the vicinity of the old Kanab fort in the late 1860s to begin resettlement efforts. They were joined in 1870 by the group led by Levi Stewart that left the Cottonwood area of the Salt Lake Valley at the direction of Brigham Young. The last group came out of the Mormon Muddy Mission in Nevada's Moapa Valley and arrived in Kane County in 1871.

Brigham Young and a party of general authorities of the Mormon church visited Kane County settlements in the spring of 1870. The church leaders laid out a fort for the settlers at Pipe Spring, hopeful that conditions were more favorable for resettlement. The fort was to be "152 feet long and 66 feet wide, the wall next to the bluff 30 feet high, with two-story dwellings inside and the wall on the lower side 20 feet high, with milk rooms etc."[1] The Pipe Spring fort was dubbed Winsor (or Windsor) Castle because of its unique two-story construction. The name comes from Anson P. Winsor, Mormon bishop of Grafton, who was in charge of Long Valley settlements and after whom the town of Mount Carmel was originally named. The variant spelling comes from the notion of some that the Winsor family could trace their origins back to the builders of Windsor Castle in England.

Brigham Young visited Kanab on 2 April 1870 with George A. Smith, Erastus Snow, John Taylor, and other Mormon church leaders. While there, Young dedicated Kanab to the work of the Lord. The area's potential for grazing was recognized and the group decided to recommend the area for cattle, sheep, and horse raising.

After Brigham Young returned to Salt Lake City, he selected Levi Stewart as the leader of a new company of families that would be sent to settle near Kanab Creek. Most of the fifty-two members of the group were from the Cottonwood area of the Salt Lake Valley. The group arrived one month after they left in May. Some stopped at Pipe Spring, but the majority of the group traveled on to Kanab where they found some of the original settlers living in the fort along with a few friendly Paiutes. While the fort was a welcome sight, it was far from ideal, and the new settlers set to work making their new homes.

The group met for religious services on 19 June 1870 and Levi Stewart assumed temporary leadership over the colonists. Within a few weeks some had moved out of the fort into makeshift shelters. Ditch digging proceeded for irrigation and community building began again. Brigham Young twice visited the Kanab fort in 1870, the second time, in September, bringing with him surveyor Jesse W. Fox. Fox surveyed a townsite, which measured one mile square, with thirty-two-rod square blocks and six-rod-wide streets intersecting at right angles. The center block was reserved for public buildings, the block to the west being claimed by Brigham Young; the street that ran between them was called Brigham Street. The remaining blocks were divided into four lots each and each family head drew lots for the land.

Levi Stewart who was called by Brigham Young to lead the resettlement of Kanab in 1870. (Utah State Historical Society)

Wells were dug, fences set up, and flowers, trees, and gardens planted to beautify the rustic environment. Efforts were made to improve the insides of homes as well. Of the residential interiors, it was reported that,

> The houses were poorly furnished with a few pieces of home-made furniture. Mattresses for the beds were ticks filled with straw or corn husks. What carpets there were, were hand woven and were tacked over a matting of clean straw. Dishes were not plenti-

ful. Many of them were made of tin. Only a few necessities were kept in a makeshift store in the early days. Bishop Stewart kept a few staple supplies on hand such as thread, calico and the like.[2]

Kanab early on became the recognized center of settlement efforts in Kane County. It was the supply station for expeditions passing through the area as well as the hub of missionary and exploration activities and pioneering. It served as a trading post, a resting stop, and a base of operations for the men of the Powell and Wheeler U.S. Geological Surveys.

When the first settlers came to Kanab, Brigham Young advised them to farm just south of Kanab Creek. He predicted: "The canyon will gut out from one end to the other and from one side to the other, and you will have all the water you need for a flourishing city."[3] He also encouraged the settlers to build an irrigation canal that would circulate around the town. A reservoir built at Big Lake a distance up Kanab Creek was an important source of water for the town. A main ditch and subsidiary ditches were dug to furnish water to the various farms, and every street in town was lined by an irrigation ditch. This facilitated the planting of fields, gardens, and orchards. John Ensign Riggs was designated as watermaster in the early 1870s. Each morning water was turned into the ditches for culinary uses. What remained was stored in the reservoir. Other water was found at a point south of town called "Square-Hole Bottom," where water could be obtained by digging holes two to three feet deep.

In 1870 the Kanab LDS Ward was organized and Levi Stewart appointed bishop. On 13 September 1870 a council of town members proposed to build a schoolhouse. The construction project was to be funded by taxes on city lots and farming land. Stewart brought machinery for a sawmill with him to Kanab, and he built the mill near Skutumpah Creek north of Kanab and soon was producing lumber for construction. With John D. Lee operating the equipment, lumber was first sawn at Stewart's mill on 31 October 1870. The earliest squared logs and sawn boards were used in cabins built for Stewart and for Moses F. Farnsworth. The four cabins were constructed along the north side of the fort.

Tragedy struck the community in the fort on the night of 14

December 1870 when fire engulfed one of the cabins of Bishop Stewart as members of his family slept. Coal oil, turpentine, and kegs of powder reportedly were also being stored in the structure, and it seems that the oil soon ignited after the fire started, trapping a number of children in the cabin. Margery Stewart, the mother of some of the children and a plural wife of the bishop, rushed into the inferno to try to rescue the trapped children and died along with three of her sons and two sons of the bishop by other wives, most likely in an explosion that collapsed the roof of the structure, blocking retreat. One child was rescued by Eke Stout, a son of noted pioneer Hosea Stout.[4]

In late 1870 the community decided to build its combination school and meetinghouse—a 28-by-36-foot structure. It was built of rock and lumber under the direction of Edward Pugh and was in use by January 1871. The school was built on the site of the burned cabin of Bishop Stewart and featured tall, small-paned windows, a board roof, and a fireplace at one end. It also served as a social hall. Other meetings and celebrations were held in an open-air bowery built of logs and branches in the center of the block north of the public square.

Although Indian troubles essentially ended with treaties signed in the late 1860s, the area forts remained into the 1870s and beyond until they were gradually dismantled and the materials salvaged to build other structures, walls, and ditches. Of the many scores of forts built in Utah Territory, few if any were ever attacked. Yet they served as a deterrent to attack while sheltering settlers, their possessions, and livestock. Also, as cooperative building projects, they had a unifying effect on the struggling communities in which they were built. The first houses built outside the fort were largely temporary structures, which provided rudimentary shelter and protection from the elements and Indian raids. The people remained cautious due to the possibility of hostilities with Indians. Edward Pugh's one-room house had portholes in the walls from which to watch for danger. The first man to finish his house outside the fort was Lyman Porter.

Zadok K. Judd, Sr., who had come west with the Mormon Battalion, brought his family to Kanab from Eagle Valley in April 1871. He drove his wagon to a town lot, put the wagon box on the ground and built a shed roof over it along with a porch. He soon dug out a cellar lined with rock beneath the wagon and laid a temporary floor. Judd and his son built a shelter over their wagon and joined a group of men going to Upper Kanab to stake out farms. The temporary home served the family well. As a later historian recorded, the younger Judd related that the family

> lived in the cellar awhile. Father and I stayed in Kanab long enough to make a shed over Mother's wagon, then we joined a company going to Upper Kanab to establish a farm. Members of that company as I remember them were: Edwin Pugh, James L. Bunting, Nathan Adams, William Crosby, F.M. Hamblin, Alma Spillsbury, Newman Brown, Zadok K. Judd, Sr., A.D. Young, Jr., Will Eager, Yance Anderson, Newman Brown, Jr., and Zadok K. Judd, Jr.[5]

That farm labor was a failure, for the wheat planted was reported as "an entire loss." After a few months, the Judds returned to Kanab discouraged with the potential of the area of Upper Kanab for settlement and Zadok helped his father build an adobe house.

By 1872 more settlers had begun moving out of the fort onto lots in the new townsite, often living in their wagons until they had built their first homes. Both Francis M. Hamblin and Edwin Ford lived in single rooms made of willow while erecting their adobe houses. Other adobe dwellings were built by William and Taylor Crosby, Ira Hatch, Gurnsey Brown, James A. Little, and Charles Oliphant with adobe bricks produced in an adobe yard not far from the center of town.

David Udall and Charles Shumway constructed two of the area's earliest rock houses. Bishop Levi Stewart's house, completed in 1872, was the largest in town at the time. It was a two-story, six-room dwelling on a fenced lot with a well. At about the same time, his son Tom Stewart built a house nearby, Ira Hatch erected a two-room adobe home, John Rider put up a residence of lumber, and George Adair made one of logs. The latter was a one-story dwelling with a full-width front porch and a fireplace at one end. A little later, after the beginning of brickmaking in the 1880s, Lacy Stiltson and William Clayton constructed the town's earliest brick-and-frame houses.

Frederick Dellenbaugh in his book *A Canyon Voyage* described his first glimpse of Kanab in late 1871 as a member of John Wesley Powell's second Colorado River expedition, giving perhaps the most complete early description of the settlement:

> I was much interested to see Kanab, of which so much had been said. I decided to take a Sunday trip in that direction. On the 17th of December about noon I put a saddle on a white mule . . . and was soon on my way. Emerging from the Chocolate Cliffs, the road led along the Vermilion Cliffs, crossing long ridges covered with cedars and pines, and soon joining a road that led from the canyon to the eastward where there was a very small settlement called Johnson. . . .
>
> I was in Kanab by three o'clock. The village which had been started only a year or two, was laid out in the characteristic Mormon style, with wide streets and regular lots fenced by wattling willows between stakes. Irrigating ditches ran down each side of every street and from them the water, derived from a creek that came down a canyon back of the town, could be led into any of the lots, each of which was about one quarter of an acre. . . . Fruit trees and vines had been planted and were already beginning to promise near results, while corn, potatoes, etc., gave fine crops. The original place of settlement was a square formed by one story log houses on three sides and a stockade on the fourth. This was called the fort and was a place of refuge. . . . One corner of the fort was made by the walls of the schoolhouse, which was at the same time meeting-house and ball-room. Altogether there were about 100 families in the village. The houses that had been built outside the fort were quite substantially constructed, some of adobe or sun-dried brick. The entire settlement had a thrifty air, as is the case with the Mormons. Not a grog-shop, or gambling saloon, or dance-hall was to be seen; quite in contrast with the usual disgraceful accompaniments of the ordinary frontier towns. A perfectly orderly government existed, headed by a bishop appointed by the church authorities in Salt Lake City. . . . I found Clem and Beaman [Walter Clement Powell, a nephew of Major Powell, and expedition photographer E.O. Beaman] domiciled with their photographic outfits with a swarm of children peeping through every crevice of the logs to get a view of the "Gentiles," a kind of animal they had seldom seen.[6]

Kanab by 1872 had become a somewhat substantial settlement composed of what Dellenbaugh described as a "stockaded square of log houses and some few neat adobe houses outside; about fifty in all. The settlement was growing strong enough to scatter itself somewhat about the site marked off for the future town." He further remarked, "One of the first things the Mormons always did in establishing a new settlement was to plant fruit and shade trees, and vines, and the like, so that in a very few years there was a condition of comfort only attained to by a non-Mormon settlement after the lapse of a quarter of a century."[7]

By 1 April 1872 the *Deseret News* could report significant growth in the area of Kanab:

> This part of the territory is being settled very rapidly. The people are busy farming and fencing their lots. Cattle have done excellently all winter and there is an abundance of feed. Fall wheat looks good and a considerable amount of spring grain has been sown. Great interest is being shown in planting of fruit trees. Probably more trees have been set out here than in any other settlement of the same size in the country. A steam sawmill is situated at Scootumpah creek where there is an abundance of grass and timber. There is a good road to the mill and business is good. Last November, Jacob Hamblin made a treaty with the Navajos, a number of whom visited Kanab and gave assurance of peace.[8]

Landscaping was a secondary consideration and also was difficult; most town land was covered with sagebrush and cactus. The lots had to be carefully cleared before gardens could be planted or flowers planted along paths between buildings. Before long, however, snapdragons, bachelor buttons, larkspurs, poppies, lilics, and roses, planted with seeds carefully brought to Kanab from other places, made the desert town look inviting.

While homes and meeting places were being constructed, early attempts at building needed industrial structures were made, not all of them successful. With the community desperately in need of a flour mill, Wandle Mace brought in a waterwheel to drive his set of millstones made of volcanic rock. However, because there was not enough water in Kanab Creek to turn the wheel consistently, Mace

The James William Thaxton Log Home. (Courtesy Deanne Glover)

sold the mill and it was dismantled and moved to Arizona. Cheese factory machinery was sent from Salt Lake City in 1871. In 1873 a tannery and gristmill were built to serve the burgeoning populace of Kanab. The mill was designed and built by the team of Reuben Broadbent and James Leithead but seems to have soon failed or been destroyed.

Edward Pugh brought the first threshing machine to Kanab when he moved there from Cottonwood. He had ordered the thresher from Chicago in 1862. It required five men to run the machine, with a team of five horses and cooperative effort to successfully maneuver it. Sawmills were established on the Kaibab Plateau near Jacob Lake and near the Divide in the northern part of the county, and a shingle mill operated on the Seaman Ranch.

Before a federal land office was established in Utah in 1869 all grants and claims of land technically were not legally binding. Nevertheless, the Mormon pioneers proceeded to claim and distribute land among themselves in the absence of the federal government, although it was not possible to secure title to that land. Mormon church and territorial government officials developed their own systems, never claiming more than temporary jurisdiction over available lands until the federal recognition was granted. Existing federal laws in force before the settlement of Utah Territory provided for a claim on public land of no less than forty acres or more than one hundred sixty acres by heads of families and individuals over twenty-one years of age, which land could be patented after fourteen months of occupancy and the payment of $1.25 per acre. Regardless of how generous this seemed to be, it was ill-suited for much of Kane County, where the distribution of land became the concern of the county court after the county was created.

During the 1870s and 1880s, the Kane County Court, or Commission, as it was later known, held its meetings in the Kanab LDS tithing office, and meetings were always opened with prayer. On 8 January 1870, the court agreed to receive produce in payment of county taxes at the following rates: wheat, $2.00 a bushel; shelled corn, $1.75 per bushel; oats, $1.50 per bushel; molasses, $1.50 per gallon.[9]

Efforts of the area's first settlers to establish an agricultural base were discouraging. The 1870 census listed only 1,244 acres of improved land in the entire county, a county which had a total area at the time of about 2.8 million acres. Furthermore, the census report estimated that there were probably only twenty more acres in the settled river valleys that could be improved. According to this census, there were 115 farms in the county, only one of which was larger than fifty acres. The census listed 341 boys and young adult males between five and eighteen years old. These were young men who would eventually need land for themselves, which put strains on available resources.[10] Already in the 1870s Kane faced the potential of significant out-migration, even before the county's towns had become fully established. One study suggests that 88 percent of the children born in the county's towns died elsewhere between 1870 and 1910.[11] Moreover, in the region which included Washington, Kane, and Iron Counties, about 71 percent of those born there during this period moved elsewhere before they died.

This suggests that one way of dealing with the difficulties of the area was simply to leave. Eventually, out-migration reached such proportions that Mormon church headquarters sent general authorities to southern Utah to rally the settlers and encourage them to stay. Kane County resident Rebecca Mace recorded a visit of regional leader Erastus Snow and his efforts to bolster the Mormons in their settlement efforts: "He found there was quite a number of families preparing to leave, move away, for like all settlements in southern Utah, it was a hard struggle to make a living, and build homes. He said he did not want this place decimated, but rather built up."[12]

John R. Young visited Kanab in 1871 and described the efforts to grow crops. He said that the grasshoppers had taken part of the wheat that was growing, and he continued, "The crop was light at the best, having been planted with a lick and a promise and not watered until too late to have a satisfactory stand."[13] Perhaps the most serious deterrent to the settlement of Kane County was the limited water resources. Kanab had always had extremely limited irrigation water for its irrigated land, among the lowest amount per acre of any place in the state.[14] Immigrants coming to the county, even those from northern Utah, were experienced at farming in a more favorable environment in terms of water. Kane County's arid environment presented enormous obstacles to farming, and most settlers soon turned to stock raising. Implicit in any decision of where to settle was the identification of nearby sources of water for culinary purposes and for agriculture. Communities were all located near predictable water sources; if they were not, they did not survive for long. The distribution of water became a matter for communities to regulate. Individuals joined together in irrigation companies; towns regulated the use and distribution of water.

The first effort at piping water into Kanab was complicated. Irrigation water was taken from a dam that ran into a settling pond, then into a cistern, then into water mains. Later, pipe was run to a spring in Hog Canyon, and another pipe was run to Cave Lakes, seven miles north of town, to supply water to farms around the area. But the water supply was unpredictable. Early crude dams were often swept away by heavy spring floods. The winter of 1880, for example, was referred to for years as the "Wash out"—days of heavy rains followed by deep snows created spring floods.

County courts were given power over water regulation, timber, and granting of mill sites, with the intent to best preserve the natural resources.[15] The work of regulation included the appointment of watermasters to oversee the regulation and maintenance of irrigation systems and to ensure that orders of the court were properly executed. Counties were divided into water districts according to the basic sources of water. The county court also regulated the location of irrigation canals and reservoirs, and controlled the use of springs and streams. Private irrigation companies provided the requisite labor building canals, reservoirs, and water systems, but county and local governments also provided support.

Many area residents soon turned to ranching and stock raising. Edwin G. Woolley, an adjutant of a unit of the Utah Territorial Militia, wrote on 27 February 1869 about the ideal grazing conditions near Pipe Spring: "This is the best stock range in this Southern Country. [The country] west from here 30 miles or more is a sea of grass, and running northeast from here thirty miles the same."[16] Some traditions maintain that Levi Stewart first brought cattle to Kanab when he arrived in the 1870s. John Ensign Riggs also brought cattle to the area during the decade. Tom Emmett ran cattle at a ranch located at Cottonwood. Francis M. Hamblin ran a united order dairy at Swallow Park; after the order dissolved, Hamblin went into the cattle business with his sons William and Frank. Other early cattlemen included Nephi and Sixtus Johnson, who ran cattle at the settlement known as Johnson and also managed John Kitchen's cattle while he went to California in search of gold. The Johnsons also brought Angora goats to Kane County. Charles S. Cram and his sons ran cattle in Stewart Canyon; Joseph Hamblin ranged herds in the sandhills bordering the Paria River.

Anson P. Winsor organized the Canaan Cooperative Stock Company in 1870 out of Pipe Spring. The Kanarra Cattle Company grazed cattle on the Markagunt and Paunsaugunt Plateaus. Others herded cattle along the rim of Bryce Canyon and along the Paria River. The Orderville United Order cooperatively owned a number of ranches and herds. It grazed one on the Kaibab Plateau in 1877; during the winter the cattle grazed in House Rock Valley.

Cattle round-ups became community affairs. Men, women, and older children all joined in the effort to drive the cows to a branding corral in the public square at Kanab. One historian reported,

At one public round-up the corral became so crowded that the fence between it and the tithing lot had to be pulled down to make room for the roping of the calves that had to be branded. The calves were roped and brought near the fire where the branding irons were heated. Some people did their branding at home before sending the young cattle to feed through the valley south of town.[17]

Later it became inconvenient to have the corral located in Kanab, and it was moved to the mouth of Tom's Canyon near the northeast corner of town. Cowboys would ride horses over the range in search of cattle that had wandered from the herd. They brought along a mess wagon, as they might be gone for weeks. After the cattle were branded, they were driven to the ranges located to the south and west for months of grazing.

By 1874, 52 percent of Kanab's farm production was in animals and animal products. Only 14 percent represented field crops such as grains and traditional agricultural produce. As much as 71 percent of the assessed wealth of Kanab was in livestock and moveable goods.[18] By the time of the next census, 15,371 head of livestock confirmed that Kane County's open spaces had proven to be better suited for ranching than farming.[19]

Lifestyle

Early residents of the county joined frequently for cooperative endeavors. In fact, it seemed that cooperation was critical for survival. Community members also met often in Mormon church conferences, where they received both practical advice and theological teaching from their ecclesiastical leaders. Much advice was practical in nature and blurred the line between the sacred and the temporal.

County government, religious institutions like the united order, and family organizations helped create a sense of community unity. People of Kane County also joined together in a variety of different organizations for recreation, education, or for fraternal or sororial connections. The Kane County Commission minutes frequently mention projects sponsored by local clubs. For example, a group organized the Philamathian Debating Society on 9 January 1872 with the following officers: W.D. Johnson, president; Lyman Hamblin, vice-president; and B.L. Young, secretary. In February 1873 a literary and lecturing society was organized, with Levi Stewart, president; David Udall, vice-president; and W.S. Johnson, secretary. Thomas Robertson addressed the first meeting of the society on the topic of cooperation. That same year, a "grand vocal concert" was given by the town's glee club on Christmas Eve in the schoolhouse under the direction of one E. Ford. Tickets were purchased for fifty cents or an equivalent amount of produce. Over the holidays a grand ball was held at Levi Stewart's home to raise funds for music books for the eleven-member choir and the glee club; dancers danced to fiddle music. Eventually an organ was purchased for the meetinghouse.

A school board consisting of Levi Stewart, Johiel McConnell, and James L. Bunting was elected in January 1871. It organized a day school with forty-seven students. Within a year there were eighty students at the school. William D. Johnson was the first teacher, and he was assisted by Persis Brown. Within another year there were about 100 students sharing the few books. The building was heated by a wood-burning stove and furnished with desks made of wood and metal for school classes.[20] Norman B. Cram walked to school and later recalled: "The kids would do their chores before school. If you missed the bucket while milking the cow you would go to school with the wet milk on your pants. Standing in front of the radiators to dry your pants would get really stinky."[21] The early teachers were strict and attempted to maintain order in their small classroom. Johnson taught school classes until 1877 when he was made local LDS bishop. Other school classes were held in private homes, some during the summer months. Ellen Meeks Hoyt, who taught at the Orderville school, was selected to teach by the school principal at Kanab. Candidates included those students who had received the highest grades while in school themselves. Hoyt received a certificate to teach in 1881 when she was fifteen years old.

The hardy settlers who came to Kane County built houses, sawmills, irrigation systems, and other elements basic to survival. But they also valued community recreation. Traditional activities like quilting bees were common and helped forge relationships between neighbors. Larger celebrations on Christmas and the Fourth and Twenty-fourth of July were community affairs. When Frederick Dellenbaugh visited Kanab in 1871, he attended a dance held on

Christmas Day. His account illustrates ways that the pioneers gathered for recreation.

> It was rainy and the men on the Powell Survey who were camped just over the Utah-Arizona State line came to Kanab in the evening to witness a dance that had been announced to take place in the school house, tabernacle, or town hall—a stone building in the corner of the fort which answered for all of these functions. The room was about fifteen by thirty feet and was lighted by three candles, a kerosene lamp, and a blazing fire of pitch-pine. Two violins were in lively operation, one being played by Lyman Hamblin, the son of old Jacob, and there was a refreshing air of gaiety about the whole assembly. The dance was opened with prayer. Two sets could occupy the floor at one time, and to even things up and prevent anyone from being left out, numbers were given each man, the numbers being called in rotation. None of our party joined as we were such strangers but we were made welcome in every respect.[22]

Dancing was by far the most popular amusement in Kane County, enjoyed by both young and old. Virtually any available combination of instruments served to accompany the cotillion and square dances, the Virginia Reel, McCloud's Reel, and the Six Nations, and the waltz was always popular as well. James E. Bunting remembered that there were strict rules about proper behavior at evening dances:

> The people celebrated four holidays a year, the Fourth and Twenty-Fourth of July, Christmas, and New Year. They held dances every Friday night, and danced the schottische, Virginia Reel, polka and the "Varsovienne." The rule was that one could not swing his partner more than once around. If he did, he had to go to church and ask forgiveness. James and six other boys had to ask forgiveness one Sunday morning. Each took his turn separately and said the same thing. "Sorry I broke the rule but will try not to do it again." Then the congregation voted to forgive them. Jim went to another dance, but had trouble stopping and swung his partner around twice. He should have asked forgiveness again, but instead he decided to stop dancing until there was a new bishop and the rule was changed.[23]

Predictably, Pioneer Day (24 July) was celebrated with particular enthusiasm in the early years of settlement. The entire town was decorated with bunting, flags, and other patriotic items. At midnight, guns began shooting salutes while bells were rung. Martial and string bands added to the fanfare early in the morning, traveling through Kanab and serenading each home. At eight or nine o'clock in the morning the entire town gathered along the center street for the parade. The band led out, followed by a float with a lovely young girl who portrayed "Utah." Pioneer wagons trailed in her wake and men dressed to represent Mormon Battalion soldiers. Another float usually was covered with sagebrush, with "Indians" hiding, although in highly visible positions. The townsfolk met under a bowery in the town center, where a program of speeches, songs, recitations, and music by the town's martial band was presented. The children attended an early dance at six o'clock in the evening; it was followed by a dance for adults that continued long into the night.

Besides vegetables and fruit trees, a household garden of the pioneer period typically would have included medicinal herbs such as tansy, anise, catnip, hops, and mint. In the early days, no professional doctors lived in the county, so folk medicine provided the only relief available. Rachael Woolley Dalley remembered the methods pioneers would take to cure ailments:

> I remember as a child we always had to wear a little red flannel bag of asafetida around our necks in the spring to keep away smallpox. Many a night my peaceful slumbers have been disturbed by that dreadful, croupy bark my brother used to give in the dark hours of the night. Mother would grab the kerosene lamp and try to pour out a few spoonfuls on some sugar to force down him as he struggled for breath.
>
> Our hired men, eight to twelve in number, always let their hair grow during the winter to protect their heads from the icy blasts while out cutting logs, etc. When spring came they could always find one among them to wield the comb and shear and what a clipping and shearing took place. . . . A few handfuls of the hair were gathered up, snipped very fine with the scissors, then mixed with honey and tame sage and choked down our unwilling throats as a cure for worms. A symptom of worms was gritting our teeth and

In 1880 Mormon pioneers on their way to the San Juan River in southeastern Utah traveled through the eastern part of Kane County and descended
through the Hole-in-the-Rock to reach the crossing of the Colorado River.
(Utah State Historical Society)

moaning in our sleep. After such symptoms we were sure to get a dose of the worm medicine. Many a night I've lain awake to avoid giving any sign or symptoms of worms.

Here is a remedy Mother insisted on. She always saved the inner lining of the chicken's gizzard, put it up to dry; then if I ever complained of indigestion, she would pulverize this dry skin, mix it with sugar and try to persuade me to swallow it. I endured many sharp pains without complaining. Bless their dear hearts they did the best they could in this desert land. . . . Oh! I mustn't forget the onion poultices on the soles of the feet to draw the fever down from the head; nor the cabbage leaf poultice for caked breast, also bees-wax and mutton tallow for the same malady. Then there was the live frog split down the belly and placed on the throat of a child dying with diphtheria. There was the woolen string tied around the neck to keep the mumps from "going down."[24]

Kanab's local cooperative branch of Zions Cooperative Mercantile Institution (ZCMI) was organized in 1872 with an initial capital stock of $1,000. Shares sold for five dollars each. Bishop Levi Stewart was the association's first chair and Moses F. Farnsworth its secretary. Vice-president Thomas Robertson and directors Elijah Averett and John Ensign Riggs voted to purchase the goods Stewart already had stored in a small store he ran out of his home. The co-op also rented the store space in Stewart's home when it first opened; it was managed by William D. Johnson. Soon a small co-op building was built to the north of the fort. Because local orchards were very successful at producing fruit in Kane County's moderate climate, the store at harvest time always had more fruit than it could sell.

The establishment of the Mormon church's United Order in Kanab in 1874 flourished for only a short time. The United Order was a cooperative living concept that varied in its application (and its willing participants) throughout Utah. The order's building plans in Kanab were ambitious. Companies were created to build a tannery, manufacturing plant, sawmill, dairy, and brickyard. The order's building committee also made plans to erect a large granary and a new rock school/meetinghouse. Disputes between the order's proponents and the much-revered Bishop Stewart divided the town, however, and only a few of the projected construction projects came to fruition. Later, the school was completed by using less-expensive brick in place of rock. Under the direction of Allen Frost, the building was erected in two stages on what has become the courthouse block. Born in London and a resident of Bountiful before moving to Kanab in 1870, Frost did carpentry for the Mt. Carmel United Order and then worked as an accomplished bricklayer in Kanab.

During the United Order period, Brigham Young established a sericulture enterprise in Kanab led by Zadok K. Judd, Sr. The order's board of directors discussed the matter at a meeting on 26 March 1875: "The labor of raising broom corn and caring for mulberry plants was discussed and Z.K. Judd was chosen to look after that industry the present season," it was recorded.[25] Judd's daughter Gertrude J. Cottom believed that her father was chosen because he and his wife were already familiar with the silkworm-raising business. She said, "Father planted mulberry trees up at Eagle Valley and later at Kanab. I remember hearing them say that the Government gave a bounty of twenty-five cents a pound for all the silk cocoons they could raise."[26] The Judds planted mulberry trees all along east Center Street in front of their Kanab home. In their upstairs room they built shelves that ran from the floor to the ceiling to hold trays filled with silkworms. The trays had to be carefully attended to as the worms hatched, fed, and matured, and the room needed to be kept warm. The worms frequently had to be fed shredded mulberry leaves. While they were eating they created a constant buzzing noise. When mature, the silkworms measured about three inches in length, at which time they would produce the cocoons that provided the thin silk fibers that were spun. A single cocoon could potentially yield from 500 to 1,200 yards of silk thread.

Gertrude Cottom helped her parents raise the silkworms and also learned from her mother how to reel the thread. She was married in 1903 in a dress made entirely out of silk from their sericulture industry. Despite the Cottom family's diligence, Kanab's climate proved unfavorable for the production of silk and by the early twentieth century they ended their efforts.

Other area businesses included a tannery and shoemaking shop run by Edwin Ford, Lyman E. Hamblin, and James L. Bunting. After B.Y. Baird introduced sheep into the area, wool was exported to

Washington and Beaver County towns for production into cloth. Molasses produced locally was traded in Sevier County for wheat and flour. Butter and cheese were transported for trade each fall to St. George or even as far away as Salt Lake City for the winter's supply of groceries and other "states' goods."

The local bishop's storehouse was an important arena for the distribution of goods. According to their principle of tithing, faithful Mormons were required to give one tenth of their harvest to the church. In a time of scarce cash, Bishop Stewart would receive vegetables, fruit, grains, and other produce, which he would store for distribution to the needy and for other church uses. Tithing office scrip was given that could be used for trade in future transactions. During times of crisis the storehouse was critical to the survival of the people of Kanab. Occasionally produce from Orderville was transferred to Kanab to help the struggling local Mormons. Barter was a typical means of transaction regardless of the circumstances.

Charles H. Oliphant opened a small store in the same building where the post office was located; he also started a nursery he ran out of a building near his home in the northern part of town. Nephi Johnson, the mail contractor, also sold supplies out of his home. His children, Joel and Vinnie, alternated selling duties. In 1876 yet another mercantile company was organized by Laurence C. Mariger, David Udall, and W.T. Stewart. They built a one-room, frame building about fifteen by twenty-five feet, with a lean-to across the back for storage. Located on the northwest corner of the Brigham Young block, the store was managed by L.C. Mariger. For a brief time another cooperative was organized based on supplies purchased from the Kanab ZCMI; it was managed by W.D. Johnson. Eventually the cooperative dissolved and L.C. Mariger bought out the store with his two wives. John R. Stewart, John Ensign Riggs, and Gurnsey Brown sold goods out of a room of the Riggs home in the west part of town for about three years.

Glendale (Berryville)

As difficulties with local Native Americans decreased, resettlement of other parts of Kane County also gradually proceded. In 1871, led by Bishop James Leithead, some members of the LDS Muddy

Mission in Nevada came to Berryville to settle. Leithead visited the site before he brought his people there and saw the evidence of prior settlement: "A few log huts with dirt roofs, rotten or broken down, water ditches filled up, land grown up with brush and weeds," he reported.[27] Joseph W. Young is reported to have erected a water-driven sawmill and built the first log house outside the Berryville fort. With lumber from Young's mill, J.W. Watson and Lorenzo Watson built frame houses in the town.

According to James William Wilson, despite their efforts, life during the first years was hard:

> It was the 3rd of March 1871 we arrived with jaded teams and tired feet. The spring began and soon the dirt floors and dirt roofs were so sloppy that they leaked onto the bed so mother had to place pans and buckets on the bed to catch the dirty drippings. We were favored to have plenty of firewood so a good fire was in action, but the rain, rain, rain seemed to be sent to try the patience of the poor pioneers. Bad colds became prevalent; some children were very sick.[28]

But Wilson also remembered their efforts to enjoy themselves despite their privations. Recalling a dance, he continued, "Some musical instruments had been brought in with the pioneers and they organized a martial band. John Harris, who knew only two tunes, that of 'Yankee Doodle' and 'Humpty Dumpty on the Wall' played these two tunes all night and people danced to them in the light of the fireplace."[29]

The new group gave the community the name of Glendale. Each family was given acreage proportionate to their number of family members—five or ten acres and also some land in the outer fields for growing hay. The group worked cooperatively on the construction of roads. Some started plowing the fields, planting corn and potatoes, and working on a system of irrigation ditches and dams.

The little town was visited in 1871 by Mormon church president Brigham Young. A craftsman himself, Young encouraged the settlers of Glendale to build their own sawmill, improve the floors of their buildings, and make the best buildings they could. Taking his advice to heart, townspeople soon erected sawmills, schools, and fine frame homes. A few masonry structures also graced the town.

James Leithead moved the gristmill machinery he had used on the Muddy River and, with the help of Reuben Broadbent, began hewing timber for use in construction of the mill itself. He reported: "We commenced hewing the timber for basement-story and pen-stock. We also had to saw the timber to line [the] penstock and scant-ling for braces. We also floored the basement and first story. We set up the stones and by fall we had it so far completed that we ground corn and made graham flour."[30] They roofed the structure in the summer of 1872, having used a temporary covering in the meantime. The two partners also ran a "whip saw" lumber mill in Lydia's Canyon.

Reuben Broadbent was trained in England by his carpenter father and had designed and superintended the building of the Farmington Rock Church in northern Utah from 1861 to 1863. He also helped with gristmills and sawmills there before plying the same trade at the Muddy Mission, American Fork, and then Kanab. In Kanab, he designed and built a gristmill along with several other notable structures, among them the Social Hall. His skill was mani-fest in Glendale in the form of well-designed and crafted structures and dwellings.[31]

Among the early buildings were a second flour mill—a water-wheel-powered burr mill south of the present Smith Hotel. The mill, adjacent barn, and first schoolhouse were built cooperatively by the citizens of Glendale. A cabin served the community as the first school, but it was replaced in 1871 by a larger schoolhouse with a fireplace at one end. The building was typical of the buildings of the period, serving as a multipurpose center, being the location for dances and funerals, church services, and social amusements. Warren M. Johnson was the first teacher as well as the local Sunday School superintendent. Eventually a rock two-story building was built on the same lot just south of the extant brick school built in 1923. This rock building looked very much like the meetinghouse but had an open belfry instead of a cupola. It too was likely designed by Leithead and Broadbent.

Already in the habit of working cooperatively on town projects,

Glendale residents organized an LDS united order in January 1874. Warren Foote recorded the event in his journal:

> We organized in Glendale under John R. Young's direction. Bishop James Leithead was elected president, Andrew S. Gibbons and myself being bishop's counselors, and James Brinkerhoff and Homer A. Bouton were elected directors. All who joined the order put in their improved lands, farming utensils, horses, cattle, wagons, harnesses, etc. All the property was appraised by a committee and each one was credited as capital stock. There were a few in the ward who did not join the order.[32]

At first, enthusiasm ran high for the potential good that would result from such total cooperation, but eventually the ardor began to cool and some members began to complain about unequal workloads and benefits. Like almost all other united order efforts throughout Utah, this one was soon discontinued.

During the 1870s and 1880s town members also built a co-op store and the Glendale Mercantile Store. The Glendale LDS Ward was organized in 1878 with James Leithead as the first bishop. The ward Relief Society was organized in July 1878, with Sarah Brinkerhoff as its first president. The women gathered funds through donations of "Sunday" eggs to the Relief Society pool. The early Primary organization for children was led by Margaret L. Brinkerhoff.

A hewn-log cabin with two rooms and small-paned windows is typical of the first generation of 1870s architecture in Glendale that still survives. Many historic outbuildings remain to remind onlookers of Glendale's agricultural and livestock-based economy. Several large barns are still serviceable. One lone vernacular building, a board structure with a symmetrical facade, appears to have been a store or other establishment.

Mt. Carmel (Winsor, or Windsor)

As peace returned to southern Utah, Brigham Young advised settlers from the Muddy River settlement mission to relocate to Long Valley, in part due to what was perceived as excessive taxation by officials of the state of Nevada, in whose jurisdiction the area had been placed in 1864. These were people tried by the desert land and its difficulties. About 300 of them proceeded to Long Valley, arriving in

An early ranch in Long Valley. (Utah State Historical Society)

March 1871. The group divided into two parties, one proceeding on to Berryville (Glendale) under James A. Leithead. The other, headed by Daniel Stark, stopped at Winsor, now known as Mt. Carmel, because local LDS stake president John W. Young later suggested that the place looked like Mt. Carmel in Palestine—both places having rich vegetation and good pasture land.

The Muddy River settlers had the advantage of being able to move into the shelters already built by the earlier group. When those earlier settlers heard about this, some returned to reclaim their property, which inevitably resulted in conflict and hard feelings. Daniel Stark was the town's first bishop; he was succeeded by Israel Hoyt, Henry B.M. Jolley, Haskell Jolley, and Hans C. Sorenson. The Mt. Carmel LDS Ward included a Relief Society organized in April 1877, and Young Men's and Women's auxiliaries after 1878. A Sunday School was organized in May 1879.

The Mt. Carmel United Order was organized 20 March 1874 by Brigham Young and placed under the leadership of Israel Hoyt, former counselor of Bishop Daniel Stark. The plan met with considerable resistance from the early group of settlers and was attempted at a particularly unpropitious time for the town. Their crops recently had been destroyed by crickets and they had experienced drought and an early frost. Famine-like conditions prevailed and tried all. Church headquarters eventually sent Howard O. Spencer from Salt Lake City to Mt. Carmel to try to make the order work more efficiently. Some members who wanted to rigorously continue the united order left town altogether and started a new town a few miles to the north—Orderville.

The town's earliest school was a log building that also served as the church and recreation hall until a rock building was completed for those purposes. The town's crowning architectural achievement was this still-extant rock structure, a substantial edifice erected in about 1875. Rock was hauled in from a hill a mile south of town and the one-room, multipurpose building was constructed.

Alton (Upper Kanab)

No one lived at Upper Kanab again until 1872, at which time Lorenzo Roundy's nephew Byron Donalvin Roundy and his wife, Matilda Ann Roundy, Lorenzo's daughter, came back in May and moved into one of Lorenzo Roundy's log cabins. Late in the fall of 1872 Byron Roundy left Matilda in Upper Kanab while he went to Panguitch for supplies to last them through the winter. While he was gone, winter weather set in and often Indians would come to the cabin to beg for food. It was later written that Matilda usually was too frightened to answer the door and would stay in her rocking chair and sing loudly to her one-year-old baby. In an account most likely embellished in the retelling, it is reported that one night she noticed her baby staring up at the ceiling, and, glancing up to see what had caught his attention, she saw a tomahawk raised over her head and an Indian standing with a group of other Indians. She was left unharmed, as they reportedly were impressed by her bravery, if not by her acuity of hearing.[33]

Others gradually came to Upper Kanab in search of land to farm. Among them were Andrew LaFayette Siler, a teacher and botanist from Tennessee, and James Swapp and Andrew Lamb and their families. Gustavus Williams arrived in 1872 and started a ranch about seven miles to the west on the Long Valley area of the Virgin River. Abundant timber for building lined the hillsides, so Brigham Young encouraged Joseph S. Young to move a steam-powered sawmill from Buckskin Mountain to Black Rock Canyon. By the early 1870s the steam-powered sawmill was producing lumber for local use as well as for export to other towns. Some of the lumber was hauled to St. George, where it was used in constructing the Mormon temple there. Graham Duncan Macdonald came to Upper Kanab to be the book-keeper for the mill and purchased land nearby. Emily Riggs Macdonald remembered his kindness to others traveling through the valley:

Snow fell deep in those horse-and-buggy days and Graham spent many days and nights helping stranded freighters and travelers over the high divide north of his ranch. His wife, Annie, spent much of her time cooking warm food and making warm beds for those trav-elers. Hundreds have slept in their home, eaten their food and had their horses cared for in a comfortable barn.[34]

Mail addressed for Upper Kanab or Sink Valley residents nearby was delivered to Ranch, Utah, and held by the Macdonalds for distri-bution. Annie Macdonald worked as the postmistress and made sure that area residents got their mail regularly. John W. and Alice Seaman's business was a shingle mill. They shipped their product as far north as Richfield. In their backroom they ran a store, selling sup-plies such as kerosene, matches, sugar, salt, soda, baking powder, overalls, shoes and boots, and food products. Both the Seamans and the Macdonalds had springs that ran on their property, including ponds with fish, ducks, and aquatic flora.

Pahreah (Paria) Area

Zadok Judd, Jr., wrote an account of the exploration of the Paria River's Buckskin Canyon that gives a view of the troubles he had in visiting that primal place for the first time:

In 1873 a company of men from St. George, Toquerville and Kanab crossed the Buckskin mountain (Kaibab) to Lee's Ferry on the Colorado River making roads across to Jacob's Pools with the teams as there was but little grass on the river. Taking care of the teams was quite a job for the horses were not contented and some of them were trying to go home all the time. Once I followed some of them for about twenty miles. One time after a wind storm at

night all the tracks were covered and I could not find a single animal and you can believe I felt pretty hard-pressed, but about noon
some of J.D. Lee's horses came in for water. I rode one of them and
finally could not follow any farther because of darkness. I must get
back to camp but my horse was tired and I was at least 15 miles
away. I had not gone far when I heard something behind me. It
was a mule, glad to see me and I glad to see him.[35]

When he returned to camp, the men were pleased to see him,
some thinking him dead since he had been gone so long.

John D. Lee and his wife Emma came to the mouth of Paria
Canyon during the winter of 1871, one of his reasons being an effort
to evade investigators of the Mountain Meadows Massacre of
September 1857, in which he had played a major part. At Paria Lee
built a dam, dug irrigation ditches, and plowed a substantial field for
planting.[36] Most dams for irrigation at the time were simple affairs,
constructed with logs, rocks, and any other debris that was handy. A
number of passersby helped work on Lee's dam, prospectors, Native
Americans, and even members of John Wesley Powell's second river
expedition as they traveled by Lee's homestead.

Lee soon reaped the rewards of his first crop. He wrote, "We are
beginning to enjoy the fruits of our labors daily as green corn, vegit-
able Marrow or summer squash, cucumbers, beets, onions, raddish,
& beans and a few mellons are in full blast. They are not only a Treat
but a great blessing to us in this Desert country."[37] Eventually Lee
constructed 1.5 miles of canals. On Saturday, 11 January 1873, Lee
first launched his noted ferry across the Colorado River. He wrote:

> We launched the Boat & called her the Colerado & the skiff we
> named the Pahreah. The Colerado is 26 by 8 1/2 feet, strong, a
> staunch craft & well constructed & a light runer. The party presant
> all crossed on her to Christen her & take a pleasure ride. We
> crossed over & back twice. Uncle Tommy Smith & son Robt rowed
> her over & I steered. Set down a good post & fastened her with a
> cablechain & reached home about dusk.[38]

The fact that Kane County's population moved so readily from
farming to ranching illustrated a basic characteristic of the population—adaptability. Men and women like Emma Lee, John D. Lee's

wife, who with him settled Lee Ferry, might have been more familiar with England's cool wet weather yet proved to be remarkably adaptable. Physical survival demanded a certain ability to accept change quickly and find new ways of doing things. The turn to ranching did have its costs in terms of village community life, as it tended to scatter individual ranches over large tracts of land.

Fluctuating Boundaries

In 1873 the Kane County Court included eleven precincts: Kanarra, Harmony, Bellvue, Toquerville, Virgin City, Duncans Retreat, Rockville, Kanab, Mt. Carmel, Glendale, and Pahreah (Paria). In 1880 the section of the county east of the Colorado River was taken to form part of newly created San Juan County. In 1882 the western portion of the county to the present western boundary (a strip of land some twenty-five to thirty miles wide) was taken by Washington County and newly created Garfield County.[39] Thus the towns of the upper Virgin River Valley were returned to Washington County. Kanab was named the new county seat of Kane County at this time, and county boundaries have remained the same since that time.

The Utah-Arizona line, which formed the southern boundary of Kane, Washington, and San Juan Counties, was not well determined in the settlers' minds until the surveys of the early 1870s. Even after the boundary was well known, the isolated Arizona towns of the Arizona Strip had natural ties to their neighboring Utah communities until (and to some degree even after) major highways and bridges were established in the twentieth century. The remote area, in fact, became a haven for polygamists in the 1880s as federal officers began to more aggressively seek to arrest those Mormons engaged in plural marriage practices.

Endnotes

1. *Deseret News,* 24 October 1870.
2. Adonis Findlay Robinson, *History of Kane County,* 40.
3. Ibid., 134.
4. Ibid., 31–32.

5. Quoted in Elsie Chamberlain Carroll, ed., *History of Kane County* (Salt Lake City: Utah Printing Company, 1970), 69.

6. Frederick S. Dellenbaugh, *A Canyon Voyage* (New York: Knickerbocker Press, 1908), 166–67.

7. Frederick S. Dellenbaugh, *Romance of the Colorado River*, 306.

8. *Deseret News*, 1 April 1872.

9. Kane County Court, Minute Book B.

10. *The Statistics of the Wealth and Industry of the United States, Ninth Census* (Washington, D.C.: U.S. Department of the Interior, 1872), 1: 636, 3:262–63.

11. Dean L. May, Lee L. Bean, Mark H. Skolnick, and John Metcalf, "Once I Lived in Cottonwood: Population Stability in Utah Mormon Towns, 1850–1910," unpublished paper given at annual meeting of Social Science History Association, Rochester, New York, November 6–9, 1980, 12–15.

12. Rebecca Howell Mace, journal, 85.

13. John R. Young, journal, Utah State Historical Society.

14. Wilbur E. Dodson, "Historical Sketch of Kane County," 6.

15. See George Thomas, *The Development of Institutions Under Irrigation* (New York: Macmillan, 1920), 45.

16. C. Gregory Crampton and David E. Miller, eds., "Journal of Two Campaigns by the Utah Territorial Militia Against the Navajo Indians, 1869," *Utah Historical Quarterly* 29 (April 1961): 154.

17. Robinson, *History of Kane County*, 114.

18. Dean L. May, "People on the Mormon Frontier: Kanab's Families of 1874," *Journal of Family History* 1 (Winter 1976): 177, 179.

19. U.S. Department of the Interior, *Compendium of the Tenth Census* (1880), part I (Washington, D.C.: Government Printing Office, 1883), 912–13.

20. Edith Bonham, interview with Keppy Petter, 6 February 1992, Kanab, Utah.

21. Norman B. Cram, interview with Erin Cram, 17 February 1992, Kanab, Utah.

22. Dellenbaugh, *A Canyon Voyage*, 173.

23. Robinson, *History of Kane County*, 246.24. 1 Ibid., 76.

25. Ibid., 116.

26. Ibid.

27. Quoted in Elsie Chamberlain Carroll, *History of Kane County*, 370.

28. Robinson, *History of Kane County*, 427.

29. Ibid.

30. Ibid., 425.

31. Allen D. Roberts, "More of Utah's Unknown Architects: Their Lives and Works," *Sunstone Magazine* 1, no. 3: 54–56.

32. Robinson, *History of Kane County*, 429.

33. Ibid., 458.

34. Ibid., 459.

35. Esther Brown Judd, "Biography of Zadok Knapp Judd, Jr. and His Wife, Ada Marie Howell Judd," 7, Utah State Historical Society.

36. Robert Glass Cleland and Juanita Brooks, *A Mormon Chronicle: The Diaries of John D. Lee* (San Marino, CA: Huntington Library, 1955), 2:182–83.

37. John D. Lee, quoted in Juanita Brooks, "Lee's Ferry at Lonely Dell," *Utah Historical Quarterly* 25 (1957): 286.

38. Ibid., 287.

39. Dodson, "Historical Sketch of Kane County," 5.

CHAPTER 6

ORDERVILLE
AND THE EXPERIMENT IN
COMMUNAL LIVING

The experiment with the Mormon church's United Order in Kane County split communities apart. Separate factions developed around Kanab bishop Levi Stewart and John R. Young, Brigham Young's nephew and a vigorous advocate of the order. Tensions ran high, and divergent attitudes toward communalism in general limited the successfulness of the effort, although Kane County was also the site of what has come to be considered the most successful of all Mormon attempts to live the United Order ideal—Orderville.

The desire to build a utopian community was not unique to the Mormon pioneers. Other idealistic millennialistic religions throughout the world during the nineteenth century reshaped expectations about community relationships and developed new ways of being members of a society. The Shakers and the Oneida Colony, among others, required much of their members, such as forsaking associations with outsiders, relinquishing former loyalties, and refining their minds and behaviors to conform to the community norms.

The Law of Consecration and Stewardship was first presented to the Mormons in Kirtland, Ohio, in the early 1830s by church founder

Joseph Smith. At that time, it facilitated the "Gathering"—the emigration of the Mormon people from their homes in upstate New York, New England, Great Britain, Canada, and elsewhere to Ohio and Missouri, then the two principal centers of the church. Because they had to leave so much behind and also pay the cost of travel, many of the emigrants were destitute and needed financial help. Pooling their resources took on theological significance as Latter-day Saints consecrated, or donated, their worldly goods to the church for the advancement of the work of the Lord.

After the Law of Tithing—paying to the church 10 percent of one's gain—replaced the grand but more difficult scheme of property pooling in the Law of Consecration and Stewardship in Nauvoo, Illinois, in the 1840s, faithful church members donated 10 percent of their resources to the church. Decades after the arrival of the Mormons in the Great Basin, however, church leader Brigham Young explored the idea of again returning to some larger scheme of cooperation, or joint property ownership and management, first in the Mormon Reformation period of 1855–56, and then at about the time of the national agricultural depression of 1873.

Mormon church leaders Brigham Young, Orson Pratt, and others eventually designed a religious economic order they called the "United Order of Enoch." Traveling throughout Utah Territory from Salt Lake City, Young organized settlers—sometimes as wards and at other places as towns—into united orders, saying: "Our object is to labor for the benefit of the whole; to retrench in our expenditures, to be prudent and economical, to study well the necessities of the community and to pass by its many useless wants, to study to secure life, health, wealth and union."[1]

At a general conference held on 9 May 1874 in Salt Lake City, and especially postponed so that Brigham Young could personally explain the policies and procedures of the order, church leaders detailed the ways members would contribute their property and jointly manage businesses. Ideally, all property would be held in common except houses and residential lots, although each united order established its own rules. Some included the deeding to the order of all property, some of which (for example, houses) could be returned. Kane County became the site of the most complete experiment with the

A view of Orderville looking to the east. (Courtesy Fred Esplin)

united order and communal living when those who wanted to more fully develop the order broke away from others in Mt. Carmel to form their own town—which they named Orderville.

In some places, the settlers reacted negatively to the proposal, but many in Mt. Carmel responded enthusiastically, particularly those, it seems, who had moved to the area from the Muddy Mission. Brigham Young's nephew (and friend of Jacob Hamblin) John R. Young organized the Mt. Carmel United Order on 20 March 1874. Officers of the order included Israel Hoyt, president; Samuel Claridge and Thomas Chamberlain, vice-presidents; William Heaton, secretary; and Henry B.M. Jolley, treasurer.

Despite initial enthusiasm for the idea, some members soon began to quarrel among themselves, as perhaps there was lingering bitterness of some earlier settlers who returned to the area after having abandoned it during the Indian troubles only to find that the Muddy Mission emigrees had taken over some of their buildings and claims. The townsfolk were divided into factions, one centering around Henry Jolley. Dissension rose to such a point that in

September 1874 Brigham Young sent Howard Orson Spencer to Mt. Carmel to settle disputes. Spencer was then called to preside over Long Valley as its chief ecclesiastical officer. Because local conflicts over the practice of the united order could not be resolved, Spencer advised Jolley and his followers to move to a different part of the valley—some two miles to the north—where all residents could be unified in their interpretation of the order, which would hopefully enable them to live more peacefully. A survey was made of a new townsite and land was secured by the order with joint ownership. The move was made in March 1875.

Because all of those who moved had sacrificed to live cooperatively, they called their new settlement Orderville. With its isolated location, remote from population centers or major transportation routes, Orderville provided a good setting for the independent social experiment. Situated approximately seventy miles east of St. George and twenty-two miles northwest of Kanab, Orderville residents took advantage of the area's natural resources, which provided the materials for building a community. Land was fertile in places, and the surrounding grazing land was ideal for stock raising. Extensive timber in the nearby mountains provided fuel and lumber for building. The Virgin River furnished water for irrigation and culinary purposes.

The majority of Orderville's original members had been schooled in cooperation in the settlement along the Muddy River organized by the Mormon church for the purpose of raising cotton. The Muddy River settlements were plagued by troubles and generally were failures. Hot and dry, the Muddy River Valley was subject to insect infestation, flash floods, and disease. The colonists were poor but united in their fight for survival. Brigham Young had visited the Muddy River settlements in 1870 and was so moved by the settlers' plight that he encouraged them to return to Utah and end their travails. This they did in 1870 and 1871. About 200 of them traveled to Long Valley, where they were instructed to take up farming and cattle raising. The beautiful valley with its abundant timber and water from the Virgin River must have seemed a veritable paradise to the destitute settlers eager for a fresh start.

The Orderville United Order was officially organized on 14 July 1875. A board of nine directors was elected and it was given the responsibility of organizing and supervising the labor and resources of the order. Directors made some decisions independent of the group, but most business transactions were brought before a meeting of the entire order for approval or disapproval. The order was incorporated for a period of twenty-five years, with a maximum capitalization of $100,000—which consisted of 10,000 shares at ten dollars each. Each donor received book credit for capital stock in the corporation according to the value of his or her contribution. It was formally agreed that such stock did not entitle the "owner" to dividends or to any share of the corporation's assets.[2]

Because the order was above all a religious effort, members were rebaptized when it was first organized in an effort to rededicate their devotion to the work of the Lord. They were placed under a solemn covenant to obey certain rules set forth by Brigham Young. Numerous accounts of the order support the conclusion that its members believed they were working for the good of the Kingdom of God, and the objectives of the order reflected the religious concepts adhered to by the Mormons. They included the ideas that

> all people are literally the sons and daughters of God, that the earth is His and all it contains, that He created it and its fullness, especially for the use and benefit of His children, that all, providing they keep His commandments, are equally entitled to the blessings of the earth; that with proper regulations there is enough and to spare for all, that every person is simply a steward and not an owner of property he has in charge, and that he is under obligations to use it, and his time, strength and talents for the good of all. They believe in living as a patriarchal family, and in common, according to their circumstances fare alike. All are required to be diligent in their labors, economical in their habits and temperate in their lives.[3]

All economic efforts organized under the umbrella of the united order were managed by a board of management composed of a president, two vice-presidents, a secretary, a treasurer, and four directors. Yearly elections allowed many to serve. The nine officers supervised property purchases and administration, directed the labor force, invested surplus funds, borrowed for investments, and regulated daily affairs of the group. Furthermore, the order consisted of thirty-three

The Orderville Co-op Building. (Courtesy Deanne Glover)

different departments, each with department heads and assigned duties of workers. Departments included blacksmithing, wagon repair, boarding house, board of appraisers, board of sisters, cabinet and carpentry, canal, commissary, coopering, cotton farm, farming, freighting, garden, gristmill, poultry, home improvement, knitting, livestock, dairy, midwifery, millinery, public works, sawmill, schools, sheep, shoe shop, soap and broom, stock feeding, tailoring, tannery, telegraph, and tin shop. Members were assigned to be assistants in the departments. A sample entry from the minutes of the board show the process by which these assignments were made.

> On motion Henry W. Esplin was sustained as foreman of the farming department the present year and C.N. Carroll is sustained as foreman of our lucern farm. And Levi Hampton as foreman of the second farm. Alvin F. Heaton was sustained as foreman of the third farm, and Allen Cox was sustained as foreman of the fourth farm. Jonathan Heaton is sustained as foreman of the Enterprise or cotton farm. John J. Esplin was sustained as foreman of the Lake Farm.

Thomas Robertson was sustained as foreman of the Blacksmith Shop. On motion F.L. Porter was released as foreman in the kitchen and boarding house. On motion Persis A. Spencer to take charge of the boarding house, with Susana Fackrell and Elizabeth Brown as assisting house [department]. On motion Carie W. Porter is appointed to labor in the kitchen under the direction of Persis A. Spencer. On motion Elizabeth Brown is released from assisting in the cloth department. On motion Albina Young was sustained as foreman of the cloth department, with Marinda and Maria Black as assistants.[4]

Changes in rules and policies later required a two-thirds vote of the membership to approve new regulations. Membership qualifications in the Orderville United Order included membership in the Church of Jesus Christ of Latter-day Saints and were in general judgments of an individual's moral and religious character rather than his or her economic status. Applicants answered questions about their expectations, why they wanted to enter the order, and what they were willing to give up. Generally, nearly everyone who applied to join was admitted.

In Orderville there would be no private property, and it was agreed that among the participants all "things shall be done by common consent."[5] When people were interviewed by the ecclesiastical leaders before being admitted to the order they were asked an extensive list of questions about their character, devotion to the idea of cooperation, and their willingness to sacrifice for the work of God:

1. What is your object in seeking to unite yourself with this Company? Do you believe the Lord requires you to take this course?

2. Have you a family? If so, what is the number? Are they one with you without exception in the course you wish to take? What is your present situation in regard to food and clothing? Do you train your family in the fear of the Lord? Do they seem to practice your teaching and walk according to your example?

3. Are you in debt, or is there any person or persons that claim to have any pretext for claim against you or yours? If so, what is the nature of the pretext or the amount of your indebtedness?

4. Is there any incumbrance on any pieces of property which you have in your possession?

5. Are you willing for yourself and all you possess to be governed and controlled by the Board of Management, or any person or persons authorized for them to act?

6. Do you think that you could come and make your permanent home with this company of people, and, if necessary, put up with all the inconveniences that older members had and have without murmuring or fault finding or become dissatisfied and wishing to withdraw from the company and thereby putting the practice to unnecessary trouble and inconveniences?

7. Are you willing to practice economy in all the points and bearings, and try to content yourself although you may think that your trials are hard at times?

8. Do you use tobacco, tea, or coffee, or indulge in drinking intoxicating drinks?

9. Are you in the habit of stealing or taking that which does not belong to you personally?

10. Are you in the habit of lying or backbiting, or slandering your brethren or sisters?

11. Are you in the habit of swearing or using profane oaths or taking the name of the Lord in vain?

12. Are you in the habit of using vulgar or obscene jests or conduct?

13. Are you in the habit of quarreling? If so, will you cease from this?

14. Are you in the habit of giving way to bad temper and abusing dumb animals? If so, will you cease from such conduct?

15. Will you take a course when you find a brother or a sister out of temper to maintain the peace by saying nothing to aggravate, and silently walk away if he or she shall not cease?

16. Are you willing to work the same as the rest of the company according to your strength and ability and for the same recompense as your peers?

17. Are you willing to be subject to those who are placed over you and do as you are told cheerfully and not sullenly?

18. Are you willing to conform to the rules of good order in all things and not appropriate to your use or the use of the company any tool or implement of husbandry or any kind of produce

without first obtaining the permission to do so from persons having charge of such tools, implements, produce or other property?

19. Will you try to the best of your ability to maintain the
peace and prosperity of this Order and as much as lies in your
power, deal honestly, impartially and justly in all transactions you
may be called upon to perform from time to time?[6]

Initially, all members were required to deed their property, both
real and personal, to the order; therefore, all wealth became common.
Individuals were made stewards over their own personal effects such
as clothing, books, furniture, and jewelry. And, although it is true that
there were no rich or poor, it was really more true that all were relatively poor. Strict accounts recorded wages and transactions. Men
received $1.50 credit for a day's work; boys eleven to seventeen years
old worked for credit of 75 cents per day. Girls from ten to thirteen
worked each day for 25 cents; those under ten worked for half that
amount.[7] Adults were charged fifty dollars a year for rent on their living spaces. The typical shanty home had a living room twelve feet
square and an adjoining bedroom that was eight by twelve feet.
Annual clothing charges were $17.50 for men and $16.50 for women.
Children's clothing ranged from one-half to three-fourths of the
adult costs.

Samuel Claridge eventually became vice-president of the order;
he originally came to Orderville in 1878 after a two-year church pros-
elytizing mission in England. Mormon church president John Taylor
advised him against liberality in admission policies to the order, saying, "whatever you do don't overload the boat for there is Danger
when there was to[o] many in of being Capsized."[8] Claridge reported
the conversation to the board of management, but, despite the advice
and attitude of the church president, "they thought the Lord had
given a command to join the Order and it would be as wrong to deny
them [as] it would be for a Repentant believer to be denied membership."[9]

Howard Spencer was chosen the original president of the
Orderville United Order; however, within two years he stepped down
to let Thomas Chamberlain become president. Chamberlain usually
is given credit for the success of the venture. His expert managerial
skills and generally affable personality made him a most suitable

leader for the group. As bishop of the Orderville LDS Ward, Chamberlain orchestrated both the temporal and spiritual welfare of his ward members. In addition to the core group who had learned to work together in the Muddy River Mission, Brigham Young also sent to Orderville emigrants from Great Britain and Scandinavia.

The fact that Orderville was established a few years after the towns of Winsor (Mt. Carmel) and Berryville (Glendale) was an advantage to the new settlers, who could obtain lumber from existing sawmills and build faster than could those in the earlier towns. In the fall of 1874, the same year the first united order was started, a water-driven pit sawmill was purchased, and with this mill Jonathan Heaton and Allen Frost produced the lumber used to construct the order's first generation of frame buildings. Thomas Chamberlain and Christopher Heaton cut the timber in a nearby canyon, while Henry W. and John J. Esplin hauled logs to the mill. Soon a second mill, a steam-powered sawmill, was purchased; it was run by B.H. Williams and Isaiah Bowers. Throughout the local order's history, nearly all of its buildings were frame structures made with lumber from these local mills. The order also purchased a flour mill from a farmer at Glendale for $3,000.

There is little architecture left to document Mormonism's most colorful and successful experience with living the United Order. Of the original complex of order buildings, as well as the later public landmarks erected by the residents of Orderville, little remains. While available materials affected the nature of the order's architecture, the united order itself influenced the town's architecture in the types, uses, styles, and placement of structures. Wealthy Howard O. Spencer, the Orderville order's first leader, consecrated nearly all he had— some $4,000 in cash plus supplies and equipment. Others did similarly according to their means. This provided an immediate cash and labor pool with which to erect buildings. Moreover, Orderville grew rapidly. The inhabitants needed quickly built housing and public facilities, and, with their unique, cooperative, religious socioeconomic system, they had the resources to rapidly create a built environment.

Upon selecting the location of the townsite, a survey was made, centered on a public block. In the middle of the block, a frame com-

The Orderville Ward Hall. (Courtesy Deanne Glover)

munity dining hall, twenty-five by forty feet, was built. Adjoining it
was a kitchen and a bakery with a large brick oven and large troughs
for bread mixing. To the northeast, a fort-like complex was built of
rows of shanties (shed-roofed buildings) put up in "sections of eight."
These housed families, and the high sides of these shed-roofed cabins, together with the tall board fences that connected them, consti-
tuted the outside walls of the "fort."

A two-story "Big House" with an upstairs porch running around
it contained many small rooms to house the families of the order's
board of directors and other leaders. Thomas Chamberlain and his
five wives lived in the Big House. Buildings were arranged in a square,
and the south side of the square was enclosed by a board fence with a
gate. The entries to the shanties faced the interior courtyard of the
square, and a wooden boardwalk ran along the fronts of the buildings. Trees and flowers were planted to beautify the compound and
a flagpole was placed in front of the dining hall. The American flag
added to the appearance of a military encampment. In fact, each
morning at 5:00 A.M. a bugler or martial band announced the begin-

ning of the work day, breakfast at 7:00 A.M., lunch at 12:00 noon, dinner at 6:30 P.M., and curfew at 9:00 P.M.

As the population grew, more buildings were constructed. A
Relief Society hall went up inside the square near the Big House. The
residential sections were connected by fences and gates. Running the
length of the shanties and fences were broad plank sidewalks, lined
with flowers, tamarisks, and box elder trees. Until a Relief Society hall
was constructed, public gatherings were held in the dining room.

After its organization, the Orderville United Order began purchasing equipment and creating businesses to provide services and
produce income for the group. The town's tannery produced a high
grade of leather, which was made into boots, shoes, harnesses, and
saddles at a leather shop. In 1879, for instance, the tannery produced
702 pairs of shoes and fifteen pairs of boots. A total of 674 pairs of
shoes were repaired that same year.[10]

Furniture, spinning wheels, and cabinets produced at the cabinet
shop rivaled the best in the region. The cooper's shop produced
buckets, tubs, barrels, and firkins. A dairy farm, located eleven miles
outside of town, produced cheese and butter for sale. An order-
owned farm in Moccasin Springs, Arizona, produced large quantities
of molasses. In 1876, the group purchased capital stock in the Rio
Virgin Manufacturing Company in Washington County, Utah. They
exchanged wool for cloth and produced woolen goods at this mill.
They also purchased a farm one mile south of town. A new town,
Enterprise, sprang up around this particular farm enterprise, which
included a cotton gin, spinning wheels, and looms to convert cotton
into cloth.

From 1881 to 1883, the order's members built a woolen factory
above Glendale at a cost of $8,500. Because the order was on the
decline at this time, this venture failed not long after its organization.
The woolen factory was a major enterprise, producing the types of
clothing needed by the community. Because secondhand machinery
was installed, however, the quality of the cloth was somewhat
reduced. The factory was a large, three-level, wooden structure with
rows of dormers across the gabled roof. In the upper part of the attic
was built a hidden room where "cohabs," as polygamists were nicknamed, could hide from federal marshals. A flume brought water

from a nearby creek to the waterwheel. Joseph Hopkins of Glendale eventually installed a new metal turbine. The building was so large that there was enough open space to hold meetings and dances there. Adelbert Webb, assisted by Warner Porter, was the chief builder. Workers lived in a row of frame shanties northwest of the factory, where a blacksmith shop was also located. A small community developed there, complete with a branch of the LDS church.

Allen Frost and his family joined the Orderville United Order after 1874. There he worked at a variety of jobs—at the sawmill, doing carpenter work, masonry, bookkeeping, and teaching school.[11] In 1877 Hattie Esplin's family moved to Long Valley and joined the people at Orderville. She reported later, "They sold all they had and turned into the common fund. They lived in the fort in a lumber cabin in the northwest corner of the fort where the Tithing Lot was."[12]

The Charles N. Carroll family joined the Orderville United Order in 1878. Daughter Emma Carroll wrote a memoir published in 1939 of her life there as a child. She wrote in part:

> Perhaps the most unique thing among us was community eating. It excited more curiosity, incited more ridicule and brought more aspersions upon us than any other one thing and much more than was warranted. The dining hall was in the center of the enclosed square, with the kitchen to the north and bakery in the basement immediately under it. About three hundred pounds of flour was made into bread each day, mixed in a large wooden mixer seven feet long by two and one-half feet wide. Occasionally a few children lingered to watch the bread mixing process which was usually left until the last thing before closing up at night. Vegetables such as potatoes, squash, etc., were baked in large quantities, as well as meats and occasionally pies, cookies, and puddings; these were a real treat, however, as they did not come often. The kitchen was a large room the west side of which was partitioned off for the furnaces. There were three standing side by side, made of brick, on which were three immense boilers. A good sized log of wood was none too much for each furnace. How would you like to see three bushels of potatoes cooked in a great boiler and a corresponding quantity of meat and vegetables in another and a third full of gravy—water gravy? It required one whole boiler of hulled corn or hominy for supper.[13]

Groups of six women cooks took turns, each having time off periodically. Between their work in the kitchen they took care of their chores at home and other types of community work. Emma Carroll's mother preferred not to eat in the community dining hall, so Emma brought her meals to her in their own home. When the order eventually allowed families to sit together in groups, she joined the family group at dinner.

Three rows of tables ran the length of the dining hall. Three older and three younger girls served meals for a week at a time. These girls set the tables, served the food, cleared the dishes when the meal was over, and brought them back to the kitchen to be washed. Sometimes they helped wash the dishes. Because the group did not have tablecloths, the table tops were scrubbed thoroughly after every meal and the benches were also washed to keep the dining area as clean as possible.

Emma Carroll remembered special friendships that grew between younger and older girls as they worked together in the dining hall:

> At the age of about eleven or twelve, a girl was eligible to appointment as a junior waiter; thus privileged she had reached the acme of her desires. The thrill of partnership with a senior waiter, aroused emotions almost bewildering. It was a supreme moment; a real affection grew up between senior and junior girls. As a junior waiter I was placed with Lucy Spencer, pretty, jolly, and very kind to me. We had the center row of tables as our charge.
>
> I have heard my sister Kezia say that she with the other senior girls would often in summer time arise early, before the time for duty at the dining room and gather the wild roses from the creek bank, placing a twig with a single rose bud under each plate. It required several hundred. The fragrance of the flowers was noticeable on entering the room.[14]

When the Orderville United Order first began the adults sat at one set of tables and the children at another, but eventually families sat together. The members of the community ate in two shifts, which required that the entire process of setting the tables and serving the food had to be done twice. Usually, the food was simple, but on special occasions it included fried pork, mashed potatoes, vegetables, pickled beets, and fresh-baked molasses cookies. After community dining was discontinued altogether due to the destruction of the dining hall by a flood in 1880, produce was parceled out to families according to need.

The order's inventory in 1878 included the town structures, 300 acres of land, a gristmill in Glendale, $1,500 worth of stock in the Kanab mill, land in Kanab, a sawmill up the canyon, 300 head of cattle, 500 head of sheep, fifty horses, and six mules. There also was machinery, merchandise, and household furniture and goods.[15] In addition, the order owned other property in the region near Harmon's Ranch, Swain's Creek, Castle Ranch, Cove Spring, Strawberry Valley, Cliff Spring, Duck Creek Ranch, and Blackburns Fork. It owned accompanying water rights and the right to use Virgin River water.[16]

Because it sought to establish a self-sufficient society, the Orderville United Order attempted to provide for its every need without importing goods from the outside world. Thus there were diverse buildings, more so than in other Mormon communities of comparable size. At the same time, the people were resourceful, utilitarian, and not given to excesses. Their buildings were plain vernacular structures. The fact that they were rapidly constructed of lumber rather than masonry helps account for the fact that none of the united order buildings have survived to the present. Buildings were provided for dairies, silkworm production, a woolen factory, animal shelters, food storage, a shoe shop, tannery, gristmill, bakery, a distant cotton factory, and a small industrial center consisting of a "blacksmith shop, cabinet and carpenter shop, broom and bucket factories, and other industrial facilities."[17] Orderville residents also were able to export lumber to St. George for the construction of the Mormon temple there, as well as provide laborers for the building of the Manti LDS Temple.

The tannery was typical of order architecture. It was a two-story, wood-frame structure with a simple gabled roof and vertical board siding. Three tall windows were placed in each side wall. There was no other architectural embellishment. Some of the united order buildings were used for multiple purposes. All religious meetings and socials were held in the dining hall for a time. After the Relief Society

The Orderville United Order Tannery. (Courtesy Deanne Glover)

hall was erected, it was used for the same purposes as well as for school classes. The first schoolhouse was a small structure, only fourteen by sixteen feet, built east of the dining hall. Due to its limited size, school classes also were held in the "garret" of the Big House. In the late 1880s a more substantial, two-story schoolhouse was built, although an attempt to make it of brick failed because the brick contained too much lime. Orderville's young children attended school three months of the year. The older children worked year-round, receiving educational instruction only at church meetings. Children were seen primarily as a resource for building up the community and as full contributors in terms of time and energy.

To the east of the town twenty acres of vegetable gardens and orchards provided food for the members. Women and girls rotated work in the gardens and tended hot beds that provided early vegetables, a flower garden, a grove of mulberry trees for silkworms, and a few beehives. South of the square, a blacksmith shop, carpenter and cabinet shops, and other industries lined the street. Other food to support the community was produced on 400 acres of land located on the periphery of town. In 1879 this land produced 4,006 bushels of wheat, 3,178 pounds of pork, 22,691 pounds of mutton, 18,256 pounds of beef, 10,456 gallons of milk, 3,745 pounds of butter, 136 pounds of cheese, 1,485 gallons of molasses, 1,888 bushels of melons, 14,000 pounds of cabbage, and 7,165 bushels of potatoes, onions, radishes, beets, cucumbers, carrots, parsnips, turnips, tomatoes, peas, and beans.[18] The group in actuality was virtually self-sufficient, and therefore changing prices of goods elsewhere had little effect on them.

The board of directors assigned duties according to skills. Besides their own household work, women took turns working in the kitchen and waiting on tables. Each day six attendants and five or six cooks prepared and served the community's food. When the first meal was served on 24 July 1875, fifteen families were present, totaling fewer than one hundred individuals. By 1877, Orderville had 370 members of the order. In 1882, the population had increased to 602, of which 259 were children under eight years of age.[19] Each day two elderly men turned a 150-pound bag of flour into bread to be baked in a large brick oven. Preserves and bottled fruit were also produced. Lunch was the main meal. Dinner usually consisted of corn meal mush, milk, and johnny cake served with butter.

Samuel Claridge enjoyed his work in the bakery and thought the women he worked with were the best in the order.

> A better set of women I never knew in my life. They were always cheerful and I never knew any of them [to] quarrel in my life. Often there would be as many as three with babies in the kitchen, for you must know we had no old maids. All got husbands as soon as they were marriageable, and it kept us busy putting up shanties and providing for their many necessities.[20]

Because there were so many people to feed, the kitchen routine was carefully organized. Workers were supervised by older women; even young girls helped clear tables and serve food. Claridge described the way they made their work more fun:

> I remember once they had a bow dance. I was in the bake-house. I told the cooks that were in the kitchen as soon as their work was done I would take them to the dance. So in a little while

we all put our clean aprons on. My wife made three large factory bows. We put them on. I had already made the arrangements with the floor manager when to let me lead on the floor. I proposed the scotch reel so I could take two sisters. At the time appointed when all was still and quiet I unexpectedly walked out with my two aged sisters which made it very amusing for all present and we were warmly greeted as we paraded through the set.[21]

The storage and distribution of supplies and resources centered in the storehouse under the charge of the bishop and the president of the order. Each department or business managed by the order had its offices there. For the first two years, resources were scarce and a committee of three women was assigned the task "to learn the necessities of the people and to decide who needed things most and issue orders on the store when things were to be given out," in order to help conserve supplies.[22]

Because families ate their meals at the community dining hall, or Big Table, there was no particular need for food preparation at home. Nevertheless, people did have certain needs in terms of personal supplies. The Orderville Account Book, kept at the community store between 1879 and 1882, provides a glimpse of what families required during this period. For example, the Samuel Claridge family purchased with credit coal oil, soap, matches, thread, pins, lye, buttons, paper, envelopes, sheeting, bleach, nails, bed casters, a wash tub, six yards of check-pattern linsey material, yarn, hats, a broom, beeswax, and an axe helve.[23]

At the end of the year, when accounts were balanced out, those who had a surplus usually donated it to the pool, and those who incurred debts had them canceled. Financial records indicate that there was always a balance of credits over debits. Strict accounting practices made everyone feel more accountable for their actions and ensured that the finances were carefully managed.

As was true of much of Kane County, the area surrounding Orderville was used for grazing. Cattle and sheep raising were natural businesses for the group to commence, and they quickly gained control over local watering places in the area. Their ranches included areas in Arizona and Utah, including House Rock, Jacob's Pools, Cane Springs, Castle Ranch, Elk Ranch, and a 150-acre ranch on the

Pahreah (Paria) River. By 1881 the Orderville United Order was pay-ing taxes on 5,000 head of sheep, and its cattle herds had increased to ten times their original size.

The board of directors appointed John R. Young foreman of the organization's twenty-one sheepherders on 25 February 1881. Samuel Claridge was one of the herders. He later wrote about his experience:

> I volunteered for one [winter's service as sheepherder] and went out for the winter with Brother Lorenzo Young, who treated me very kindly. I would do the cooking and went to the herd when I got ready. He was an old hand and understood it better than I did, but I enjoyed it very much. I read my Book of Mormon, Doctrine and Covenants, and other books and I enjoyed much of the Good Spirit and the time passed away very pleasantly. We would live on fat mutton all the time and with our molasses and pottatoes we fared well. Our herd done splendid, and they gave us great credit for being such good shepherds.[24]

Claridge also helped care for the horses and cows, assisting with the milking.

> We now put up a large shed or stable. Our cows were placed in stalls on one side, the horses on the other, and one man appointed to do all feeding, the hay and grain for the horses. The cows would all know their places. A man would go along and just lift the top catch and they would all be fastened in a few minutes. We raised lots of mangrel-wurzel which was all chopped up and fed to each cow. The haycart would go down the center and the horses and cows were fed from each side. Regular milkmen were appointed and the stables kept clean. Every day the man with his team would have nothing to do only to curry his horses.[25]

For a time, Mary Fowler's mother was the supervisor of the diary. She brought her children along while she worked. Family members braided straw hats or sewed clothes from home woven cloth. Their days seemed to be devoted to church and spiritual work; work stopped periodically for family prayers or group meetings. "The atmosphere and proceedings of these meetings were the same pattern whether concerned with civil or ecclesiastical matters." a relative of Fowler wrote.[26]

The members of the order joined together for social activities as well as for work. The religious auxilliaries provided the backdrop for dances, parties, and educational activities. The local Young Men's and Young Ladies Mutual Improvement Assocations began when the order was first organized. The women's Relief Society published its own weekly newspaper, with such articles or regualar columns as "Our Interest," "Home Composition," "The Pearl," "The Clipper," and "The Mutual Star." Every Saturday the young men's organization published the *Honey Bee,* a sixteen-page broadside.[27]

The Demise of the Orderville United Order

Ironically, when the economy of southern Utah improved during the 1880s, the Orderville United Order started its decline. Even so, it has been considered the most successful of all the efforts at creating united orders throughout the Mormon church. Most failed within six months, and relatively few lasted more than a year. Some other successful variants, such as that at Brigham City in northern Utah, did not include the rigorous communal living arrangements of Orderville.

The dedication of Orderville residents to the concept well suited the establishment of a relatively isolated community in a region whose residents of other towns themselves practiced little more than subsistence economies. As towns and enterprises developed, however, and as new technologies such as the railroad and the telegraph came to the region with their promise (and threat) of outside goods and increased trade, the more spartan united order concept came under seige—a seige compounded after Brigham Young died in 1877 and other church leaders became less committed to that ideal and more interested in pursuing a traditional American capitalistic economic system. At the same time, the troubles of the Mormon church and all its members due to the practice of plural marriage left little leisure to devote to the United Order or any other principle that needed reinforcement from the pulpit.

In the 1870s Orderville was among the most successful settlements in the territory. By the 1880s, however, other communities in Kane County began to challenge Orderville's success at farming, mining, and stock producing. Also, the practitioners of the order maintained its relatively simple, original lifestyle, yet by comparison to other settlements it began to seem to many that their town was backward and unprogressive socially.

As perhaps a signal of the trend toward growing individualism and independence, the town's policy of communal dining was discontinued in 1880 after a flood destroyed the dining hall. This had an immediate and serious impact on the communal atmosphere of the order. Three years later, with the prodding of Apostle Erastus Snow, a wage system also was differentiated to reflect diverse levels of talent, skill, and education. Thus the original leveling effect of cooperation and communalism was later tempered or weakened by a growing emphasis on differences.

It was also significant that by the 1880s Orderville's chief outside supporter had died. During his lifetime, Brigham Young had done much to aid the town's efforts. He visited the town on occasion, advising and blessing the members' labors. On 17 January 1877 he wrote the president of the order and urged him to keep careful accounts and to set specific day rates for all work done: "A little girl can take account of the time and enter each day's credit under the respective names of the workers. This record can be taken, say every evening about supper or prayer time." He further wrote: "Credit a man for what he does. It is a true principle that every person shall be rewarded for the labor he performs; that is, he shall be credited for all good he does, but the fruits of his labors must be added to the general fund of the United Order."[28]

Apostle Erastus Snow, the regional church leader, did not view the Orderville United Order's efforts as favorably as did Brigham Young, and after the church president's death Snow assumed more direct responsibility for Orderville. He visited the town on 20 April 1877 and found much with which he was dissatisfied. In a sermon before a group of the town's adults he said:

> I have been exercised much in regard to the method adopted at Orderville. I do not think the Lord is particular how we make the garments with which we are clothed, or as to the manner in which we prepare our food. Neither do I think the Lord cares much about whether we sit down to one or more tables.[29]

In a later statement, Snow further commented:

> I am just as sanguine now as I have been in time past that the Lord wishes His people to be united as the Nephites [a people described in the Book of Mormon] were, when there will be no more poor among them; when all will be faithful in their labors. The people of Orderville or those that are organized in the United Order deserved credit for what they had done, but that they are exactly on the line, I cannot say, I can see some defects in their organizations that will show themselves at some time, and will cause some to feel disaffected.[30]

In reflecting on the troubles the Orderville United Order eventually met, Thomas Robertson wrote in a letter dated 18 August 1883 to Reddick Allred:

> Accumulating wealth was not our object, that was furthest from our minds; our aim was to establish a principle of equality— as near as our fallen natures would admit of, striving always to grade upwards to the mark. We found it necessary to make changes from time to time as our experience in living together with united interests brought us in contact with difficulties that people in other circumstances knew but little or nothing about, consequently new developments had to be met with new arrangements, and occasionally one would become dissatisfied and leave, and in such cases we invariably paid them their capital invested and their accumulations for that year up to the time they quit work for the company.[31]

Rather than continue to alter the system, perhaps beyond recognition, the members looked to church leaders for guidance. In the spring of 1884 Thomas Chamberlain and a few other men traveled to Salt Lake City to talk with church leaders about possibly closing down the Orderville United Order. The general authorities did not issue any firm directive, it seems, being content to praise the order's members for their dedication, and urging them to continue, while at the same time saying that the Lord had not revealed a definite plan for the Latter-day Saints to follow. Kanab Stake President L. John Nuttall recorded the meeting in his diary.

At 7:30, Presidents Taylor and Cannon and Elder Nuttall met

with Bp. Thomas Chamberlain and Elder Thomas Robertson [of Orderville]. . . . The affairs of the United Order of Orderville was considered, it having been said that it was the design to break up the Order next September [1884]. Prest. Taylor said he did not want the people to thus break up, but to continue their labors in the United Order. [He] referred to other institutions wherein, when the capital stock is put in, it becomes the company property, and cannot be drawn out without the consent of the company. Bro. Chamberlain explained the circumstances and condition of the people of their ward. After consideration Prest. Taylor promised to write a letter to the people of Orderville giving his mind as to how they shall continue their labors.[32]

The Orderville leaders returned somewhat discouraged and thrown upon their own resources for deciding the fate of the order.

In a letter to Chamberlain, general authority of the church George Q. Cannon placed the blame for the order's failure on its inability to maintain the cooperation of the members and also on its changed policy toward equalized wages. Cannon said: "When you changed your system from that of equal labor credits and disbursements to that of giving men credit according to their skill etc., just as is done in society elsewhere, you opened the door for selfishness and other feelings to enter, which such society has to contend with. By this change you dropped back to the old level. With such a change it cannot be reasonably expected that your organization can hold together for any length of time."[33] It is clear in hindsight, however, that changes in the state's economy and the attitude of church leaders toward the order impacted the order as well.

Orderville suffered the blow of losing the support of Mormon church leaders at the same time that many of its leading polygamist members went into hiding to avoid arrest under the provisions of the federal Edmunds Act. Because so many Orderville residents were polygamists, the community was seriously impacted by the larger prosecution of polygamists by the United States government. Men like Thomas Chamberlain spent months in hiding and were eventually apprehended, prosecuted, and imprisoned. Without effective leadership, the order increasingly weakened, and church leaders kept urging a weakening of the original system, such as allowing personal

Pioneers of Orderville in March 1931. (Courtesy Fred Esplin)

luxuries and encouraging plans to share the stock with the rising generation—a shortcoming of the original plans that had somewhat
alienated the youth of the order. Some church leaders also favored the
dissolution of the order to help reduce Mormonism's peculiarities in
the eyes of federal authorities they were trying to placate.

E.D. Woolley, president of the Kanab LDS Stake after Nuttall,
described the outcome of a series of meetings in late 1884 and early
1885 with church leaders about the continuation of the order:

> We were a week laboring and counseling, talking and praying
> with the people as a whole and with the leaders separately. Finally
> they voted unanimously to discontinue their operations in Utopia.
> As soon as that was done the apostles skipped back home and left
> me to the reconstruction. . . . It was a pretty job for that time and
> for my abilities.[34]

A committee was appointed to come up with a plan for the dissolution of the order. "After exercising all the faith we could and calling for Divine aid," Woolley wrote, "we evolved the following plan.
We had the Secretary go over the capital stock, and list everything
that had been put in at inventory price. After that was done, teams,

land, etc., being named so that we knew what and where it was, we held an auction sale in 1885 of all the community belongings."[35] The men sat through the auction "like Quakers," Woolley said, each waiting so that he could get his own property back. Payment was made with credits that the order's members had accumulated. Woolley himself was the auctioneer. The order retained ownership of three entities: the tannery, the woolen factory, and the sheep enterprise. These businesses were leased out to individuals who managed them, however. By 1900, when the original charter of the order expired, the Orderville United Order had effectively ceased to exist.

The Orderville United Order had lasted for more than a decade and was the most successful example of the communal mode of living among the Mormon pioneers. Andrew Jenson visited Orderville in 1892 with the intention of writing a history of the town. He concluded:

> The good Saints of Orderville gained an experience that will never be forgotten by those who passed through it and I was assured by several of the brethren who stuck to it till the last that they never felt happier in their lives than they did when the Order was in complete running order and they were devoting their entire time, talent and strength for the common good. Good feelings, brotherly love and unselfish motives characterized most of those who were members until the last.[36]

Many contemporarily written reminiscences detail life under the order, making frequent mention of the spirit of true communalism that existed there. Henry Fowler remembered: "I have lived in Utah, Arizona, California, Idaho and in many different towns and I never was so much attached to a people, I never experienced greater joy nor had better times than during the period of time I was connected with the United Order in Orderville."[37]

Although the Orderville experiment in communal living was relatively short-lived, it provided a unique example of both the benefits and the pitfalls of living cooperatively. While requiring the sacrifice of its members, the community's strong bonds spanned generations and family divisions and facilitated the people's efforts at taming the wilderness and making a living. The Mormons' efforts at cooperation in the creation of the United Order linked them symbolically to communitarians across the country who were seeking new ways of interacting in communities, of equalizing wealth, and democratizing experience in social settings.

The United Order was practiced in Orderville for some ten years, far longer than in any other Mormon community. When it was abandoned in 1885, it marked the end of an era. Some of its businesses continued to operate cooperatively, and most of the buildings continued to serve in similar or adapted uses. After the demise of the order, a small amount of construction occurred each decade despite decreases in population. Rube Jensen was the chief carpenter for many late-nineteenth century homes. In 1969 long-time resident LeGrande C. Heaton wrote:

> Some of the houses were made of hand-hewn logs; others of native yellow pine lumber were sawed locally and were shingles with steam-split shingles made by local mills. . . . The houses were finished on the interior with lath, covered with lime and horsehair plaster (and) white washed with a lime finish. The nails were square iron nails, some of which were made in Orderville. Some were purchased in Cedar City. Each house had one or two open fireplaces. On cold nights they glowed brightly with wood gathered in the nearby hills. . . . Each home was surrounded by a fence. Some of the fences were picket, some board and some barb-wire. Most of the yards had flower gardens.[38]

LeGrande Heaton summarized what had become of the physical town first known as Order City: "Gradually the old houses have been replaced until today, there are 95 quite modern homes. . . . Some of them appear old, but all have been built or added to since 1890. None of the original buildings remain, except a replica of the old stone house, rebuilt with the original rock by the Daughters of the Utah Pioneers."[39] Heaton's assessment may not have been entirely correct, as it appears that several dwellings from the 1870s and 1880s remain. One may be a tall, two-level, frame building in the middle of the commercial district on the east side of U.S. Highway 89. Featuring a cornice trimmed with nineteen pairs of ornamental brackets, this building appears in old photographs of Orderville and may be the former co-op or some other store of that era. Still, Orderville today bears little resemblance to its appearance during the united order years of the 1870s and 1880s, or even to its turn-of-the-century look. Gone are the united order buildings the rock school, the church, and the social hall so proudly erected.

ENDNOTES

1. Brigham Young, quoted in Mark A. Pendleton, "The Orderville United Order of Zion," *Utah Historical Quarterly* 7 (October 1939): 144.

2. The original "Articles of Incorporation" are in the Bleak Manuscript Collection at the Huntington Library in San Marino, California. See *Deseret News,* 1 October 1875.

3. E.M. Webb, in "Manuscript History of Kanab Stake," LDS Church Archives.

4. Joel E. Ricks, "Forms and Methods of Early Settlement in Utah and the Surrounding Regions, 1847–77," (Ph.D. dissertation, University of Chicago, 1930), 152–54.

5. Pendleton, "The Orderville United Order of Zion," 146.

6. Ibid.

7. Ibid.

8. Samuel Claridge, autobiography, 35–36, typescript, Utah State Historical Society.

9. Ibid.

10. "Partial List of Products and Manufactures of O.U.O. for 1879," Bleak Manuscript Collection, copy at Utah State Historical Society Library.

11. Sibyl Frost Mendenhall, "Biographical Sketch of Allen Frost," 10, Utah State Historical Society.

12. Hattie Esplin, Life Sketch, 4, Utah State Historical Society.

13. Emma Carroll Seegmiller, "Personal Memories of the United Order of Orderville, Utah," *Utah Historical Quarterly* 7 (1939): 33.

14. Ibid.

15. E.M. Webb to John R. Young, Orderville, 21 May 1878, "Memoirs of John R. Young," 223–24, Utah State Historical Society.

16. Water Commissioner's Certificates, 13–44, Kane County Recorder's Office, Kanab, Utah. The awards of water rights were made a matter of record in 1881 in accordance with legislation of the Legislative Assembly of the Territory of Utah approved 20 February 1880.

17. Adonis Findlay Robinson, *History of Kane County,* 318.

18. "Partial List of Products and Manufactures."

19. Pendleton, "The Orderville United Order of Zion," 149.

20. Quoted in S. George Ellsworth, *Samuel Claridge: Pioneering the Outposts of Zion* (Logan: Utah State University Press, 1987), 190.

21. Ibid., 190–91.

22. Kate Carter, ed., *Heart Throbs of the West* (Salt Lake City: Daughters of Utah Pioneers, 1936–51), 4:28.

23. Orderville United Order, Account Book, 1879–1882, 25, 163, 276. LDS Church Archives.

24. Ellsworth, *Samuel Claridge,* 192–93.

25. Ibid., 193.

26. Fred M. Fowler, "Mary Fowler: A child of Pioneers," 8, Utah State Historical Society.

27. Ibid., 194.

28. Brigham Young, quoted in Pendleton, "The Orderville United Order of Zion," 155.

29. Quoted in Elsie Chamberlain Carroll, *History of Kane County,* 322.

30. Erastus Snow, 19 April 1877, quoted in *Deseret News,* 9 May 1877.

31. Pendleton, "The Orderville United Order of Zion," 156.

32. L. John Nuttall, diary, 28 April 1884, Utah State Historical Society.

33. Pendleton, "The Orderville United Order of Zion," 158.

34. Edwin Dilworth Woolley, "Final Settlement of the Order," in Carter, *Heart Throbs,* 4:47–48.

35. Ibid.

36. *Deseret News,* 4 March 1892.

37. Henry Fowler, in Carter, *Heart Throbs,* 1:59.

38. Quoted in Robinson, *History of Kane County,* 391.

39. Ibid.

CHAPTER 7

COMMUNITY BUILDING, 1880–1900

Life in Kane County

Kane County has always been somewhat isolated because of its uniquely challenging landscape, its lack of connections to railroad lines, and its relatively small population. During the nineteenth century, life there was in part dictated by one's occupation, by connection to the Mormon church, and by one's home. The interconnectedness of the three created an interesting mesh in which religion, family, and community often almost seemed to be one and the same.

The lack of railroad connections limited both settlement and development of Kane County. Marysvale in Piute County, 132 miles away, was the nearest railroad terminal; before the railroad reached there, area settlers had to travel to the terminus of the railroad, wherever it happened to be as the tracks were laid from Nephi into and through Sevier County in the latter part of the nineteenth century. This had an effect on agricultural production for market, as well as mining, manufacturing, and the settlement of towns in Kane County.

131

In some ways, however, isolation was an asset; the dry climate and expanses of land provided a very good setting for the stock raising industry.

The 1880 census reported a total of 3,085 people and 15,371 head of livestock in Kane County. Population had more than doubled from the 1,513 people counted in 1870. By that time the area had become a center of ranching rather than subsistence farming, which it continued to be in the twentieth century.[1] The settlers in the region were quick to adapt and to search out other ways of making a living. They saw the land as a resource to be used for their economic gain. Thousands of acres of land unsuitable for agricultural use were fine for grazing. Ranching was a more appropriate economic use of the land, as was the case in much of the region. By the time of the census of 1890, stock raising was by far the most important industry in the region. In 1900 it was second in importance only to mining in Utah Territory.

Edwin D. Woolley, Jr., was an early area cattleman. In the 1880s he and John W. Young ran the Grand Canyon Cattle Company headquartered at the V.T. Ranch. Their cattle ranged through the Kaibab Forest. In the 1880s John W. Young and other Kane County leaders were moving herds of cattle across the Arizona Strip country. Town dwellers by preference and church calling, these men hired herders and line riders to do much of the work. Many southern Utah cowboys were an interesting hybrid—tied to specific towns and places but also drawn to the independent life on the range.

The Grand Canyon area during this period was a place where bands of thieves and cattle rustlers sometimes hid out, as this era was noted for its cattle rustling throughout the territory and general region. Trails from the Grand Canyon's North Rim also were important to Kane County residents as they explored the area and attempted to make use of its resources, particularly the timber.

James A. Little and Royal Cutler brought sheep to the area in 1871. Little's sheep ranch north of Glendale was the location of the first shearing corrals used by many local sheepmen. The sheep industry became more important to the area after 1890, as sheep began to supplant cattle on the ranges, ranchers believing that they made better use of the range, although, in fact, they actually hastened its dete-

The Stevens Home in Mt. Carmel. (Courtesy Deanne Glover)

rioriation with their close cropping of the grasses. Kane County's towns serviced sheep herders and cattlemen alike.

Cattlemen would drive their herds of cattle to distant markets or railheads. In the earliest stock raising days, Salt Lake City was the best shipping point for markets outside Utah, and a round trip to Salt Lake could take a full month. By the 1880s, Nephi became a more convenient and closer shipping point because of the extension of the railroad to the south. The journey to Nephi was ninety miles shorter and took about eight fewer days. Later, cattle were shipped from Cedar City and Flagstaff.

Much early trade was conducted on the basis of barter, or payment in goods. For example, Brigham Young paid William James Frazier McAllister to interpret in Spanish for a period of time in Kanab. McAllister reported that he was paid with a team, "harness and wagon, some factory cloth, dried beef and pork, 1 ton of flour and one which I went to S.L.C. and received from Br. Eliju F. Sheets." He continued, "I traded a span of mules, harness, and wagon to James Emmit for the lot with house and water where Eddie Riggs lives now. The lot was to be well fenced, a new lumber room house.

Half were—so that my first lesson in trading with the 2 rooms not fit for a barn, the naked lot and no fence."[2]

Mail service in and out of Kane County was difficult, compounded by the difficult terrain, climatic conditions, and the threat of attack by unfriendly Native Americans. The first men reported to carry mail along with other supplies were brothers Nephi and Justin Johnson and Joel H. James. Joseph Hamblin and Charley Hilton also occasionally transported mail and other parcels. They would usually travel the rough county from Toquerville to Pipe Springs to Kanab to Johnson. Other times the mail was carried on horseback over the Schunesburg Trail, a dangerous, circuitous route that led from Kanab to Tenny Canyon across the northern portion of Cottonwood Ranch, then to Rock Canyon and to the Schunesburg mill. At the mill the carrier transferred the mail to a back pack and carried it the rest of the way down a steep, rough trail down a 1,000-foot cliff. At the bottom of the cliff he met up with another carrier who carried the mail the rest of the way. Eventually, a wire cable was devised to carry the mail packet down the cliff.

Zadok K. Judd carried the mail to Lee's Ferry along with his sons Zadok Jr., Eli, and Samuel. Richard and Charles Smithson met the Judds at the east end of the Paria route and carried the mail the remainder of the distance from Johnson. Eventually mail was carried on horseback from Kanab to Panguitch by John R. Findlay. Buckboards soon replaced horsemen despite the precarious condition of many of the roads between the distant towns. The sandy roads of Long Valley were particularly precarious in places.

During the late 1880s and early 1890s Kane County received some relatively large appropriations, about $2,500 per year, "for constructing, repairing and maintaining roads from Kanab north to the Garfield County line in Kane County and "for constructing roads across the North Fork country in Iron and Kane counties."[3] This facilitated mail service and other area transportation.

Kanab

After Levi Stewart served as bishop of the Kanab LDS Ward, L. John Nuttall became the local ecclesiastical leader in 1876. When the united order effort there was abandoned, he moved to Orderville to join the more zealous attempt at cooperative living being conducted there. William D. Johnson served as Kanab's bishop until 1884; Laurence Maringer then was bishop for five years. Maringer resigned in 1890 and John Rider became the presiding religious leader for a short time until Joel H. Johnson became bishop. Johnson served until after the turn of the century, being replaced in 1901 by Harmon Scott Cutler.[4]

In 1881 another gristmill in Kanab was completed by Reuben Broadbent and James Guthiar in Kanab Canyon about three miles north of town. According to one local history, the men were sent by Mormon church president John Taylor to build the mill. This mill was soon destroyed by a flood, however. Others followed, including a small mill on the east side of town built in the 1890s by Zadok K. Judd that used an overshot waterwheel and provided coarsely ground meal. Wheat generally soon ceased to be produced in the area; until that time, residents generally took what wheat they raised to be ground at a mill in Glendale in Long Valley.[5]

First organized on 14 December 1881, the Kanab Irrigation Company became closely connected to the history of Kanab, and the fortunes of both later were closely intertwined. Besides developing and maintaining irrigation canal systems and building reservoirs, the company was concerned with the distribution of water for culinary use. Shares in the Kanab Irrigation Company in the first years sold for prices ranging from a few cents to three dollars. Ten percent of the value of the capital stock was used each year for repairing the water courses, dams, and flumes. The minutes of the company mention the need to clear streams of debris, construct new dams, and build storage reservoirs. One passage from a WPA-sponsored history of irrigation describes the local custom of drawing water for use in the house from a ditch or other water source in front of the house:

> The word "Pond" used in connection with water shares recalls a practice of the first settlers in securing drinking water. Ponds were made here and there about town to which people came for water for house use. The practice grew out of necessity because the stream dried up during some of the hot summer days. Water again at night reached town so ponds were made as reservoirs more for drinking purposes than for irrigation. Not all the settlers held

ponds but many of them did and, judging from what early settlers have said several people in the same neighborhood combined to make a point. Ponds were used until sufficient water for daily use was always available.[6]

One enterprising young man hauled water out of canals for up to fifteen cents a barrel, depending on what part of town he was working in.[7]

The Kanab Irrigation Company, still active today, was initially chartered for fifty years. Its stated purpose was to operate all necessary irrigation ditches, construct reservoirs and other means of water storage and distribution, and maintain a consistent water supply for its shareholders. Water came from Kanab Canyon, Big Lake, Hog Canyon, John R. Canyon, and other smaller tributaries. The first company board of directors included William D. Johnson, John L. Bunting, James Leithead, J.E. Riggs, and John R. Stewart. A committee to hear water claims from stockholders was composed of William T. Stewart, John G. Brown, and B.Y. Baird.

The Kanab Irrigation Company purchased two lots southwest of town from the local school trustees for a new reservoir. A second reservoir was built in 1882 northeast of Moquis Knolls, the land purchased from Zadok K. Judd at fifteen dollars per acre. The water in each reservoir was variously graded: city water (or primary) water, original (or secondary) water, and surplus water. Original water was available to irrigate 269 acres and was divided by the company between families according to their need.

Problems plagued the company, and many were reported in the minutes of the company. Service complaints were made that the water was not coming to town early enough in the morning and that if necessary there should be proper division of the water at the head of the district ditches according to the shares of water to be drawn in each district. Consequently, the general watermaster was instructed to have the water turned to town at 5:00 o'clock each morning and turned off at 5:00 in the evening.

The company started to build another dam of dirt and logs and an irrigation ditch in 1883. Due to a misunderstanding, the water was backed up before the spillway was completed, and the dam was destroyed. In the words of a local historian,

> This dramatic event was known as the "great washout." The creek bed was sunk forty to fifty feet below the intake irrigation ditches, and the underseepage caused the wall to become dry. The entire supply of water was cut off since the dam afforded both culinary and irrigation water. Then in the same year came an even more devastating catastrophe. It was Sunday, July 29th while the people were in church that a great flood swept down the canyon into the valley, removing masses of earth and trees and forming a deeper chasm where the original creek had flowed.
>
> The worshiping citizens were startled by loud claps of thunder, soon followed by a frightening roar of rushing water which swept everything before it. James Brown recalled that . . . "Father's field which was below town was covered with water and shocks of grain standing in the field were buried to the binding bands in sands."[8]

John Rider sent a report of this flood to the *Deseret News* which described the damage caused locally:

> A wave of debris ten feet high reached clear across the canyon. It destroyed 300 acres of hay and drowned several head of cattle. . . . The city dam was washed out and the channel of the creek cut down about forty feet. The gristmill door was broken away and two feet of debris and sand lodged in the lower story. The face of the canyon was altered. About 1300 bushels of grain in the upper and lower fields were lost where the flood was about one mile in width. A great many springs were opened, showing an increase in water. On Monday following the flood a survey was made for a new town ditch to connect with the millrace. It was to be completed in thirty days at a cost of $4,400.[9]

After the devastating events, the townspeople immediately started rebuilding. They built three-foot flumes secured with cedar posts at the location of the original dam two miles north of town, and kept a close watch on the structure. They then contracted with Samuel Adams in 1885 to rebuild a more sturdy dam, paid for with an extra tax levy. Those short on cash could work for water rights. A new ditch to town was finished by May 1885. In 1890, however, heavy

The Edward T. Lamb Home in Mt. Carmel. (Courtesy Deanne Glover)

winter snows and rain caused another flood, which washed away the twenty-five-foot dam. Interestingly, Frederick S. Dellenbaugh of the second Powell expedition earlier had predicted difficulties for the town in maintaining a regular water supply:

> In February, 1872, while we were camped below Kanab, Clem and I were walking one day and saw a place where the creek which flowed on a level with the surroundings, suddenly plunged into a deep mud canyon. This canyon had been cut back from far below by the undermining action of the great Canyon several miles above, but I did not dream that it would accomplish this work as it actually did continue its retrogression till it eventually reached the mouth years later. During a great flood it washed a canyon not only to Kanab, but for miles up the gorge, sweeping away at one master stroke hundreds of acres of arable land and leaving a mud chasm forty feet deep. Had the fall we examined then been arranged so that the water might glide down, the fearful washout would not have occurred.[10]

The townspeople's next attempt at dam building was at a site just below Three Lakes recommended by Erastus Snow. The head of the ditch was created by blasting a hole in the rock of the canyon wall with three tons of blasting powder. Finished by 1891, the dam was 200 feet in length, 200 feet in width, and 40 feet in breadth. Patrolling the dam became a civic responsibility built out of necessity. Between 1898 and 1899 Thomas Chamberlain helped form a pipeline company to build a settling pond at the north of town and to pipe water to homes by means of iron pipes. This helped facilitate the division of irrigation water and water used for culinary purposes. Edwin D. Woolley and H.E. Bowman piped water from Hog Canyon also in the 1890s. After the dam was washed away by floods in 1900, water was hauled into town until a new dam was built in 1908–09. Culinary water was transported to town from a water source 1.5 miles away in barrels that moved on "lizards," or log sleds, that facilitated their movement along the bumpy dirt roads. Soon, entrepreneurs were hauling water for fifteen to twenty-five cents a barrel for those who didn't want to do the chore. The water was thick with red sand and had to settle for a period before it could be used. Housewives found that clothes washed in this water had a distinctive pinkish tint that spoke of their native environment. Nevertheless, the water was a precious commodity; it was carefully rationed for washing clothes as well as for an occasional bath.

On 29 June 1885, a group of citizens of Kanab petitioned for incorporation.[11] Kanab incorporated with Allen Frost as town president and William S. Lewis, A.L. Stewart, W.H. Clayton and Zadok K. Judd, Jr., as council members. Their first meeting was held at Frost's home on 28 September, and W.H. Clayton was appointed clerk, Zadok K. Judd treasurer, and W.S. Stewart town marshal. The men opened and closed their town council meetings with prayer.

The primary business of the second town council meeting was to create and file a plat defining the corporate limits of the town, and to assess a tax of one-fourth of one percent on all town property values according to law. During October the council began designing local ordinances to regulate local affairs. For instance, anyone discharging firearms within the town limits would be fined; other lawbreakers would be imprisoned or fined for their offenses; and trustees would be paid twenty-five cents per hour for their attendance at council meetings. During 1886, the council passed ordinances that dealt with the fouling of water that flowed into town and with adultery and prostitution. It also authorized a survey of a town cemetery. St. George's code of laws were often looked to as a guide as council members established rules and ordinances for the town.

After a general body of laws was created, the council generally dealt with more routine matters of maintenance—tax matters, land questions, and the making of new laws. Licenses given to new businesses (such as a drugstore in 1896) give some picture of the growth of the town's services and population. Periodic projects like fencing the cemetery, sprinkling town roads to control dust, and digging new irrigation canals help provide a picture of daily life and the efforts to make Kanab a more beautiful town.

The cooperation that typified the early settlement efforts continued to play a role in community building. One resolution passed by the board was sent to the LDS bishop to be read in a church meeting. It read:

> Whereas; the streets, sidewalks, ditches, both company and individual road crossings are dilapidated and in some instances dangerous for pedestrians to travel, and in view of the fact of the approaching quarterly conference, be it resolved that the residents of the town be respectively asked to assist in clearing and repairing said ditches, sidewalks, etc. and the same will be highly appreciated by the town council.[12]

Besides celebrating the Fourth and Twenty-Fourth of July as they had for several decades, Kane County residents celebrated an annual Old Folks Day after the 1890s. Originally celebrated as part of the Pioneer Day events, it became a separate festivity. On Old Folks Day, horse races were held on a half-mile track located about a mile from town.

A school building known as the Academy was built on the northeast corner of the site occupied by the present elementary school in Kanab. It replaced the existing school and housed grades one through eight. It was begun and partly constructed about the year 1890 by a Mr. Foremaster and brothers Elisha and Elijah Averett, pioneer stonemasons and builders of the fort at Pipe Spring. The first stage of construction was a one-story brick building with a flat roof, which leaked during stormy weather; a pitched roof later replaced the flat one. This structure was used as a social center as well as for church and school.

In 1896 a new story of brick was added. A belfry on the top housed a bell that served for church and school call, fire alarm, and curfew.

Kanab had 409 inhabitants in 1890. In 1892 H.E. Bowman, Daniel Seegmiller, A.D. Young, Edwin D. Woolley, and F.A. Lundquist joined together in a company they called Bowman and Company. Bowman managed the business, which was housed in a brick building on the corner of Center and Main Streets. He sold out to Thomas Chamberlain in 1896.

Kanab's first doctor arrived in 1894, a Doctor Harvey, who supplemented the services already provided by local midwives. Annie S. Riggs and Lucinda S. Brown, both informally trained midwives, went to Salt Lake City to take a course in obstetrics and nursing.

Kanab's commercial architecture began as stores moved out of homes and onto Main Street. Competitors soon put up small stores in the center of town, where the present business district emerged. It included the Johnson Brothers Store, which later became the Elephant Store and then the Highway Hotel, in a one-and-one-half story wood structure with a two-story false front of wood siding and tall windows.

Bowman and Company built one of the town's first brick stores. It was a substantial two-story structure with large storefront windows flanking the centered front doors, with a pair of tall double windows on the second floor. Other early commercial establishments and buildings included the Exchange Building, Kanab Equitable Building, Glazier Store, Stockman's Store (in the Jepson Building), Marinda Halliday's Ice Cream Parlor and Millinery, and Honey's Barber Shop, among many others. In 1900 the town collected $265.17 taxes in the form of labor and $6.98 in cash, which gives some indication of the limited amount of hard cash in the county.

Glendale

Glendale's early prosperity was largely due to large sheep herds in the hills nearby. Glendale's first building of prominence was a handsome, Greek Revival style meetinghouse. Serving as designers, LDS bishop James Leithead and Reuben Broadbent drafted plans for the twenty-six-by-forty-foot frame edifice. John Averett laid the stone foundation; N.J. Levanger and James W. Watson did the carpentry work. Built mostly in 1891 but not dedicated until 1895, the church featured a twenty-foot-high ceiling, a columned portico, ten tall windows with thirty-six panes of glass each, and an octagonal cupola/belfry containing a 400-pound bell. The bell was made especially for the church by a Mr. Jensen, who had been a bellmaker in Sweden. In 1928 the church was expanded with an addition built on the east end.

Another significant public building erected near the time of the meetinghouse was the Social Hall, a thirty-three-by-seventy-foot frame structure. It included a high ceiling, a stage at one end, doors at each end, and rows of tall windows on the sides. During the winter of 1891–92, men went into the hills and cut timber for the hall as well as a surplus amount to pay for the milling of the lumber. They hauled the logs to the Macdonald sawmill above Black Rock Canyon. Cultural life centered primarily on activities sponsored by the Mormon ward. Plays such as *The Black Heifer, Silas the Chore Boy,* and *Snow White* were staged there; dances and LDS stake conferences were also held in the Social Hall. The hall had the misfortune of being struck by lightning three times. The last time, in 1929, it caught fire and burned to the ground.

Among the most architecturally significant dwellings remaining are a double-wing, Gothic Revival house with two angular bay windows and ornamental boards trimming the gables. A Victorian house with Queen Anne windows and trim dates from the 1890s, while two similar triple-dormered, central-passage homes seem products of the 1880s.

Mt. Carmel

Mt. Carmel was an important way-station for mail carriers traveling through Long Valley and a supply and rest station for travelers, where they could stable their horses and rest before continuing their journeys. According to B.H. Sorensen, a mail rider,

> the carrier would leave Mt. Carmel at 2 P.M., ride north to MacDonald's Ranch, meet the carrier from Hatch, exchange mail bags and return, delivering mail at other communities along the way, arriving back in Mt. Carmel between 8 and 10 P.M. Fifty to seventy-five cents per day was the going wage for this route. Going south, the rider would leave at 4 A.M., climb the Mt. Carmel hill,

The Mt. Carmel Church. (Courtesy Deanne Glover)

pass Red Knoll, into Cave Lakes Canyon, where he would water his horse and proceed on to Kanab. In Kanab, he'd feed and rest his horse, exchange mail bags and leave in time to be back in Mt. Carmel by 2 P.M. $1.00 was the daily wage for this rider.[13]

The earliest method of school transportation was a covered wagon with a wood-burning stove in the center to provide warmth for the children. Some of Mt. Carmel's earliest teachers were Frank Little, Bessie F. Little, Seymour McAllister, Margaret Melling, John H. Beatty, Fanny Kleinman, Edwin Stucki, Mary Hicks, Ivor C. Iverson, Artimisha Palmer, and Wilmirth Johnson. Mt. Carmel's children were brought by Heber Covington in a wagon to Orderville to attend school there, and during bad weather the children were often late because the horses had a difficult time pulling the wagon through the muddy rutted roads. Eventually the town bought a school bus that was first driven by the schoolteacher himself and eventually by William and LeGrande Heaton.

Alton (Upper Kanab)

The architecture of the small, isolated community of Alton reflects its builders taking advantage of the town's proximity to sources of timber. Alton consisted of only a few developed blocks and was mainly an agricultural and ranching town. No commercial or industrial districts developed, although a few stores were in business over time.

After brothers Byron and William Roundy came to Upper Kanab, they settled on 160-acre homesteads and organized a cattle company they called the Canaan Cooperative Stock Company, which was headquartered in St. George. They imported stock herds and began a dairy business. The upper Canaan Ranch had four shares of water, the Roundys two shares, and the lower Canaan Ranch six. They were joined in 1882 by the Edwin D. Woolley and Daniel Seegmiller families.

In 1882, Edwin Dilworth Woolley, Jr., and Daniel Seegmiller were called by Apostle Erastus Snow to Upper Kanab to manage the Mormon church cattle ranch there. Woolley accepted the call, believing that the area would be the perfect environment to help his wife recover from a recurring illness. His daughter Mary remembered it as a beautiful site at the base of the red rock. "We found the ranch to be a very picturesque spot, beautifully situated under a row of pink cliffs, the same formation as Bryce Canyon and was unknown to the world," she wrote.

The Woolley family's journey from St. George to Upper Kanab took eight days, the family camping each night in a different locale. Mary Woolley Chamberlain remembered the journey:

> Just a series of long weary days of travel over rough roads or through deep sand. . . . We finally reached our destination. It was early evening and as we passed Byron D. Roundy's home, he and his good wife Matilda insisted on our stopping there for supper. They were our nearest neighbors and were anxious to get acquainted. They were very hospitable and the friendship formed at that time lasted throughout the years.[14]

Despite the difficulties of the journey to Upper Kanab, the family was overwhelmed by the beauty of Long Valley and particularly of the settlement area, informally called Ranch. Mary Chamberlain continued:

> Our ranch was situated at the mouth of two canyons, one on

the north called Main Canyon which was most beautiful and had several canyons leading off from it, Pole and Quaking Asp, being the ones I remember best. The canyon on the east was Rush Canyon in which was a ten-acre wheat field which could be seen from the house. Good streams of water came from these canyons, supplying plenty of irrigation for our land and all the farms below owned by the Roundy Brothers, Byron D. and William, and Richard Robinson who had a large family of boys and girls with whom we soon became acquainted and formed lasting friendships. These three families were our only neighbors within six or eight miles.

Down in Sink Valley lived James Swapp and his large family whom we seldom saw except when there was a celebration or some special occasion. About six miles over on the other side of a small divide at the head of Long Valley Canyon, Brother John Seamon operated a sawmill. He had a large family and also hired a number of young men, so there was always a crowd there. Rube Jolley lived close by and kept the post office where we went for all our mail. About two and a half miles farther down the canyon, lived Graham Macdonald, his good wife, Annie and a large family of boys and girls. . . . Our neighbors were all very hospitable, and we enjoyed the friendship of everyone.[15]

Her father rented one hundred cows, which the family and hired workers would milk by hand. A neighbor and dairyman, Richard Robinson, taught Woolley how to make cheese. Each fall, Woolley traveled to Salt Lake City to purchase supplies for his family. Mary Woolley remembered that it was always a great day when her father returned from one of these trips, "as the house became a veritable store, with bolts of factory bleach, cheese cloth, gingham, shirting, geans, demin, calico, . . . boots and shoes for the entire family including the hired man, dozens of boxes of thread, tape, buttons, . . . bales of yarn, carpet warp, candle wicking, sacks of sugar, rice, beans, boxes of raisins, barrels of coal oil, cases of matches, kegs of nails, bolts, screws, brooms, blankets, etc."[16] She related an account of one trip north Woolley made in February 1884 that was a particular adventure. Her father's buckboard got stuck along the way and he was forced to spend a night on the rim of the Great Basin, in four feet of snow, the temperature below zero. He had no food and was ill prepared for spending a night camping in the canyon. "A very thrilling account of the whole trip of eleven days all of which were spent in breaking track through snow often up to his arm pits, through which he had to wallow," and how he fell fifty times was published in the newspaper, his daughter reported.

Two public buildings were eventually erected in the lovely valley at the head of the Virgin River—a schoolhouse that also served as a meetinghouse, built in 1885 by Edwin D. Woolley and the Roundy brothers, and a recreation hall built in the cove north of Macdonald Lake. There the members of this rather diffuse community joined together for dances—with Hyrum Roundy playing the violin, Rube Jolley second violin, John W. Seaman the bass fiddle, and Graham Macdonald the drums. Reluctant to go back to the isolation of their individual homesteads, the settlers would dance until long past midnight. Children would be cuddled up in big homemade quilts along the sides of the room as the adults danced through the night hours. Another schoolhouse later was built about halfway between Byron Roundy's home and the Woolley home. Jed F. Woolley (Edwin Woolley's nephew) taught school there to local children, who often had to come to school on skis when the snow was too deep to walk in.

Horse racing was a particularly favorite local pastime; in fact, the horses raised on local ranches were well known throughout the region for their speed and quality breeding. Elizabeth W. Jensen, in her father's biography, quoted an interview with W.W. Seegmiller about the quality of stock raised locally:

> The main progress of the country during the nineties and a few years in the new century, depended upon the maintenance and improvement of the rangelands. E.D. Woolley and Daniel Seegmiller, partners in the upper Kanab Ranch, were the first to import blooded horses and purebred bulls for breeding. The blood is still here. I remember when I was a little boy of going after the purebred cattle to Salt Lake City. There was great curiosity through the country. People would come out for miles around a settlement to see them as we passed by.[17]

The cowboy and ranching culture was not welcomed by all Mormon settlers. Rebecca Mace noted in her journal in March 1895:

> The General Stake Conference convened on the 2nd and 3rd, March 1895. On the 4th Horse racing took place just out of town about 4 or 5 miles, or as some expressed it, the After Conference.
>
> On the 7th the Relief Society met in a general monthly meeting. . . . Sister Harriet Brown was called upon and she opened upon the evils of Horse racing, and all the sisters sustained her in the position.[18]

Edwin Woolley was made local LDS stake president in June 1884 and functioned in that capacity for the next twenty-six years, traveling throughout the area of Kane and Garfield Counties and to Lee's Ferry and the Colorado River to the south. In 1887 the three communities of Ranch at the head of the Rio Virgin, Upper Kanab at the top of Kanab Creek, and Sink Valley joined together to form a LDS ward. Graham Macdonald became the first bishop, with Byron D. Roundy, Sr., and Franklin B. Woolley as his counselors. It was considered an extension of the Glendale LDS Ward. Graham Macdonald was a professional plasterer and used his craft to make many local meetinghouses more beautiful.

The women of Kane County LDS Relief Societies engaged in churchwide grain storage projects. After harvests, Relief Society women would go into the fields to glean the remaining wheat, which they then saved. The women also made quilts and rugs and sold "Sunday" eggs to raise money for other causes or needs. The Relief Society wheat was used when crops failed; some was sent to San Francisco after the earthquake in 1906, and some was even sent to China to help in times of famine there. The women initially stored the wheat in wooden bins at the tithing office but eventually built their own granary, which had bins lined with tin.

Federal Prosecution of Polygamists

After the Civil War, the issue of the Mormon church's practice of polygamy aroused increased attention from United States government officials and put the territory in a state of confusion. A series of increasingly strong anti-polygamy bills went before the U.S. Congress—the Morrill Act of 1862, the Cullom Act of 1870, the

Edmunds Act of 1882, and the Edmunds-Tucker Act of 1887—and
focused attention on Utah. A crusade began to put down the power
of the theocratic government of the Mormon church in Utah
Territory.

Polygamists in Kane County as elsewhere reacted to the pressures
put on them by federal marshals and went into hiding, or "on the
underground," as it was termed. Polygamists throughout the region
were hunted and prosecuted—particularly in the 1880s. Family and
community life was upset. Many Mormons showed that they were
willing to sacrifice enormously for their religious beliefs, but the cost
was frequently quite high.

For Edwin Woolley and his family, living on the ranch in Upper
Kanab proved to be an adventure that none of them could have predicted. Beautifully situated at the base of the Pink Cliffs, the ranch
became a haven for polygamists on the run during the underground
period. Woolley's home in Long Valley was used as an underground
station. Many church leaders stopped there while in hiding, coming
from as far away as Salt Lake City for a few days and sometimes weeks
at a time. According to Mary Woolley, "We lived in constant fear and
dread and were always on the look-out for a white-top buggy coming up the road, as the Deputy Marshalls were about the only ones
who drove them at that time and even the little children were taught
to be on the watch and to give the alarm if one approached."[19]

Edwin Woolley moved one of his wives, Flora, to the region of
Pipe Spring, Arizona, a rendezvous area for many plural wives that
soon boasted its own town, called Fredonia. Some of the couple's
children were born in hiding there. According to his daughter Mary's
account:

> Some built comfortable homes and lived there for many years,
> while others lived in wagon boxes, under willow sheds, etc. until
> the "Raid" was over and then returned to their homes. The place
> was named "Fredonia" by Apostle Erastus Snow, which in Spanish
> means "free women," but it was not interpreted by him nor the
> people of that day, in the modern sense.[20]

William Morley Black first moved to Kane County in 1873, settling one of his plural families in Long Valley. During 1888 he was

forced on the underground and spent the next several months in hiding and traveling from place to place to avoid arrest. He wrote in his autobiography:

> Then I spent one year playing hide and seek with the U S dept Marshalls but got tired of the play so I took Louisa the youngest family and skipped for old Mexico I went with two teams leaving Huntington Nov 13 1888 passing thru Rabbit Valley and up the Sevier by Johnsons then across the Buckskin Mt, to Lees ferry. The nights were cold but no storms. We passed up the little Colorado in Arizona and the day before Christmas reached St. Johns where my son Sm G lived. I spent a pleasant week with them. Then moved on in Round Valley I met prest David Udall and found employment for the winter in his grist mill.[21]

Black left Round Valley in May 1889 and then crossed the border into Mexico. He wrote: "here I was in a foreign land not of choice but of necessity in my own land a criminal yet I had not injured a living person. The law that makes me a sinner was encested [*sic*] on purpose to convict me. . . . To me it is leagly unjust which adds a sting to it's cruelty."[22]

William James Frazier McAllister bought a lot in Fredonia and built a house for his wife Angie. Two of their three children were born during the underground period there. Ida Udall went to Snowflake, Arizona, during the period to live in her father's home. Despite careful efforts, during that time her husband, David King Udall, was prosecuted and imprisoned for cohabitation.[23]

Delaun Mills Cox also remembered the buggies, because they were a luxury the pioneers could not usually afford themselves. They were also taught never to answer questions from a stranger, even if money were offered to induce them. Thomas Cox built a secret hiding place in the hayloft of his barn. According to Delaun Cox, "On one occasion he was hiding there when the boys were hauling hay, and not knowing anything about it they ran the pitch-fork through his leg, wounding him quite seriously, so he did not try that place again and was often forced to ride all night to get beyond their reach."[24]

Mary Woolley reported that marshals named McGeary and

Armstrong often patrolled the area. Coolly, her mother would feed
them dinner, entertaining them in the house while her husband hid
out in the hayloft. She even cared for an ailing marshal: "Once when
Mr. Armstrong came he was desperately sick and mother proceeded
to give him a lobelia emetic, soak his feet in hot mustard water, etc.,
Which was her unfailing remedy for everything."[25] Edwin Woolley
was finally apprehended and arrested in October 1887 but was
acquitted at a preliminary hearing before a United States commissioner at Silver Reef. In 1890 he was again arrested and taken before a
grand jury at Beaver, Utah. There, his case was dismissed for lack of
evidence because Flora, his plural wife, was in Arizona and they could
not force her to testify as a material witness.

Kane County Government

Despite the tension between the federal government and the
Utah Mormons over the Mormon practice of plural marriage, county
life and activities continued. Although the quality of Kane County's
commission minutes varies, they do over time include at least the
names of local elected officials, a sense of local political issues and
personalities, and the problems that county government had to con-
front during the last decades of the nineteenth century. The first
extant record book is Book B, which covers the period from 1883 to
1902.[26] Book B starts with 5 March 1883, the commission meetings
being held in Kanab in the tithing office. At that time, besides the
selectmen (county commissioners) county officials included a justice
of the peace, a road supervisor, a pound keeper, and a sheriff. After
1884 the school superintendent was made a county position elected
by Kane County voters. This brought the local superintendent under
authority of the Utah Territory Superintendent of Public Instruction.

County business was frequently concerned with the construction
of roads, regulation of stock grazing in public fields, or the interaction between neighbors. Public welfare was a concern of officials; on
5 November 1883, for example, German Buchanan solicited financial
assistance from the commission for his "insane" wife. The topic of the
organization of a new school district to meet the needs of the children of Orderville and other Long Valley towns came before the commission on 9 March 1885. In March 1892 county voters supported

repairs on the county courthouse, including the erection of a new privy.

In 1883 one M. Slack was the court clerk and L.C. Mariger was the deputy officer. Selectmen included Nephi Johnson, who also was considered road commissioner, Lemuel H. Redd, and George Spilsbury. W.A. Bringhurst was the judge of the county court and William J. Jolly the justice of the peace of Mt. Carmel. Brigham Y. Baird served as road supervisor for the Kanab district and William Worthen for Mt. Carmel; Nephi Jolly was the pound keeper for Mt. Carmel, and William W. Hammond justice of the peace for Mt. Carmel. James Leithead was road supervisor for Glendale, William H. Laws road supervisor for Johnson, and Francis Kirby had the responsibility at Pahreah. The county attorney was identified simply as "Halladay."[27] Another important group of county officials were the board of examiners for teachers, which in 1883 included E.M. Webb, A.W. Brown, W.A. Bringhurst, and M. Slack. Officers for Pahreah appointed in June 1884 included Joseph A. Stewart as justice of the peace; Thomas Smith, constable; and Esly Stewart, Thomas Stewart, and George A. Smith school trustees.

On 25 June 1883, the names of other positions were recorded: Taylor Crosby, deputy sheriff; C. Stapley, county treasurer; and W.D. Johnson, Jr., county superintendent of schools. Johnson submitted his first report to the commission that same day. The roster of selectmen often varied due in part to the number of men who had responsibilities that took them out of the county, including missions for the Mormon church, freighting businesses, or plural families located in other towns. In November 1883 the selectmen included John Rider, Brigham Y. Baird, William D. Johnson, and Robert Moncur. Resignations and replacements were relatively easily made during these years and depended as much as anything else on one's willingness and availability to serve. Roads—construction, maintenance, and regulation—and animal control seemed to be the two topics most often addressed.

The county commission in 1884 paid $18.00 rent to William D. Johnson for space for the county clerk and recorder's office. Selectmen in attendance in December 1884 were William D. Johnson, R. Moncur, and Willard Carroll. Brigham Baird resigned that year as road commissioner of the eastern part of the county. In March 1885, the selectmen read a petition from Thomas Stateworthy and forty-two others requesting creation of a school district for the Orderville factory above Glendale. This petition was approved on 1 June 1885, and designated as District 8.[28] The school organized that year operated until 1892.

In 1890 the county's population was counted at 1,685—a great drop from the 3,085 counted ten years earlier, as many had found that the available land could not support them. Between 1887 and 1891 county selectmen included James Leithead, B.Y. Baird, G.D. MacDonald, Joseph S. Emett, and Charles W. Carroll (1890). Carroll was also serving after 1887 as county assessor and collector of taxes. Various requests came before the Kane County selectmen; for example, A.D. Young asked for a certificate entitling his deaf son to the benefits of the territorial appropriation for deaf mutes, and a petition in March 1889 from citizens of Long Valley asked that an election be held to change the county seat to Glendale.[29] When the issue of the removal of the county seat from Kanab to Glendale was placed on the ballot later in 1889 eighty-six voted against and fifty-eight for the measure. Kanab continued to be the center of county government.[30]

In May 1889 there was a proposal for bids for a courthouse to be constructed. The selectmen received bids from William McAllister, from Broadbent, Hopkins and Averett, and from C.S. Cram; the bid was awarded to Broadbent, Hopkins, and Averett for $2,500. By December 1889 the courthouse was being rented for dances for two dollars per night.

In 1890, selectmen received fifty dollars per month; the county clerk, $300; county recorder, $100.00; superintendent of schools seventy-five dollars; and the surveyor received one dollar per month.[31] In 1893, the selectmen included Joel H. Johnson, H.S. Jolley, John Rider, and H.S. Cutler, with John R. Findley as sheriff and John F. Brown as county attorney. The tax assessor and collector was M.D. Harris.[32]

In 1895, county government was led by Judge J.S. Bunting and selectmen John Rider, A.D. Findley, and M.D. Harris. Joseph E. Robinson was paid one hundred dollars to compile a county census for Kane County that same year, just before Utah statehood.[33] John

Rider resigned as selectman and county auditor in December 1895 and was replaced by H.S. Jolley.

On 9 November 1896, H.E. Bowman asked for a road franchise for a toll road from Kanab Canyon to the top of Mt. Carmel Hill via Three Lakes; county commissioners took the matter under advisement. In the general election of November 1896, county residents cast a total of 520 votes and supported Lafayette Holbrook for their congressional representative. At the turn of the century, county officers included Joel Johnson, Jonathan Heaton, and Hans C. Sorenson, commissioners; Wallace O. Bunting, clerk; James Swapp, sheriff; Hattie Spencer, recorder; and Thomas Chamberlain, treasurer.[34]

News of county, state, and national affairs was circulated by a series of weekly newspapers. News of the earliest episodes in Kane County's history were reported in the *Deseret News* of Salt Lake City. The *Piute Pioneer* published in Marysvale briefly supplied news to much of southern Utah on a weekly basis during the late 1890s and for a time was the only newspaper that regularly appeared in Kane County. In the 1890s local news was reported by Elmer Johnson in the *Kanab Index.* This paper carried news of local events, announcements of births, deaths, and marriages, and occasional editorials and advertisements. In 1899, J.T. Camp and his family moved to Kanab and brought with them an old printing press. Having established his reputation as a newspaperman as editor of the *Sevier County Times,* Camp soon published the *Kanab Clipper,* starting on 1 January 1900. This twelve-by-fourteen-inch broadsheet was only four pages long, but it carried news from towns across the county.

Like other Utahns, residents of Kane County rejoiced when Utah was finally granted statehood in early 1896. Rebecca Mace recorded in her journal the impact the announcement of statehood had on the county:

> 1896 opened auspiciously for Utah and its inhabitants. On the 4th of January 1896 President Cleaveland issued a Proclamation admitting Utah into the Sisterhood of States. As soon as the message (2 oc. PM) was received guns were fired, Flag hoisted. Bands played. Shouts of joy arose from the heart and lips of all, with ringing of bells and everything which could be used to sound a note of joy was brought into requisition. Some of our young men formed

themselves into a military company calling themselves the Home Guard, and with the Martial Band, George Mace leader, marched and countermarched, serenading prominent Men. . . . And thus the day was made one of general rejoicing. From the moment the telegram arrived, never had all Utah joined in such hilarious rejoicing.

On the 6th—Monday, the officers of the new State, who was elected in the previous election held in November 1895 was inaugurated, the day being set apart as a holiday to be remembered as such forever. It was enjoyed to the utmost.

Guns were fired at daybreak. 10:00 a procession was formed, lead by the Band of Home Guards—followed by citizens, also a juvenile corps, or Bell Brigade. At two o'clock the citizens met in the Social Hall and partook of a Pic Nic Dinner, then followed speech and Song, closing the day with a grand Inaugural Ball.

The day was all that could be desired. The weather was pleasant and all enjoyed themselves, there was nothing to mar the occasion, and it will be a day long to be remembered by the inhabitants of Kanab both old and young.[35]

Beginnings of Kane County Tourism

Residents of Kane County quite early began to benefit economically from their proximity to the Colorado River and the great natural wonder of the Grand Canyon. As part of an elite education in the nineteenth century, European monuments—the Louvre, Chartres cathedral, and the Pantheon, among others—were essential parts of the Grand Tour, romanticized in travel literature throughout the eighteenth and nineteenth centuries. Many American and European travelers followed a relatively predictable journey through the centers of European culture; Paris, Rome, Vienna, and London attracted the privileged with their history, art, and culture. Sometime during the late nineteenth century, the Grand Tour for some expanded to include North America, and—for a few—the natural wonders of the canyonlands that included Kane County.

European and American explorers, travelers, and adventurers came to Utah Territory and marveled at the rock formations, canyons, and rivers of southern Utah—detailing their adventures in travel accounts, journals, government reports, and other forms of literature, which brought the relatively unknown territory greater attention. The region's beauties were painted by Thomas Moran, drawn by W.H. Holmes, and photographed by Jack Hillers and Timothy H. O'Sullivan, each of whom brought the wonders of the area to the eyes of the world. Once the influx of tourists began, except for very short intervals caused by wars or natural disasters, it never stopped, growing to impressive numbers by the late twentieth century.

One early visitor to Utah from Italy was travel writer and adventurer Carlo Gardini, who in his book *Gli Stati Uniti*, written in 1887, detailed four separate journeys through Utah Territory. Stopping at the predictable railroad towns—Salt Lake City, Ogden, and Provo—he also visited less well-known sites like Toquerville, Pipe Spring, and Kanab. Despite the fact that Gardini was treated well by his Mormon hosts, he came with assumptions about the secrecy of their religious activities and called them a "bizarre sect." When he arrived, he had read travel accounts by Baron Von Hubner and William Hepworth Dixon, both of whom had already passed through the area. He went to southern Utah primarily because of his curiosity about Indians. His understanding was that Mormon missionary activity among the Native Americans had been based on the belief that they were descended from an ancient tribe of Israel. Gardini's guide said that the Native Americans were of a very peaceful nature and reported that "they not only do not suffer in the midst of the settlers; the passengers in the stages are never molested by them."[36]

Despite the difficulty of traveling the terrain between Pipe Spring and Kanab, that locale was unlike anything Gardini had previously experienced and everything seemed more grand and dramatic than anything in his previous experience. He wrote: "The distance from Pipe Springs to Kanab is approximately 25 miles; the road, which is sufficiently good, first takes us directly east, then passes by the spectacular and gigantic low-permian-terrace; and, after having turned in a northerly direction, arrives in Kanab, it being built on the banks of the river and protected on the other side by a large formation of red rock." He was impressed by the inhabitants of the town of Kanab, which population he guessed at being approximately 400, most of whom were Mormons. He wrote, "Kanab is not as pretty a city as

Cedar City and Toquerville, nonetheless all of its habitations have lawns with full flowers and trees, similar to the style of all the Mormon villages."[37]

His guide asked for information about the location of the nearest Indian encampment and was informed that the Native Americans had recently moved to the south to camp near a spring. The guide explained the importance of being well prepared for the journey, as the terrain and weather were unforgiving and unpredictable in their extremes. According to Gardini: "The most important object consisted in obtaining two good horses, not an easy thing in and of itself, on account of the fact that these animals, do not have horseshoes and they therefore suffer from wounds at the top of their feet. However, with the help of the head of the house where we were lodged, we were able to obtain two excellent horses and provisions sufficient for at least three days, since in the mountains where we would travel there were no eating establishments or water or anything else civilized."

The men purchased supplies in Kanab and were able to get a variety of canned goods, dried meat, and a supply of water:

> We were able to obtain various boxes of conserved meat—in America they are better prepared than in either France or in England—coffee, cognac and some canteens full of water. With respect to items to prepare food, we could not take anything except a small kettle to boil water for use with our coffee and tea, the only hot item that we were able to procure without putting us behind in the small amount of that we would be in the hills. I also utilized the moccasins, a special type of shoe utilized especially by American explorers, that I had bought to climb Pike's Peak, but the thing that was most useful at the same time, were two magnificent buffalo skins which were loaned to us by the good head of household, and they are almost indispensable when one has to spend a night in the desert.[38]

They began their journey before sunrise, capitalizing on the cool air, eager for what lay ahead.

> At 4:00 A.M. the next morning we had already begun our journey and our Indian boy was setting the pace with admirable shrewdness, choosing the least difficult path. Along the scene that

we were traveling through there were giant rocks almost stripped of any vegetation and in their appearance not much different than the vermillion caves which we saw on the way from Pipe Springs to Kanab. We walked until almost midday when we stopped, based on the advice of our guide, near a [spot] which terminated in a ravine and at the end of which were located pools of relatively clear water deposited from those hurricanes which commonly rage in this region. Nearby there were also located a few parcels of ground covered with grass, so that our horses were allowed to roam free to search for their own food. We only took the precaution to attach [hobbles] to their front legs, so that they would not wander too far.[39]

As was frequently true of European visitors to the West, the party was fascinated with the behavior, appearance, and lifestyle of the Native Americans they encountered and carefully noted their "foreign" way of life. Gardini's writings reveal contemporary stereotypes, limited knowledge of Indian life and history, and a general fascination with the novel and exotic.

After about three hours of rest, we started our journey again heading toward evening to the spring which we had been told about in Kanab, and a little distance from there we noticed in fact a group of attentive Indians in a very straight valley in which around noon our perspective was blocked. That camp consisted of about a dozen tents which were spread among a few shrubs. The tents were made from branches of trees stuck in the ground and tied together at the top with varying pieces of canvas or dirty skins of animals. The Indians who live in them amounted to less than two dozen and when good words were directed toward them by the missionary and our guide, only the men responded with some signs demoting a little courtesy whereas the women and children looked at us firmly without speaking a syllable.

In an effort to befriend them, we gave them a little tobacco, a few pieces of multicolored cotton and various pieces of glass beads, objects that we had purposely brought from Kanab but they failed to change the attitude of the savages, and my gifts were accepted with such coldness that I was almost mortified, if the missionary had not made me realize, that such a way of acting is innate to the

Indians who still being in extreme misery maintain their haughti-
ness and impassiveness.[40]

Gardini came away "convinced that the Indians were an original
variety and in fact unique among human species."

French traveler Albert Tissander spent six months traveling in the
United States in 1885. In his travel account *Six Mois Aux Etats-Unis
(Six Months in the United States)* he mentioned, like Gardini, his awe
at the natural environment of Kane County.[41] Among many other
sites, Tissander visited prominent Kane County destinations including Kanab, the Kaibab Forest, and canyons of the area. His guide
through Kane County was a former whaler, miner, and member of a
prominent Canadian family who had squandered his fortune and
ended up in Silver Reef, Utah, where he drove hired carriages for travelers through the area. Tissander wrote of the journey across the
rugged terrain, giving a glimpse of Kanab at the time.

> We settled into a carriage as uncomfortable as the one that
> had driven me to Silver Reef, and the roads no less bumpy.
> Fortunately, the landscape was as splendid as before. The Virgen
> [*sic*] River rocks were pink and silver-gray, and I looked in amaze-
> ment at their outline, carved and filigreed into thousands of fan-
> tastic shapes. . . . The lonely wastes resumed; nothing but desert all
> day. Then we ran alongside the Vermilion Cliffs, a long mountain
> chain of red sandstone standing tall above the wide prairies where
> numerous flocks grazed. The moonlight shone a faery light on all
> this grandiose scenery. . . . The following day, at noon, we were at
> Kanab. It lies beside a river that is almost always close to dried-up,
> but in the snow-melt seasons, it swells and overspills extensively in
> floods, washing away sand and putting the entire country there-
> abouts under water. Huge red-sandstone rocks (the Triassic
> escarpment) sheltered the village on one side; on the other, the
> scrublands stretch away out of sight. It housed perhaps 500 inhab-
> itants. Their isolation would have been complete, but by their own
> industriousness they have succeeded in forging links with the most
> prosperous and civilized in their country. The telegraph was
> installed there![42]

Edwin D. Woolley often has been given credit for promoting
Kane County as a tourist destination. Elizabeth W. Jensen recalled a

The Thomas S. Tate House in Mt. Carmel. (Courtesy Deanne Glover)

time in the latter part of the nineteenth century when he was riding with John W. Young and was so overcome by the beauty of the landscape that he reportedly exclaimed: "This is one of the Wonders of the World! People will come from all quarters of the globe and will pay great sums of money to gaze on what we now behold."[43] According to family members, the idea of developing a local tourist industry was never far from his mind, and he was always ready to expound on the subject. John W. Young helped Woolley bring the area to the attention of would-be travelers as far away as England during the late 1880s when he was on a mission in Great Britain for the Mormon church. Young came up with the idea of attracting English aristocrats to the Kaibab Forest area as a private recreation area. Young purchased land there which he used to graze cattle and horses. He envisioned the Kaibab as a hunting ground and center of tourism with hotels and lodges, primarily with the British nobility in mind.

Coincidentally, William "Buffalo Bill" Cody was also in England at the time of Young's stay, and Young invited him to come to the Kaibab and serve as a guide for British visitors. Cody came to Kane County in the summer of 1891. He and various English aristocrats were met at the railroad terminus in Flagstaff, Arizona, by Dan

Seegmiller from Kanab, who was placed by John Young in charge of the enterprise. The group traveled to Kanab by way of Lee's Ferry, Houserock Valley, and the Kaibab Forest.

The party included Junius Wells, Buffalo Bill, John Barker, and some Englishmen—a Major McKinnon, Lord Ingram, and Lord Milmey. The visitors eventually concluded that although the land was beautiful it was too difficult to travel to and did not pursue the idea of establishing a resort. The failure of the venture placed John Young and other large landholders in the region in some financial difficulty, a fact which eventually helped lead to the establishment of the national forest and national park in the area, as some private land-holders were willing to relinquish their holdings in the area. The group saw the Grand Canyon, and the presence in the region of Buffalo Bill was a major event for local inhabitants. Travel in the area was risky, with narrow roads and steep precipices. The company was ferried across the Colorado River at Lees Ferry on a rather primitive raft made of logs and ropes.

Regardless of their reasons for visiting the area, the explorers, sci-entists, tourists, and others who passed through Kane County and wrote about their experiences were moved to express what they felt about the land. In doing so, they helped to advertise the area's grand beauty and make the isolated place a destination for those desiring an unusual experience in the wilds, but a wilds that was also con-nected to the rest of the world by modern communication devices.

ENDNOTES

1. *Compendium of the Tenth Census* (1880), Part I (Washington, D.C.: U.S. Department of the Interior, 1883), 912–13.

2. William James Frazier McAllister, Autobiography, 8, Utah State Historical Society.

3. Ezra T. Knowlton, *History of Highway Development in Utah*, 824.

4. Elsie Chamberlain Carroll, *History of Kane County*, 180–81.

5. Ibid., 24–25.

6. Julius S. Dalley, "Maintaining an Irrigation System," Utah Writers' Projects, Box 83, Fd. 3, Utah State Historical Society.

7. Ibid.

8. Adonis Findlay Robinson, *History of Kane County*, 138–39.

9. Quoted in Carroll, *History of Kane County,* 128.

10. Quoted in Carroll, *History of Kane County,* 129.

11. Kane County Court, Minutes, 7 September 1885.

12. Quoted in Robinson, *History of Kane County,* 90.

13. Carroll, *History of Kane County,* 451.

14. Ibid., 461.

15. Ibid.

16. Mary E. Woolley Chamberlain, "Edwin Dilworth Woolley, Jr., 1845–1920," 3–4, Utah State Historical Society.

17. Ibid., 464.

18. Rebecca Mace, Journal, March 1895.

19. Chamberlain, "Edwin Dilworth Woolley," 7.

20. Ibid.

21. William Morley Black, Autobiography, 19, Utah State Historical Society.

22. Ibid.

23. Vera A. Christensen, "Biography of Ella Stewart Udall," 6, Utah State Historical Society.

24. Delaun Mills Cox, "History of Delaun Mills Cox," 20, Utah State Historical Society.

25. Chamberlain, "Edwin Dilworth Woolley," 7.

26. A copy of Kane County Minute Book B is housed in the Utah State Historical Society Archives in Salt Lake City.

27. Kane County Court, Minute Book B, 5 March 1883.

28. Kane County Court, Minutes, 1 June 1885.

29. Ibid., March 1889.

30. Ibid., 2 September 1889.

31. Ibid., 5 May 1890.

32. Kane County Court, Minutes, 6 March 1893.

33. Ibid., 9 September 1895.

34. Kane County Commission, Minutes, November 1900.

35. Mace, Journal, January 1896.

36. Carlo Gardini, *Gli Stati Uniti* (Bologna, 1887), trans. by Michael W. Homer, from forthcoming book, as yet unpaginated, *On the Way to Somewhere Else: European Travelers in Utah, 1853–1930,* to be published by Arthur Clarke, Glendale, CA.

37. Ibid., 3.

38. Ibid

39. Ibid.

40. Ibid.

41. Albert Tissandier, *Six Mois Aux Etats-Unis* . . . (Paris, 1886), trans. by Hugh MacNaughton, from forthcoming book, as yet unpaginated, *On the Way to Somewhere Else: European Travelers in Utah, 1853–1930,* to be published by Arthur Clarke, Glendale, CA.

42. Ibid.

43. Quoted in Robinson, *History of Kane County,* 185.

CHAPTER 8

KANE COUNTY ENTERS THE TWENTIETH CENTURY, 1900–1920

Life in the County

As Kane County's residents entered the twentieth century, life continued pretty much as it had. Life in the shadow of the Vermilion Cliffs was relatively simple, driven by the need to provide for families, find ways of joining together in communities, and enjoy the beauties of the natural environment. The Mormon church provided most of the religious and social structure for county residents, even though the more rigorous experiment of the United Order was now gone in the county as elsewhere and the church no longer publicly sanctioned plural marriages (and soon would denounce them altogether), leading to better relations with federal officials and non-Mormons in the new state.

Kane County began the twentieth century with a relatively stable economy and a population of 1,811, up from the 1,685 counted ten years previously. The gain was even more substantial than the numbers reflected, as they did not now include people in land that had been annexed to Garfield County during the previous decade. The

Wagons loaded with sacks of wool ready for shipment. (Courtesy Fred Esplin)

economy was based in large measure on ranching and livestock. Local ranchers were optimistic—the demand for cattle and sheep products was good and would continue to be such through the time of World War I. The market stagnated during the 1920s, however, in Kane County as throughout the nation.

The impact of Utah statehood, U.S. involvement in the Spanish-American War, the revolution in transportation with the advent of the automobile, and changes in communication like radio and eventually television initially affected the county less than they did more urban areas, since many changes were late in fully coming to the county. Dirt roads were the norm, and many residents of Kane still carried their water into their homes from a nearby ditch as late as the 1940s.

Kane County residents were not self-sufficient, having to ship in staples from other parts of the state. Because of this, freighting became an important occupation for some locals. Before regular freighting was established, local farmers would sometimes take their dairy products and other surplus produce to other regional towns and barter for their needs. The earliest shipping into Kane County came out of Beaver, Utah, and Pipe Spring, Arizona.

Freighting was particularly important to the sheep raising business. Kane County had abundant good grazing land. Sheepmen sheared their sheep twice a year and hauled their wool to markets in the north for sale. The *Kane County Independent* reported on 11 April 1912 that 13,000 head of goats were sheared at the Dry Lake pens. The men who freighted the wool to market often would return with wagons loaded with supplies either to sell in the county or to support their own families. With the extension of the railroad south into the Sevier County area by the turn of the century, Salina, Richfield, and Marysvale all became shipping points for both cattle, sheep, and wool from the Kane County region.

Many residents of Kane County towns—both Kanab and the Long Valley communities—owned ranches in nearby canyons where they spent their summers. The abundant grasses of mountain meadows and the more easily accessible water sources made for excellent conditions for dairying. For instance, Francis M. and Elizabeth Hamblin established the Swallow Park Ranch during the period of the united order in Kanab. Their daughter, Sytha S. Johnson, dairied there between 1908 and 1910, specializing in the production of cheese. Her process was relatively simple:

> The milk was strained into a cheese tub at night. Next morning the cream was skimmed off and the morning milk added. It was then heated and rennet added to form the curd. Next the curd was scalded until it "squawked" when tested, then drained and cooled and salted and placed in the cheese press until the next morning. After it was removed it was rubbed with butter and turned each day until it ripened and was ready to cut.[1]

In 1905 Edwin D. Woolley and Daniel Seegmiller helped organize the Utah Cattle Company to improve the state of the stock-raising industry in southern Utah. They sponsored experiments with Persian sheep and imported special breeding horses and bulls to improve stock lines. The Utah Angora Goat Association formed in 1906 to promote the use of mohair; Benjamin Hamblin was its first president.

Some local cattlemen also attempted to set up a buffalo-raising business. According to Helen Burgoyne:

> A unique experiment in livestock breeding was begun in 1905. Col. C.J. Jones, "Buffalo" Jones, who first came into this section to

A Sheep Camp above Long Valley. (Courtesy Fred Esplin)

explore the feasibility of establishing a national park, sold Ernest
Pratt and Edwin D. Woolley on the possibility of creating a new
kind of cattle by breeding buffaloes with Galloway cows. Mr. Pratt
said, "Jones' story of elegant robes sounded big! We bit and a company was formed with Jones at the head."[2]

The buffalo were shipped to Lund from Los Angeles, and Pratt,
Scott Brown, and Tim Hoyt headed them across Cedar Mountain.
The animals became sore-footed and had to be shod with oxen shoes.
By the time they reached Kanab, Pratt had had enough and withdrew
from the company.

Edwin D. Woolley's responsibility in the company was to trade
300 three-year-old cows for 100 Galloway cows, a transaction he had
to make in Kansas. Their party reached Bright Angel Point in 1906
and the cows were herded along with the buffalo. The experiment
was considered a failure because the two species failed to interbreed.
The company dissolved after four years. Jones returned to the East
with some remaining money, the cows, and a few buffalo; Owen
began herding buffalo in the House Rock Valley for wages and eventually bought out the local owners, eventually selling the herd in
Arizona.

Mrs. Rachael Woolley Dalley, who as a girl helped her father move the buffalo, said that the Woolley estate only received $1,200 for the company's 300 choice heifers and that for years letters came from eastern stockholders asking what had become of the company. The local sheep men resented having the company's Persian sheep on the range, for their wool was very coarse. "The men did not want the breeds mixed and the value of wool thus depreciated." The Persian sheep soon disappeared from the country, but for many years the state of Arizona reportedly sold permits to hunt buffalo.[3]

National Parks, National Forests, and Federal Land Use Policies

An important land use consideration in Kane County long has been the large amount of land in the county that is controlled by the federal government. The agencies that managed these resources have played an increasingly important role in Kane County affairs. During the first two decades of the twentieth century, a national conservation movement increasingly turned its attention to the creation of agencies and legislation that would protect and regulate the public domain in the interests of future generations.

Federal land management policy can be seen to have developed in five stages: 1. acquisition of lands for the nation, 2. disposal of some federal lands to private and state ownership, 3. reservation of certain areas for permanent federal management, 4. custodial management of public lands, and, 5. more intensive management of those lands. Congress created the General Land Office in 1812; until 1910, the General Land Office commissioned outside firms to survey lands prior to their sale to private interests and had no directives to manage the federal land except for those areas designated as national parks or forest reserves.

The conservation movement near the turn of the century helped create a national forest system. In 1891 Congress passed an act with a Forest Reservation amendment that allowed the president to "set apart and reserve, in any State or Territory, lands wholly or in part covered with timber or undergrowth, whether of commercial value or not," and a National Forest Commission was appointed in 1896.[4]

Gifford Pinchot became the head of the Division of Forestry in the Department of Agriculture in 1898 and turned the division into a professionally managed operation. Pinchot also introduced the concept of ranchers leasing public forest lands for grazing for their animals. A succession of bills strengthened his position, allowing the Secretary of Agriculture to acquire and manage forest lands. Under Pinchot's direction, the Forest Service developed and protected national forest land in both the spirit of conservation and the application of forest management principles allowing grazing and timber cutting in the forests.

Lumber continued to be produced from the forests, including the forest reserves and national forests of the region. J. Edward Crofts purchased John Stout's water-powered sawmill, located near the Hoyt Dairy above Glendale. Crofts had worked at the mill, which had been in operation for several years, since 1905. During the five years he ran the mill, it produced about 1,000 feet of lumber each day.

Kaibab forest areas had been set apart as a forest reserve in 1893, and the Kaibab National Forest was created in 1908, although not without opposition from area ranchers, who feared that increasing regulations would limit the grazing of their livestock herds in the forest. On 11 January 1908 President Theodore Roosevelt established Grand Canyon National Monument, a separate entity from the Kaibab Forest also created at that time, and plans were soon established to make the great canyon a national park. Grand Canyon National Park was finally created on 26 February 1919 after President Woodrow Wilson signed the bill authorizing it. This did not come about without controversy—some of it from ranchers of the Arizona Strip area and Kane County.

In 1912 the *Kane County Independent* noted the discussion about turning large portions of the Kaibab National Forest into a national park. Despite the increased tourism which the park designation would bring, there was significant opposition to the idea, especially from ranchers who saw their personal livelihood threatened. "Do we want to stay in the cattle and sheep raising business, or be lackeys for big brewers, soap-makers and stock gamblers and their wives, for the wages a tourist agency would pay?" asked the Kanab paper.[5]

The attempt to make a national park out of the Kaibab Forest was met with considerable resistance from local cattlemen and ranchers who anticipated that it would cause great injury to their personal cattle and sheep operations by excluding them from that range. In one article of the *Kane County Independent* their point of view was articulated:

> The proposed park would cut into the grazing area on the Forest materially, and this at a time when stockmen are facing a cut in their grazing permits because the range is already becoming overcrowded, and when the price of beef is beyond any but the rich on account of their being so little public range left to raise beef on.
>
> The loss of so much grazing land, while it would be felt seriously in this country, could be borne without a word if it would benefit the nation in any way. But the game on the Forest is already fully protected by the game preserve, and the natural wonders of the region are protected for all time by being set aside as a national monument. By these measures the Nation is already taking care of its scenic wealth.[6]

Despite their self-interested protests and rather limited vision, in September cattlemen were ordered to remove 1,000 head of cattle from the west side of the Kaibab National Forest.[7] Ranchers were more successful in their attempts to eliminate wolves and other predatory animals on forest lands, in part because President Roosevelt had established the Grand Canyon National Game Preserve in 1906, with the intent to protect deer. In October 1912 a bounty of $150 was offered for each wolf killed.[8]

The battle over public lands continued throughout the century, with ranchers resisting any government attempt to more strictly manage the public lands or increase grazing fees. Many area ranchers in Kane County as elsewhere in the West seemed to believe that their lengthy use of the land entitled them to permanently control it or at least not have any of their previous privileges reduced or eliminated.

In October 1912 the Indian agent on the Kaibab Indian Reservation just across the border in Arizona received instructions from government officials to charge cattlemen one dollar per head per year for grazing fees for running cattle on the reservation. Then as now, white ranchers in the area were upset at any charges or restrictions on their use of the land, although the land in this case technically belonged to Native Americans. As reported in the *Kane County Independent*, "this fee is to be charged despite the fact that water owned by the Indians is in such places that 300 head of cattle could hardly find grazing to support them within watering distance of any water they own."[9]

Apparently, the only major watering sources nearby were claimed by B.A. Riggs, Edward Lamb, the Heaton family, and Edwin D. Woolley, men who were particularly impacted by the ruling. According to the newspaper, "These men will now have to pay a dollar a head each year to water their cattle with their own water." It continued, "This order will effect all cattlemen in Kane County, as well as some in Washington and Iron, who own cattle that have drifted from their home range onto the Reservation and may be taken up for trespass."[10]

Regardless of efforts on the part of the government to regulate grazing lands, area cattlemen ran their herds pretty much where they wanted without much interference, damaging the public rangeland with overgrazing when they weren't trespassing on Indian lands. The *Kane County Independent* commented on the number of cattle grazing in the county and the "advantages" to ranchers of working in such a wide expanse of isolated land. It said of a Forest Service "effort to force a count of cattle on the west side of Forest Reserve," that "it is admitted by most of the grazers that the west side is overstocked. However the 'Service' seems helpless to enforce the rules."[11] A pattern was early established of area opposition to any kind of range management that would affect the short-term economic gain of ranchers, even if the improved rangeland would benefit them in the long run.

Until this time, the grazers had been paying a twenty cents grazing tax, imposed by the Department of the Interior. Expressing the local outrage at this so-called federal interference in local affairs, the paper said, "The sheepmen do not get off scathless, they are now to pay $2.00 per 1000 for the privilege of driving their sheep across the Reservation, on roads that have been open to the public for 35 years. They will be allowed 36 hours in which to cross. This is one of the grandest little schemes to put cattlemen out of business ever hatched.

Who is behind it?" the paper asked in conclusion.[12] No attempt was made to understand the Indians' point of view, that their own range was being depleted by the herds belonging to white ranchers that freely crossed it.

Although at one time the area that became Zion National Park was mainly within the earlier enlarged county boundaries, today only a small portion (and later addition) to Zion National Park and only a portion of Bryce Canyon National Park are in Kane County. Still, the region's national parks and monuments have been very important to the county's economy.

Mormon pioneers settled small communities at the edge of Zion Canyon beginning in 1861. Some agricultural land about a mile in width was found along the canyon floor. During the winter of 1864–65 a wagon road that crossed the stream many times was built along the Virgin River bed. This road continued to serve as the main road into Zion Canyon until the National Park Service built a road to replace it. In 1930 that second road was replaced by a well-graded highway that was constructed between the river and the older road.

One early account of the startling beauty of Zion Canyon was written by Clarence Dutton of the U.S. Geological Survey, who, in a report published in 1880, wrote of his wonder at first seeing the canyon: "In an instant, there flashed before us a scene never to be forgotten. In coming time it will, I believe, take rank with a small number of spectacles each of which will, in its own be regarded as the most exquisite of its kind which the earth discloses. The scene before us was the Temples and Tombs of the Virgin."

Major John Wesley Powell had a similar response to Zion Canyon. He wrote in his journal, "Entering this, we have to wade up the stream; often the water fills the entire channel, and although we travel many miles, we find no floodplain, talus, or broken piles of rock at the foot of the cliff. The walls have smooth, plain faces, and are everywhere very regular and vertical for a thousand feet or more, where they seem to break in shelving slopes to higher altitudes; and everywhere as we go along, we find springs bursting out at the foot of the walls."[13]

In 1908, Deputy United States Surveyor Leo A. Snow first recommended making Zion Canyon a national park:

A view can be had of this canyon surpassed only by a similar
view of the Grand Canyon of the Colorado. At intervals along the
west side of the canyon streams of various sizes rush over the edge
of the chasm forming water falls from 800 to 2000 feet high. The
stream in the bottom of the canyon appears as a silver ribbon
winding its way among the undergrowth and occasionally disap-
pearing form view. In my opinion this canyon should be set apart
by the government as a national park.[14]

Zion National Park was created by an act of Congress on 19
November 1919. It originally had been designated as a national monument by President William Howard Taft on 31 July 1909, and was
first known as Mukuntuweap, from its Indian name. The park
presently embraces 94,888 acres. Utah Highway 15, called the Zion-
Mt. Carmel Highway, connects the park with U.S. Highways 89 and
91, a distance of twenty-four miles. Travelers of the road at one point
move through the Zion-Mt. Carmel Tunnel, which is 5,607 feet in
length, with six cut-out galleries for canyon views.

Political Life in Kane County

Kane County resources were managed and regulated by various
governmental entities, from the federal government to the state,
county, and townships. Each had separate jurisdictions and frequently overlapping interests in local affairs. In important ways, however, each built on and enlarged services provided by the others.
Often, however, agencies of these separate governmental bodies have
come into conflict with one another. Government in Kane County
reflects a complex mesh of conflicting interests and powers.

County government could be considered an administrative
extension of the powers of the state. The Utah Constitution delin-
eates county responsibilities and powers, describing counties as "legal
subdivisions of this state."[15] The county functions as an agent in
statewide programs. Numerous county projects are in part funded
with state monies, the county receives federal grants-in-aid, shared
state revenues, county property taxes, local option sales taxes, and
other fees such as licensing fees gathered from area residents. The
main local sources of revenue for Kane County are property taxes
and sales taxes. Additional funds come from state and federal sources.

These various sources of funding are used in a variety of different ways: flood control and fire protection, mental health and substance-abuse services, the construction of public buildings, the care of the sick and destitute, and the construction and maintenance of county roads and bridges. Cities such as Kanab provide various services; in unincorporated areas of the county, the county government provides services such as law enforcement and fire protection.

County employees such as the county recorder, county assessor, and county treasurer try to ensure that all business conducted by the county is fair and legal. Some services provided by the county are mandated by law, such as a county health department responsible for the providing of basic public health services within the county's boundaries. Local elections are also regulated by the county commissioners, who establish, abolish, or revise election districts, appoint election judges, canvass election returns, and issue certificates of election. Until there was a newspaper published locally in Kane County, election notices had to be posted around town in election districts for four weeks before elections. As do all counties in Utah, Kane County has the right to sue and be sued, to acquire and hold land for county purposes, to make contracts and purchase property, to manage and dispose of property, and to levy and collect taxes as authorized by law.

When the new century began, the county commission included men whose ancestors had helped build Kane County. Joel H. Johnson, Jonathan Heaton, William Smith, and Henry N. Esplin were all children of families who helped settle the area and had done much to ensure that it would grow. Commission terms were either for four or two years. County leaders generally came from a small group of more economically successful men, many of whom also were prominent in Mormon church affairs. Over the next two decades commissioners included the following men, many of whom served at different times: George F. Carroll, Joseph W. Hopkins, William H. Swapp, Charles R. Pugh, John C. Carpenter, and Myron A. Holgate. In 1912, Henry W. Esplin was elected again, as was James E. Bunting. Others included Thomas Chamberlain, Joseph W. Hopkins, Willis C. Little, Fred G. Carroll, and John F. Brown.[16] Besides roads, tax assessment and collection, and the supervision of school districts, the commission occasionally heard requests from ranchers to hunt down wolves and other predators as well as improve the water supply.[17] Since many commissioners were ranchers themselves who would economically benefit from such measures, such requests generally were favorably received.

In the early decades of the twentieth century, commissioners offered bounties on rabbits, gophers, and squirrels from a county bounty fund to stop these foraging animals from destroying crops. The minutes leave much to the imagination; they never mention the country entering a world war or the nation falling into economic depression. The issues the county leaders attended to were local in nature. From the minutes one gets a sense of familial networks, of generations that stayed over time and built up power and connections as part of their tradition of community involvement and service.

Key issues for the Kane County Commission as well as expenses to the county continued to be road work, schools, printing of laws, regulations and other informative material, fencing, and the maintenance of county-owned land. To facilitate road work, the commissioners were members of an Intermountain good roads association. Dividing money up between the various school districts was always complicated, and every attempt was made to be fair. In March 1914, the commission divided Kane County into two high school districts as part of consolidation efforts throughout the state. Kane County High School was in District 1; Mt. Carmel, Orderville, Glendale joined in District 2.[18]

The era saw the growth nationally of the temperance and prohibition movements, both of which were supported by many Mormon church members, although a few also were known to occasionally imbibe during the period in which the Word of Wisdom was not considered the strict test of good fellowship in the Mormon church that it became in subsequent years. Also, county and state officials increasingly sought to curtail bootlegging or distilling operations, as they had a financial interest in the licensing of liquor establishments. In December 1912, for example, Kane County officials seized twelve gallons of liquor, which the marshal dumped out onto the ground.[19]

In June 1913, the county was approached by dry farming advocate Dr. John Widstoe and others of the Utah Agricultural College,

A parade in Glendale in August 1917 in support of Prohibition. (Courtesy Deanne Glover)

who asked to lease forty acres of land for a demonstration farm to test dry-farming methods. The county agreed to the proposition on 1 July 1913 and agreed to prepare the land, clear it, and provide it with a "rabbit proof fence."[20] Dry farming never achieved great success in the county, however.

An interesting episode in Kane County politics during this time was the election in November 1911 of a woman mayor for Kanab, Mary Elizabeth Woolley Howard. She held the office for two years and reportedly was only the second woman mayor ever to be elected in the United States. Even more interesting was the fact that the entire town board was composed of women—Vinnie Jepson, Tamar Hamblin, Blanche Hamblin, and Luella McAllister. Each was married and had a family of between two and seven children. Three of the women gave birth while in office, and some held offices in the local church. Howard wrote of the experience:

> Our election was intended as a joke and no one thought seri-
> ously of it at the time. When the election day dawned, there was
> no ticket in the field; no one seemed interested in the supervision
> of the town, so the loafers on the ditchbank (of which there were
> always plenty) proceeded to make up a ticket (of women) as a bur-

lesque. But there was no other ticket in opposition, so, of course, we were elected. When Father came and told me about it, I was disgusted and said I would not think of qualifying and I knew others would not even if I did, but he insisted that we take it seriously and put the job over as he knew we could, and he would give us all the support and backing possible. . . . So, after due consideration and much debating, we decided to tackle the job and see what we could do.[21]

Under Howard's leadership, the city taxed peddlers traveling through town (thus supporting local merchants), sponsored a "clean town" campaign, canceled horse races and ball games on Sundays, passed prohibitions against gambling, and also passed a liquor-control law. The women campaigned for temperance, making Kanab a "dry" town. Attempting to make Kanab a more beautiful city, they had the town cemetery surveyed and platted, bought lumber for new bridges to be built over town ditches, and joined the Kanab Irrigation Company to help build a large dike to protect the town from floods. They designated 12 September 1912 as "Stink Weed Day" and gave cash prizes for the best neighborhood clean-up projects. Perhaps the most important contribution they made to Kanab's history was making the work of the town council more visible. However, after the 1914 election, the town council was again only composed of men.[22]

Tax assessment records provide interesting insight into local economic conditions. Principal property considered of value included horses, cattle, sheep, real estate, machinery, and even "ice cream parlor fixtures." State and national election results were recorded in the commission's minutes, providing insight into local political affiliations. In the November 1914 election, for example, Republican senator and Mormon apostle Reed Smoot received 453 votes to Democrat James H. Moyle's 127 and J.F. Parsons's ten votes. In the 1916 election, Republican George Sutherland received 329 votes for U.S. Senator and Democrat William H. King received 301; for the House of Representatives that year, Kane County also supported the Republican candidate—Timothy C. Hoyt received 409 votes and Milton H. Welling garnered 223. For governor, the county gave Nephi L. Morris 356 votes and Democrat (and winner) Simon Bamberger 278. County offices were occupied by both Republicans and

Democrats; for example, County Clerk Fuller S. Broadbent was a Republican and County Treasurer J.G. Spencer was a Democrat.

Road work was the most typical county expense; fencing and land maintenance problems followed. Tax assessments provide interesting insights into economic conditions: in good times, assessed values rise; in times of depression or recession, they plummet. In 1916, for example, taxes were levied for schools, state district court, general court, county poor fund, state road tax, Kanab town general maintenance, and the Kanab town library, among other things. County commissioners worked part-time for the county and, while they received fair salaries, those salaries were modest and were not anyone's principal source of income. On the other hand, county clerks and recorders worked full-time for the county. Until the second decade of the twentieth century, the county sheriff, attorney, and assessor offices were also part-time positions.

Discussion of a proposed county courthouse building began in March 1920. A sketch and preliminary plans prepared by architects Ware and Traganza for $250 pictured a three-story building, with a jail on the third floor. Within the year, plans were made for a celebration for the laying of the cornerstone. The planning committee included local leaders—county officials, LDS church officials, members of the Commercial Club, and the Kanab Town Board.

Water

In Kane County, as elsewhere in Utah Territory, availability of water was the key to settlement. Few settlements in the Mormon region had a more difficult time than most Kane County communities locating and providing a consistent supply of water. Kanab Creek was the most basic source of water for Kanab; but even it frequently dried up and at other times flooded. The flow normally was insufficient for much agricultural development. Kanab settlers always looked to find other sources of water.

In October 1909 the Kanab Irrigation Company's board of directors solicited help from the governor and state land board to help them fund a new dam, which they estimated would cost about $25,000, to be built on the site of the dam destroyed in Kanab Canyon in 1900 by floods. Three local contractors—H.S. Cutler, the Cram

Maintaining irrigation ditches and canals was hard work in Kane County. (Courtesy Fred Esplin)

brothers, and the Ford brothers—bid on tunnel work required for the dam. Cram Brothers contracted to do the work for about $3.20 per linear foot. On 19 November 1910, according to the minutes of the Kanab Irrigation Company, "The board met at the dam and it was decided to complete the dam by building up the front of it at a width sufficient to raise the crest of the dam 4 ft. higher and be 20 ft. wide on top. And if there is a surplus number of hands, put them to work placing the rocks at the top of the dam. And put a temporary wooden headgate in the spill to turn the water into the ditch."[23] In 1911 the East-Side High Ditch water system was established.

A consistent source of good water was lacking for many county residents. On 22 April 1912 the *Kane County Independent* commented on the water coming into town from the "Pipe Line": "Have you noticed that the Pipe Line water tastes like the drizzlings from a sewer?" it asked. It also claimed that "the cistern needs cleaning to prevent a typhoid epidemic." By August, the Kanab Pipe Line Company was adding another spring to its main line.[24]

A group of men organized a private water company in 1914. They included Neale Hamblin as president, along with Frank Hamblin, Sr., Frank Hamblin, Jr., Gid, Donald, and Alex Findlay, Jet

Johnson, Will Dobson, Walt Hamblin, and a Dr. Norris. The company built a new pipeline to furnish water for Kanab.

Kanab

Ownership of some of Kanab's businesses changed through the years and some new companies were organized. Marinda Halliday in 1900 began an ice cream parlor and millinery shop in her home located in the northeast part of town. After a time, she began selling groceries, confections, and children's clothing as well. Heber Cram began a confectionary and bowling alley on Center Street, in time selling other items; he called the enterprise "Kanab Wonderland."

John W. Glazier came to Kanab in 1904 and with H.S. Cutler began a mercantile company, called Cutler and Company, in the Exchange Building. In 1906 H.E. Bowman brought his family back to Kanab and purchased the Bowman and Company business. After two decades, the business was sold to Othello C. Bowman. The company stayed in business until the Depression, when it was sold to ZCMI. It was later sold to Pickett Lumber Company. Eventually the building housed a machine and hardware store. In 1909 a group organized the Kanab Equitable; stockholders included James E. Bunting, Charles R. Pugh, Leonard B. Pugh, H.S. Cutler, Jet Johnson, Brigham A. Riggs, and Eleanor J. McAllister. They purchased the Kanab Wonderland Store building and began their business. A letter written to Leonard Pugh by Elizabeth Swapp provides a sense of the types of products sold:

> People are getting quite anxious over their winter flour, wanting to know what you can deliver it for. We are out of sugar and been out for three weeks. We need dishes–plates, bowls, mush dishes, tea-cups and saucers. Also: 12 wire hair brushes, 3 bolts black outing flannel, 1 bolt blue sateen, 3 pieces dark naped outing flannel for house dresses, 4 nice bed spreads, carpet warp in brown, green, yellow, orange; tobacco 10 cents and 5 cents also cigars, except Little Toms and Henry Georges. . . . Len order me a pair of those rough kid shoes, buttoned and one pair of low heel shoes—buttoned, and have them sent by mail—size 5.[25]

In 1914 a large group organized the Stockman's Store, an enterprise housed in the Jepson Building, with John W. Glazier as the manager.

Charles Harmson Esplin about 1918. (Courtesy Fred Esplin)

Kanab was without high school classes until 1900. By then the county had reached the point that it had a sufficient population base to warrant the establishment of a high school. The first principal was Joseph L. Horne, who ran the school out of two rooms in the Academy. The school term lasted from October to March, and teachers were paid sixty dollars in 1912. Academy teachers included Marinda Halliday, Bertha Halliday Cram, Rose Fuller, Frank Cutler, Malcolm Little, Bessie Woolley Day, Caroline Findlay Roundy, Dana Farnsworth (Findlay), Clara McAllister (Shields), Addie Little Swapp, Bessie F. Little, Will Dobson, Josephine S. Major, Bessie Spencer, Hazel Johnson (Mackelprang), Blanche Hicks (Mace), Mary Riggs, Sarah Dye (Major), Linda Burnham (Hamblin), and Rose H. Hamblin. In September 1912 the *Kane County Independent* noted that there were 214 students enrolled in school in the county, that the school buildings were all overcrowded, and that there was a serious shortage of teachers.[26]

By 1914 the Academy was very crowded and some classes were held in the old tithing office and at the local LDS ward hall. In 1914 a second two-year high school was established in Kanab in the Jepson Building on the southwest corner of Main and Center Streets under the supervision of J.L. Horne. Subjects taught included mathematics, history, science, English, oral expression, domestic science, wood-work, athletics, and art. Tuition was forty dollars per year and students were required to purchase their own books.

In 1917–18 the elementary classes moved with the high school to a new fourteen-room school building on the hill on Center Street. It was funded by the county and the state school board. Justin and Lloyd Chamberlain tore down the Academy, using the bricks to build their homes. Eighth grade students had to pass state examinations before they were allowed to graduate.[27]

The Bull Pups Club began in 1908 as a social club; eventually becoming the Commercial Club, members worked on civic projects as well as staging social events. A reinvigorated Commercial Club was led by President W.W. Seegmiller after 1922. Members declared their mission: "We the citizens of Kanab, feeling the need of an organization for the promotion of the interests of our community, and the welfare of the county at large, deem it necessary to establish a Kanab Commercial Club. We further pledge ourselves to support such an organization and to maintain it on a strictly business basis."[28]

In 1910 Will Dobson ordered a small press and type and began publication of *Lone Cedar,* a self-described "midget, all-home-print weekly." According to one source, "It won the support of the loyal people of the town and county, however, even of those who laughed at its unimpressive appearance. Sometimes it went out on wrapping paper which won it added ridicule."[29] Charles H. Townsend bought the paper in 1911 and changed its name to *Kane County News.* In addition, he changed the typeface, bought a bigger press, and increased the size of the sheet.

In 1913 Dr. Ellis R. Shipp traveled to Kanab from Salt Lake City to give a course in nursing to local women including Laura Broadbent, Alice Robinson, Nellie Pugh, Kate Greenhough, and Eva Hortt.

Early in 1914 a group of interested individuals joined together to propose the establishment of a library in Kanab. The meeting was held in the town hall and, although the attendance was not great, those who attended were enthusiastic. At first conceived of as little more than a reading room, plans were made for local book drives and fund-raising efforts. By December forty-six dollars had been raised, a library board appointed, and several hundred books donated from family libraries and private sources. In January 1915 a Library Benefit Ball was held by the Kanab Ladies Literary League, which raised a grand total of $4.20 from the event. The library cause received support from the Bay View Club, Federated Womens Clubs, and the Salt Lake College Club. The local LDS Relief Society and Young Ladies Mutual Improvement Association also held book drives for the library.[30]

The Mormon church and Kanab High School each sponsored a number of celebrations and other activities for locals, including theatricals, concerts, ball games and other sporting events. Bishops of Kane County wards in the early twentieth century included Joel H. Johnson, Harmon Scott Cutler, Herbert E. Riggs, Zadok K. Judd, Jr., and William W. Seegmiller. Between 1913 and 1922 Israel H. Chamberlain served as bishop, also serving again between 1928 and 1934.

Between 1912 and 1916, the Kane Kounty Karnival included a rodeo, barbecue, horse races, and dances. Local cowboys showed their skills at roping and bulldogging steers and rode bucking broncos and steers. Edwin D. Woolley attempted to include some of his buffalo in the celebration. At the end of the period, the city built a race track and rodeo grounds in town. Later, the local Lions Club and American Legion both sponsored horse races and rodeos held on these public grounds. Sometimes at the same time as the Karnival, young men would organize rabbit hunts. The hunts had a practical as well as recreational benefit (since the rabbits destroyed crops), and teams of married men competed against the area's single men to see who could kill the most rabbits.

Glendale

Glendale had a population of 319 in 1900; it then declined to 244 by the next census. During 1906–07, pipe for a water system was installed that transported water from a local spring. During that period stockholders in the local water company were assessed thirty dollars for water per year. In 1911 the irrigation company was incorporated and stock certificates issued.

Built up on both sides of the old state road, today's U.S. Highway

The Mt. Carmel Relief Society in 1911. (Courtesy Deanne Glover)

89, Glendale eventually developed a small commercial district catering to the needs of residents and travelers alike. Homer Bouton's store on 200 North was the first; it was followed a little later by the Glendale Co-op, which opened just west of the school. A rival store, the Glendale Equitable, was built south of the Smith Hotel on the west side of Highway 89, which was the town's Main Street. A new building for the Equitable later was erected at the northeast corner of the highway and Mill Street, the eventual site of the Glendale Mercantile Store.

Mt. Carmel

The Mt. Carmel rock building of the mid-1870s was used as a school until 1917, at which time students were bused to Orderville after the consolidation of school districts. A fire in December 1919 destroyed the building except for its stone walls.

Since the turn of the century, LDS bishops in Mt. Carmel have included Osmer Lamb, Edward T. Lamb, Roland S. Esplin, David W.P. Stevens, and Wilbur Covington. Besides church activities, the town gathered for musicals and dances, basketball and baseball games, and horse racing. Mt. Carmel's Main Street was one of the longest stretches of level road in the county and was a particularly favored location for horse races until traffic prohibited racing. A swimming hole located near the local irrigation dam on the Virgin River was popular for young people seeking respite from long, hot summer days.

For several decades, farming and livestock raising were the principal means of providing a living at Mt. Carmel. Eventually some local men supplemented their income from farming with jobs as teachers or working for the Kaibab Lumber Company, as carpenters, or on government projects. Even though a few businesses were established—a small mercantile and a few grocery stores operated from private homes—the town was always quite small.

The settlers hauled culinary water from the Virgin River in barrels on the sleds called lizards or in wagons. In 1915 a pipeline from a spring brought water two miles to the irrigation dam. A cement tank built on a knoll at the north edge of town, a pump house, and a pump completed the system. In 1961 the spring started to fail, so the townspeople drilled a well near the old pumphouse. A good source of water was discovered at a depth of sixty feet and a new pump pulled water from the well to be stored in a tank on the knoll.

The architecture of Mt. Carmel reflects its agrarian history. One of the earliest outbuildings of importance was the tithing barn, a wood-frame structure built to house produce, hay, grain, and horses. The barn also served as a way-station for mail contractors.

Alton

The original townsite of Alton was the area along the junction of present U.S. Highway 89 and a road east that now leads to the present town. The main road went to the head of the Sevier River and then on to Alton through Johnson Canyon. The Ranch–Long Valley Road was built later. Homes and ranches were scattered according to the lay of the land rather than a survey grid.

The establishment of present-day Alton occurred at the beginning of the twentieth century. The town was originally known as Upper Kanab before 1908, when the name was changed to Alton. It was planned in the style of a Mormon settlement, but its founder, Jonathon Heaton, had more capitalistic intentions. In 1901 Heaton

bought out the Seegmiller estate for $8,000 and moved his family—
Amy Hoyt and her fifteen children—to the ranch. Some of the children had gained experience in helping to found nearby Orderville.
Heaton owned quite a significant amount of land, also having bought
a number of the homesteads of old-timers who had left the area. He
hired Lysander Porter to survey the land to the west called "Oak Flat,"
named for its dense groves of scrub oak. Along with William Cox and
Junius and Daniel Heaton he laid out a town, which was organized
in nine ten-acre blocks, each divided into four lots. The men reserved
the center block for a public square, and one lot for a recreational
hall, another for a chapel, one for a school, and one known as the
tithing lot, which was to be used for storing the tithing contributions
of Mormon church members. In addition, Heaton had Porter survey
a few small farm lots in the lower fields, which he then sold. The town
lots slowly were sold at a considerable profit, and the center street
became known as Main Street.

A sacrament meeting held 26 April 1908 in Ira Heaton's home
became an organizational meeting for the town. A committee was
appointed to get estimates of the cost of piping water into town;
another committee was given the task of planning the building of a
social hall. It was also decided that on 1 May the members of the
town would gather to decide on a name for their town.

A one-room schoolhouse complete with a bell tower was built in
1908 on the southeast corner of the public square. It was a one-room,
wood-frame structure with a Greek Revival cornice, belfry, and four
tall windows along each side. It sat on the southeast corner of the
public square. The well-crafted school was also used for church meetings, dances, and socials. A party was held on May Day 1908 in the
schoolhouse. Homemade ice cream and crackers, a musical band, and
decorations indicated that it was a festive occasion of great importance. A variety of different names were recommended: Heatonville,
Oaktown, Snowville, and Klondyke, among many others. Charles R.
Pugh, who had come to Upper Kanab from Sink Valley Ranch, had
been reading a book about the Alton Fjord in Norway, which was
known for its altitude. Because the new town's altitude was some
7,200 feet, the name seemed appropriate to consider. Each of the suggested names was written on a small piece of paper and put into a

hat. A two-year-old child, Gwen Heaton, drew the winning name from the hat—and Alton, Utah, began its story.

Completion of the schoolhouse building was cause for a major celebration that July Fourth. At daybreak a flag raising began the festivities; a string band then began a program that ran through the day and included patriotic speeches, songs, musical numbers, readings, and jokes. The "Goddess of Liberty," Clarissa Heaton, who sat on an elaborately decorated, bunting-draped throne spoke, with her two attendants at her side. Almost every girl in Alton later had her turn at being the goddess at the annual event. A community picnic and dance finished off the day.

The Alton LDS Ward first met in the schoolhouse in September 1908. At that meeting, Mormon Apostle Francis M. Lyman dedicated the new town. The next steps were building internal improvements. In 1911 a separate social hall was built, a frame structure meant to accommodate the many visitors who came to Alton's cool summer night dances. Hinter Siler sawed the lumber for the building and the carpentry was done by men from Orderville. In 1914 a culinary water system was begun by the Alton Farmer's Association. The group completed a high-line canal that transported canyon water to a storage reservoir northeast of town. Individual property owners also built small cisterns on their own property and allowed them to fill with rain and/or ditch water that would then settle. That same year, a pay telephone was placed in the town store. Paved streets followed. After the Donalvin Roundy barn burned down in 1916, the town voted for a tax levy at a cost of $300 per family to pipe water in from Birch Springs, three miles north of town.

Some of the residences in Alton were moved in from their scattered ranch sites. Arthur Glover wrote:

> The ranchers in the valley decided to get together and build up a town, which would be called Alton. Our house was one of the first to be moved in. This house was . . . moved about three miles up the valley. This was a big undertaking in those days. The snow was about four feet deep, so they figured by jacking the house up and putting two logs under for runners, they could pull it with horses. Twenty-four of the best horses in the valley were hitched to these logs, by the use of plenty of chains, in such a way that they

could all do their share. After about ten days of hard and some-times heart-breaking struggle, the house was finally set down on the chosen lot.[31]

As the community slowly grew, it eventually felt the need for a larger chapel. Due to insufficient funds for a new building, the existing facility was improved with a stage and classroom wings built on the east side of the old hall. A Relief Society hall was included in the addition. Initially the church's heating system was primitive and of questionable safety. It consisted of little more than a bonfire built on a large box filled with sand in one of the corners. Later, a huge pot-bellied stove was placed in the center of the hall. The first lighting was provided by kerosene lanterns. These were replaced with gasoline lanterns and, eventually, by electric lights, at first powered by a small electric plant located in a home.

The last of Alton's public buildings was its two-room school, which was constructed in 1917 and is still extant. Essentially unaltered since it was built, the rectangular, gable-roofed structure has a large front porch shielding two entry doors, one for each of the two large rooms. Each room is illuminated by five tall windows.

In Alton many distinctive frame structures were built which seem to be the product of a single builder. Dating from the World War I bungalow era, the designs are original to Alton and feature hip and "jerkinhead," or clipped-gable, roofs, angle-bay windows, and dormers. Taken together, Alton's collection of public buildings and residences make a harmonious ensemble with their clean, white-painted exteriors. The town's agricultural structures—small barns and outbuildings—are vernacular wood buildings.

Orderville

Two major public structures marked Orderville's entry into the twentieth century. The LDS meetinghouse, erected in 1900–01, was a tall, dignified edifice with a L-shaped floor plan and three-story, steepled bell tower looking over the pastoral town. Also built in 1900–01 was the social hall, an interesting brick building with polygonal ends and a large hip roof. No longer extant, it sat on the east side of the highway, one block east of its companion church.

In the city, some signs of the Mormon village remain. The regu-

The Orderville Relief Society. (Courtesy Fred Esplin)

lar, gridded town layout, square blocks, and Mormon wardhouse are the most visible markers. Mormon house types of several materials, styles, and floor plans also remain. A couple of one-story, hall-parlor houses with wood or stucco siding and small-paned windows appear to date from the 1870s and 1880s, as do also a few 1–1/2 story, wood-sided, central-passage homes with full-width porches. Some Victorian houses remain with crosswing plans and ornamental trim. The period cottage era is also represented.

Tourism and Roads

For the first six or seven decades of Utah's road building history, both transportation and roads were primitive by today's standards. Roads were cut out of the sometimes rugged terrain of mountains, canyons, and hard plains, and roadbeds at times were built up with stone retaining walls and covered with compacted gravel and earth. It was only after the advent of the automobile that roads were paved with more durable materials such as asphalt and concrete.

Having established the basic routes still most important in

Ruins of buildings at a coal mine on Warm Creek. (Utah State Historical Society)

county transportation, improvements and extensions of the main system were funded in subsequent years. After statehood, allocations came every two years on a fairly consistent basis. In 1901, six small road projects were funded in the county, with three more coming in 1903. In 1907, the sizable sum of $5,500 was earmarked to build a bridge over the Virgin River on the main road from St. George to the Territory of Arizona and Kanab in Kane County.[32]

Edwin Woolley continued to be a prime mover in bringing Kane County to the attention of outsiders as a potential tourist destination. Around the turn of the century, he often invited politicians to the county to tour the region. In September 1905, for example, Senator Reed Smoot, T.C. Hoyt, Edwin D. Woolley, his nephew E.G. Woolley, Graham McDonald, James Clove, Lewis T. Cannon, and Congressman Joseph Howell came to Kanab. This was such an important event for the small rural southern Utah town that school was canceled and community members lined the streets for an informal (and very brief) parade down Main Street. The group toured the Kaibab Forest Reserve and the North Rim of the Grand Canyon.

D.D. Rust claimed credit for introducing novelist Zane Grey to the county, accompanying him on a cougar hunt in the Kaibab Plateau with Colonel C.J. Jones, journalist Grant Wallace, and others in 1907. Woolley said of such expeditions, "some [were] for enjoyment, others for publicity or promotional purposes, all of which served to focus public attention more and more on the area."[33] Between 1912 and 1916 Governor William Spry traveled three times through the county.

Edwin Woolley held public meetings about the feasibility of building a railroad into the Kaibab Forest region for transporting tourists, and he was determined to build a trail down into the Grand Canyon, establish a camp at the bottom, and construct a tramway across the river. After several years of planning, beginning in 1901 he and Jim Emmet did build a trail twelve miles long down Bright Angel Canyon to the Colorado River. The trail included 500 feet of heavy wire cable and 1,000 feet of smaller cable. By 1908 a cable supporting a tram had been established over the river with the help of an investment of $5,000 from Utah mining magnate Jesse Knight. The government did not permit tolls in the area, however, so the operation never flourished.[34]

After automobiles came into popular use, Wooley worked to bring autos to the Grand Canyon, to encourage the establishment of gasoline stations in Kane County towns, and to create better road systems. What roads did exist in the region were difficult to use during wet times of the year. Between Kanab and Long Valley a large sandy expanse existed. Sand was also found to the west, as were also imposing cliffs preventing travel west into Zion Canyon. Woolley believed the auto had great potential for bringing tourists into the area and could potentially launch a new era for Kane County.

The first automobiles to travel through the Kaibab to the North Rim passed through Kanab in June 1909. The trip was engineered by Edwin Woolley and included three cars. Ten gallons of gasoline was distributed every thirty miles, and the group carried with them extra water and sand as well as tools and equipment for car repairs. Frequently, they had to get out of the cars to remove high road centers, level or fill other spots, and cut timber that had fallen and blocked the road. Two cars completed the journey. They traversed sandy patches by laying canvas tarps in front of the cars. In areas washed out by swollen creeks, straw was placed to make a more solid footing, and the automobile passengers moved rocks off the road. Mary Woolley Chamberlain detailed events at Kanab:

> When the long, loud honk was finally heard as the party approached the outskirts of town from the east, everyone rushed into the street to get a glimpse of the wonderful contraption. Father sat upon the engine, waving his hat in midair and shouting "Hurrah! I told you so!" at the top of his voice. The people followed the procession until they arrived at our home where the machine stopped. . . . There were not a dozen people in town who had even seen an automobile before.[35]

The trip demonstrated the automobile's potential for bringing tourists to visit the area's natural wonders, and it also focused attention on the natural beauties of the region. Nevertheless, it would be almost ten years before a passable road for automobiles would be built through the county.

Roads were improved in the region in 1913 when a group of convicts were assigned to area road construction. The United States Forest Service spent $2,750 for a road from Jacob's Lake to the North Rim that same year. In 1914, a five-county region of southern Utah held a convention in Hurricane to discuss the road situation. The result was the organization of the Grand Canyon Highway Association, which added impetus to tourist promotion.

In 1909, not long after the first cars and trucks appeared in the early 1900s, the Utah State Road Commission was created. The commission divided the state into four geographical divisions, each placed under the direction of a member of the commission. Kane County was under the supervision of state engineer Caleb Tanner during the eight years of Governor William Spry's administration, and it continued to be directed by other commission members in subsequent years as part of the southwest region.

As the region became increasingly known by means of the books published about it, others began to come to the area to see the wonders for themselves. The books written by Powell, Dellenbaugh, and others became guidebooks for later adventurers like brothers Ellsworth and Emery Kolb, whose book *Through the Grand Canyon from Wyoming to Mexico,* published in 1914, typified a new genre of travel books which focused not only on the dramatic sites seen but also on the danger of the journey undertaken. The Kolbs made frequent mention of their predecessors, acknowledging their importance. As had been true of earlier travel accounts, they described local vegetation, animals, and rock formations seen along the river and gave vivid descriptions of the rock walls of the canyons traveled through, emphasizing the dangers of the natural wonderland. Nevertheless, the message was clear: the journey was worth every risk it presented.

ENDNOTES

1. Adonis Findlay Robinson, *History of Kane County,* 111.

2. Ibid., 114–15.

3. Ibid.

4. *The Principal Laws Relating to Forest Service Activities,* Agriculture Handbook No. 453 (Washington, D.C.: Government Printing Office, 1974), 112.

5. *Kane County Independent,* 3 October 1912.

6. "Attempting to Make a National Park of Kaibab," *Kane County Independent,* 5 September 1912.

7. Ibid.

8. *Kane County Independent,* 12 September 1912, 3 October 1912.

9. *Kane County Independent,* 24 October 1912.

10. Ibid.

11. *Kane County Independent,* 30 May 1912.

12. Quoted in Angus M. Woodbury, "A History of Southern Utah and Its National Parks," 185.

13. Ibid., 186.

14. Ibid., 187.

15. Utah Constitution, Article XI.

16. See Kane County Commission, Minutes, various years.

17. *Kane County Independent,* 22 August 1912, 12 September 1912.

18. Kane County Commission, Minutes, 9 March 1914.

19. Robinson, *History of Kane County,* 97.

20. Kane County Commission, Minutes, 1 July 1913.

21. Quoted in Susan Arrington and Leonard Arrington, *Sunbonnet Sisters* (Salt Lake City: Bookcraft, 1984), 147.

22. Mary W. Howard, "An Example of Women in Politics," *Utah Historical Quarterly* 38 (1970): 61–64.

23. "Minutes of the Kanab Irrigation Company," 19 November 1910, Utah State Historical Society Library.

24. *Kane County Independent,* 29 August 1912.

25. Robinson, *History of Kane County,* 152.26. 1 *Kane County Independent,* 19 September 1912.

27. Robinson, *History of Kane County,* 226.

28. Ibid., 269.

29. Robinson, *History of Kane County,* 221.

30. Blanche H. Mace, "Public Library from Scratch," 1–7, Utah State Historical Society.

31. Arthur Glover, "A Brief History of the Life of Arthur Glover," Utah State Historical Society Library.

32. Ezra C. Knowlton, *History of Highway Development in Utah,* 807, 812, 837, 842, 849, 854.

33. Quoted in Robinson, *History of Kane County,* 191.

34. Woodbury, "A History of Southern Utah and Its National Parks," 191–92. See also Mary W. Chamberlain, "Edwin Dilworth Woolley, Jr., 1845–1920," 9.

35. Chamberlain, "Edwin Dilworth Woolley," 9.

CHAPTER 9

KANE COUNTY AND THE DEPRESSION YEARS, 1920–1940

Beginning with the farming recession of the 1920s and acceler-
ating with the Depression of the 1930s, rural Utah along with the rest
of the state and much of the nation slipped into dramatic economic
decline. These were decades of significant change, generally reflected
by out-migration from the region. Many people moved to other areas
of the state or out of the state altogether. Population growth slowed
and in some areas even declined. One study suggests that between
1920 and 1930, the number of Utahns who lived in other states
increased by 50,000 individuals.[1] Kane County, however, maintained
its population better than some other areas. In fact, during the 1920s
it experienced an increase of 181 people, reaching a total of 2,235 by
1930. By 1940 another slight gain in population was recorded—this
time to 2,561 county inhabitants.[2]

The growth was due in part to the resourcefulness of the residents. The agrarian lifestyle of most residents was less dependent
upon national employment and economic trends and problems, and
most residents were able to grow their own basic food. Since mining,
industry, and tourism had never been important sources of revenue,

the downturn of the cash economy did not impact Kane County as much as it did most other regions of the country. Still, county residents did suffer. Livestock values, which had dropped dramatically in the years after World War I, stayed low until the 1940s.[3]

County Life in the 1920s

The Kanab Library, first organized in 1914, was expanded in 1920 under Mayor David D. Rust. The library board requested that local tax rates be raised by one mill to help fund improvements and the purchase of new books; the town council responded with a unanimous vote in favor. The board still had to do private fund-raising, and most library work was done on a volunteer basis. In 1920 the board also made an unsuccessful bid to have the library made a county institution.

The library was housed in a number of different locations during its first years. Three years after it opened in the Jepson Building, it was moved to the new Kanab High School building. Despite the assistance of many of the high school teachers, a number of books were lost or stolen, so the board decided to move the library again. A cramped room above the Opera House housed the library for two years until it was moved to the Kane County Courthouse, where it remained for the next nineteen years.

In 1920 Willis Little became chair of the Kane County Commission; in 1922 Israel H. Heaton and G. Duncan McDonald were elected to serve the county. Through the years, the Kane County Commission minutes speak to the fine line that existed between church and state. Kane County was not overtly run as a theological state, but it was the case that the leaderships of the county, towns, and local Mormon churches were often almost one and the same. The same families dominated both the secular and religious arenas. Also, church groups and activities are mentioned casually in the minutes, illustrating how deeply the Mormon church and its institutions ran in county affairs. For instance, in February 1921, the Kanab Relief Society sewed quilts for the jail, the county furnishing $24.82 for supplies.

During April 1921 plans were made for the celebration of the laying of the cornerstone of the new courthouse. The planning com-

A horse-drawn float in Orderville during the 1920s. (Courtesy Deanne Glover)

mittee included LDS church officials, representatives of the Kanab Commercial Club, and the Kanab town board. While the courthouse was under construction, the commissioners rented a room for meetings in the library for five dollars per month.[4] The county purchased the furnishings and hardware from ZCMI, the Mormon church-owned department store.

The commission minutes describe the way poverty relief was handled in the pre-Depression era. For example, one entry read: "Bishop Richard S. McAllister, was appointed as a commissioner of the Poor for the purpose of caring for the Atkin family. He was authorized to expend the sum of $25.00 to secure food for their temporary relief and he was further authorized to arrange for their transportation to Washington County, Utah which is the home of the family, at the expense of the County of Kane, and was instructed to see to it that the expense of such transportation was as small as possible."[5] This passage is interesting because it illustrates the county's attitude toward welfare; clearly the poor were considered a responsibility of the county, if only to remove them from its boundaries. Also, the casual reference to "Bishop" McAllister, as if that were another sort of first name, shows the familiarity between county government and the Mormon church that existed in the county.

The A. Clair Ford Post was organized in Kanab in 1922, honoring veterans of World War I from the county. The Legion sponsored boxing matches and races as well as fireworks at holiday times.

Kane County voters have generally supported the Republican party; in fact, the county has been considered perhaps the most Republican county in the United States. In the November 1922 election Kane County voters supported Republican Ernest Bamberger (444 votes) against Democrat William H. King (166 votes) for United States Senator. They supported the winning candidate in the House election, Republican Don B. Colton receiving 475 votes to Milton H. Welling's 134. They also supported other Republicans: Charles R. Mabey, Israel H. Heaton, and Duncan McDonald were elected to the county commission; Delos R. McAllister was elected county clerk and recorder, Walter E. Hamblin county sheriff, John F. Brown county

The Kanab High School Pep Club 1935–1936. (Courtesy Deanne Glover)

attorney, Joseph G. Spencer county surveyor, and William S. Swapp county assessor.[6]

For United States Senate in the 1926 election, Kane County overwhelmingly supported Mormon church apostle and Republican incumbent Reed Smoot with 264 votes to 90 cast for Ashby Snow. Again supporting Don B. Colton for Congress, the county also voted Republican in most local contests. Charles R. Pugh and Charles S. Anderson were elected to the county commission that year. Other county officers included D. Mayrell Tietjen, county clerk; Lloyd Chamberlain, sheriff; and William S. Swapp, assessor.[7]

In 1927, the county's budget included $900 for salaries for the county commissioners, $900 for miscellaneous expenses, and $4,257 for the county road fund. These figures were based on a total county income of $9,207.08 collected from licensing fees, property taxes, and other sources. A principal topic of discussion recorded in the minutes of the commission was the distribution of resources. Funds were distributed for general purposes, district school use, county road construction and repair, relief to widows, a fund for the needy, the Kanab Library, stocking nearby streams with fish, and general maintenance of the county infrastructure.[8]

By 1928 Kanab High School had graduated a total of ninety-eight students; current enrollment that year was eighty-seven, and the total population of students in Kanab schools was 286. Helen B. Chamberlain headed a committee which attempted to raise funds to begin a kindergarten in 1928. The teacher, Mary Holt, was paid by the school board, and students had to pay a ten-dollar fee for an eight-month period; however, classes were only held for four months. After this attempt, private kindergartens were held at the LDS ward hall in Kanab, the tithing office, or in the volunteer teachers' homes.

In the 1928 statewide election, the majority of Kane County residents again voted for the Republican party candidates from Herbert Hoover on down, although in Utah many Democrats were elected, including incumbent governor George H. Dern and Senator William H. King. Republicans Charles Anderson and G.D. Macdonald were elected to the county commission.[9]

The commission minutes provide an idea of the nature of the local issues that demanded the commissioners' attention. The 7 July 1930 entry read in part: "After long consideration of the Board in regards to the license's on pavilions or open air dance halls, they decided to issue a license. . . . The license fee should be $7.50 per nights dancing for dancing only. That said dances shall be closed at 12 o'clock P.M. each night."[10] The county leaders generally tried to support Mormon church standards. The next year they decided there would be "no Sunday night dances," that they would charge a "clean and respectable business fee of $5.00 per night in advance," that there would be no more than two dances per week, and that the commissioners could call special dances.[11]

County Life in the 1930s

G.D. Macdonald was reelected to the commission along with Neaf Hamblin in 1930. Other county officers included D.M. Tietjen, clerk; Lloyd Chamberlain, sheriff; Willard Mackelprang, county attorney; and William M. Cox, surveyor.[12] In 1933, because of the economic difficulties of the Depression, the commissioners cut their salaries—commissioners were paid $25.00 per month; the county assessor was paid $50.00 monthly, the county sheriff $75.00, the county attorney $62.50, and the county clerk $85.00.[13]

In the years before the Depression fully developed there were those in Kane County who extolled the progress they had made in meeting the challenges of the twentieth century. The *Kane County Standard* described Kanab as a "Modern City," in an article boosting the area's attractions on 5 June 1931. It read in part:

> Kanab is taking on new life the last week. Tourist traffic is increasing daily and everyone is busy. The garages are full of cars and custom at the stores is increasing. At one time last Saturday night Center street was so crowded with cars in front of the stores and hotel that there was scarcely room to pass. In spite of the fact that we are all crying "depression and hard times," Kanab people drive good cars, have good homes, wear good clothes and eat good food. We also live in one of the most picturesque and progressive little communitites in the country. We have a good water supply, a splendid electric light and power system, excellent telephone service and good amusements. When one looks back to five years ago and compares conditions then and now, he can see that Kanab has progressed a great deal.

The writer attributed the progress largely to the construction of U.S. Highway 89 through Kanab, saying it had probably "done more to give the town an atmosphere of progress than any other one thing. However," he maintained, "local people have done a great deal to improve conditions here. Today a tourist can buy as good a variety of vegetables, fruits, meats and groceries at the stores, groceries, meat markets and bakery in Kanab as elsewhere." He continued enthusiastically in the language of a good booster.

If a group of joy seekers wish to spend a day or night in Kanab they can find entertainment and amusement at the Talkie at the Star Theatre, or a dance in the open air at Hillcrest or they can spend an afternoon at our Free Public Library or if it is Sunday they can attend a good LDS service in our comfortable ward chapel. This summer, a swimming pool north of town, and a tennis court on the ward "square" will add to our means of public entertainment. The men and boys at the garages and service stations expect to give their customers excellent service and if one needs a shave, haircut, wave or re-set, they can get them at our barber shops and beauty parlor, or they can even get their shoes fixed while they wait. . . . Let's adopt and live up to the slogan, "Kanab, the Best for Accommodations, Eats, Service, Entertainment and Hospitality."[14]

Bringing in a load of winter wood. Mt. Carmel about 1930. (Courtesy Deanne Glover)

Kanab sported an opera house, and the town's first theater was operated by Ray B. Young. The building also housed a barber shop operated by Young. The Star Theater was destroyed by fire on 2 October 1931 by a fire started by a child playing with matches near the film projector. In 1934 Elmer Jackson built another theater as part of the Huish theater chain. "Large crowds of people flocked to the new Kanab Theatre every night since it has been open," the *Kane County Standard* reported, "and everyone expresses himself as being pleased with the productions. Not only have the Kanab people been attending the talkies but people from nearly all the surrounding towns have been there. We are pleased to note that Mr. Jackson has employed home people to help him run the show."[15]

The *Kane County Standard* was the successor to the *Kane County News,* which had been started in 1911 by Charles Townsend. The *News* had been printed in Panguitch, as was the *Standard,* which was established in 1929 under the editorship of Rose Hamblin, who was also instrumental in the establishment and growth of the Kanab library. Although edited in Kanab and circulated locally, the paper was published by the News Publishing Company in Panguitch. The *Standard* was a quality weekly newspaper, chronicling local news items along with national news and wire service columns and features.[16]

Until 1929 electricity was furnished to the county by an electrical plant managed by city government and located in Kanab behind the LDS ward meetinghouse. During the Depression, several local residents found it impossible to pay their electrical bills or their taxes, and even the town found it difficult to come up with revenue to pay installments for electric power. The North American Electric Gas and Coke Company, a New York business with holdings in Portland, Oregon, and in Canada, proposed in 1930 to purchase the power plant and provide Kanab with an alternate electrical source.[17] That deal was rejected; however, in 1932, the city council and mayor Carlos W. Judd decided to sell the plant to Dixie Power (later known as Southern Utah Power Company). After 1932 Kane County was supplied electrical power by the Southern Utah Power Company.

The Mountain States Telephone and Telegraph company began installing a new line to Kanab in August 1929 to improve outside communication with the county. The company also announced plans to update service throughout Kanab, including placing telephone poles in four of the streets and running additional lines to homes along fences to avoid obstructing traffic. The company had begun service in Garfield County a month earlier and planned to bring it to Kanab as soon after as possible. The exchange would be located in the home of Mrs. Janey M. Johnson.[18]

The telephone line was completed in October 1929, greatly facilitating communication with areas outside the county as well as internally. The *Kane County Standard* announced the names of those parties who had the first forty-five phone lines in its 18 October 1929 edition. Among them were businesses, service enterprises, and private individuals. They included the Highway Hotel, the Highway Garage, the Palmer-Esplin Garage, the Kane County Courthouse, the Kanab Equitable Store, the Jepson Cafe, the Utah Service Station, Dr. U.H. Norris, the Kanab LDS Stake office and Kanab High School. A telephone directory was published by December that gave the names, numbers and addresses of those with phones. The Kanab newspaper reported that the phonebook was a "neat little booklet measuring nine by six inches and the names of Panguitch, Junction and Kanab are included, as well as the U.S. Forest Service stations on Buckskin mountain."[19] In 1937 a new line was installed from Kanab across the border to Fredonia, Moccasin, Pipe Spring, and the Kaibab Indian School in Arizona.[20]

During the New Deal years, frequent mention was made in the commission minutes of federal programs that employed and benefited the county as well as efforts of local organizations to provide relief to the needy and to improve local facilities. For example, in June 1933, the Kanab Lions Club built a wading pool at the courthouse for children. The Lions Club also staged an annual rodeo over Labor Day weekend. A better record of New Deal activities in the county is provided by the *Kane County Standard,* which recorded the process of bringing federal funds into the county to employ local men and women, improve local facilities, build new facilities, and help county residents survive the Depression.

In the 1934 election, William S. Swapp and Easton Blackburn were elected to the county commission. Other county officers included D.M. Tietjen as clerk, Z.J. Ford as sheriff, Hattie J. Swapp as recorder, D.L. Pugh as attorney, and Robert Chamberlain as assessor. In 1936 E.J. Ford and Arthur Glover joined the commission. Even with the conditions of the Depression era pressing on the struggling farmers and ranchers of the county, the commission attended to other business, including the construction and maintenance of roads, "policing dances at Three Lakes," expressing a particular concern about cigarette smoking among the county's youth, and weed control.[21]

Mail came to Kane County from Cedar City, although it was often interrupted during the winter months because of bad weather.[22] In March 1930, representatives of Salina, Richfield, Gunnison, Marysvale, Circleville, Panguitch and other towns along U.S. Highway 89 met with the Kanab Lions Club to discuss the matter of their present mail route along the highway. The decision was made to continue to have the Denver and Rio Grande Railroad bring the mail to Marysvale, so that it would arrive there the same day it left

Salt Lake City.[23] It would then be routed to the various communities by motor vehicles.

Kane County's mail service was important in connecting the isolated county to the world outside. Through the decades mail was carried by a number of hardy men through county towns. Julius Dalley, Kanab's postmaster from 1920 to 1934, recalled that in the 1920s a Mr. Hanks had the mail contract and that "Norman Sargeant and Theodore Chidister delivered the mail regularly by means of trucks for almost the entire time of his contract. Occasionally Walter Daniels was the carrier." In 1926 Harold I. Bowman of Kanab received the mail contract and carried the mail for the next four years. Frank Gowans of Kanab began working at the beginning of July 1926 and served until 30 June 1930, the end of the contract, carrying the mail from Kanab to Panguitch. Charles Whipple and Moyle Sergeant also helped. Barton Brothers were the next contractors and delivered the mail by truck from Marysvale.

The completion of Zion-Mt. Carmel Tunnel in 1931 opened another truck mail route, which was served by Wilson Lunt of Cedar City in 1931–32. With the washing out of the Coal Hill Bridge mail had to be put over the wash on a cable. Burton Banks came to Kanab in 1932 as a mail contractor. Frank Robertson and Robert Burch were two men who worked under Banks. Charles Cooper, a one-armed man, delivered mail by horse along the sandy road and down Kanab Canyon. After the Colorado River Bridge was completed in 1929, passenger buses carried mail from Arizona cities across the river.[24]

The fact that Kane County failed to attract a railroad line limited its ability to grow economically and exchange with the world outside. Over the years, discussion did occasionally arise about the benefits and possible plans for bringing railroads into the area. In 1932, for instance, the Denver Pacific Railroad Company applied to the United States Interstate Commerce Commission for permission to build a railroad from Denver to San Pedro Harbor, California, a total distance of 815 miles. By building the line through Kane County and other areas identified for the route, the line would pass through a significant amount of territory that had no railroad within a distance of one hundred miles on either side. O.C. Bowman of Kanab received a letter from Coleman Crenshaw, president of the Denver Pacific

A celebration in Mt. Carmel. (Courtesy Deanne Glover)

Railroad Company in Salt Lake City, establishing his intention to build the railroad directly through Kanab. Crenshaw wrote that his letter was an inquiry about Kanab's natural resources, how many carloads Kanab stockmen presently used for the transportation of their livestock from other railroad hubs, and how far local cattlemen had to ship their stock to railroad hubs for shipment to market. Bowman read the letter to the Associated Civic Clubs of Southern Utah meeting in Beaver on 15 October 1932. He reported that Crenshaw's letter also asked for

> an estimate of the distance from Kanab to Moab and from Kanab down the Kanab gulch to the Colorado river. Inquiry was also made as to the coal, minerals, and oil in the area. If the people in this vicinity are interested in the contemplated railroad, . . . [he] asks for them to send a man to represent Kanab's interests at a hearing which will come up in the near future at Los Angeles, California.[25]

Nothing came of the project in the long run, however.

The local enterprises reveal a moderately varied economy with a variety typical of a rural county. Local construction businesses each specialized variously in buildings, highway and street construction, and carpentering and wood-flooring installation. Four sawmills and planing mills were located in the area, as was one newspaper. Three local trucking businesses transported goods both locally and outside the area. A telephone company and an electrical power plant provided services for locals. A variety of stores were located in Kane County towns—general merchandise and grocery stores, a confectionary store, a clothing store, a drug store, a hardware and farm implement store, and various restaurants and gas stations.

A study of Kane County produced by the Utah State Planning Board in 1935 identified change in the county between 1900 and 1935. The population of Kane County increased from 1,811 in 1900 to 2,235 in 1930. Kanab had a population of 710 in 1900 and 1,195 in 1930. Caucasians born in the United States represented 97.9 percent of the total population in 1930 and 77 percent of the total population received at least part of their income from a farm. In 1900 all individuals on the census stated some identification with a farm; in 1930, 1,722 described themselves as non-farmers. In 1930 the greatest number of workers worked in agriculture, 364 of the total. The next highest category was thirty-four people who worked in garages or in greasing stations. Thirty-one residents were professionals or worked in semi-professional capacities; twenty worked in the building trades, eighteen in wholesale and retail. In 1930, 135 individuals were unemployed; most of this group were common laborers.

The total number of farms was 54 percent greater in 1935 than in 1910. The number of individuals who owned their farms was 23 percent higher. The assessed value of farmlands increased between 1910 and 1930 by 183 percent but then decreased by 1935 by 31 percent during the Depression. In 1930 there were 200 farms in the county; in 1935 there were 255. The value and production of crops declined steadily after 1919. The number of sheep on local farms in 1910 was 106,534; this had decreased to 80,346 in 1935. The total number of cattle also decreased over the same time period—from 13,157 in 1910 to 7,725 in 1935. The principal farm product was hay and forage, although some farmers planted corn, potatoes, and wheat. The assessed value of real estate increased between 1910 and 1930 but then decreased 17 percent between 1930 and 1935.

Kane County's population increased by 322 between 1930 and 1940 to a total population of 2,557. Town populations fluctuated—Kanab went from 1,195 to 1,396 residents; Mt. Carmel increased in population from 133 to 184, Orderville from 439 to 449, Glendale from 289 to 297, and Alton from 193 to 240.[26]

Kanab

Although life in Kane County was impacted by national programs of the New Deal, the everyday exigencies, including a local outbreak of scarlet fever in 1931, also impacted people. Communicable diseases were terrifying to those in rural towns. The *Kane County Standard* reported precautions taken in Kanab during the quarantine established in 1931, including measures that seem excessive at the present time, such as the report that "the librarian at the Free Public Library has been forced to burn books this winter that have been sent back to the library from quarantined homes."[27] The library closed down altogether in January 1934 because of lack of funds. Kane County schools closed early in April 1931 because of a lack of funds, and parents had to teach their children at home if they wanted them to have more schooling.[28] The school board worked on finding new ways of funding salaries and stretching available resources. Local teachers offered to work for reduced salaries, and, by the end of the summer, the board had come up with a stringent budget that would allow the district to run schools for an eight-months term during the 1932–33 school year.[29]

Dr. George Aiken purchased land in the northwest part of Kanab to build a hospital in 1934. By June 1935 the *Kane County Standard* reported that work by local contractor Albert Anderson on the twenty-nine-room structure was proceeding "nicely." Charles Plumb designed the hospital, which was in the "ranch house style." Next door, a residence was also being built to house Dr. Aiken and his family.

The hospital included two wards, four bathrooms, two doctor's offices, a dentist office and laboratory, an operating room and delivery room, a nursery, and a waiting room on the first floor. A full basement housed an x-ray room, sterilization room, two nurses' rooms, a janitor's apartment, and a mechanical plant. The new hospital was

The Hotel Highway in September 1921. (Utah State Historical Society)

ready for opening in February 1936 and was described as attractive, modern, and up-to-date in every way.[30] Within the week every room in the hospital was occupied. Mr. and Mrs. H. Maxwell of Glendale were the parents of the first baby born in the new hospital. It was delivered free of charge and nicknamed "Freeborn" by Dr. Aiken.[31]

The library finally gained its own home through the devoted efforts of a number of individuals. The Works Progress Administration (WPA) agreed to furnish labor for the project, but Kanab City was required to locate and purchase a building site. Land near the high school was purchased, the city council purchased the Johnson sawmill located in the Kaibab Forest, and a WPA crew cut the timber for the library itself as well as a surplus to sell to provide funds for doors, windows, and other necessary building components.

The city council also built a brick kiln in the northeast section of Kanab to produce bricks for the building. Mark E. Pope was hired to manage the project. The building cost $8,000 to build. When the library was relocated to its new home there were 6,000 books and between 2,000 and 3,000 magazines in the collection. The library's collection was supplemented by donations from various sources including Kanab schools, the Missoula Public Library, the St. George Public Library, Sears Roebuck and Company, and the Brigham Macdonald Memorial. The Ladies Literary League has also been a major contributor to the library through the years.

A proposed airport to be built at the Chamberlain farm southeast of Kanab was also approved by the local Civil Works Administration (CWA) committee and sent to the state committee for approval. It was proposed that the costs for this project be shared by the state and the town of Kanab (which would purchase the property), and that the labor would be paid for by the CWA to the amount of $1,570.[32]

The Kanab LDS Ward was divided into two wards–the Kanab North Ward and Kanab South Ward—in 1936. According to an earlier history, the idea had been discussed for quite some time:

> For twenty-five years during both the administrations of Stake President William W. Seegmiller and Heber J. Meeks (1910–1934) there had been talk of dividing the Kanab Ward. No action was taken because of the reluctance of the people to divide, the difficulty of dividing the wards equally, the problem of finding officers for two complete organizations, and the lack of pressure from the General Authorities. However, during President Charles C. Heaton's incumbency (1934–1945) the ward had grown to over twelve hundred members and a division seemed imperative. The matter was carefully considered and the proposed plans were presented to the Presiding Authorities, who approved. After a great deal of preliminary detail was completed, the division was made final July 12, 1936. . . . The dividing line was Center Street on Highway 89.[33]

Alton

In 1929 the local church building was further improved by the construction of a chapel area and a furnace room. A recreational facility that brought large crowds out for its opening was the Twin-Pines Open Air Dance Pavilion, which was built by Dan Heaton, Frank Hurd, and William Swapp about a half mile up the road from the town in the late 1920s. The main dance floor was located around

Orderville in the 1930s. (Courtesy Deanne Glover)

two tall pine trees, creating a green bower for musicians. When it originally opened, locals partied for three full days, camping nearby, being thrilled by airplane stunts overhead, and enjoying rodeo events, horse races, boxing and wrestling matches, and more traditional activities such as dances and musicals.

Alton gained a flood-control system in 1933. During the Franklin D. Roosevelt administration, Alton received municipal power from the Garkane Electric Power Company. The town's population peaked at 350 in the 1930s.

Orderville

In 1922–23 the town's first high school was completed. Harry R. Wilson and William J. Monroe, Jr., designed the building, which was built by Albert Anderson of Toquerville for $30,000. A mechanical school was also built for $8,000. The modern facility had reinforced-concrete footings, cut-stone foundation walls, and superstructure walls of native brick made on site by Elijah T. Holgate. Lumber was cut by Edward Crofts from a forest some seventeen miles to the north. The first local garage and service station was built in 1925 by the Heaton brothers. In 1937 the Valley Theatre opened its doors to motion picture audiences.

Mt. Carmel

The LDS church purchased the Mt. Carmel rock building of the mid-1870s, rebuilt the original rock section, and added two matching rock wings in the back, giving the building its present T-shaped floor plan. The schoolhouse was remodeled in 1923–24. The rear contained a stage and two classrooms. A new hip roof and belfry unified and improved the exterior appearance. The landmark served as a church until 1963 when members were included in the Orderville LDS Ward.

With the advent of the automobile, service areas soon were developed at the junctions of major traffic routes. Thus by the early 1920s, Mt. Carmel Junction, two miles south on U.S. Highway 89 at Utah State Road 9, began to grow and draw attention away from the town proper. Here two gasoline stations served motorists' needs. Motels, a restaurant, and a golf course also catered to travelers. Eventually homesteads were built along the road between the junction and the town.

Mt. Carmel's size has always been limited by its available resources. In 1930, for example, the total population was 133. Irrigation efforts were key to the development of the small town. Local men built a dam on the Virgin River about two miles north of town and directed water onto the Mt. Carmel fields. Dams were usually constructed with brush, trees, rocks, and dirt. Occasionally, after a severe rainstorm, the dams would break and flood the fields. Weeks of laborious repair required the cooperation of all local farmers impacted by this type of disaster.

Glendale

In 1922 J. Edward Crofts moved his sawmill from the Glendale area to Cedar Mountain and installed a steam engine to power it; eventually he converted it to diesel. His sons—Arlos, Josiah, Alfred, John, and Leo—joined in the business, which thrived until the 1950s when it merged with the Pearson and Crofts mill located near Bryce Canyon. Crofts was honored by Utah State Agricultural College in

1954 with a conservation award which recognized his outstanding leadership in national resource management.

On 29 March 1935 Glendale was incorporated, with David A. Smith as the town's first mayor. Other mayors have included Charles C. Anderson, Merle J. Spencer, James L. Esplin, Howard Spencer, and Charles Wilbur Brinkerhoff. The town's first postmaster was Warren Foote in the late 1880s; others have included John S. Carpenter, Elizabeth Hopkins Carpenter, Lois Harris Spencer, Rachel Jolley, Ella Anderson, David A. Smith, John Levanger, Alvin Black, Sarah Black and Ive Maxwell.

Transportation and Roads

During the first decades of the twentieth century, Zion Canyon, Bryce Canyon, and the Grand Canyon all became national parks, and the state of Utah built roads to make the region more accessible. The sandy stretch between Kanab and Long Valley was paved in 1922, and in 1930 the Zion–Mt. Carmel tunnel was built, connecting Kane County's towns with the rest of southwestern Utah and U.S. Highway 91, which was built in the 1920s.

In the late 1920s, funding to complete the Zion-Mt. Carmel Highway, called "Utah's most spectacular and most publicized road project," came from the federal government to help provide access to Zion and other national parks of the region. One of the most incredible engineering feats in the history of road building, the twenty-five-mile road, located in Kane and Washington Counties, moves from the canyon floor to Pine Creek Canyon and the four-mile roadway spirals upward to a tunnel paralleling the face of the vertical cliffs for 5,615 feet. Construction within the park cost $2,000,000; from the park to Mt. Carmel it cost the state and the federal government another $500,000 for the road.

The Zion–Mt. Carmel tunnel was an important engineering feat. It was no longer necessary for travelers between St. George and Kanab to take the long roundabout route through northern Arizona. After two years of work, the Nevada Contracting Company shut down its camp in early 1930, according to the *Kane County Standard*, "thus making the end of their job of building the major part of what is perhaps the most spectacular highway in the world."[34] The Zion-

Lee's Ferry on the Colorado River near the mouth of the Paria River provided access between Kane County and northern Arizona. This photograph was taken 19 March 1935. (Utah State Historical Society)

Mt. Carmel tunnel road was officially dedicated on 2 July 1930 by Governor George H. Dern and later served as a vital link between U.S. Highways 89 and 91 after Highway 89 connected Kane County towns to Bryce Canyon and other northern areas with a direct north-south highway through the county.[35]

In 1929 Arizona had announced plans to improve the roads to the new Colorado River bridge at Marble Canyon. It would spend $20,000 during 1929 surveying and laying out a route from Flagstaff to the state line south of Kanab and put $88,000 into the construction of the road itself. Two possible routes were discussed for the road—one joining the Grand Canyon road in the Kaibab Forest at Jacob's Lake and the other skirting the rim of the Kaibab Plateau on the edge of House Rock Valley.[36] The National Park Service reported that inquiries about road conditions leading to the bridge had increased dramatically since its completion, and that approximately fifty cars passed over it each day.[37] In December 1929, Arizona officials announced that they would improve the road between Flagstaff and the Navajo Bridge and on through Fredonia to the Utah state line.[38]

In 1930 the state of Utah committed to spend $100,000 on road improvements and construction in Kane County for grading and structures on the road from Kanab 4.5 miles south to the Utah-Arizona line, construction of about three miles of road in the Three Lakes section extending from six to nine miles north of Kanab (a dangerous stretch through a tortuous canyon), and the graveling of both sections.[39] In February 1930 the *Kane County Standard* reported that the road crew was "anxiously waiting for the construction of the road through Kanab and Three Lakes Canyon to start." The county commissioners had approved the right of way and had begun the process of condemning properties in the way of construction, making every attempt to "purchase the necessary right of ways and in every way have also tried to be fair with the property owners, and at the same time do justice to their offices."[40] The *Kane County Standard* reported in an article entitled "More Than a Million for Roads" in its 28 November 1930 issue that contracts were under negotiation for more than a million dollars worth of highway construction for the region, including $200,000 for the road in Arizona between Jacob Lake and the Navajo Bridge.[41]

The people of Kane County recognized the importance of U.S. Highway 89 when it was completed in the area in the early 1930s and the improvements in the region's roads to the county's future well being, opening trade, recreation potential, and communication and cultural exchange with other Utah counties and with Arizona.[42] The *Kane County Standard* reviewed proposed area road construction and improvement projects for the summer of 1931 in its 24 April issue. Funding sources included the state of Utah, the National Forest Service, the National Park Service, and Kane County; they would collectively spend $1,646,237 on the projects. In addition, another $95,000 was to be spent on general maintenance of roads. This included grading graveled surfaces, building bridges and culverts, and spending $12,000 on various improvements. The road from Toquerville to La Verkin junction, a fourteen-mile stretch from the eastern boundary of Zion National Park on the Zion-Mt. Carmel

Tunnel road to the Mt. Carmel junction, and the twelve-mile road from Three Lakes north of Kanab to the Utah-Arizona line would be improved for $105,000. J.C. Compton contracted to complete these jobs.

The largest of the new road construction jobs in the region was a new road in Zion Canyon which would be constructed for $250,000. Ten miles of road would be constructed from Hatch to the junction of the Bryce Canyon road for $60,000. Another contract was for the Mt. Carmel dugway (three miles of heavy construction for $125,000), a job that started at the junction of the Zion-Mt. Carmel Road, going south up the canyon toward Kanab to the summit of the sandy plateau. Six miles of road from the sandy plateau to Three Lakes would cost $75,000; three short road sections in Kanab Canyon cost $80,000, and thirteen miles of road from Jacob Lake to Pleasant Valley in the Kaibab Forest area for $60,000 were also planned. The House Rock Valley road from Jacob's Lake to Pleasant Valley was to be constructed for $300,000.[43] The *Kane County Standard* reported the progress of each project through the summer, as all affected the local economy, even if all were not in Kane County.[44]

Natural Resources and Public Lands

Besides the road construction during these decades, the town and county governments continued to maintain and improve their existing infrastructures, particularly in the search for additional sources of water. The Kane County Water Conservancy District was the primary agency involved with water-resource development in the county. Kane County extracted water from a number of reservoir sites, including Alton, Alton Lakes, Cave Lake, Duck Lake, Kanab Sink, Johnson Creek, Little Meadow, Long Valley, the Paria River, and Shirts Creek. A study conducted in 1935 provides a picture of how much land was irrigated, and the canals that fed fields with water from nearby streams, reservoirs, and other sources. In the county there were forty-six miles of irrigation canals. The total number of farms in 1930 was 200; of those, 167 were irrigated. The total area of those farms was 94,968 acres.[45]

In September 1937, the Elbow Dam project was planned to tap a water source that was anticipated to bring agricultural expansion to

Kanab farmers. The water would be conveyed to land in and around Kanab through Kanab Creek and a system of canals, and it would irrigate thousands of acres of land for cultivation.[46]

A single coal mining business was located and operating in the county near Alton. During the 1930s efforts were made to locate coal deposits in the hope of developing further mining industries in the county. The *Kane County Standard* reported one such effort in July 1931 that was conducted by the government and supervised locally by Ray Lightner and Don A. Lightner of St. George. The coal field was located near the eastern boundary of Zion National Park fifteen miles northwest of Orderville, and 24,000 acres were involved in the lease.[47] Considerable interest was aroused by the coal field, which was leased by a group of men from Richfield and southern California. The vein of coal was up to twelve feet thick and continued for miles to the east and west. The group leased 2,600 acres from the government and considerable acreage from private farmers. To access the vein they constructed a four-mile road from Esplin's ranch to the Cedar-Long Valley road in Dry Valley near Navajo Lake.[48]

The Kanab Lions Club met on 11 February 1934 to discuss with Benjamin Cameron of Panguitch a plan to develop a coal mine on Cedar Mountain. Apparently, the coal in this district was considered ideal for stoves and fireplaces because it was relatively smokeless.[49] It was anticipated that coal mining could produce a stable economic resource for the county from the abundant natural deposits. "Kane county will have a permanent pay roll, when the coal mines in the north-west part of this county are opened up," one writer enthusiastically predicted in 1939. "A road which takes off at the Clear Creek road, east of tunnels on the Zion-Mt. Carmel highway, leading to these coal beds is now in the course of construction," the newspaper reported. It was predicted by Kane County Clerk D.M. Tietjen that the road would take about two months to complete.[50] The mining did not develop to the large extent hoped, however.

In 1929 permission had been requested from the Federal Land Office in Salt Lake City by a number of Salt Lake City investors to prospect for oil and gas on 56,320 acres of public land in Garfield and Kane counties. All the applications were denied.[51]

Ranchers endeavored to continue the lifestyle they knew and

loved during the difficult times. About this time, the lifestyle of cattleman William T. Dobson of Kanab was portrayed in a story called "Sinister," which appeared in serial form in the *Westerner* magazine. Dobson was born four miles north of the Arizona-Utah border. The nearest railroad station was in Nephi to the north; Kanab was farther from a station than was any other town in the state. The diversity of ways Dobson worked to support his family typifies those of other Kane County residents. As a boy he worked in both cattle and sheep camps—he was familiar with roundups, shearing corrals, and working in sawmills. When World War I began, he had a large family and had become a forest ranger in the Kaibab National Forest. "This life," he reportedly said, "was so fascinating he always felt ashamed to take pay for it. It was like being paid to go a vacation to the wonderland of America."[52] He later tried his hand at fruit growing and attempted to start a newspaper in Kanab. He eventually moved to Salt Lake City.

Local cattlemen had participated in a range protest in Salt Lake City in August 1930 in conjunction with the convention of the Utah Cattle and Horse Growers Association. They focused on proposed plans for making House Rock Valley and the Sandhills into a buffalo and antelope preserve. This range in southern Utah and northern Arizona had long been used as grazing ground for thousands of cattle and sheep. The area cattlemen felt it had become time to draw a line against further parts of the area being made into national parks or reserves. They referred to the fact that a large area of good grazing land in northern Arizona had already been taken away from the stockmen when the Kaibab Indian Reservation had been created at Moccasin and when Pipe Spring National Monument was established. They also resented the creation of the deer preserve in the Kaibab National Forest and maintained, "If much more land is taken away and made into game preserves, . . . it will be impossible for [us] to remain in the business."[53]

Managing local resources was an increasingly pressing concern during the farming depression years of the 1920s and 1930s. The use of the water of the Colorado River provided another test of different attitudes toward utilization of resources during the first decades of the twentieth century. Although Mormon settlement had been located along the irrigable banks of the Virgin, Paria, and Kanab

Rivers, there was no acreage along the Colorado River suitable for major agricultural uses. In 1922, the seven states of the Colorado River basin, in the effort to find a more equitable way of using this important resource, developed a formal agreement, the Colorado River Compact, which created a division of the river's water between the upper basin states of Utah, Colorado, Wyoming, and New Mexico and the lower basin states of Arizona, Nevada, and California, the dividing point being Lees Ferry. This agreement established claims to the water and allowed for future negotiations between states willing to form alliances for special projects. For instance, the Hoover Dam, completed in 1936, created an enormous source of hydroelectric power, the Lake Mead National Recreation Area, and economic benefit to nearby cities, particularly Las Vegas.

In 1930, the Kaibab Investigative Committee, including representatives from nine national associations, spent ten days in June on location in the national forest. The found that the forest rangeland had been seriously depleted by domestic grazing animals and deer; in fact, the forest was only producing about 10 percent of the forage that it had once produced. Overgrazing was leading to the disappearance of aspen trees and cliffrose bushes. Conifer reproduction was almost impossible because few seedings were escaping the notice of hungry deer. The study emphasized the importance of taking a planning approach in the future in dealing with the management of game and other forest policies to ensure growth rather than deterioration.[54]

National Parks—Bryce Canyon

The automobile more than any other technological advancement impacted Kane County and made Zion National Park much more accessible. Visitor totals into Zion reflected that change—between 1919 and 1920 the number increased from 1,914 to 3,692; by 1930 park visitation had reached 55,000. In 1930 Zion National Park was expanded to include land in Kane County—an area made accessible by the Zion-Mt. Carmel tunnel and road. Prior to this time the park boundary had ended at the Washington-Kane County line.

Kane County also houses a sizable portion of Bryce Canyon National Park and benefits from the location of the park in the region. The economic impact in this case is not as great as it is from Zion National Park, however, as the portion of Bryce Canyon National Park in Kane County is only accessible by motor vehicle from within the park through Garfield County. Such scenic attractions of the park as Yovimpa Point, Rainbow Point, and Ponderosa Canyon are located in Kane County, which benefits from general tourist visitation to the area; many who visit one of the great national parks of the region continue on to visit the others.

Bryce Canyon gained increasing attention and consideration as either a state park or national monument beginning in the 1910s—a process that had accelerated by the early 1920s. In 1916 Reuben C. Syrett homesteaded near the entrance of what would eventually become Bryce Canyon National Park. By 1920 Ruby and Minnie Syrett had built tourist facilities in the canyon. In 1919 the Utah State Legislature asked Congress to consider making Bryce Canyon a national monument, and this was accomplished by declaration of President Warren G. Harding in 1923. The monument initially was under jurisdiction of the U.S. Forest Service, and increased national attention focused on the area. By 1924 Congress passed a bill to establish the canyon as a Utah National Park after all private and state holdings in the area were eliminated. In the process of fulfilling the conditions, Utah officials worked to change the proposed name of the park to Bryce Canyon, and on 25 February 1928 Congress formally authorized Bryce Canyon National Park, almost doubling its size from the earlier authorization, including land in Kane County, which could now boast of having a national park within its boundaries.[55] Soon, after the expansion of Zion National Park, Kane could claim portions of two national parks.

E.T. Scoyen, superintendent of Utah's national parks, spoke to the Lions Club of Kanab in January 1931 about the important tradition of protecting the wilderness and the public domain for future generations. Scoyen said that the interest in national parks had accelerated in the years after World War I. National parks visitation in the country had increased from an average of 450,000 a year to 2,800,000 per year. He articulated the government's attitude toward federal involvement in the protection of the country's public areas:

> The National Park is a peculiar type of government reserva-
> tion. It is also the one distinct contribution of the people of the
> United States to land administration. The principle of wilderness
> preservation for the benefit and enjoyment of the people is an
> American principle. After originating this idealistic idea we went
> to work with characteristic American energy and developed to a
> point where it has attracted the interest of other nations.
>
> I said the fundamental park policy is peculiar. By this I merely
> mean that we have gone beyond accepted policies of land conser-
> vation previously in use. Conservation of our forests and other
> resources is a factor which we can trace back almost to the dawn
> of civilization.[56]

Scoyen continued by articulating the value of a national park to
an area. First, he said, beyond the obvious value of living near a place
that is wild and beautiful, is an economic value to the area. "If there
were not some actual cash value involved, groups and organizations
in all parts of the country would not be trying so desperately to have
a park operating in their vicinity," he maintained. A national park
also promotes travel in general to an area. He mentioned that as he
had traveled around the county he had often heard the criticism that
this economic value benefits outsiders rather than those living in the
county itself, saying: "I have frequently heard it said that this park
business and tourists is something outside, it is not operated for the
benefit of local people, and that its ever expanding operation will
greatly cripple, if not eventually destroy the livestock industry in this
section." Although conceding this might be true, his response was
that a national park was an integral part of the entire social and economic life of a county as well as the rest of the region and should not
be limited by its impact to a few at the expense of the many. The area
would benefit, according to Scoyen, by roads that would be built and
funded by the government through the county and by service businesses that could start up and supply tourists through the area. In this
he both anticipated criticism of national preserves and a response
that has continued between citizens on both sides of the issue up to
the present day.

In January 1931 Superintendent Scoyen spoke with an old-time
resident of one of the towns bordering Zion National Park. The old

man stood in front of his family home. Scoyen asked how old the home was, and the man said it was almost fifty years old and that it was still as tight as it was when first built. Scoyen responded, "Well! Times have changed since that was built!" "Yes," the old-timer responded, "but they have changed more in the last five years than they did in the first forty-five."[57]

The Depression and the New Deal

For people in all of Utah's counties, the Great Depression was a time of fear and anxiety. Kane County had already felt the effects of the declining market in agricultural goods after 1919 with the drop in demand for farm products after the end of World War I. Farm prices and production dropped dramatically during the decade of the 1920s. Farmers continued to plant their fields and were able to feed their families, but there were few markets for their surplus produce. Most did have enough to eat, however; they had garden plots and generally a number of chickens.[58] To get a piece of candy at the store, children could bring an egg to trade for it. Most women made their family's clothes, and many never threw anything away, finding uses for everything.

According to one Kanab resident growing up during the era, the lives of children were little different during the farming depression years of the 1920s and 1930s:

Being young in the 1920s was not all hard work even though it was during the depression. After the work was done the neighborhood children would gather for a nightly game of kick the can, or join the many races that were always being held. During the colder months they would gather at someone's house and play cards or go to the school where dances were being held for everyone. The dances even allowed the first and second graders to come and encouraged them to participate.[59]

The majority of Kane County voters had voted for Republican presidents Warren Harding, Calvin Coolidge, and Herbert Hoover, and they were overwhelmingly Republican in their voting preferences and conservative in their outlook, proclaiming the ideas of free enterprise and little government regulation. Even during the Depression the majority of county voters consistently favored the Republican presidential candidate, although most Utahns and other Americans voted to elect Democrat Franklin D. Roosevelt four consecutive times, beginning in 1932. Nevertheless, after Roosevelt was elected president, county residents looked to his New Deal programs for federal assistance.

Roosevelt was convinced that it was the government's obligation to help end the Depression. He called upon the United States Congress to enact laws that would create programs that would involve the government more with the lives of the people. The group of programs created in this effort to reverse the economic decline were called the New Deal. Programs under Roosevelt's New Deal had three main purposes: provide relief for the needy, create jobs and encourage business expansion, and reform business and governmental practices to arrest the Depression's development. New Deal legislation created numerous agencies, called "alphabet agencies" after their abbreviations, that provided the organizational network necessary to frame programs and put them into action.

Perhaps the most pressing need in Kane County as elsewhere was immediate relief for the hungry and homeless and unemployed workers and their families. Kane County benefited from a variety of New Deal programs. The federal government directed the disbursement of funds, the efforts of agencies, and the establishment of programs toward development and recovery for the county. The number of people receiving aid under the Public Welfare Program in Kane County generally increased between 1930 and 1940. In 1936, for example, the average number of cases was sixty-seven; the next year, the number increased to ninety-five, and in 1938 it went to 117. The Works Progress Administration (WPA) assigned fifty-one workers to the county to various projects in 1935, 104 in 1936, fifty-one in 1937, and eighty-seven in 1938. The Welfare and Works Program spent $131,543.77 in Kane County between 1932 and 1938. About 54.3 percent of the funds for this program came from the federal government, 34.3 percent from the state, and 11.4 percent from the county.[60]

The Agricultural Adjustment Administration (AAA) helped local farmers learn methods of increasing the fertility of depleted fields, conserving their lands, and reestablishing their purchasing power. The state AAA committee included a representative from Kane

County—James A. Brown from Kanab. Several agencies served the needs of local farmers. The Farm Security Administration (FSA) office that oversaw the projects proceeding in Kane County was located in St. George. The local supervisor was Willis Dunkley and the home management supervisor was Eleanor Smith. The purpose of the organization was to further rural rehabilitation. Among other programs, the FSA provided long-term loans to qualified farm tenants to help them purchase farms.

The Federal Surplus Commodities Corporation purchased, exchanged, processed, transported, handled, stored, and distributed surplus agricultural commodities on a non-commercial basis, redirecting farm surpluses to the poor and the needy. Kane County's representative in the agency was Florian W. Johnson of Kanab. Long-time residents recall the program and in particular what some considered the senselessness of such an approach, feeling like it was getting money for nothing, although at the time locals accepted the aid. Calvin Johnson remembered a time when the government paid cattlemen ten dollars a head to destroy their substandard cattle.[61] Although many didn't understand it, the program was designed to help increase prices while eliminating diseased or malnourished animals. Ranchers were allowed to use the meat unless it was diseased.

Because much of the county's grazing land was public land that was managed by the federal government, cooperation between those in the cattle industry and governmental agencies was important. In August 1934 the U.S. Forest Service conducted a study of grazing conditions in the Kaibab National Forest. Because it had been a year of drought, the deer population was at risk. A series of public meetings was held that was attended by local cattlemen and representatives from the state governments of Arizona and Utah and the Forest Service.[62] An advisory committee of the Cattle Emergency Relief group of Kane County met in the county courthouse in Kanab on 1 August 1934 to organize the government's purchase and shipment of cattle out of the county; some 250 head of cattle had already been shipped out of Alton and another 136 calves had been condemned.[63]

Other farm relief efforts continued for several years. In 1937, for example, $2,500 in "rural rehabilitation" funds was granted to area livestock owners for families in "urgent need of subsistence and without feed for their range sheep, milk cows, pigs, or chickens."[64] The government also contributed to immediate relief efforts by extending the food stamp plan in 1940 to benefit those in certain rural counties of Utah, including Kane. This program was described by the local newspaper as a "means of distributing over-abundant crops through neighborhood markets to the 6,700 families receiving public assistance in the twelve counties."[65]

Among the most popular and effective government programs was the Civilian Conservation Corps (CCC), established to help put unemployed young men to work, generally in a rural setting, to work on public range, national forest, and national park conservation and improvement projects. Some twenty CCC camps were created at public land areas in Utah, including one in Zion National Park. The Zion Park camp spent some time in erosion-control work along the Virgin River. The insular nature of rural Mormon Utahns was challenged by the program which was aiding them, creating mixed feelings among many. Old-timers remember when the CCC workers came into town, as the workers would sometimes come into Kanab for Saturday night dances. They were well regulated by their supervisors, but most were still quite different in culture and outlook from local men and came primarily from cities throughout the country. The CCC men competed against local teams in intramural baseball games. The girls in one family who lived in Alton were told by their parents that they couldn't date the CCC workers when they came into town—they could only date Utah boys. As they remembered it, most of the CCC men were Italians from New York City. Some would come to the Mormon church in Kanab on Sunday for worship services and occasionally families would invite them to dinner. Mormon prejudice was deep-rooted, however. One time, the girls reportedly were driving from their ranch to Alton and had a flat tire. A truckload of CCC men drove by and stopped to change the tire. While they were working, a neighbor drove by, jerked his car to a stop, and starting yelling at the CCC workers to leave the young women alone.[66]

During the 1930s, CCC workers created hiking trails, camping grounds, and numerous other improvements to Zion National Park. Locals increasingly began to recognize the importance that the region's national parks played in their economy. The CCC Duck

Creek Recreation Camp was officially dedicated on 25 June 1933. Governor Henry H. Blood came to the celebration to deliver the keynote address. Representatives of four southern Utah counties participated in the program, in which W.R. Palmer related a story of the naming of Navajo Lake, a male chorus from Kanab sang several numbers, the Parowan band played during a late night dance, and community singing was also featured. Duck Creek was heralded by the local newspaper, which wrote that it was an "ideal place to establish a recreation camp, the air being cool and refreshing, the scenery enchanting and there is good fishing along Duck Creek. There is no doubt but that this camp will become a popular retreat as soon as it is know to all who wish to spend a few days or weeks camping in a shady and quiet place among the pines and aspens."[67]

Crews from CCC camps in the area worked on projects in Fredonia, Zion National Park, Grand Canyon National Park, and Bryce Canyon National Park. The CCC men only received five dollars of personal spending money each month (the remaining twenty-five dollars being sent to their families at home), but collectively this was a great deal of money during the period and helped bolster businesses in the area long before tourism picked up. Both CCC and WPA projects greatly benefited the area and its towns, including helping build the county courthouse and new school buildings. These projects also had the benefit of putting some local people to work and had the incidental effect of teaching many people trades they might not have learned otherwise. Some became rock masons, carpenters, and builders from working on CCC and WPA projects.[68] The beautiful rock work done by CCC workers in Zion National Park created a number of professional masons. They were proud of their work in addition to being able to survive through the difficult years of the Depression.

The U.S. Forest Service also played a role in the area's economic recovery during the New Deal years by administering grazing programs, protecting watersheds for domestic agricultural and industrial purposes, and developing recreational opportunities for visitors in the national forests. Kane County came under the direction of the Forest Service district headquartered in Panguitch, Utah. About twenty-nine men from Kanab were hired to work with the Forest

Service on range improvement funded under the Public Works Act. Some protest was organized in Arizona about hiring Utah men for projects that were mainly located in other states, particularly referring to the Arizona area of the Arizona Strip. The Kanab Lions Club solicited help from Utah's senators in negotiating a reinterpretation of the provisions of the PWA so that the residents of Kanab could work on the Kaibab National Forest.[69] They justified their request on the grounds that Kanab residents had grazed stock in the area for several years, and that the Forest Service had been careful in the past to employ men from both Utah and Arizona on a relatively equal basis.

The high school struggled during the Depression years to pay salaries and expenses. During the 1932–33 school year students came to school only half a day. In part funded by the WPA, the school building underwent significant remodeling in 1934 when the exterior walls were rebuilt and a new roof added. Other improvements included the surfacing of sidewalks, rebuilding a retaining wall, and creating terraced seats above the athletic track. In 1934 the school term was extended from eight to nine months for the first time since before the Depression.[70]

County officials made the decisions as to who needed relief. In the opinion of the *Kane County Standard*, "Kane county needs more relief than it is getting, and we should use every effort to see that we get our just dues."[71] Like many throughout the state and nation who proclaimed the merits of self-sufficiency and limited government, when government programs were made available, county residents did not want to be left out. In 1934, however, Kane County actually was receiving less relief than any other county in the state according to statistics compiled by the state relief committee: only 6.13 percent of the population was receiving aid (this in contrast, for example, to Beaver County with 30.60 percent, Duchesne County with 53.50 percent, and Iron County with 37.40 percent). At the time, there were only three projects that were employing men needing relief—the laying of a new pipe line, building shops for vocational training at Kanab High School and Valley High School, and repairing the grounds of the courthouse.[72] In August 1934 a Federal Emergency Relief Administration (FERA)-funded road project was surveyed from Panguitch to Glendale. In October 1934 two other FERA pro-

Braiding the May Pole in Kanab on 1 May 1929. (Courtesy Deanne Glover)

jects began in Kane County—a project for grading, improving, and repairing Kanab town streets and the Kanab cemetery, and another project involving maintenance of the Kanab public library.[73] Kanab Mayor Edwin J. Ford had applied for a $15,000 WPA appropriation for library expansion. At that time, the library included 5,000 books and thousands of magazines, and it was estimated that circulation in 1933 was as high as 13,000 items per year.

During May 1934 Kanab officials passed an ordinance to improve and repair the existing waterworks system.[74] In 1935, Kanab revamped much of its water system with funding from the Public Works Administration, adding larger mains and a new large cistern high on the side of a cliff north of town, and re-laying pipe.[75] The Lions Club worked on a transportation project during 1937 to provide three blocks of "full width, hard surfaced highway through the main business section." The group planned to help surface the road and build curbs and gutters for three blocks of streets in Kanab.[76] Many local men and women worked on WPA projects; for example, Genieve Millett Cutler BlueJacket remembered working on a WPA project lining Kanab's ditches with rock.[77]

At one meeting held at the Kane County Courthouse on 13

September 1934, Lowry Nelson of the Agricultural College at Logan spoke about the FERA program and how to access funds. Nelson described FERA as a relief program, not a work program, and said that individuals employed on such projects needed to be eligible for relief before they could be assigned to a project. "The only purpose of the projects is to allow the people receiving relief to work for what they get, and they are allowed only sufficient to satisfy their minimum subsistence requirements, as determined by the investigation of the case worker," he said. Kane County's FERA committee estimated that one hundred families in the county were added to the county's relief list by June 1934. The *Kane County Standard* suggested in July 1934 that "few of the men employed in Kane at the present time are working on permanent jobs."[78]

In 1934, fifty-seven men from Kane County worked on Civil Works Administration (CWA) projects, and forty others worked on the federal project on campgrounds underway in Zion Canyon that year. The state CWA committee approved the following projects for the county: repairing streets and sidewalks in Kanab, $915; repairing streets and sidewalks at Orderville, $525; repairing streets and sidewalks at Glendale, $225; repairing streets and sidewalks at Alton, $195; repairing and improving school grounds and buildings at Kanab, $1,455; repairing roads and bridges at Kanab, $2,550; repairing school grounds and buildings at Orderville, $787; repairing and improving school grounds and buildings at Glendale, $225. Women's projects included hiring two county nurses—one from Long Valley and one from Kanab—one social worker from Alton, and one library worker from Kanab, with total salaries and wages of $738. After the salary for a librarian was approved by the state CWA committee, Kanab's public library was able to reopen, after having been closed for three weeks. The library was to be opened for four hours five days a week, and for two additional hours each day the librarian would classify, organize, and repair books.[79]

The women's county committee of the CWA at Kanab organized efforts to register women in need of work through the county relief agent. Although registration was no guarantee of employment, when work did become available these were the first women to be considered. The committee also reviewed proposals sent to the state committee regarding the county's women and also sought ways to bring work from other towns to local women. The CWA specifically called for women who could do clerical work, nursing, library work, work in connection with securing relief, work in connection with vocational or adult education, janitorial work, and social work.[80] Kanab's committee—which included Nabbie S. Mace, Rose H. Hamblin, and Elsie Hamblin—worked in close cooperation with the local Mormon Relief Society.

The Kane County Reemployment Service, managed by R.B. Young, endeavored to place workers with private employers. "We invite all employers to use the reemployment office as the agency through which he may best secure qualified workers," Young announced. "Merchants, farmers, stockraisers, housecleaners, anyone wanting to hire any kind of help may secure through the reemployment office workers of any kind for short-time or long-time jobs. We also want," he continued, "to impress the civic organizations that are stressing such programs as remodeling, clean-up campaigns, municipal construction and repair work with the fact that the Reemployment office is now ready and eager to refer workers to the projects which result from local organized effort."[81]

In October 1935 the Kane County Board of Education received a grant from the federal government for $24,600 for construction of two new school buildings in the county. The first of the two structures would be a four-room building to house the industrial shop and home-economics classes at Valley High School; the second was for a six-room school building for Orderville elementary classes. The Talboe Company of Provo received the contract to build the two buildings.[82]

Kane County schools received $6,000 in WPA funds in May 1936 to improve school grounds and buildings, with the single specification that no more than $2,100 be used on any single project. Many local men were employed on the projects. From the total appropriation, $1,800 was used to build a retaining wall and stadium at the Kanab High School. The stadium would eventually seat 1,400 people.[83] During 1937, WPA projects included construction of a new county jail, a race track, and fairgrounds, as well as work on the public library.[84]

When the new arena, racetrack and grandstand were finally completed in 1937, Kanab staged a three-day race and rodeo. Each day, six races were held on the new circular track. The *Standard* reported on 3 December 1937, "To hold the interest of the crowd between races wild, bucking horses and mangy cattle were turned loose in the arena with riders clinging to 'bucking strap' or saddle leather in order to stay. Rope tricks were performed by experts in the art and pranks were played between the acting cowboys and pick-up men as they went about their performing."

Tourism

Brothers Whitney, Gronway, and Chauncey Parry played roles in shaping the county's tourist economy during these decades. The Parry brothers capitalized on area developments and began the new business of busing tourists to Zion and Bryce canyons. In March 1931 Chauncey Parry began preparations to open up a hotel—the Parry Lodge—on his property in Kanab. Remodeling soon was underway, adapting the historic house into an "up-to-date" hotel and building modern two-room cabins equipped with good beds and running water on the lot to the north.[85]

In 1935 the *Kane County Standard* enthusiastically maintained that the county was "coming into her own, via scenery." The article continued: "Year by year since tourists have been attracted to southern Utah by the scenic wonders and natural beauties, home folks have realized that many of our most unique, and interesting places, and scenic spots have been missed almost without exception by the tourist as they pass along the highway at high speed." For this reason, the editor continued, each month he was going to devote a column to describing the county's unique attractions. For example, he reported,

> Last year over 2,000 people were at the Kane county celebration at Aspen grove on Cedar mountain July 24. This year at the Home Coming we want to see more there. The balmy mountain air, the enchanting scenery and clear, cool, water, make this place an ideal outdoor recreation center. Beautiful Navajo Lake which is only a short distance from the grove is equipped with an open air theater, camp grounds with tables, benches, stoves and sanitary

rest rooms. Swings and teeters have been erected to delight the children and a large space has been cleared which affords ample room for out door sports such as base ball, races, and games of various kinds.[86]

Also mentioned was the Caves Lakes area in Kanab Canyon, which was a site of Anasazi Basketmaker ruins.

Kanab was featured in the September 1937 issue of what the Kanab newspaper called "See Northern Arizona Magazine" as a tourist mecca of southern Utah. The article said in part,

> Kanab is known for its sunshine and wonderful temperature. The elevation is 4925 and with the protection of the mountains, makes it one of the delightful spots all seasons of the year. In winter, the sun is warm and bright and in summer the cool breezes from the canyon make it one of the most pleasant places in the country.[87]

The article mentioned that Kanab offered several options in lodging, two large department stores and four grocery stores, a bakery, drug store, and "three of the best places in the state to eat." It elaborately praised Kanab as a beautiful rural town welcoming tourists to the region.

> Kanab is the home town of the sheep and cattle man. Well painted homes and well kept lots bespeak the thrift and industry of its people. The home accommodation for the tourist population is no less beautiful and attractive. The native sand stone is to be found worked into paths, curbs, fences and homes of the community and public buildings. One cannot enter Kanab without being attracted by the long strip of green lawn on the slope of the hill in front of the main building at the school campus.
>
> Kanab is a heaven of rest. Each night the camps are crowded with pleasure-seeking travelers stopping for a space to rest in quiet contentment. The courtesy of the people, the cleanliness of the accommodations, the green of the gardens, and the cool of the breeze make Kanab an ideal spot for a rest from traveling.[88]

Salt Lake City's KSL radio station featured Kanab in a broadcast during February 1938 which outlined the town's history and presented a colorful description of some of its first inhabitants and the many scenic attractions and opportunities for recreation in nearby canyonland areas. Among other allurements, the broadcast mentioned the county's proximity to three national parks—Grand Canyon, Zion, and Bryce Canyon—the Zion-Mt. Carmel highway, Navajo Lake, and caves and cliff dwellings near Kanab.[89]

An informal survey conducted by F.D.B. Gay of Provo of cars passing through Kane County along U.S. Highway 89 noted the various state license plates of cars traveling through Kanab on 19 July 1939. Gay counted a total of 137 cars from thirty-eight states between 9:00 A.M. and 4:30 P.M. California travelers and those from Arizona were by far the most common—twenty-seven and fourteen, respectively—but even the District of Columbia and Hawaii were represented. Cars from as far away as Massachusetts, New Jersey, Alabama, Arkansas, and Wisconsin also were seen.[90]

Movie Industry

The earliest motion picture made in Kane County was filmed in 1922; it was a silent western film called *Deadwood Gulch* starring Tom Mix. The Parry brothers attempted to capitalize on the great potential the area had for the movie industry by preparing a portfolio of scenic photographs of Kane County that they sent to major Hollywood studios, promoting the area as a location for western movies. Locals also started businesses that provided lodging and supplies to movie crews. Their efforts were successful; eventually more than 200 films were made entirely or in part in Kane County, bringing thousands of dollars into the local economy.[91]

The *Kane County Standard* regularly reported on movies being filmed locally and movie stars who were spotted eating at local restaurants. On 27 August 1937, for example, the paper read, "A troupe of moving picture stars from Hollywood, California" have been in town "making films for the talkie 'Badman of the Brimstone.' It is reported that they will be in this vicinity for about ten days. They have employed quite a crew of local men to assist them with their equipment and other work. Several horses have also been hired as well as trucks."[92] Some of the scenes were filmed at Zion Narrows and others at the Joel Johnson ranch. The crew was staying at the Parry Lodge in Kanab.

Typically, a film company would come into town with trucks filled with equipment, trailers for the stars' comfort on site, and movie crews. But almost every movie filmed locally also employed a number of locals for extras, to drive trucks and haul sets, and for a variety of other purposes. In one case, according to the local newspaper, "Every evening a large crowd of employees gather at the cabins at the west entrance to the Parry lodge grounds, where a large pay roll is distributed. Business houses, hotels and auto camps are all doing thriving businesses. The company [the Columbia Film Company] is certainly spending a great deal of money here in making the films for their production."[93]

Kanab has been the setting for more than one hundred westerns, some filmed right in town. Kanab even was known as "Utah's Little Hollywood." Early films included *The Green Grass of Wyoming* and *Bad Day at Black Rock,* among numerous others. Marilyn Monroe, Clark Gable, Barbara Stanwick, Gary Cooper, and John Wayne were among the movie stars who stayed at Parry Lodge while they filmed locally. Dennis Judd's mother told a story about waitressing at Parry's Lodge and serving Clark Gable; she brushed up against his arm and reportedly wouldn't wash her arm for a week.[94]

The *Kane County Standard* kept residents informed about local movie developments. For example, it announced in 1934 that the "advance men of the talkie of one of Zane Grey's novels will build a house at Johnson which will be used in the reel to be made here in the near future. It is reported that several local cowboys will be used. I.O. Brown was visited recently with the object of obtaining vines and shrubbery for some of the scenes."[95]

Joel McCrea made a series of movies in Kanab including *Union Pacific, Boots and Saddles,* and *Bugles in the Afternoon.* One year he starred in a movie that needed an Indian attack three hundred strong. The movie makers invited all the local Native Americans to participate but still came up short, so several white men from Kanab dressed up for the roles in long black wigs and painted skin. According to the story, they were required to ride their horses bareback, and the plan was for thirty of these riders to fall off their horses when the firing commenced. The Indians lined up along the ridge ready for the attack, including the thirty Indians who would fall according to the script, mixed in with all the others on horseback. The thirty had been offered an extra dollar for falling off their mounts, but before the filming they had talked about the extra money they would receive for their daring. The director called "Action," and the three hundred Indians attacked the wagon train. Then all three hundred reportedly fell off their horses. The scene obviously needed to be refilmed.[96]

Much of the action that accompanied the movie industry centered around the Parry Lodge. The three Parry brothers actively pursued business from the movie industry, even traveling to Hollywood to promote Kanab as a location for filming westerns. Leah Hannah Button remembered working at Parry's Lodge when Lloyd Bridges was on location. Once when she served him, he put his arm around her and put a tip in her pocket.[97] Genieve BlueJacket worked as a waitress during the same time; she remembered being in a scene of *The Green Grass of Wyoming* and often waited on movie stars at the restaurant at Parry's Lodge.[98] Theo McAllister got work as a carpenter building movie sets.[99] David Swapp met both John Wayne and Barbara Stanwyck, whom he considered overly bossy. He preferred being around the roadies and extras.[100]

Jackie Rife remembered how the movies connected Kane County to the world outside. Isolated beforehand, some residents were startled by how different their lives were from those of the outsiders.[101] The movie business helped the local economy weather the Depression, providing an excellent source of revenue for many Kane County residents.

The *Kane County Standard* painted a typical scene as a movie company came into town in 1938 and locals sprang into action:

> This week Kanab is again astir. A large movie company is again located in Kanab with headquarters at the Parry Lodge. Large trucks full of equipment lined the street from the court house to the post office and many cars and busses obstructed the streets east of the Parry Lodge Monday evening. Many local men have been employed to work for the company. The films are being taken for a serial "Wild Bill Hicock." Scenes have been filmed in Johnson canyon, at the "Y" junction in Long Valley, at the Tavern on the Utah-Arizona line and other places. A dam was constructed at the

"Y" by local men early this week, which will be used as a scene in the production.[102]

Also in 1938, a western entitled *The Kanab Kid,* starring Gertrude Messenger and Bob Steele, was filmed in Kane County by Metro-Goldwyn-Meyer. Area resident Jean Crawford portrayed the part of a little girl, and Kanab locals Chauncey and Whitney Parry also acted in the film. The production crew included twenty-seven men and women and several large trucks full of equipment. The movie was filmed near Cave Lakes and in Johnson Canyon. Between fifty and one hundred local residents were hired to play the roles of cowboys and other "western characters." Local cattle herds were featured in the film as well.[103]

In December 1938 Hollywood director Denver Dixon organized an independent film company with fifteen Kanab residents to establish a studio and frontier town "Main Street" set on a more permanent basis. Israel Heaton's farm south of the Kanab cemetery was chosen for the site. Crews began construction almost immediately, anticipating the filming of *The Mormon Conquest,* which was scheduled to commence in the near future.[104] The company was to be called the Security National Picture Corporation, headed by Dixon as president and Guy Chamberlain of Kanab as vice-president.[105] The setting of the "western town" was carefully selected and was described as being "picturesque in every way. The beautiful vermilion cliffs a short distance to the north and east of the studio, which are broken with gaps and large boulders in places, the lower rolling hills and open country to the south furnish variety enough for scenes in several productions."[106] The company staged an opening dance on the new set on 20 January 1939, bringing people from all the surrounding towns together to celebrate.

For a 1939 film based on Walter O. Edmond's popular novel *Drums Along the Mohawk,* published in 1936, the paper reported, "Many men from Kanab and Long Valley recently signed up to do construction work on Cedar mountain for the Twentieth Century Fox company, which will begin filming a $2,000,000 picture in July. It is reported that a stockade, fort, cabins and varied scenes will be built at Sidney Valley, Duck Creek, Navajo Lake." Henry Fonda and

Claudette Colbert co-starred, and the picture employed a reported 2,000 people, many from local towns as well as from Garfield, Iron, and Washington Counties. According to one observer, "The camp which is really a modern tent city, affords practically all the conveniences of home. . . . Quarters for the stars are super-deluxe, tent cabins and have hot and cold running water, private baths, and a modern, sanitary sewage system. Community bath houses have been constructed for use by extra help and are, also, connected with the sewage system, which includes septic tank and sub-surface drainage."[107] In addition, a kitchen serving between 150 and 400 people each meal, complete with refrigeration and sterilization facilities, was constructed on the site. To entertain the crew and extras, "recreation features" were provided in the camp. "A huge recreation tent, provided with benches, screen and projecting machines for moving pictures has been constructed. Several full length features have been shown for entertainment and other features have been presented. A stage has been built and is equipped with foot lights and curtains for legitimate performances," it was reported. Audiences sat on flattened logs arranged in a huge circle around a bonfire in front of the stage.[108]

Many doubtless hoped general better times were coming to the county with the Great Depression finally ending. The expenditure of funds for local internal improvements had been an obvious benefit to the county, particularly during the Depression years. It improved the infrastructure, provided jobs to local residents, and gave new hope to county residents. It was made possible through various government agencies, particularly those of the federal government, and was visionary in its potential impact on the county.

ENDNOTES

1. Richard D. Poll, Thomas G. Alexander, Eugene E. Campbell, and David E. Miller, eds., *Utah's History* (Provo, Utah: Brigham Young University Press, 1978), 690.

2. Allan Kent Powell, ed., *Utah History Encyclopedia*, 432–33.

3. U.S. Bureau of the Census, *Historical Statistics of the United States: Colonial Times to 1957* (Washington, D.C.: Government Printing Office, 1960), 289–90, 297–98.

4. Kane County Commission, Minutes, 18 April 1921, 21 February 1922.

5. Ibid., 18 April 1922.

6. Ibid., 13 November 1922.

7. Ibid., 3 November 1926.

8. Ibid., 18 July 1927.

9. Ibid., 10 November 1928.

10. Ibid., 7 July 1930.

11. Ibid., 4 May 1931.

12. Ibid., 14 November 1930.

13. Ibid., 10 April 1933.

14. *Kane County Standard*, 5 June 1931.

15. "New Kanab Talkie Has Large Crowds," *Kane County Standard*, 19 October 1934.

16. Elsie Chamberlain Carroll, *History of Kane County*, 223.

17. "Shall Kanab Sell Electric Light Plant," *Kane County Standard*, 28 March 1930.

18. "Development Work Inaugurated to Improve Kane County Service," *Kane County Standard*, 9 August 1929.

19. "Telephone Directory Gives Street and No. Of Patrons," *Kane County Standard*, 13 December 1929.

20. "Telephone Co. Building New Line," *Kane County Standard*, 16 April 1937.

21. Kane County Commission, Minutes, 12 November 1934, 9 November 1936.

22. "Mail Route to be Maintained," *Kane County Standard*, 3 October 1930.

23. "Large Meeting Held At Kanab," *Kane County Standard*, 14 March 1930.

24. Robinson, *History of Kane County*, 129.

25. "Railroad Officials Drawing Tentative Plans for Extension of Denver-Pacific to Kanab," *Kane County Standard*, 21 October 1932.

26. United States Bureau of the Census, Reports for 1930 and 1940, various pages.

27. "Observe the Quarantine," *Kane County Standard*, 13 March 1931.

28. "Public Library at Kanab is Closed for Lack of Funds," *Kane County Standard*, 12 January 1934.

29. See "Teachers Ask to Accept Notes," *Kane County Standard*, 19

February 1932, and "Full School Term Assured," *Kane County Standard,* 19 August 1932.

30. "New Hospital Will Be a Big Asset to Kane County People," *Kane County Standard,* 21 June 1935; "New Kanab Hospital Ready for Opening," *Kane County Standard,* 21 February 1936.

31. "Many Patients at Kanab Hospital," *Kane County Standard,* 13 March 1936.

32. "Kane County Aided by CWA Projects," *Kane County Standard,* 19 January 1934.

33. Robinson, *History of Kane County,* 204.

34. "Contract Work Completed," *Kane County Standard,* 14 February 1930.

35. "Road Dedication to be Held in Tunnel," *Kane County Standard,* 23 May 1930.

36. "Arizona to Improve Road to the New Colorado Bridge," *Kane County Standard,* 26 July 1929.

37. "Lee's Ferry Bridge Attracts Travel," *Kane County Standard,* 20 September 1929.

38. "Arizona To Build Road to Utah State Line," *Kane County Standard,* 6 December 1929.

39. "Kanab Road to Cost State Over $100,000," *Kane County Standard,* 14 March 1930.

40. "Road Work Now Open For Bids," *Kane County Standard,* 28 February 1930.

41. "More Than a Million For Roads," *Kane County Standard,* 28 November 1930.

42. "Highway 89 Opens Up Southern Utah," *Kane County Standard,* 16 March 1934.

43. "Nearly $2,000,000 for Southern Utah Roads," *Kane County Standard,* 24 April 1931.

44. See, for example, "Highway 89 Being Re-Capped and Oiled," *Kane County Standard,* 24 July 1931.

45. Kane County Basic Data of Economic Activities and Resources, Utah State Planning Board, 27.

46. "Elbow Dam Project is Nearing Commencement," *Kane County Standard,* 17 September 1937.

47. "Development Work Started on Coal Mine," *Kane County Standard,* 17 July 1931.

48. "Kane Coal Beds Being Developed," *Kane County Standard,* 21 August 1931.

49. See *Kane County Standard*, 15 February 1935.

50. "Cannal Coal Road Being Constructed," *Kane County Standard*, 14 July 1939.

51. "22 Ask for Oil Seeking Rights," *Kane County Standard*, 11 October 1929.

52. "Native Son of Kanab Gains Recognition," *Kane County Standard*, 2 August 1929.

53. "Cattlemen Enter Range Protest," *Kane County Standard*, 18 August 1930.

54. "Kaibab Forest Investigative Committee Report Findings," *Kane County Standard*, 3 July 1931.

55. See Angus M. Woodbury, "A History of Southern Utah and Its National Parks," 207–8; and Linda King Newell and Vivian Linford Talbot, *A History of Garfield County* (Salt Lake City: Utah Historical Society and Garfield County Commission, 1998), 260–68.

56. "National Parks and Their Relation to Developments of Southern Utah," *Kane County Standard*, 2 January 1931.

57. Ibid.

58. Calvin Johnson, interview with Martha Bradley, 13 July 1995, Kanab, Utah, transcript in possession of author.

59. Verla Lewis, interview with Angie Lewis, 15 February 1992, Kanab, Utah.

60. Kane County Basic Data of Economic Activities and Resources, Utah State Planning Board, 1967, 6.

61. Johnson, interview.

62. "Kaibab Forest Grazing Study is Promised," *Kane County Standard*, 3 August 1934.

63. "Advisory Committee Meet on Cattle Relief," *Kane County Standard*, 3 August 1934.

64. "$2,500 to be Issued in Grants to Relieve Livestock Owners," *Kane County Standard*, 19 February 1937.

65. "Stamp Plan Will Be Set Up Here," *Kane County Standard*, 20 December 1940.

66. June Cox Hepworth, "The Oak Grove Farm: History of William M. Cox and His Family," 10, Utah State Historical Society.

67. "Governor to Speak At Two-Day Fiesta," *Kane County Standard*, 23 June 1933.

68. Johnson, interview.

69. "Kanabers May Yet Have Chance to Work on Kaibab," *Kane County Standard*, 23 March 1934.

70. "Kane County Schools to Have Nine Month Term," *Kane County Standard*, 9 March 1934.

71. "Kane County is in Need of More Relief," *Kane County Standard*, 14 September 1934.

72. Utah State Planning Board, "Basic Data of Economic Activities and Resources," 1934.

73. "Kanab Gets Two New FERA Projects," *Kane County Standard*, 19 October 1934.

74. See *Kane County Standard*, 10 May 1935, 24 May 1935.

75. See *Kane County Standard*, 12 July 1935.

76. "Kanab is Assured Improved Highway," *Kane County Standard*, 19 November 1937.

77. Genieve Millet Cutler BlueJacket, interview with Buddy Millett, 5 May 1993, Kanab, Utah.

78. "FERA Estimates Kane County Needy," *Kane County Standard*, 13 July 1934.

79. "Kanab Free Public Library Now Open," *Kane County Standard*, 28 January 1934.

80. "Women's County CWA Committee Begins Work," *Kane County Standard*, 29 December 1933.

81. "Use Local National Reemployment Office," *Kane County Standard*, 13 July 1934.

82. *Kane County Standard*, 18 October 1935, 13 December 1935.

83. "Kane County Schools to Get $6,000 WPA Funds," *Kane County Standard*, 22 May 1936.

84. "Kane County Derives Much Good From Government Relief Funds," *Kane County Standard*, 2 July 1937.

85. "Kanab to Have a New Hotel," *Kane County Standard*, 27 March 1931.

86. "Kane County is Coming into Her Own, Via Scenery," *Kane County Standard*, 21 June 1935.

87. "Kanab As Tourist Headquarters Boosted in Arizona Scenic Magazine," *Kane County Standard*, 10 September 1937.

88. Ibid.

89. "Kanabers Enjoy Radio Program," *Kane County Standard*, 18 February 1938.

90. "Tourist Count Shows Many Traveling '89' Through Nation's Scenic Area," *Kane County Standard*, 4 August 1939.

91. See Robinson, *History of Kane County*, 99–108, 177–83.

92. "Movie Scenes Are Taken Near Kanab," *Kane County Standard*, 27 August 1937. The film *Bad Man of Brimstone* was shown to "large and appreciative" Kane County audiences 9, 10, and 11 January 1938 according to the 14 January 1938 issue of the *Kane County Standard*.

93. "Movie Company Employs Many," *Kane County Standard*, 9 June 1939.

94. Dennis Judd, interview with Martha Bradley, 10 July 1995, Kanab, Utah.

95. "House to Be Used in Talkie Will be Built at Johnson, Utah," *Kane County Standard*, 10 August 1934.

96. Judd, interview.

97. Leah Hannah Button, interview with Jeremy Button, 5 May 1992, Kanab, Utah.

98. BlueJacket, interview.

99. Theo McAllister, interview with Rob Smith, 13 May 1993, Kanab, Utah.

100. David Swapp, interview with Jeremy Free, 6 May 1993, Kanab, Utah.

101. Jackie Rife, interview.

102. "Moving Picture Co. Taking Scenes Here," *Kane County Standard*, 3 June 1938.

103. "'Kanab Kid' Title of New Scenario," *Kane County Standard*, 30 September 1938.

104. "Movie Company Organized Here," *Kane County Standard*, 9 December 1938.

105. "Local Men Start New Industry in Kane County," *Kane County Standard*, 23 December 1938.

106. "Gathering Data For New Movie Film," *Kane County Standard*, 20 January 1939.

107. "Movie Group Expects to Complete Outdoor Shots for Picture This Week," *Kane County Standard*, 28 July 1939.

108. Ibid.

CHAPTER 10

WORLD WAR II AND LATER DEVELOPMENTS, 1940–1960

It has always been true in Kane County's history that using the resources of the land has been seen as the means of economic survival. Particularly after World War II, however, the natural scenic beauties and wonders of the area were increasingly touted in order to draw visitors to the area. Tourism increasingly yielded significant revenues for local businesses, and locals have increasingly attempted to provide goods and services to tourists drawn to the region by its natural scenic wonders.

By the end of the first half of the twentieth century, trends in Kane County's economy had been firmly established: a declining emphasis on cattle raising and agriculture because of declining prices and increased competition in the national marketplace, a new interest in developing mining and oil exploration, and an emphasis on encouraging tourism to bring business to the area. The September 1940 issue of *National Geographic* magazine featured Kane County in fifty-eight pages of photographs and text that brought the area's beauty's to the attention of the world.

The building of Hoover Dam in the 1930s was of significance to

Kane County because it stimulated interest in the Grand Canyon and, more particularly, in river travel. River running became yet another tourist activity in the 1940s after Haldane "Buzz" Holmstrom's solo journey down the Grand Canyon. Soon recreational river runners were exploring and enjoying all the region's rivers, including the Colorado River at lovely Glen Canyon on Kane County's eastern border.

The Kanab Lions Club helped promote the county's attractions, publishing in 1941 a pamphlet complete with maps, descriptions of favored sites, and general information. It began,

> Each summer 100,000 tourists from every state in the Union make Kanab, Utah, their headquarters while visiting the Parks in Scenic Southern Utah and Northern Arizona. A typical western Mormon town of 1500 people, Kanab is located four miles north of the Arizona line at the foot of Vermillion Cliffs on U.S. 89. At an elevation of 5,000 feet, it lies in the Heart of the Canyon Country, only 90 minutes drive from the Grand Canyon, Bryce Canyon or Zion Park. It is the center of a large livestock and range district, where sights and the romance of the Old West still lives.[1]

Some New Deal programs continued until early 1942 and the outbreak of World War II. The Agricultural Adjustment Administration (AAA) funded eleven projects that benefited farmers and ranchers during 1941 under the direction of the Kane County range examiner, although not all were popular since some mandated restrictions in numbers of animals grazed or limited grazing areas in order to help restore the severely overgrazed land. During that growing season, grazing was not allowed on 12,493 acres of rangeland, 527 pounds of seed were planted on 176 acres of depleted rangeland, and 400 acres of sagebrush terrain was cleared and planted with vegetation more desirable to local stock raisers. To prevent erosion and help control potential floods, three spreader dams were built which put riprap on eroding gullies and contoured twelve acres of rangeland. These projects also were designed to help provide water for livestock. In addition, fences were built to facilitate handling of stock on the range—1,102 rods of net fence, 540 rods of barbed wire, and fourteen rods of wooden-pole fence were built in the county in 1941.[2]

The U.S. Fish and Wildlife Service attempted to serve some interests of local cattlemen, trapping and killing "predators" and removing them from rangeland. In 1941, the agency reported trapping a total of 1,044 coyotes, bobcats, mountain lions, and bear in the region. Wolves had long been eliminated from the area. According to Edward Rasmussen, assistant district agent, coyotes posed the biggest problem to ranchers.[3]

World War II

World War II finally pulled America out of the Depression, although many of the New Deal programs had helped. Many of the world's difficulties that created the backdrop for the war were connected to the economic depression that had spread across much of the world. Poor economic conditions helped give rise to German and Japanese militarism. The German people rallied to Hitler's call to arms because they believed he could make better lives for them. The Japanese justified their movement into Manchuria with the prediction that it would improve economic conditions in Japan.

War certainly impacted the lives of those who served and their families. Responding to a request from local unions to utilize courthouse rooms for public meetings, the Kane County Commission voted in December 1940 to "let Union meetings be held in court rooms providing that no smoking be allowed in the building either in the rooms or halls."[4]

Many residents remembered initially being afraid of Japanese attack. Civil defense preparations, air raid drills, and blackouts were practiced. Christmas lighting was forbidden outdoors during the war years, and local civilian defense groups were organized in each town. Of course, families whose sons and daughters served in the war felt a personal loss and concern. Lester Y. Johnson reported that during the war the government restricted the number of LDS missionaries allowed draft deferments.[5]

The county experienced a reduction in tourism after the bombing of Pearl Harbor; out of a total of thirteen gas stations in the county, only eight remained open during the first year of the war. Shortages of rubber and the subsequent rationing of tires for motor vehicles were national programs that impacted the ability of tourists to travel the distances required to come to the area's national parks.

During this slump, the Parry Lodge in Kanab closed its dining room and only rented cabins.[6]

The Kanab hospital generally remained open during the war, serving Kane County residents and patients from northern Arizona. In 1941, Dr. G.R. Aiken, perhaps tired from running the hospital on his own, solicited help from community organizations. A group of representatives from the Kanab Lions Club, county commission, city council, and Kanab LDS Stake met to discuss alternative ways of running the hospital as either a community or county project. The hospital was strained because of limited funds in 1942, closing for a time; it reportedly had to dismiss most of its staff to stay open.[7] The county purchased the hospital from Aiken in March 1943 for $15,000. This price included the grounds, the buildings, and the equipment.

The War Manpower Board's procurement and assignment service informed Dr. Aiken at the hospital that doctors would not be taken into the armed services if they were still needed in local communities. The attempt was made, however, to train high school students as nurses' aides to help the hospital increase its efficiency.[8] Ironically, however, Aiken himself enlisted and left for the Puget Sound Naval Yard in February 1943 as a lieutenant commander in the Navy Medical Corps.[9] Although Dr. Aiken had decided to discontinue practicing in Kanab, other doctors were considering coming to Kanab and working at the hospital. Marvel Moffit was appointed public health nurse for the county to provide additional health services in 1944.[10]

Jackie Rife was seven years old when World War II began. The patriotism that marked the war years was unparalleled in her experience. All the people sacrificed; for example, they would wear their shoes only when they needed to, and they even saved the tinfoil from gum wrappers.[11] People pulled together, raising large victory gardens. "I remember, I had to weed them," Rife said. She also remembered the war-related telegrams that came to area families. Her father went to the induction center three times, but she reported that officials wouldn't let him enlist because of health problems. It was a difficult time. Patriotism began in school with the Pledge of Allegiance, and prayer was routine. Calvin Johnson remembered how few men were around; the town was just "naked," he said. The community joined together for dances and other activities to keep up their morale.

Part of the war effort was seen as making a special effort to improve conditions in towns and cities. Dr. George R. Aiken, Kanab's mayor in 1942, issued a proclamation which read in part:

> Whereas, throughout the state a special effort is being put forth for a general clean-up, paint-up, fix-up and beautification endeavor in the name of the cleaner communities within the state to aid the war effort, and
>
> Whereas, in protection of health and happiness of citizenry and detraction from the possible beauty and inviting appearance of the community, it is desired that the citizens of Kanab remove any debris and rubbish, which has accumulated during the winter months, and
>
> Whereas, in compliance with what is conceded to be the wishes of practically all citizens and in furtherance of an established custom, in cooperation with local and State Board of Health; and that weather conditions are seemingly favorable to a successful removal and disposal of such debris, tin cans and rubbish, as well as to a general repairing and beautification campaign . . .

Aiken designated the week of 27 April to 2 May a special clean-up period for Kanab City, "to instill in the minds of everyone the spirit of the necessity of a clean, healthful, beautiful and attractive community."[12]

A local newspaper article hinted at tension that existed just beneath the surface during the war years. The article, headlined "Former Kanab Citizen Under FBI Investigation," said, "Dr. William H. Taylor left Kanab about Sept. 4, 1943. On September 10, a few days later a special agent from the Federal Bureau of Investigation was here looking up his record. It seems Dr. Taylor is wanted for subversive activities. His sympathies were with the Nazis."[13] It is not known if the allegations were true, but conservative rural Utah could shelter such people without them raising undue suspicion for many of their beliefs. Still, patriotism appealed to most; nativism and bigotry might occasionally surface, but they did so usually under the guise of patriotism. In a rather extraordinary but telling editorial in the *Kane County Standard* dated 27 March 1941, editor Burnham Ford expressed his outrage as well as his racial and political biases. Referring to the establishment of relocation camps for Japanese-Americans from the West Coast, it read in part:

> It was expressed in last week's issue of the Standard that Kane county definitely did not want any of the yellow Japs migrated, settled or employed in its communities. This question is right now of such strategic importance to the future standard and wellbeing of our county, our communities and our homes that a great many of our progressive citizens have asked publication of such an article, expressing our views as a people, to uphold our standards of living and protect our heritage, our county, our homes and our loved ones from being over run and paluted [sic] by the migration, penetration, infiltration of the yellow Japs into our country.
>
> With great respect we honor the heritage our fathers and our forefathers gave unto us, by the grace of God. Never, have the records shown that Kane county has ever had a Japanese resident.
>
> The people of Kane County are, and always have been, high in morale [sic] standards, clean morally and spiritually, always devoted to the care and wellbeing of their homes and families, with ever a ready hand to help their neighbor and fellowmen. These qualities and standards are not a thing of chance, they are inherited qualities that have been handed down from generation to generation. And these qualities we intend to protect.
>
> If you don't think that heritage counts, did you ever stop to think that the only reason you don't kiss cows and worship snakes is because your mother and father were not Hindu and that you were not born on the banks of the Bramin River. And the only reason that you are not a rattle snake is because your parents were not rattle snakes. If your ancestors had been rattle snakes you too would have been a rattle snake, and nothing but the hand of God could ever change you.[14]

While one can perhaps hope this was an exaggerated viewpoint, even more inflammatory sections could also be found in the editorial, which does show a provincialism and lack of cultural understanding.

This attitude actually became public policy during the war years. Kane County Sheriff George Swapp pledged his support in April 1942 to cooperate with the highway patrol to stop "Japs" at Kane

County borders, with the exception of those Japanese-Americans who had "government permits to farther destinations," who then would be escorted through the county and safely delivered elsewhere. "Signs will be posted on the three main highways at the county line to the effect of notifying all transits, that no Japs are allowed in Kane County," Swapp reported, continuing, "Rumors that three or four Jap families were due to arrive in Kane county very soon caused feelings to run high throughout the county and a special meeting was called Wednesday to protect Kane county from any form of Jap exploit." Swapp claimed that Governor Maw had expressed his support of their efforts to "protect themselves."[15]

Not all residents favored such expressions of bigotry. Soon after one such sign was posted between Kanab and Fredonia, it disappeared; the "vandals" were never apprehended and it can be assumed that they represented many who had more tolerant feelings for their fellow citizens and other human beings. Americans in general have much to look back in shame upon at their attitudes during these years, particularly in the establishment of relocation camps for Japanese-Americans from the West Coast.

The Kanab newspaper also reported on personal disasters during the war as at other times, such as a fire that destroyed Glen Johnson's sawmill and burned seven square miles of forest timber in 1942.[16] Kaibab lead mines, located near Jacob Lake, Arizona, forty miles south of Kanab, produced 115 tons of ore for use in the production of war products during 1944. The ore was delivered to Marysvale, 165 miles to the north, for shipment by rail from there to defense plants.[17] This was one example of the benefits county residents felt from increased markets for local raw materials during the war years; the increased demand for agricultural products was another.

The human cost of war was profoundly felt in rural Utah communities, as elsewhere. On 15 July 1945 a dual funeral was held for Private Winsor A. Asay and Sergeant Deveroux W. Bowman, both of Kanab. Asay, twenty-five years old, was killed in action after just a year in the armed services. Bowman, a graduate of Kanab High School, had been in the army since October 1943 and died in a German prisoner of war camp after his airplane was shot down over enemy territory. Locals J.L. Bybee and Mardeane, Delenna, and Lyle McDonald participated in the memorial service.[18]

Residents of Kane County celebrated the end of the war in August 1945 along with others throughout the nation and much of the world. In 1945 the Office of Price Administration (OPA) began to try to make the transition to peacetime without causing inflationary pressures, as shortages during the war period began to ease. Its program would increase supplies of reasonably priced essential goods, trying in the process to protect both manufacturers and consumers. In the euphoria of the early postwar period, however, most chafed under any restrictions; and those in Kane County, like their fellow citizens nationwide, looked to a future of unbridled prosperity after the trials of the Depression and war years.[19]

After the war years, life in Kane County began to return to normal routines. Kanab's schools, for example, had a full roster of teachers and a total enrollment of 351 students in 1947; 175 students were at the high school. Several new high school teachers had joined the faculty; they included Claude Y. Lundquist, C. Duffin Pugh, and David Q. Gates.[20]

In October 1947 some Kane County women organized a local unit of the Utah Federated Republican Women's Club, with Vera Swapp as president, Helene McAllister vice-president, and Amanda Robb secretary and treasurer. When first organized, the group included twenty women, who decided to hold six meetings a year in a room in the courthouse. According to the newspaper account, the purpose of the club was to "further republican standards, and ideals, to become an active part of the national organization." Yet it was also reported that all meetings were open to both Democratic and Republican party members alike, "in order to do the most good for the community."[21] The Kanab Women's Business and Professional Club donated a public drinking fountain to Kanab City that was to be located near a corner of Main and Center Streets. The women's club donated the materials and the American Legion and the Lions Club donated the labor to place the fountain.[22]

By 1946 the county was investigating the idea of selling the hospital to a private party, with the condition that the hospital continue to be used as a hospital or revert back to the county.[23] The hospital underwent extensive improvements in January 1949—floors were covered with asphalt tile and the rooms, offices, and operating rooms were painted and redecorated. Several of Kanab's civic organizations raised funds for new kitchen equipment. In January 1949 the women of the American Legion Auxiliary met at the hospital at various times and sewed and repaired hospital linens and made blankets and other badly needed supplies. On Friday, 21 January, men of the Kanab Lions Club spent the evening at the hospital and laid the flooring. The Lady Lions served their husbands sandwiches, cake, and coffee. After the work was done, the groups got together to stage a Hospital Benefit Ball to celebrate the successful effort. A new hospital board was organized on 14 March 1949 in the county commissioners' chamber at the courthouse. The board included N.B. Roundy of Alton, Elsie Brinkerhoff of Glendale, John H. Crofts of Orderville, Rena Talt of Mt. Carmel, Mrs. George Aiken, and Daniel Frost of Kanab.

Kane County Hospital expanded in 1950. Funds were raised in a drive conducted throughout Kane County and northern Arizona. Renovation included a more modern operating room, delivery room, x-ray facility, and emergency room to handle minor cases. At the time, the hospital had ten beds, but that soon would be increased to thirteen with the addition of a small maternity ward.[24]

After World War II and the Korean War the American Legion A. Clair Ford Post held patriotic-oration events, financed local boys and girls to attend Boys and Girls State events, and built an open-air pavilion for Saturday night dances.

Economic and Demographic Profile

In terms of the assessed value of local businesses, in 1945 bus companies were valued at $7,673, power companies at $46,044, telephone companies at $58,552, and mining companies at only $3,280. The Industrial Commission of Utah as part of the Department of Employment Security conducted a study of industry in Kane County in September 1947 that provides a look at economic conditions and trends in the county at mid-century. It studied a total of fifty-two different entities employing local residents in government, agriculture, railroads and transportation, domestic service, and religious and

The Kanab Automobile Garage. (Utah State Historical Society)

non-profit organizations. Of those industries included in the study, the largest number (sixteen) were in wholesale and retail trade, another sixteen were labeled service industries, five were manufacturers, two were construction firms, and three were placed under the category of transportation, communication, and utilities.

Determined to share in the booming tourist industry that developed after World War II, county boosters tried to present their best face to the world while capitalizing on the county's proximity to nearby national parks. Tourism was rapidly overtaking agriculture as the county's economic mainstay. In 1947 there were four hotels and four campgrounds in the county. Other businesses included three beauty or barber shops, two automobile repair shops, two bowling and billiard halls, and three doctor's offices. According to an enumeration based on industries subject to unemployment insurance, of a total of 820 workers in the county in November 1947, 415 worked in agriculture, 405 in non-agricultural jobs, twenty worked for the government, eighty-five in public schools, thirty-one were employed in manufacturing businesses, eight in transportation, eighteen in retail trade, and thirty-seven in service industries.

In 1947 the Daughters of Utah Pioneers helped organize a statewide celebration of the 100-hundred-year anniversary of the arrival of the Mormon pioneers in Utah Territory, instructing local units on ways to commemorate the event. J. Reed Moore, Kane County centennial chair, worked with a committee of representatives from county government, public institutions, and private concerns and individuals. Governor Herbert Maw was invited to head a parade on the morning of 12 June under the direction of the American Legion. At local pageants, county queens were to be chosen to compete in a statewide competition. Competitors had to be at least eighteen years old, a descendent of the pioneers, "be of good character, and have some special talent."[25] Geraldine Judd, who was twenty-one years old, won the Kane County contest; her attendants were Alta and Junice Sorenson.

The local celebration included a historical sketch read by Helen Burgoyne, a string duet by Julia Young and John Burgoyne, a pioneer story read by Adonis Findlay Robinson, and singing of a male chorus directed by Don Moffitt. A trio—Nabbie Mace, Ramona Johnson, and Ruth Roberts—sang, and the local seventh-grade class danced a pioneer dance. John H. Brown played a mandolin solo, and the community joined in singing the Mormon hymn "Come, Come Ye Saints" and "Utah, We Love Thee."

Governor Maw did come to the county for the day's festivities, leading the parade. The American Legion Post 69 sponsored the parade, which included some thirty floats presenting such things as the history of Kane County, the Orderville High School band, and the Kane County centennial royalty. The most amusing entry was a replica of the early Kanab culinary water-delivery system—a barrel mounted on a "water lizard." A program welcoming all to the three-day celebration was given at the town park. Horse racing and other sporting events were staged during the celebration, as was a play, "Angel Street," produced by the Utah Agricultural College, and a light opera presented by University of Utah players. A final banquet held at the Parry Lodge was held after a parade of show horses down Main Street. Later, a fireworks display entertained the celebrants.[26]

In 1950 Kane County's population was 2,299, a drop of 12 percent (about 300 inhabitants) since 1940.[27] Still, the period was marked by building growth in certain parts of the county—Kanab's business district, for example, experienced the construction of a new motel, numerous homes, and a new post office building.[28] In 1958, the *Kane County Standard* under its new name of the *Southern Utah News* reported a population increase of 23.1 percent in a single year.[29] That same year, the Bureau of Economic and Business Research at the University of Utah projected that by 1975 an additional 1,400 people would live in Kane County.[30] Those projections were slightly off, population in 1970 was only 2,421. More than any other single factor, available jobs impacted population totals. It was important to many area residents to find ways to entice young people to stay in the county rather than leave for better jobs and economic security elsewhere. It was also important that the county find new ways to attract outsiders to the area who would bring needed revenue, greater diversity in population, and help reenergize an area that could be considered stagnant or in decline.

The decades after 1950 were years of shifting values, economies, and social systems in the United States. As American families adapted to the post-war world, they found new ways of earning a living, residing in neighborhoods, and relating to the world outside. It was no different for people in Kane County. Because of changing economic conditions it was necessary for Kane County residents to find new ways to survive economically, and in this they proved to be quite resourceful. Increasingly, however, they came to view the federal government as an opponent of sorts as they tried to claim effective control over the public lands in the county. Outside interests—environmentalist groups in particular—also came to play a larger role in local affairs and promoted policies that sought to alter traditional land-use policies, protect wilderness, and oppose the funding of building projects on public lands at taxpayer expense for the benefit of a few—in this case, the ranching, timber, and mining interests in Kane County.

At mid-century, the Kane County Commission included LeGrande C. Heaton, Cecil C. Pugh, Antone R. Hamblin, and Merle V. Adams; D.M. Tietjen was the county clerk. Discussions at that time were underway about a Utah-Arizona power cooperative, to be a subsidiary of the Southwest Power Federation. Dr. George R. Aiken,

Kanab in the 1940s. (Utah State Historical Society)

Maurice Judd, Fred Heaton, Millard Black, and Odell J. Watson were local board members. This utility cooperative initially was to be funded by a $300,000 loan from the federal Rural Electrification Administration.[31]

Kanab

Development of water systems was a constant priority of Kanab City officials. A city reservoir was built in Kanab City in 1948. This 1,000,000-gallon reservoir had concrete foundations and floor and was built by contractor W.E. Thatcher. Fifteen local men were employed on the project.[32] The culinary water supply was increased in 1952 an additional 165 to 200 gallons per minute by the digging of a well in the north end of Three Lakes Canyon. Mayor Daniel S. Frost predicted that the well would bring in a new era of agriculture for the town. The well required one-half mile of pipe to connect it with the existing system, which had yielded 232 gallons of water per minute, an amount that had been insufficient during the peak-usage months of July and August. Until that time, the culinary water source had never been chlorinated because the springs were tapped at their source and cemented.

Because of the population increase in Kanab related to the building of Glen Canyon Dam, a second well was drilled by the city, the

"Big Well," located west of the highway at the top of Three Lakes Canyon. In May 1958, Kanab City hired the engineering firm of Coon and King from Salt Lake City to draw up plans for a new water and sewer system. Until that time, sewage waste had been dumped into Kanab Creek. City voters passed a bond in the amount of $375,000 and city officials applied for a federal loan.[33] They received notification of approval on 8 May 1958. It was estimated that the total project would cost $483,730 and would be funded in part with a federal grant of $51,814 from the Department of Health, Education, and Welfare under the Water Pollution Control Act, and $56,916 from the city itself.[34] Ultimately, all waste water in the system ended up at a modern sewage disposal plant outside town. It was claimed in 1959 to be the only complete disposal system at the time in southern Utah. The new sewage plant prevented polluted water from draining into northern Arizona.[35]

A Volunteer Fireman's Association was formed in Kanab in May 1949 with Locklon Cram as fire chief. The Kanab City Council organized the sixteen-man crew and equipment, which included a three-ton fire truck, 600 feet of fire hose, and smoke masks for the crew.

Orderville

The stately, architecturally eclectic church built at the turn of the century was razed in 1956 when plans were made for the present meetinghouse. A typical red brick, white-trimmed Mormon product, the present church was built in two parts; the recreation hall was constructed first, and the chapel was dedicated in 1959. The 14,898-square-foot complex cost $150,000, half of which was donated. It included a bishop's office, Relief Society room, Junior Sunday School, baptismal font, sixteen classrooms, and storage areas. The brick facade was topped by a squat steeple over the main gable.

Further educational enhancements came when the Valley High School gymnasium was built in 1955 by Chytraus Brothers contractors. In 1958 the building was expanded to include a foyer and music rooms. Ten years earlier, the LDS seminary building, a twenty-four-foot-square cement-block structure, was erected for $3,000 with the help of donated labor.

Twentieth-century Orderville has benefited and grown due to

increases in local industry and tourism. While two regional coal mines, a lime kiln, and area sawmills bolstered the economy, the largest source of income has come to be tourists and road trade along U.S. Highway 89. Orderville had earlier developed lodgings, such as the Palmer Hotel, a turn-of-the-century Victorian inn, for travelers. With the emergence of the automobile came new motels and inns, among them the Orderville Motel, the Valley Motel and Cafe, the Fisher Motel, the Coral Cove Trailer Park, and the Parkway Motel, originally Hattie's Inn.

Orderville features homes from every decade over the last 120 years; its newer houses exhibit Ranch style and split-level designs common to most American cities. Writing in 1959, LeGrande Heaton summarized that,

> There are about eighty homes in the community. They are all wired for electricity, and all but two have modern plumbing facilities. The present homes are built of various kinds of material—lumber, brick, and cement blocks. About twenty-five percent have outside stucco finish. Most of them are painted and are landscaped with lawns, shrubbery and flowers.[36]

Only a few of the earlier outbuildings remain to document the town's agrarian past. To commemorate Orderville's history, the Daughters of Utah Pioneers salvaged stone from the old rock school and erected the Pioneer Memorial Building, a partial replica of the school. A one-story structure with a gable roof and small-pane windows, the hall serves at present as a meeting place and museum. The commercial district at present is small and consists mostly of architecturally nondescript shops and older, remodeled stores.

Mt. Carmel

In 1955 a concrete dam replaced the more makeshift efforts at retaining water and helped provide a more consistent water supply. Newer dwellings in the town are much larger than previous structures and employ Ranch and other more contemporary styles.

Life in the County

Kane County has always been a rural county whose residents' lifestyle has been bound to traditional values and a strong sense of history. Old-timers speak fondly of family outings in Johnson's Canyon; they reference the location of ranches and farmsteads by their proximity to the Vermilion Cliffs or Kanab Creek. The natural landscape and the social landscape form a delicate web of meaning. A sense of place, a sense of being at home in a town or a city or a natural environment, grows as we learn its seasons and rhythms, the way individuals interact. A sense of place is something that is created over time and space and comes in part from the interaction with features of the natural setting or the manmade physical environment. Old-timers interviewed about their youth remembered the time when Kanab's only school was one room and when all area roads were dirt and frequently covered with sand difficult to maneuver in. More recent stories about the motion picture industry abound, photos on the walls of many homes show locals standing shoulder to shoulder with such movie stars as John Wayne, Dean Martin, and Barbara Stanwyck.

The county fair became an increasingly important activity after World War II, bringing together for recreation Kane County's farmers, business people, and families. Traditionally held during the first week in August, the fair included stock exhibits, the display of handicrafts, and a variety of activities. The Kane County Fair was held at Orderville in 1947 and grew to become a countywide activity. First organized by Valley High School's Future Farmers of America Club under the direction of agriculture teacher J. Bryant Anderson, the fair began as a livestock show for young people. Anderson's work was noticed by the Utah Mormon pioneer centennial committee and became part of a plan for future fairs that would combine traditional livestock shows with other recreational activities. Odell Watson, county commissioner and fair chair in 1947, joined with Charles T. Hepworth, mayor of Orderville, Rachel Dalley of Utah State Extension Services, and J. Reed Moore to organize the event.[37]

County residents joined together for a "49ers Celebration" in May 1949 that included a cowboy dinner. Much of the fun took place on the streets, where men, women, and children dressed in "western garb" to join in the festivities. One of the day's highlights was a horse race. The racing committee brought together the best stock horses in the county as well as from northern Arizona. A dance continued long past midnight. Sponsored in part by the Kanab Lions Club, the day was intended to bring the community together. Prizes were given out at the end of the day. The *Kane County Standard* reported:

> For noble and stout-hearted Kanabites who bore those itching beards, prizes will be awarded you at the dance in compensation for your efforts. Whitting Bros. Lumber Co. Will lead off with a ten dollar bill for the best dressed couple. Dan Frost will part with a big, juicy ham for the best adorned face (meaning whiskers). Following are the rest of the prizes for the beards and costumes: Gift Shop, a hand tooled belt; Kanab Equitable, a prize in merchandise; Bahen's, an Arrow Shirt; Virge's Cafe and Bakery, two free meals and three pies; Bunting Market, five dollars in groceries. Fenton's Pharmacy is giving a Parker pen for the most sparse beard and Whit Parry is offering two meals at his dining room (less desert) to the second best couple. Other prizes have been promised but it has not been indicated just exactly what they will be.[38]

In 1950 the county fair featured a dance held at the American Legion pavilion, with local orchestra the Moonlight Serenaders playing long into the night. The highlight of the night's activities was the selection of Miss Kane County. The *Standard* promoted the event: "These lovely girls will parade and dance for your approval and the approval of the imported judges. The winner will reign over the Fair at Orderville the following day and will be presented with an inscribed watch. The Fair Committee is expecting a huge turnout of all Kane County—plan to be there."[39]

The fair began with a flag ceremony. The day's activities included films "depicting farm, home and traffic safety," wildlife and national parks, agriculture, homemaking, and comedies. There was judging of the county's finest livestock, produce, and poultry, and youth groups such as the 4-H Club displayed their entries. The day ended with a barbeque and outdoor talent show.

The area was profoundly affected by the nuclear testing in Nevada beginning in the 1950s. Many remember being able to see the lights of the tests and wondered at their significance. Leah Button recalled that "while we were living down there [a house six miles east of Kanab], we used to get up quite early in the morning to gaze south-westward to watch the Atomic bombs go off at the test site in

Nevada."[40] Most residents were patriotic supporters of the government, which was engaged in an nuclear arms race with the Soviet Union in the midst of the Cold War that lasted from the late 1940s to the late 1980s. They supported the atomic testing program despite some protests against it and warnings that nuclear fallout could be harmful to those in the vicinity of nuclear tests. Only much later did some county "downwinders" begin to question government authorities on the matter and seek redress for ailments and cancer-caused deaths many claimed were related to the atomic testing of the early Cold War.

Kane County's close-knit communities have been described as inclusive, although residents say that it is only those newcomers who try to change things who are considered outsiders, an insider being someone who is respectful of Kane County as it is. The twentieth century's technological, political, and social changes nevertheless have increasingly impacted county residents. Increasing restrictions on the use of public lands have been especially unpleasant to many county residents.

County residents valued their heritage and the hard work of settlement of their forebears. Many, in fact, seemed to feel that they were entitled to special claims on the public lands they and their ancestors had utilized over the years. Clearly life for most in Kane County had never been easy. Men like Jacob Hamblin, John Mangum, and Levi Stewart were strong-willed, robust men who battled to make their mark on the land. Many were also adventurers. For instance, Peter Shirts's settlement on the Paria River was greatly isolated from other whites. Breathtaking vistas in each direction may have helped him and his family endure the difficulty of living in their desert home. The stone remains of his house are quiet testimony to his efforts.

Folktales abound about Shirts, one of which is a story of him plowing the land with a team of Paiute Indians hitched to the plow. Even if exaggerated, such stories indicate not only the resolve of men like Shirts, but early attitudes toward Native Americans. The economic growth that Kane County residents celebrated after World War II brought a greater awareness of the land to other Americans, who began to claim their own input into how the land should be managed. This and increased global market economics threatened the traditional extractive uses of the land.

Besides the numerous businesses established earlier in the century, new organizations started up after 1950. For example, Lowell M. and Zelma J. Johnson started the Kanab Construction and Lumber Company in the early 1950s. Also in the 1950s, Boyd Y. and LaVerde P. McAllister began a sand-and-gravel plant in Kanab. Dan M. Ogden started a similar business—the Herring Ready-Mix plant—along U.S. Highway 89. The Salt Lake branch of Dun and Bradstreet financial services reported in 1955 on the financial well-being of Kanab's business scene. "There are 4 more business concerns in Kanab today than there were four years ago," said D.E. Smith, district manager. This brought the total number of businesses up to fifty-two from the forty-eight reported in 1953.[41]

In 1940 Southern Utah Power Company extended power to Fredonia, Arizona. In July 1941 the company was able to reduce rates for business customers.[42] The company added new generating units in 1933, 1940, 1947, and 1952. In 1947 a 360-horsepower diesel electric generating unit was installed in the power house of the company's building in Kanab. Local distribution was enlarged and improved with the addition of new transformers at this time as well.[43] Kanab resident Elgin H. Morris managed the plant between 1934 and 1954.

Southwest Utah Power Federation purchased Southern Utah Power Company in August 1949 and promised new transmission lines, a new generator plant, and the extension of power lines to Moccasin, Cane Beds, Hurricane, Short Creek, and Johnson. The officers of the Southwest Utah Power Federation included Gronway Parry, mayor of Cedar City and president of the company; Wilford Brooksby of Fredonia; George R. Aiken and Odell Watson of Kanab; Millard Black of Cane Beds; and Fred C. Heaton of Moccasin.[44] By 1952, 449 local customers were using 1.3 million kilowatt hours of electrical power. Electricity was supplied to different areas of the county by Garkane Power Association and Southern Utah Power Company, which installed a new unit in its Kanab plant in October 1956. Earlier, the plant had a capacity to service a population of up

The Kanab Fire Department in August 1952. (Kane County News)

to 3,000 individuals. The addition gave it more than ten times the capacity it had when it was purchased from Kanab City in 1933.

Southern Utah Power merged with California-Pacific Utilities Company on 19 June 1958. The former president of Southern Utah Power, Warren H. Bullock, was installed on the board of directors of the new company and all employees continued to work for the new entity. The company supplied electricity to Cedar City, Kanab,

Hurricane, Enterprise, and a number of small communities near Zion National Park.[45]

Despite improvements in facilities and transportation, Kane County at mid-century was still a place apart—isolated by a rugged natural environment. For many this was the principal draw to the area—here was a place that felt untouched, raw, and boldly primitive, different from almost anything they could see anywhere else. After 1950, tourists came to the Kane County region in increasing numbers, drawn by the rugged plateau and canyon lands, rock formations, and the vibrant hues and textures of the natural environment.

Kane County entrepreneurs and boosters were anxious to take advantage of the influx of visitors, and new businesses related to the tourist industry are an important part of the story of the economic development of the county during the second half of the twentieth century. In the spring of 1957, it seemed that a business boom reflecting tourism was beginning in Kanab. New construction for businesses included two new service stations. Outside of town, a trailer court was being constructed by Kenyon Little on Johnson Road. Also, the Roman Catholic church had purchased land near Main Street for a new church.[46]

Part of the boom was due to the construction of Glen Canyon Dam, which officially began in 1956. In fact, a new city—Glen Canyon City—was built during the late 1950s near the Glen Canyon dam site. The town was located fourteen miles from the dam and seven miles from the Utah-Arizona border. The small town included residential areas, trailer lots, commercial zones, public playgrounds, an area for churches and schools, and a section for future industrial development. In 1957, internal improvements included four wells for water, a commercial well, and electric power relayed from Henrieville until the dam began its own production of power.[47]

County commissioners managed county business and supervised county officers and departments. For instance, on 10 June 1957, the commission took up the problem of increased traffic due to development of Glen Canyon Dam, reporting that any buildings erected along or near highways in Kane County must be approved by the Kane County Commission.[48] In some ways this could be considered the beginning of centralized planning of development in Kane

County. The salaries listed in the commission minutes in 1957 provide insight into the positions. County commissioners Cecil C. Pugh, Burton Banks, and Clark F. Swapp received $2,000 annually for their part-time duties, the county assessor was paid $3,000, the county attorney, $1,800, the full-time county sheriff earned $12,000, the county recorder and the county clerk each received $4,000.

Issues faced by county commissioners were usually local in their nature—weed control, supervision of the tourist visitor's center in Kanab, animal control, disposal of waste, and increasing crime—although the latter was generally of a minor nature. In 1958, for example, law enforcement officers and school, church, and community leaders held a series of meetings throughout the county to discuss increased crimes among young people and others, as well as the general observance of the law. According to the newspaper: "Heading the list of problems are at least two places of business which are not governing their establishments in controlling juveniles in smoking in public and not observing the curfew hour."[49] In June 1959 an inquiry into complaints of illegal sale of liquor, gambling, prostitution, and the failure of public officials to enforce the law was begun at the Kane County Courthouse.

In 1958 a Salt Lake City corporation, Tourists Enterprises, announced a $800,000 investment in a development and in regional bus tours. The facility was planned to include a dude ranch, motel, nine-hole golf course and club house, tennis courts, cafe, photo shop, and sound stages for movie companies. President S. Wayne Clark said the company planned to capitalize on the tourist boom as well as the continuing interest in the area as a scene for motion pictures. The 393 acres of land purchased for the development was located on Johnson Road.[50] Tourists Enterprises hired the Hogan and Tingey construction company of Centerville to construct its motel. By February 1960, however, the ambitious project had been reevaluated and put on hold.

Agriculture

The Bureau of the Census report for 1945 categorized farming in the county. Of a total of 155 farms, one produced a specialty crop, fifteen others harvested a variety of crops for sale, nineteen were dairy farms, two were poultry enterprises, eighty-three were livestock ranches, and twenty-seven were simply subsistence farms. In terms of total acreage, the largest category of 1,000 acres or more included thirty-eight farms; eleven farms each were found in three categories: 260–379 acres, 380–499 acres, and 500–699 acres. Twelve farms had between three and nine acres; fifteen farms were thirty to forty-nine acres in size. Other categories included from three to ten farms each.

Assessed value of property in the county in 1945 according to Utah State Tax Commission reports was $1,684,285. Of that, $799,166 represented real estate, including $22,372 in improved dry-farm land, $141,575 in improved irrigated farmland, and $1,286 in unimproved farmland. Grazing land represented another $518,362 in value, and land in towns was valued at $99,565. Improvements on town land were valued at $312,085. Range cattle were by far the most valuable farm product—listed in 1945 at $117,638. Other livestock—including horses, mules, sheep, pigs and poultry—brought the total value of livestock to $237,129.[51]

The Guy Chamberlain dairy began production of pasturized milk in July 1947 with new equipment that brought the dairy in compliance with state grade A regulations. The pasteurization process involved the movement of milk from the cow immediately into the pasteurizer and then to the cooler. It was then poured into bottles and capped—all by machinery. Many local dairy farmers sold their milk directly to Chamberlain's dairy, where it was pasturized and distributed for sale. The dairy expanded in 1950 after three years in business, installing new equipment—a cottage cheese machine, a buttermilk machine, and a cooler for raw milk. State inspector Lyman Willardson said that "Kanab and area served by the dairy were fortunate in having such an up-to-date plant and as modern as any in the state."[52] The dairy served the entire county and several communities in northern Arizona.

In 1950, Kane County and neighboring Garfield County were suffering from the consequences of a drought in the fall of 1949. The Panguitch office of the Farmers Home Administration had designated the region as a disaster area, which opened up the availability of federal loans for local farmers and livestock raisers who were in financial trouble.[53] Three years later, severe drought conditions again brought emergency aid to Kane County stockmen and farmers. Normal rainfall in the area was scarcely enough to sustain crops, but between 1952 and 1953 the county received only 2.55 inches of rain, and area rangeland was producing much less feed than normal.[54] By 1957, however, Kanab received more moisture than it had at any other time in the past fifty years. Welcoming the end of the long severe dry spell, cattlemen adjusted to the extremes of the environment.[55]

Natural Resources

The water users of Kane County met regularly in the late 1940s to decide how best to use appropriations from the state legislature to develop and improve small irrigation projects and power resources. The county's Water Uses and Power Board was organized in June 1947 with Preston Bunting as president, Lawrence Esplin as vice-president, and Reed Moore as secretary. Henry Carroll, Dee Roundy, and the county commissioners were the directors of the group.[56] Discussion about a Glen Canyon Dam project also began during this time. The hydroelectric dam would be one of twenty-three proposed power projects affecting Utah, but the only one directly impacting Kane County. Federal Power Commission surveys suggested that the Glen Canyon Reservoir would have a capacity to generate 618,000 kilowatts of electricity, have a level 408 feet above the streambed, and hold some 8,600,000 acre-feet of water. The local newspaper later reported that "the storage capacity at Glen Canyon site is enormous and that proposals have been made for a reservoir with a total capacity of 50,000,000 acre feet."[57]

The Glen Canyon Dam was recognized for its great potential in creating a recreational playground for southern Utah. Commissioners Merrill MacDonald and William J. Smirl and local stockman Floyd Maddox visited the proposed site in February 1954. According to Commissioner Smirl, however, it was no recreational playground at the time:

> Huge monuments of rock rise for hundreds of feet into the dry desert air, and rival the mammoth pinnacles found across the Colorado River in Monument Valley, . . . The area is still one of the most primitive and least known in the United States and should be

traveled at present only by those having proper desert equipment and knowledge of the region.[58]

The lumber industry was a major economic factor locally during the period. Hundreds of Kane County men were employed by the Kaibab Lumber Company mill that was located just below Fredonia and was operated in the 1940s by brothers A. Milton and Jay Whiting of Holbrook, Arizona. Other local men worked for other logging companies or milling operations in the area. J.L. Bybee set up a sawmill in 1943 at the north end of Kanab. He sold the business to Jack Mognett and Glenn Johnson the next year. During the years they ran the mill, the two men improved operations until they sold in 1947 to Rowley Brothers, who moved the machinery to the north fork of the Virgin River.

Kane County residents gradually realized the value of the prudent harvest of timber from both public and private forested lands in the county, although aggressive lumbering practices did necessitate increased federal protection of the area's resources. What had earlier been a small timber harvesting operation in Kane County began to provide timber to national markets in the 1940s. The Kaibab Lumber Company sawmill in Fredonia, Arizona, became a year-round employer of area men in 1954. In the 1950s this mill was producing about 100,000 board feet of lumber per shift.

The history of the area's lumber industry has been closely linked with changing policies of the U.S. Forest Service toward timber cutting. The Kaibab National Forest is located in Arizona, but forested areas of the Kaibab Plateau spill over into Kane County. The forest contains a large amount of ponderosa pine that was historically inaccessible, limiting lumbering in the area. In the twentieth century, the Forest Service developed programs to induce lumber manufacturers to establish modern mills to cut timber logged in the Kaibab. It spent more than $500,000 on timber access roads, facilitating the transportation of Kaibab timber to the Fredonia mill. The mill itself

Opposite: A rafter on the Colorado River in Glen Canyon in 1942. (Utah State Historical Society)

received national attention and was often visited by lumber representatives from companies across the country.[59]

Lumbering was big business in the region. The Forest Service announced that a timber sale of about 125 million board feet was scheduled for the Kaibab National Forest in 1950. This news was received enthusiastically locally and was applauded by most residents for the potential economic benefit it could bring to the county. "Letting of bids for the new and enlarged timber cut will be the first large scale attempt to selectively manage the world's largest known stand of virgin ponderous pine—[the] stand is estimated at four billion feet. Bids will be let that, through section cutting, the entire forest will have been cut over once in a period of twenty years," according to one Forest Service official.[60] Although such a large-scale harvesting of virgin old-growth timber would be condemned and opposed by many in later years, at the time there was little organized opposition, and agencies like the Forest Service were seen as cooperative partners and facilitators of private economic interests. This expansion of timber harvesting meant additional employment, the building of new roads in the county to better access forest land, and greater traffic through the area—all of which in turn would mean more revenue for local businesses.

In 1950 the Kaibab Lumber Company successfully competed for a contract to cut 168 million feet in the Big Saddle Unit, about thirty-five miles south of Fredonia in the Kaibab Forest.[61] In 1953 Croft's Lumber Company of Orderville was awarded a contract to cut 3 million board feet of Western yellow pine saw timber on a 2,500-acre tract in the Strawberry Knolls district of the the Dixie National Forest.[62] The Kaibab Lumber Company, with five different lumber operations, centralized its operations in Flagstaff in February 1957. Two years later, Kaibab sales reached 100 million board feet and the company had seven full-time salesmen who worked the western region.[63]

After World War II, attempts proceeded to identify new sources of revenue for county residents, including continual investigation of the area's mineral, oil, and coal reserves. The Smirl-Alton coal mines reported an "impressive output" during the busy winter months at the mine in 1949, extracting an average of forty tons daily. The mine was worked from a central shaft, ore taken from underground rooms.[64] The Carter Oil Company was exploring in the county at the time for possible drilling sites.[65] A uranium strike was recorded that same year thirteen miles from Kanab at Navajo Gap; M.E. Noel and E.W. Ford claimed an area of 1,000 feet of exposed uranium.[66] The claim set off a rush on land nearby, some claims reportedly yielding rich deposits. These reports were often exaggerated in the uranium frenzy, and Kane County never became a major source of uranium in subsequent years.

In October 1953 a report from the oil industry suggested that the Kanab Basin was land with great potential for the extraction of oil and gas. The Valen Oil and Gas Company, with offices in Fredonia, Arizona, was one of the largest holding companies in the area. Company president Van D. Bennett said that the company was continuing its leasing program from the federal government and "will have exploratory drilling rigs in the area in a matter of a few months." He said that each test well would cost from $150,000 to $250,000 and that it would take at least five wells to conclusively test the area.[67] Drilling at the Byrd Oil Company well in eastern Kane County had progressed to a depth of 5,226 feet in October 1953; but it had yielded no oil by the time it had reached a depth of 10,000 feet.[68] The Great Western Drilling Company was drilling to depths of around 7,000 feet in Reese Canyon about three miles south. This well encountered oil saturation at a depth of approximately 6,430 feet. This find was particularly significant because of the geological conditions of the Kanab-Fredonia Basin. According to one geologist, if "structural geological traps are determined in this area [it follows] that commercial oil production is highly probable where these formations are found at a much shallower depth than in the wells mentioned above."[69]

By March 1954 the focus was on uranium deposits, and, according to the *Southern Utah News,* claims were being staked by the hundreds in the county. Most of the filings were east of Kanab, starting at Johnson Gap and extending over to the Paria River country.[70] In June 1954, *Time* magazine featured a story about a murder committed in Kane County during the uranium-craze years. Sixty-two-year-old Leroy Albert Wilson was an excommunicated Mormon and "leader of a strange band of men and women," according to *Time*. He was found dead on a slope outside of Kanab with six .45 caliber bullets in his back and head, his Geiger counter in hand. Founder of a small colony called "Veyo" 100 miles northwest of Kanab, he was a large and imposing man, considered by some as being belligerent and crude. Kane County Sheriff Mason Meeks explained the occurrence as an inevitable result of the greed that drove this new version of the "gold rush." He was quoted by the newspaper: "Terrible thing it was. Many a man was murdered in cold blood because of it. Well, we got a new one now, uranium fever, and as long as the fever lasts and people keep on claimin' everything in sight and them outside promoters keep swarmin' in here with their big-money offers, there's bad trouble ahead."[71] By June 1954, 1,850 filings of location notices had been submitted to the county. House Rock Valley was described as a particularly "hot" area for claims. Residents from the nearby haven for polygamists of Short Creek, Arizona, including Roy Johnson, Orval Johnson, Lewis Barlow, Edwin Jessop, filed more than one hundred claims in that area alone.[72]

During the Boyle's Company uranium drilling activities east of Kanab in April 1955 near the Von Hake and Foote Hamblin ranches, an artesian well was discovered at a depth of 150 feet. Water initially sprayed twenty feet into the air, creating a natural fountain and attracting excited visitors from nearby towns. The newspaper focused on the value of this water—perhaps the most scarce and critical commodity for living in the area—rather than on the potential of discovering more uranium.

The Drilling Company was originally drilling for uranium, but for now most of the local people have forgotten about uranium in favor of a more valuable resource for this area—water. This undoubtedly will start some extensive drilling by ranchers in that area, and some have already made preliminary investigations into it. With water being so important to this area it is hoped that these wells along with others that might be drilled will yield a great amount of water for our thirsty land to drink up.[73]

The Kanab Uranium Corporation, a penny-stock firm created during the wild and little-regulated era, hit a natural gas deposit in May that same year in Grand County, again during a search for uranium. It was estimated that the well would produce from 4–6 million cubic feet of natural gas a day from the Morrison Formation, located at a depth of about 3,260 feet, and additional gas from the Dakota section at around 3,177 feet, for a total potential of some 8 million cubic feet of natural gas daily.[74]

An incidental effect of the uranium boom was that the number of part-time prospectors for wealth created labor shortages in southern Utah. A report issued by the Agricultural Marketing Service, the Utah Extension Service, and others suggested that many local workers had been "absorbed by uranium mining activities" rather than helping harvest farm crops.[75]

Oil drilling continued throughout the period. In 1957, for example, the Tidewater Oil Company of Oklahoma drilled to a depth of 3,200 feet twenty-five miles to the east of Kanab.[76] The J. Ray McDermott Company of Denver planned to drill an 11,000-foot test well near Kanab in 1959. By July the drilling was underway, testing various geologic formations near the Virgin Oil Fields.[77] Mountain States Drilling Company of Denver drilled yet another well, twelve miles northwest of Kanab near Red Knoll in 1962.[78] The Pan American Petroleum Corporation drilled in the Paria area in 1967 to depths of 6,000 feet.[79] Between 1953 and 1968, eight test wells—all coming up dry—were drilled in the county. Three were in the Mt. Carmel area, two in Reese Canyon, and one each in the Soda Springs, Kaibab Gulch, and Kanab areas.[80]

The development of coal mining was an idea that various entrepreneurs returned to throughout Kane County's twentieth-century history. For example, Preston Peterson, former member of the Utah State Road Commission, was considering a partnership with R.A. Gillis in the development of coal property in the western part of the county in 1941.[81] Gaining access to the coal deposits was not possible without a great economic investment—one that no one ultimately was willing to make during the mid-part of the century, however.

Education

In the 1954–55 school year, the high school and elementary schools each had their own principals for the first time since 1935. In 1952 Kanab had received supplemental state aid—$581,261—under the School Building Act for two new school buildings. An elementary school described as "modern" was designed by architects William J. Monroe, Jr., and Harry R. Wilson. It included seven classrooms, a multipurpose room, and offices. It was located on the northern half of the public square at the center of town and was constructed for a cost of $206,804. The new high school was to be built at the foot of the hill where the older structure was located and contained seven classrooms, a gymnasium and stage, and administration offices. It was built for a cost of $339,569 and was designed by architect Claude S. Ashworth.[82] In 1957, the district approved plans to add five additional classrooms to the Kanab Elementary School, a reflection of the addition of some ninety students to the original total of 210.[83]

Despite the new facilities, Kane County schools decreased in student population in the mid-1950s, with a loss of twenty-five pupils in 1955 from the year before, for a total of 626 students. Kanab Elementary housed some 200 children between the ages of five and twelve; Kanab High School had another 164 students; and Valley High School had 133 students. Valley Elementary had seventy students; Glendale Elementary had thirty-four, and Alton Elementary had twenty-five students.[84] Students from the Kane County schools were pitted against each other and other teams from the region in sporting events.

Consolidation of certain Kane County schools became a topic discussed both locally and by the Utah State Board of Education in the 1950s because of the potential savings it would bring to the county, particularly the consolidation of Valley and Kanab High Schools. It was anticipated that this would save the district $25,000 per year.[85] Even so, this was a very controversial issue in Kane County towns. In May 1960, Utah Board of Education personnel made a room-by-room inspection of the county's schools along with county, state, district, and local representatives. Although the state furnished about 81 percent of the total funds of the district, it was left to the Kane County School Board to make the final decision.[86] However, the state board did decide to withdraw special approval for the operation of the small elementary schools at Alton and Glendale beginning with the 1961–62 school year, a decision that met with significant disfavor locally. The board did promise to build a new elementary school in Orderville for Long Valley children.[87] Valley Elementary was constructed in 1967 for $276,250 and included six classrooms, a multipurpose room with wall tables, a modern kitchen, instructional material center, kindergarten room, and suite of offices.

Higher education opportunities could only be found outside the county. The nearest junior colleges were Dixie College at St. George and Southern Utah State College (now University) in Cedar City. A vocational school located in Richfield, Sevier Valley Technical College, also attracted a number of Kane County youths.

Communication and Transportation

The *Kane County Standard* was edited after 1941 by Lloyd Lovestedt and was printed in Kane County for the first time in its history in February 1941. This shift from a Garfield County printer was made with the purchase of the paper by the Standard Publishing Company. Centering its operations in Kanab, the company installed linotype equipment and a cylinder printing press. The publisher announced the intention to provide the most up-to-date news and pay close attention to local affairs: "And so we delve into the task of printing a paper for Kane county in Kane county; a task we will enjoy in the midst of these colorful surroundings. We encourage all our readers to write or phone their news to this office not later than Tuesday evening or early Wednesday morning in order that it may appear in that week's publication."[88] While Lovestedt served during World War II, Clair Ford edited the paper.[89] A.C. and Jess E. Saunders published the paper in the early 1940s. The paper was bought in July 1945 by Myron W. Martin of Whittier, California. Martin, his wife, and two daughters moved to Kanab to operate the business.[90]

In 1950 the *Kane County Standard* again changed management; Errol G. Brown was the new publisher and editor, and he was backed by the belief that a "progressive" newspaper was important to a community's well-being. He wrote, "We believe that one of the greatest assets that any city, town or locality can have is a progressive and informative newspaper. To be progressive and informative a newspaper must have the cooperation and support of the people at all times and to the extent that it can operate on a sound economical basis, to be able to present its format to the public in a way becoming to the trend of modern times and in a manner that will be a credit to an up-and-coming community or locality."[91] The *Standard* was awarded a second place in "General Excellency" at the Utah State Press Association's annual convention in February 1953 and received that association's top award for newspaper excellence the next year.[92] After 1954, the paper became known as the *Southern Utah News,* and Brown was nominated for a Pulitzer Prize in Journalism for his work in local publishing.[93]

A $130,000 building was constructed in 1956 in Kanab for a branch of Mountain States Telephone Company. The structure was constructed of cement block with brick facing and native flagstone trim and housed Kanab's new telephone dial system and a business office. Part of the process of shifting to the new dialing system included home visits by company employees to demonstrate to customers how to use the latest equipment.[94] Under the new system, which was completed by February 1957, when Kanab residents picked up their phone, instead of speaking directly to an operator and cranking the phone to operate it, they heard a humming sound which signaled they could dial a number directly.

In October 1943, R.W.F. "Bob" Schmidt, a regional superintendent of airport services for the Civil Aeronautics Administration, and Joseph Bergen, commissioner of aeronautics for the State of Utah came to Kanab to discuss the location of an airstrip.[95] Mayor L. Elmer Jackson proposed that the Kanab Lions Club co-sponsor the airstrip, an idea the members enthusiastically responded to.

After World War II ended, a number of men returned to Kane County who had served in the Army Air Corps. Many brought with them the ability to fly aircraft and some foresaw the potential impact that regular airline service in and out of the county might have on the local economy. Emron Findlay Robinson, a flight officer during the war, flew home from the war in his own two-passenger airplane, which he landed in a pasture on the bench east of Kanab. Chester Shuttleworth and Alfred Brooksby also owned planes, which they kept in Fredonia. Besides petitioning the city council for a local airstrip, Robinson began teaching flying lessons locally. Eventually four of his students—Thomas Parkes, Bob Baardseth, Romell Young, and Richard Von Hake—became professional pilots.

On 11 June 1946, Mayor Jackson called a special city council meeting, with councilmen Claud M. Glazier, Elgin H. Morris, John M. Burgoyne, and C.H. Ackerman in attendance. The Lions Club announced in October of 1946 that it would donate $1,500 for the purchase of land for an airport.[96] The U.S. government and the Utah state government each provided part of the funding in return for provisions that the airport be built near a highway and be supplied with water, electrical power, and telephone service. The city purchased agricultural land owned by Carlos W. Judd, Merlin G. Shumway, Dana F. Findlay, and Clara E. Spencer for $425 per acre. During the post-war movie boom and the years when Glen Canyon Dam was being built, the airport proved to be enormously beneficial to the county. In fact, the needs of the motion picture industry doubtless served as a major motivation for the airport construction.

The first plane to land at the new Kanab Municipal Airport had passengers from the Universal International Motion Picture Company. A crowd of people gathered near the field in anticipation of the flight's arrival in early October 1948, getting out of their cars to watch the landing. The first to depart from the plane was movie star Howard Duff, followed by Lloyd Bridges. The pilot and co-pilot expressed enthusiasm about the new airport, applauding the length and the general appearance of the field and saying that they were surprised to see such a modern airport in this part of the country. The airport was officially dedicated on 24 October 1948 by Governor Herbert Maw. The Utah State Road Commission donated $3,000 to the Kanab Municipal Airport for the purchase of three hangars.[97]

A new city airport was completed in 1959. The federal government contributed $11,600 to the system, the city paying the additional $7,100.[98] In March 1959 Bonanza Airlines announced it would begin service in and out of the county and maintain a consistent schedule of flights to Arizona, Nevada, and northern Utah.

In 1943 the idea of building a Paria area road was being investigated by a group including Frank Moore of the regional U.S. Grazing Service office, Frank O'Brien of the Utah Department of Publicity and Industrial Development, men from the state highway department, the county attorney, and other citizens of Kanab. The group traveled from Warm Creek on horseback to try to identify the best

The LDS Church in Kanab. (Utah State Historical Society)

route. In May it was announced that work would start immediately on the dirt road. The Utah Publicity and Industrial Development Department appropriated $4,700 for the project in July.[99] A year earlier, Lester Little and Fred Fleming of Kanab helped negotiate a commitment from the same department for $4,500 to help construction of a road to Coral Pink Sand Dunes, which would greatly facilitate the movement of movie film crews and their equipment in and out of that area.[100]

In the 1950s, the national interstate highway system, including more than 600 miles of roadway in Utah, was planned and funded with federal monies. Included in the system was Interstate 15, which ran north-south through the state of Utah.

The Glen Canyon Dam project created an immediate need for improved transportation to and from the building site and eventually to recreation sites around the dam area and the resulting reservoir, Lake Powell. Roads were built in Kane County an the surrounding region as part of the overall project. Kanab was chosen as the northern junction point for a major roadway (which became the route of U.S. Highway 89) running southeasterly to the proposed

Glen Canyon Dam, where the Colorado River would be crossed. The highway would then return to rejoin old U.S. 89 in Arizona south of the river crossing. The fifty-seven-mile Utah stretch of roadway was to cost $5.5 million. Funding for the project was completed in 1957–58 at an eventual cost of $6 million. The highway was dedicated in a 19 September 1958 ceremony as a unit in the federal primary highway system.[101] The *Southern Utah News* announced on 18 June 1959 that the "wonderfully scenic, just completed highway leading east from Kanab, Utah" connected Kane County to activity at the dam site.[102] This road, Utah Highway 259, became U.S. Highway 89 in 1960.

Motion Pictures

Between the 1930s and 1950s, Kane County's canyon vistas became a regular backdrop for Hollywood motion pictures. Clarence A. Locan, a public-relations man for the Metro-Goldwin-Mayer film company, said that Kane County residents were excellent hosts—taking their visitors on fishing trips and staging barbecues, campfires, and horseback rides. "These people treated us as neighbors and human beings and forgot all about moving pictures. In Hollywood we can't be ourselves; there are certain appearances we have to keep and so on, because fans expect it," he was quoted. "Out in Utah we can wear old clothes, gossip with the cowboys and people in the general store, act as we please, and be perfectly natural. Personally getting away from Hollywood into these mountains has done me a world of good, physically and mentally."[103]

Buffalo Bill was a film produced by Twentieth Century Fox in 1943 that caused quite a stir in Kane County. After a complete fort was built in Johnson Canyon, a crew of about one hundred men and women arrived in Kanab from Hollywood. Parts of the movie, starring Joel McCrea and Maureen O'Hara, also were filmed at the old townsite of Paria. Almost as soon as it was built, the stage set was threatened by flooding from the Paria River. The crew built two dams to divert water, but water rolled over the dams.[104] Nearly 250 local residents were employed by the company for the picture; they included Della Pugh, who acted as a stand-in for Maureen O'Hara. Also, more than 200 Navajo Indians were hired to camp nearby for scenes in the film.[105]

The townsite of Paria with its old western look was also used for many other movies, and continued to be used for films, television programs, and commercials in the following decades. The entire area benefited from the film industry in the early 1940s as in the years before. The production crews, actors, and directors all needed places to stay and eat, local laborers worked on sets, waitresses, shop owners, and all other local businesses benefited from trade associated with the presence of crowds of outsiders in town. The movie industry needed teamsters, drivers, stuntmen, horse trainers, and carpenters; and virtually everyone in town was an extra on one film or another. The *Kane County Standard* commented upon the way the movie industry enlivened the sleepy little southern Utah town: "The movies have surely revived the town. The hustle and bustle is here once more. Every one who wants a job is busy. Those who are working receive a substantial check for the week's work. The Kanab Equitable was crowded to capacity and it also took on the capacity of a bank last Saturday. There was quite a line-up to have Mr. Ackerman cash checks."[106]

Use of the region for motion pictures continued after World War II, as that period into the 1950s was in many respects the heyday of movie making in Kane County. In its 19 September 1949 issue, *Life* magazine highlighted Kanab as "Utah's Hollywood," "a tiny town earning a big town living supplying locale, extras and props." The land clearly was the county's most significant asset. Photographs of the movie days line the walls of Dennis Judd's restaurant at the time of this writing. One shows Judd seated next to Dean Martin for a film in which he worked as Martin's double. Another shows Jackie Rife and other local women dressed as Indian women for a western that featured women pioneers—*Westward the Women*. About 150 women worked on the film, including some recruited from outside the area. Women also worked as saloon girls or as farm wives. A person who could drive a team of horses could find a lot of work. Wranglers with their teams could get a dollar a day per horse and a dollar a day for labor. Rife remembered big productions when the whole town was filled with movie crews and money was spent freely.[107]

In order to see that local residents received pay commensurate with that received by movie extras from California, Calvin Johnson organized a local filmworkers union that was affililated with the Teamsters Union. Johnson himself worked in some films as a double for stars; he also played both cowboys and Indians and drove wagons for the companies. Fay Hamblin worked as a public relations man, identifying locations for particular films, traveling to Hollywood to negotiate deals, and serving as a sort of liason between Kanab and southern California movie makers. In September 1949 the county commission considered renting county equipment to movie companies working in town to further attract the companies.[108]

During the mid-1950s fewer and fewer movie production companies came to town. This has been attributed to the changed technology of filmmaking; more scenes could be produced in studios, with dubbed-in backgrounds filmed on location. Kane County still attracted the movie industry to a lesser degree after 1950. Howard Koch, an assistant director at MGM studios in Hollywood, came to the area in 1951 to find a location for a film called *Lone Star* starring Clark Gable and Ava Gardner. He remembered: "We needed horses and riders and good country that would look like Texas."[109] He was advised to contact Fay Hamblin. Koch drove to Kanab and with Hamblin's help arranged for animals, a location, and arrangements to house and provide for the cast. According to Koch, that visit began a friendship that spanned twenty-five years and resulted in the production of twelve films.

The landscape was the obvious draw to Hollywood producers, but the townspeople facilitated their efforts, and movie makers received enthusiastic local support in their work in Kane County. The citizens benefited as well. Besides the revenue the film industry produced (Howard Koch estimated that the pictures he made produced four or five million dollars for Kanab), many residents continued to work as extras in the films—everyone "from the Mormon bishop, to the mayor, to the butcher, got a chance to take part in several movies."[110] All town businesses benefited—motels were filled, restaurants catered meals or fed movie workers late into the night, carpenters and artists built sets, and ranchers and farmers leased out their land.[111]

In June 1953 a film entitled *Camel Corps* was filmed in Kane County near Johnson Canyon. It was a new special effects three-dimensional (3-D) film, and director Ray Nazarro reportedly required a "good deal more careful study and times for all shots. A large number of animals, besides the camels, are being used in the film as well as wagons, and a lot of local props owned by local men," the *Kane County Standard* reported.[112] Motion pictures were attempting to use 3-D and other innovations and special effects to combat the rise of television, which had begun to cut into the entertainment market. Some scenic movies, particularly westerns, continued to be filmed in the county. In 1955, for example, Howard Koch and Aubrey Schenk of Camden Productions came to Kanab to shoot the film *Fort Yuma*, starring Peter Graves. The company hired twenty locals for the film as well as another sixty for two days of shooting. This work was appreciated by many in Kanab who longed for the bustling days of the movie boom and missed the added revenue which came to the county from Hollywood. The *Southern Utah News* noted,

> Having suffered from the loss of movie making in Kanab for the past year or two, this company will be a great uplift to the feelings in this area. It is hoped that with the reorganization of the Screen Extra's Guild and several other matters being cleared up that the movie-making men of Hollywood will consider our beautiful locations for many more of their pictures in the future.[113]

Many local men and women chose to join the Kane County extras organization. Clara Pratt, secretary and treasurer of the group, collected an initial fee of ten dollars and the subsequent annual fee of two dollars. All extras were hired through this organization.[114] One major motion picture to be filmed in Kanab in 1955 was *The Lone Ranger*, produced by Warner Brothers. The company imported a crew of one hundred film workers and employed seventy-five extras as well as eighty Indians from the area. The Parry Lodge housed most of the company members.[115] Despite the general lull, a few films continued to be made, employing local men and women and bringing needed revenue into the county. The Kanab Chamber of Commerce and the Kane County Commission continually worked to attract movie companies throughout the period.[116]

Besides motion pictures, an increased number of television shows were filmed in the area. For example, "My Friend Flicka" television episodes were filmed locally; later, the series "Death Valley Days" began filming in 1959. The drama "Route 66" filmed an episode in Kanab that employed locals Bert Brinkerhoff, Debra Walley, and Tony Haig, and the popular western series "Gunsmoke" filmed several episodes in Kane County canyons.[117]

Motion pictures began to counter television's threat with color extravaganzas, grand epics, and other technical innovations. This to some extent benefited southern Utahns, but westerns remained the films most commonly shot in the area. Frank Sinatra came to Kanab in 1961 to star in the Hollywood film *Sergeants Three* along with Peter Lawford, Dean Martin, Sammy Davis, Jr., and Joey Bishop. Filmed near the old Paria townsite forty miles east of Kanab, the movie was described as a "rollicking, action-packed, gutsy story of the winning of the American West," and was said to be the largest western to be filmed in Kane County.[118] While in town, Sinatra gave a check to Kanab High School for the purchase of football uniforms and other badly needed sports equipment.[119] *The Greatest Story Ever Told* was one movie epic of the 1960s that was filmed in part locally.

After the movie industry boom died down, the Parry brothers among others campaigned for the bus tour business of foreign visitors, offering package deals that included lodging, entertainment (melodramas or musical presentations), and tours of area attractions. The residents of the county looked for a general expansion of business in the years ahead as the decade of the 1960s approached.

Endnotes

1. "100,000 Tourists Can't Be Wrong," *Kane County Standard*, 19 June 1941.

2. "Projects Completed on Range in Kane County," *Kane County Standard*, 20 May 1942.

3. "Government Trappers Aid Stockmen in Control of Predators," *Kane County Standard*, 17 April 1941.

4. Kane County Commission, Minutes, 9 December 1940.

5. Lester Y. Johnson, interview with Bayden Grover, 27 April 1993, Kanab, Utah.

6. "Slump in Tourist Trade Forces Close of Stations," *Kane County Standard*, 24 July 1942.

7. "Kanab Hospital Closes to Care of Patients," *Kane County Standard*, 10 July 1942.

8. "Kanab Hospital Reopens This Week," *Kane County Standard*, 13 November 1942.

9. "Dr. G.R. Aiken Receives Commission in Navy," *Kane County Standard*, 26 February 1943.

10. *Kane County Standard*, 5 March 1943, 8 December 1944.

11. Jackie Rife, interview with Martha Bradley, 9 July 1995.

12. "Mayor's Proclamation," *Kane County Standard*, 24 April 1942.

13. "Former Kanab Citizen Under FBI Investigation," *Kane County Standard*, 16 September 1943.

14. "Who Wants the Jap?" *Kane County Standard*, 27 March 1941. See also "Send the Japs to Fight the Germans," *Kane County Standard*, 1 May 1942.

15. "No Japs Will Be Resettled in Kane County," *Kane County Standard*, 24 April 1942.

16. "Fire Causes Loss of Sawmill and 7 Sq. Miles Timber," *Kane County Standard*, 3 July 1942.

17. "Huge Fleet of Trucks Busy Transporting Ore," *Kane County Standard*, 17 November 1944.

18. *Kane County Standard*, 20 July 1945.

19. "OPA Gives Outlook on Clothing Project," *Kane County Standard*, 2 February 1945.20. 1 "Kanab Schools Now Fully Organized," *Kane County Standard*, 19 September 1947.

21. "Women's Republican Club Organized," *Kane County Standard*, 17 October 1947.

22. "Kanab Women's Club to Donate Fountain," *Kane County Standard*, 8 October 1948.

23. *Kane County Standard*, 20 September 1946.

24. "County Hospital Proposal Will Make Addition," *Kane County Standard*, 20 October 1950.

25. Adonis Findlay Robinson, *History of Kane County*, 171.

26. "Kane Centennial to Start Next Thursday," *Kane County Standard*, 6 June 1947.

27. "Census Shows Decrease in County," *Kane County Standard*, 12 May 1950.

28. "Building Boom in Kanab," *Kane County Standard,* 24 February 1950.

29. "Kane County Population Increase Notes High Percentage," *Southern Utah News,* 15 May 1958.

30. "University Survey Shows 1400 Increase in Kane County by 1975," *Southern Utah News,* 20 February 1958.

31. "Dr. Aiken Explains Federation Operation to Business Women," *Kane County Standard,* 24 February 1950.

32. "Concrete Work Starts at City Reservoir," *Kane County Standard,* 28 May 1948.

33. "Kanab City Government Reports Complete Data on Water and Sewer," *Southern Utah News,* 1 May 1958.

34. "Telegram Assures Kanab of Funds for Water, Sewer," *Southern Utah News,* 8 May 1958.

35. *Southern Utah News,* 4 June 1959, 10 December 1959.

36. Quoted in Robinson, *History of Kane County,* 391–92.

37. "Kane County Fair Has Grown Up," *Kane County Standard,* 29 August 1947.

38. "Program Outlines Full Day of Eating, Horse Racing and Dancing," *Kane County Standard,* 6 May 1949.

39. "Dance Will Open Fair Program," *Kane County Standard,* 25 August 1950.

40. Leah Hannah Button, interview with Jeremy Button, 5 May 1992, Kanab, Utah. See also Rife, interview.

41. "Four More Business Firms in Kanab Today Than There Were Four Years Ago," *Southern Utah News,* 29 December 1955.

42. "Commercial Rates Reduced in Kanab Says Manager Morris," *Kane County Standard,* 17 July 1941.

43. *Kane County Standard,* 20 December 1946.

44. "Southwest Utah Power Federation Purchases Southern Utah Power Company," *Kane County Standard,* 26 August 1949.

45. "Approval Given On Southern Utah Power Co. Merger," *Southern Utah News,* 28 June 1958.

46. "Business Boom Taking Place in Kanab As Spring Starts," *Southern Utah News,* 7 March 1957.

47. "Glen Canyon Townsite Progressing Toward Completion, Will Offer Convenience to Workers," *Southern Utah News,* 8 August 1957.

48. Kane County Commission, Minutes, 10 June 1957.

49. "Law Enforcement Problems Increase in Kane County Area,

Officers Study Solutions—Ask Public, Parents Help," *Southern Utah News,* 23 January 1958.

50. "Salt Lake Corporation Will Invest $800,000 in Kanab Tourist Program," *Southern Utah News,* 3 April 1958. See also *Southern Utah News,* 22 May 1958.

51. Utah Tax Commission, "Report for 1945," Utah State Historical Society.

52. "Pasturized Milk Now Produced in Kanab," *Kane County Standard,* 1 August 1947; "Chamberlain Dairy is Making Rapid Growth," *Kane County Standard,* 28 July 1950.

53. "Drought Places Kane County in Disaster Area," *Kane County Standard,* 1 December 1950.

54. "Severe Drought Conditions," *Kane County Standard,* 17 July 1953.

55. "Weatherman Reports Near Record for Moisture in 1957," *Southern Utah News,* 2 January 1958.

56. "Water Users Saturday Meeting Postponed," *Kane County Standard,* 24 October 1947.

57. "Glen Canyon Dam to Make a Kane County Lake," *Kane County Standard,* 2 January 1948.

58. "Glen Canyon Dam Site Viewed As Recreation Area," *Kane County Standard,* 4 February 1954.

59. *Southern Utah News,* 25 March 1954, 26 June 1953.

60. "Increased Kaibab Cut is Indicative of Major Industry," *Kane County Standard,* 24 February 1950.

61. "Local Concern Gets One of Biggest Contracts in Southwest, 168,000,000 ft," *Kane County Standard,* 22 September 1950.

62. "Kane Lumber Men Win Timber Bid on Dixie Forest," *Kane County Standard,* 27 March 1953.

63. *Southern Utah News,* 14 February 1957, 5 February 1959.

64. "Alton Coal Mine Has Impressive Output," *Kane County Standard,* 4 March 1949.

65. "Oil Company Official Explains Operations," *Kane County Standard,* 11 March 1949.

66. "Uranium Strike Recorded 13 Miles From Kanab," *Kane County Standard,* 20 May 1949. See also *Kane County Standard,* 13 May 1949.

67. "Oil Report Says Kanab Basin Best Unknown Area," *Kane County Standard,* 2 October 1953.

68. "Local Interest in Oil Development Heightens as Nation Observes Oil Progress Week," *Kane County Standard,* 16 October 1953.

69. "Oil Drillers Find Good Oil Saturation in Kane County," *Southern Utah News*, 17 February 1955.

70. "Hot Uranium Discoveries Hit Kanab Area," *Southern Utah News*, 11 March 1954.

71. "Time Magazine Gives Highlights Uranium Murder Here," *Southern Utah News*, 10 June 1954.

72. "Uranium Boom Progresses, Drilling and Mining Activities Expected to Get Underway in Near Future Here," *Southern Utah News*, 24 June 1954.

73. "Uranium Drilling Company Runs Into Water East of Kanab," *Southern Utah News*, 10 March 1955.

74. "Kanab Uranium Corporation Strikes Natural Gas Instead of Uranium During Grand County Drilling Saturday," *Southern Utah News*, 5 May 1955.

75. "Uranium Boom Creates Farm Labor Shortage," *Southern Utah News*, 7 July 1955.

76. "Local Drilling for Oil and Gas Goes Forward by Tidewater Oil Company," *Southern Utah News*, 3 January 1957.

77. *Southern Utah News*, 25 June 1959, 23 July 1959.

78. "Oil Well Drilling Below 4200 Depth Tuesday This Week," *Southern Utah News*, 4 October 1962.

79. *Southern Utah News*, 2 February 1967.

80. "Kane County Mineral Report," *Southern Utah News*, 1 February 1968.

81. "New Coal Fields Being Developed in Kane County," *Kane County Standard*, 2 October 1941.

82. "Save Two New School Buildings," *Kane County Standard*, 10 July 1953. See also "Proposed Kanab High School Building Site Approved," *Kane County Standard*, 19 November 1953.

83. "Kanab Schools Receive $118,000 for Additional Classrooms as Elementary Plans and Blueprints Being Approved," *Southern Utah News*, 28 November 1957.

84. "Kane County Schools Suffer Decrease in 1955 Enrollment," *Southern Utah News*, 29 September 1955.

85. "Consolidation of Kane County Schools Discussed," *Southern Utah News*, 31 March 1936.

86. "Room by Room Survey Completed by State and Local School Boards on Consolidation," *Southern Utah News*, 12 May 1960.

87. "Utah State Board of Education Holds to Decision to Consolidate

Kane Schools Within Coming Two Years," *Southern Utah News*, 14 July 1960.

88. "Kane County Standard Now Being Printed in Kane County," *Kane County Standard*, 27 February 1941.

89. "To Our Readers,"*Kane County Standard*, 8 June 1943.

90. "Standard Changes Ownership," *Kane County Standard*, 29 June 1945.

91. "Standard Assumes New Management," *Kane County Standard*, 21 July 1950.

92. *Kane County Standard*, 27 February 1953; *Southern Utah News*, 18 February 1954.

93. "S.U.N. Publisher is Nominated for Pulitzer Prize Award," *Southern Utah News*, 11 February 1954.

94. "New Telephone Building Slated for Construction This Month," *Southern Utah News*, 9 August 1956.

95. "Work Starts at Once on Air Port Runway," *Kane County Standard*, 14 October 1943.

96. "Airport Gets Boost," *Kane County Standard*, 11 October 1946.

97. *Kane County Standard*, 15 October 1948, 22 October 1948, 26 November 1948.

98. "Airport Lighting System is Approved," *Southern Utah News*, 10 December 1959.

99. See *Kane County Standard*, 14 May 1943, 28 May 1943, 29 July 1943.

100. "Completion of Road to Sand Dunes Assured by Additional State Funds," *Kane County Standard*, 22 May 1942.

101. Ezra C. Knowlton, *History of Highway Development in Utah*, 579.

102. "Road Building in Utah Opens New Travel," *Southern Utah News*, 18 June 1959.

103. "Picture Folk Enjoy Southern Utah Hospitality," *Kane County Standard*, 3 September 1937.

104. "Buffalo Bill, the Greatest Picture to Be Filmed in Kane County, Will be Done in Techni-Color," *Kane County Standard*, 5 August 1943.

105. "Over 200 of 20-Century-Fox Co. In Kanab Filming Picture," *Kane County Standard*, 12 August 1943.106. 1 "Movies Create Hustle and Bustle in Kanab," *Kane County Standard*, 8 July 1943.

107. Rife, interview.

108. Kane County Commission, Minutes, 1 September 1949.

109. "Kanab Has a Long Tradition as a Place to Make Movies," *The History Blazer,* 8 July 1995, Utah State Historical Society.

110. Ibid.

111. See Howard Koch, interview with Dennis Rowley and James D'Arc, 10 November 1976, Special Collections, Harold B. Lee Library, Brigham Young University.

112. "Filming of 'Camel Corps' Gets Underway Here," *Kane County Standard,* 26 June 1953.

113. "Warner Brothers Studios and Belair Productions to Film Three Movies Near Kanab" *Southern Utah News,* 28 July 1955.

114. "Camden Productions to Film 'Fort Yuma' in Kanab Presently," *Southern Utah News,* 14 April 1955.

115. *Southern Utah News,* 28 July 1955.

116. "Kanab Chamber of Commerce Works With Movie and TV Committees to Assure Kanab Area More Productions," *Southern Utah News,* 10 July 1958.

117. See *Southern Utah News,* 20 August 1959, 25 August 1960, 20 May 1971.

118. "Areas Largest Movie Production Gets Underway Friday With Star Studded Cast, Should Help Boost Local Economy," *Southern Utah News,* 1 June 1961.

119. "Kanab High School Receives Gift From Frank Sinatra of Much Needed Athletic Equipment and Accessories," *Southern Utah News,* 15 June 1961.

CHAPTER 11

DEVELOPMENT AND CONTROVERSY, THE 1960s AND 1970s

The 1960s have been considered a turbulent decade in American history—in great part due to the youth of the nation rebelling against certain established ways, or the Establishment, as it was termed, and protesting the conflict in Vietnam. This rebelliousness and protest did not generally extend to conservative, Mormon, rural Utah, including Kane County—but the decade of the 1960s and those that followed were turbulent in the county as well, particularly in terms of the debate over policy and use of public lands.

Glen Canyon Dam

Perhaps the most important public dialogue that portended great changes for Kane County at mid-century was the debate concerning the construction of Glen Canyon Dam. A joint meeting of the Colorado River Basin states committee and the Upper Colorado River Commission called for a billion dollar upper basin states' storage program with the Bureau of Reclamation. The ambitious storage plan called for the construction of nine reservoirs on the Colorado River and its main tributaries, to result in some 48 million acre-feet of water storage capacity. It was anticipated that the economic bene-fits to Kane County would be great.[1] Opposition to the plans would also surface, beginning a debate over the environment and land uses that has continued to the present day.

The passage of the Upper Colorado River Storage Project Bill by the U.S. House of Representatives in 1956 initiated one of the largest reclamation projects in the history of the United States. The total cost of the project was estimated at $756 million, a major portion of which would be spent on the construction of Glen Canyon Dam southeast of Kanab near Page, Arizona. The resulting reservoir, later named Lake Powell for early Colorado River explorer John Wesley Powell, would cover eastern Kane County (the border of which was the center of the Colorado River channel) as it filled Glen Canyon, greatly impacting the area physically and in terms of its use by recre-ationists.

Utah's leaders of government praised the move—Senator Wallace F. Bennett, no doubt speaking of the construction phase of the dam, said that "the passage of the bill would mean more urgent industry for this area than can now be comprehended." Utah Governor J. Bracken Lee said, "It is just the beginning of a long range program that will build up the west."[2] After the passage of the bill, discussion centered on access in and out of the area. The *Southern Utah News* asserted, "It has been determined that the best route for an access road to the Glen Canyon damsite would be from Kanab, a distance of some 70 miles. There have been rumors, however, to the effect that the roads would go through Garfield County by way of Cannonville and leave Kanab out. This will be discussed Tuesday by the Kanab City Council and possibly a delegation will be sent to Salt Lake City to look into this and do all they can to help get the roads built from Kanab."[3]

The effort was reminiscent of earlier battles over the location of county seats or railroad hubs. Other counties vied for the route to the dam site, realizing its importance to their economies. Groups out of Panguitch, Richfield, and other towns feeding off tourist visits to Bryce Canyon supported the construction of roads through their areas instead of through Kanab.[4] Kane County officials understood the significant revenue that could be generated by travelers through the area on their way to Lake Powell if the road was built from Kanab; which it subsequently was.

The Kanab newspaper kept area residents informed about developments regarding the dam project. In a meeting held in Phoenix in April 1956, Arizona highway officials, Arizona governor Ernest McFarland, and Wilbur A. Dexheimer of the Bureau of Reclamation met to discuss the location of townsites and roads for the $420 million project. According to the *Southern Utah News*, Dexheimer was reluctant to make any commitment, "and in a very blunt manner, in the project matter Mr. Dexheimer went on to say, 'I would like to first learn to what extent the two states, Arizona and Utah, will aid in building access roads to the construction site.'"[5] By May 1956 the Bureau of Reclamation opened up competition for bids for the rental of heavy road-making equipment for "roughing in a road to the Glen Canyon Damsite." In June, it opened bids for three other contracts associated with the dam construction: an access road from Bitter Springs on U.S. Highway 89 north of Flagstaff to the dam site; a bridge across the Colorado River three miles downstream from the dam site; and the excavation of a diversion tunnel on the Utah side of the river.[6] Each successive project brought revenue into the general area.

The Bureau of Reclamation arranged to use the north part of Kanab High School for offices and drafting rooms where fifty men would work on projects related to the dam.[7] Increased signs of activity were in evidence in the Kanab area. The county commission anticipated a building boom in relationship to the project. It initially would be related to the construction workers, but eventually tourist trade and other movement through the area would be a source of much-needed revenue. Access roads to the dam were the first construction projects to employ local men and provide better communication and transportation between Arizona and southern Utah's remote areas. The *Southern Utah News* detailed each step in the development process with enthusiasm and acclaim for the potential benefits the dam would bring to the area. Each new portion of road, tunnel, or bridge that was built employed locals and brought federal dollars into the economy as it improved the infrastructure of the area.

President Dwight D. Eisenhower began official construction of the dam on 15 October 1956 by remote control from the White House in Washington, D.C., when he set off the first blast, which dislodged a huge slab of rock above the location selected for the upper portal of the right diversion tunnel. From that point on, the building site and surrounding area were the scenes of complex activity.

A townsite soon developed close to the dam site. Glen Canyon City was located in Kane County and largely developed to facilitate the smooth operation of the project, provide housing for workers, and begin an initial permanent base for recreational uses of the area. The BLM saw it as a headquarters for government activities and construction. It was estimated initially that the population of the town could reach as high as 10,000 during the construction phase of the project, but that it would likely eventually stabilize at about 4,000 persons. The permanent population would include personnel operating and maintaining the dam, providing recreational and tourist services, and operating other service businesses. The townsite was located at about 4,200 feet and had temperatures that ranged from a low of 2 degrees to highs of 114 degrees Fahrenheit, with low humidity.[8]

The state of Utah sold land west of the dam site in June 1957 at public auction at bids ranging from ten dollars to $380 an acre. Much of the land was located on the highway being built from Kanab to the dam site. The sale met with concern on the part of some local cattlemen who feared that unrestricted building would interfere with cattle grazing.[9]

The first town meeting at Glen Canyon City was held at the Rusmar Boardinghouse in June 1958 to organize a fire department, appoint a temporary town manager, and discuss options for education of the children in town. Twenty-eight residents took part in the discussion; at the time, there were thirty families in town, with about twenty-six children. The residents also considered ways of providing medical care, mail service, communication by phone or radio, and maintenance of roads.[10] Eventually, Glen Canyon City students would be bused to schools in Page, Arizona, or Kanab until local schools were built.[11]

The highway from Kanab to Glen Canyon opened in 1958 with

a dedicatory speech given by Governor George D. Clyde, who said in part, "This is a true milestone in the history and development of Kane County, of this whole vast and spectacular region, of all Utah, and of the entire West!" The hard-surfaced, all-weather highway was constructed for $5,767,000 by five different contractors. It was fifty-seven miles long, thirty-six feet wide, and included six bridges along its course.[12]

The Glen Canyon Bridge provided access to both sides of the river for construction needs and was built by the Kiewit-Judson Pacific Murphy Company, which placed the first steel for the arch span on 7 May 1958 and the last on 6 August 1958. The bridge is 1,271 feet long and rises some 700 feet above the river. It was the world's highest steel arch bridge and was dedicated on 20 February 1959.

The contract for Glen Canyon Dam was the largest single construction contract in the history of the Bureau of Reclamation. As designed, Glen Canyon Dam would be the third highest dam in the world, 700 feet above the lowest bedrock (Hoover Dam was 726 feet high and Mauvolsin Dam in Switzerland was 780 feet in height). The dam would contain approximately 4,770,000 cubic yards of concrete in the dam itself and 5,200,000 cubic yards in the dam appurtenance structure. The 900,000-kilowatt power plant installed at the dam would be the seventh largest in the world.[13] The first electricity actually generated by the plant was transmitted to Shiprock, New Mexico, in September 1964.[14]

Merritt-Chapman & Scott Corporation was awarded the building contract and anticipated completing the project in eight years. Concrete for the dam itself was first poured in June 1960 after a dedication ceremony.[15] The left diversion tunnel, which provided for the flow of the Colorado River during construction, was closed in March 1963 and initiated storage of water in Lake Powell. This event began the boating and other recreational use of the manmade lake while ending river running and other uses of Glen Canyon, much to the sorrow of many lovers of the natural landscape. It was estimated that Lake Powell eventually would be more than 150 miles long and reach a point near Hite, Utah, for a total area of sixty-five square miles.[16]

The National Park Service built numerous recreational amenities along the shores of the lake in Utah; one was near Hite and another was at Hall's Crossing. A marina at Bullfrog Basin was built in the northeast corner of Kane County, although access was from Garfield County to the north. Wahweap Marina, just across the line in Arizona, included a swimming beach and fuel dock operated by Canyon Tours, an Arizona firm. In addition, the National Park Service invested $2 million in recreation sites at Wahweap, including a sixteen-unit campground.[17]

Glen Canyon Dam was officially dedicated on 22 September 1966 by First Lady Ladybird Johnson after ten years of planning, designing, and construction. The *Southern Utah News* reported, "Today, the canyon lies serenely and comparatively silent except for the hum of the huge hydro-electric generators and the sound of thousands of people who come to see this newest of Reclamation dams on the Colorado River and its sparkling clear sky-blue reservoir, Lake Powell."[18] Congress approved the Glen Canyon National Recreation Area Bill in October 1972, providing funds for other area improvements. The Glen Canyon National Recreation area included Lake Powell and about 1.2 million acres surrounding it in northern Arizona and Kane, Garfield, Wayne, and San Juan Counties in Utah.

Not all were pleased with the new developments, however. Particularly outside of southern Utah, and even of the state itself, a growing chorus of voices began to call for greater protection of the remaining wild and undeveloped lands of the West. A growing conservation movement began to seek increased management of the nation's public lands. The loss of Glen Canyon to the dam and reservoir became a rallying point for environmental activists in years to come.

Public Lands

Federal land management prescribes environmental and policy regulations which apply to public lands. Kane County includes approximately 2.5 million acres of land, and more than 95 percent of that land is controlled by various federal and state agencies; only 5 percent of the land base is privately owned or controlled. Most of this private land is located near Kanab, although other private land is found in the Long Valley area, Big Water, Church Wells, and Cedar

Mountain. Only a small amount of land is irrigated. Most land in Kane County is public land that has been and currently is used for livestock grazing.

As public use and awareness of public lands increased after World War II, increased demands for both recreational use and conservation were voiced by many of the nation's citizens. In response, during the 1960s the Bureau of Land Management developed new programs to protect and improve wildlife habitats, develop recreational facilities, and build roads through BLM lands. With the Multiple Use and Classification Act of 1964, the BLM moved to facilitate many different uses for public land and more intensive management.

One BLM publication in 1967, for example, promoted local recreational, scenic, and economic activities on BLM land, including the enjoyment (and protection) of the many sites of ancient Indian rock art and ruins in the Kanab BLM District. It also identified the potential for excellent hunting, fishing, and other outdoor activities in the area, articulating a policy of multiple use. "One major use of public lands is for livestock grazing," it maintained. "In Kanab BLM district approximately 17,000 cattle and 14,000 sheep graze part of each year on public lands. Stockmen and BLM technicians cooperate in proper management of the range resource—improving soil cover, reducing erosion and increasing forage for both livestock and wildlife." Although this publication painted a rather rosy picture, the actual relationship was frequently strained. Finally, the pamphlet stated, "Many other products come from public lands: juniper fence posts, pinon Christmas trees, firewood and minerals. And BLM-administered lands are a source where expanding communities can obtain needed living space—for recreation, industrial and residential development." It was difficult to argue with the objectives of the BLM, but in reality each use had the potential to create a battle-ground.[19]

Another important development was the 1960 Multiple Use and Sustained Yield Act which modified the U.S. Forest Service practice of encouraging timber harvesting to advocating stricter harvesting regulations as well as promoting a variety of uses of national forest land.

The Wilderness Act of 1964 represented a major victory for conservationists throughout the nation in setting aside some undeveloped areas, greatly restricting their use. The act stated in part:

> In order to assure that an increasing population accompanied by expanding settlement and growing mechanization, does not occupy and modify all areas within the United States and its possessions, leaving no lands designated for preservation and protection in their natural condition, it is hereby declared to be the policy of the Congress to secure for the American people of present and future generations the benefits of an enduring resource of wilderness.[20]

Wilderness areas were identified from federally owned lands and managed by the same agencies that had managed them before. The preservation concept embodied in the Wilderness Act was a particular concern to residents of Kane County and many others throughout the West. They feared the potential economic losses that could result from closing those areas to traditional extractive uses such as mining and lumbering. In subsequent years, moves were made to set aside additional lands as protected wilderness, and the process of identifying and setting aside such land has polarized many of those in the West and throughout the nation, including residents of Kane County.

Agriculture

In 1964 some 10 percent of the county's total land was farmed. There were 128 farms with an average of 2,019 acres each. The total value of local farm products raised was $548,225—which included about $21,000 in crops, $2,000 in dairy products, $511,000 in livestock, and $11,000 in poultry products. The crops Kane's farmers raised helped feed local residents and their livestock, any surplus was exported. Farmers raised some wheat, oats, barley, and alfalfa. There was a significant amount of fruit raised in orchards in the area, including a crop of 79,000 pounds of apples and 8,000 pounds of peaches.[21]

Stockmen, farmers, and other businessmen shared a common growing concern during the 1960s and 1970s about the use of public lands. They met frequently with representatives of the Bureau of

Since the founding of Kane County, cattle have been an important part of the area's heritage and livelihood. (Kane County News)

Land Management to discuss the changing policies and regulations that affected grazing, roads, leasing, and other developments on public property managed by the government. In December 1964, one such gathering included officials Robert E. Wold, R.D. Nielsen, Donald G. Gipe, and several local stockmen and other county residents dissatisfied with the way the public lands were being managed. They voiced their concerns about water use, reseeding of grazing lands, and fencing on private land that abutted public land. Many of them believed they were being discriminated against by what they termed the unnecessary tagging of animals, building and use of corrals, and unnecessary handling of cattle going onto and coming off public lands, which they believed resulted in weight loss and sometimes death to the cattle.[22]

Other environmental concerns occupied the county as well. In 1969 Kane County Agricultural Agent Harold Lindsey suggested aerial spraying by helicopter to try to eliminate an elm leaf beetle infestation. The problem had plagued local elm trees since 1956; however, officials decided not to spray, anticipating that the chemicals would affect beneficial pollinating insects as well. The United States Census of Agriculture revealed that there were a total of 127 farms in the county in 1969; the average farm sold $2,500 or more of agricultural products per year. The average size of county farms was 1,806 acres, and the average value was $92,170. The value of all farm products sold in 1969 was $1,041,035—almost double that sold in 1964. Livestock, poultry, and other animal products represented another $1,003,021 in sales—an increase again almost double the 1964 figure.[23] Despite these increases, farmers and livestock men had concerns about future land use.

Public policy through the years was changing, as other Americans, their elected representatives, and various agency directors began to pay more attention to the public lands. The agencies that earlier had essentially tried to facilitate use of the land by ranchers or timbermen now were asked to foster and accommodate other uses, including growing recreational uses and an environmental conservation movement. A new office was established for the Kanab BLM District in December 1969. The center included offices, a warehouse, a vehicle storage shed, and a blacktopped parking lot for twenty-five vehicles. This replaced the office headquarters that had previously been housed in an old CCC barracks, in use since the 1940s. The BLM Kanab District oversaw some 2,680,000 acres of the public domain.[24]

In August 1971, local stockmen again met with representatives of the BLM. Fred Howard, director of the Kanab BLM District explained to the group the process the BLM used to make multiple-use decisions. Each resource was to be examined independently, according to Howard, and then conflicts were considered in the context of the particular resource. Resources in the region included the land, minerals, recreational use, wildlife, the watershed, livestock use, and protection of the environment. The BLM made some recommendations about multiple-use options of the public land. The recommendations included restricted mining of coal on the Kaiparowits Plateau, with strict pollution controls being established; continued oil exploration, with certain restrictions; that public lands be made available for urban development near Glen Canyon City with the use of Housing and Urban Development funds; and that a high-quality road system be built in the Warm Creek area. Other recommendations related to school-trust lands, the creation of recreation areas in the Moquith area, Kanab Sand Dunes, Canaan Mountain, Virgin

River back country, and the Paria River area. Many of these recommendations would push cattle out of traditional grazing lands.[25]

The general local reaction was that the already strained relationship between the BLM and local stockmen had deteriorated. Believing their traditional livelihood threatened, stockmen felt the BLM's plan failed to recognize the needs of long-time inhabitants and workers of the county and that it brought the BLM into the business of managing the cattle industry. Not surprisingly, the local newspaper supported the stockmen. An editorial ran in the *Southern Utah News* on 19 August 1971 that summarized local objections to the plan.

> They are trying to run livestock men out of business. Some stock growers are beginning to believe this is actually true. They are getting beyond the bounds of land management into operations: recreational, wildlife, re-establishing forage on the lands, etc.
>
> Overstaffed and under worked on taxpayer dollars. It does seem significant that in the past 20 years the local staff has grown from two people to over 20. Add to that the two used to keep the yard clean and the building. Now these two duties are put out on bid. . . . The problem is, there is a problem. And despite public relations work from the BLM, the problem gets worse rather than better. We're not sure what the solution is, but we are sure that Uncle Sam (the government agencies) better find some before the taxpayers do so themselves.

Conditions were changing; something local residents were right to see as a threat to their traditional operations, although it was not the conspiracy by an unfeeling bureaucracy against them that some claimed. It was other citizens wanting other uses for public land. Six months later, stockmen again met with BLM officials, having felt increased pressure to conform to the new policies. The *Southern Utah News* described their reaction: "Stockmen have felt that pressure, even to the point of threats, have been pressed upon them, making their livelihood somewhat questionable, and they have progressed to the attitude, 'we are going to stand up and fight!'" At the meeting, held in Kanab with state BLM director Robert Nielson, they claimed they were being threatened with such statements as "Cattle will all be out of the area pretty soon" and "None of this country is cattle country, it is recreational area." Some said they had received letters stating that if they did not build improvements or bring existing fences and water systems up to standards their permits would be revoked by the government. Nielson responded by saying that the BLM should try to be more cooperative with those holding permits to graze livestock on public lands.[26]

Another concern of local cattlemen was predator control. Federal laws prohibited them from protecting their cattle by killing certain species. They claimed this prevented them from protecting their property, which they believed was unconstitutional. Nielson replied that the BLM's job was to carry out the laws made by Congress and that Congress was under increased pressure from environmentalist and conservation groups. He did say, "Where there is a pattern of losses to predators a control program may be set up." A representative of the stockmen voiced a common attitude: "We are natives of this country and feel we have rights here, we have never tried to keep people off the public lands. We are believers in the multiple use concept, but when confronted with the recent master plan you proposed we became extremely alarmed."[27]

This attitude of special rights has colored the debate over public land use to the present day. Beneficiaries of public policy (or lack thereof) in the past understandably did not want those privileges denied or revoked. A group of livestock men and other interested citizens met with U.S. Representative Sherman P. Lloyd on 2 September 1971. They voiced their concerns that increased restrictions on grazing on federal lands would force them out of business and claimed that the government should not be able to change land-use regulations.[28]

The county's sheep industry steadily declined during this period. On 7 June 1971 about half of the county's total sheep, some 3,000 sheep, left the yards of Roland Esplin and Sons's sheep ranch at Mt. Carmel to board trucks headed north to Oregon markets. Esplin reflected just how different the situation was from when the family began the business in 1928: "In those days the sheep industry touched every community in the area." He reflected, "I bought my first hundred head of sheep from my father in the Fall of 1928 for $10.00 a head. I was working for him at the time for $60 a month. A year later I bought another hundred head. These sheep and a homestead were my start." At one time, his ranch had as many as 5,500 ewes.

Esplin said he would be quitting the business, and he blamed the federal government: "Government regulations along with hired help are almost forcing us to quit. A dead wool market kills the profit in sheep raising. Government interference is the worst however. When a man can't even protect his own livestock from preditory animals on his range [referring to laws protecting mountain lions and coyotes] it's time a man was quitting."[29] Unmentioned in this analysis, however, was the fact that it was the free enterprise system the ranchers claimed to favor that was changing the market, reducing profitability, and raising wages for hired help, and that the grazing land in question was public land, not the ranchers' own land. As was the case with most citizens throughout the nation, both rural and urban, people readily accepted government assistance but then cried "interference" when changing policies did not favor their particular interest.

Natural Resources

Federally managed lands in Utah include national forests, national parks, national monuments, and national recreation areas, and Kane County has examples of each. Much of the public land controlled by the government is rich in natural resources. Kane County reportedly contains some of the richest coal reserves west of the Mississippi River.

The *Southern Utah News* reported that the Kaibab Lumber Company contributed a million dollar payroll to southern Utah at the beginning of the decade of the 1960s.[30] More than three-fourths of the company's regional employees lived in Kanab in 1960; but, in August of that year, because of the depressed lumber market, the company began a thirty-day curtailment that would put sixty men out of work within the week. Many of the workers had been with the company for years, but the company could not afford to maintain its production figures in the face of economic trends.[31]

The Kaibab Lumber Company underwent reorganization the next year in an attempt to more efficiently stay in business. Kane County workers responded in October 1961 with the organization of a local sawmill union. Union president Clifton Young, vice-president George Brinkerhoff, and Aurie Henrie met with the company management on 3 October. After commenting on the general slump in the lumber industry, company president E. Jay Whiting said he believed the national market would improve and that the company would face better times. Union secretary Aurie Henrie described the union as existing to help employees who suffered financial dislocation, sickness, or death in the family. The union also saw a role in negotiating special situations, like arranging time off for interested men during the annual deer hunt.[32]

The union appealed to Senator Wallace F. Bennett in January 1963 for congressional help for lumber-producing states during the slump in lumber prices. At the time, many of the workers were experiencing seasonal layoffs and others were doing reduced-pay maintenance work.[33] However, the timber industry was part of an increasingly global marketplace and faced intense national and international free-market competition—ironically, the very thing most Kane County residents claimed to support—and the local timber industry continued its decline. In March 1970 Kaibab Industries temporarily shut down its sawmill because of lack of markets for its products.[34]

In an effort to take the initiative in the development of local resources, a group called the Kanab Watershed Land Use Planning Committee was established in December 1973 to recommend policies and shape local attitudes towards land use issues. The group believed "land use planning is a means whereby local people have a procedure to develop their area along the lines that they feel are most important. This planning can and must be done only by local people."[35] They were making this effort to protect local interests and because of their shared belief that "outside experts cannot and do not know of the unique problems and opportunities that are available in each individual area. They know of the general types of things that can be done but they have no knowledge of the frame of reference of the local people." A technical assistance committee would assist the advisory committee in gathering information about resources. The group was headed by Verl Matthews and conducted inventories and researched and reported on possible options. The committee was a pilot project of the area's Five-County Association of Governments (composed of Kane, Garfield, Washington, Iron, and Beaver Counties) and was supported by the Kane County Commission.

Construction of a pipe line in Kane County. (Kane County News)

The Kaiparowits Plateau

Some plans for future economic expansion were focused on the
Kaiparowits Plateau, where many hoped that coal fields could be
located and a coal-fired electrical power plant built. Extensive coal

deposits, although primarily of a low grade, were found in various areas of Kane County. During the period, the only active coal mine was in Alton, north of Kanab, which produced between 1,000 and 2,000 tons per year. However, national mining attention began to focus on the Kaiparowits Plateau, in part in response to the general and projected future growth of the southwestern United States and that area's need for energy development.

In the 1960s, enterprising mining companies began to apply for coal prospecting permits for various areas on the Kaiparowits Plateau, mapping, exploring, and prospecting for claims. In January 1964, for example, Resources Company, Inc., a group of three southwestern utilities companies, applied to the Bureau of Land Management for permits to mine 6,566 acres of plateau land. Walter T. Lucking of the company said to the newspaper that "development of a future coal supply for power production could prove to be a tremendous boon not only to Arizona and Southern Utah but to other states as well. We know that tremendous quantities of electric energy are going to be needed in coming years to support the growth in this region, and perhaps a development such as this would be the key to ample fuel supplies to provide this energy."[36]

Resources Company applied to the Utah State Water and Power Board in November 1964 to build a coal-fired power generating station in Kane County. The company intended to draw 102,000 acre-feet of water yearly from Lake Powell for cooling purposes and boiler use. This company was a spin-off creation of the Arizona Public Service Co., San Diego Gas & Electric Co., and Southern California Edison Co., which joined forces for the project. It was the intention of the group to mine coal on the Kaiparowits Plateau and transport it by rail about ten miles to the site of the power plant. Ultimately, the plant would have the potential of generating 5 million kilowatts of electricity for the Southwest market.

University of Utah Assistant Professor of Geology Richard A. Robison spoke in Kane County in January 1964 and suggested that the Kaiparowits Plateau coal deposits were richer than had previously been thought. He encouraged county leaders to apply for mineral leases for the use of this land. Because of increasing costs of energy production in recent years, even though the coal deposits were diffi-

cult to access in certain locations, the effort could be of considerable
benefit, according to Robison, and perhaps would qualify for various
aids from the federal government.[37]

Also in 1964, the U.S. Geological Survey completed an evaluation
of 115,000 acres of potential coal land in Kane and Garfield Counties
in order to permit the U.S. Bureau of Land Management to lift the
withdrawal order that had controlled and limited use of such lands.
"This should ease the process of transferring title of sections of land
to the State of Utah and remove any legal clouds over the economic
development of this resource," said Utah Representative Sherman P.
Lloyd. The study determined that 101,653 acres had significant
deposits of coal, another 1,120 acres that earlier had been classified
as non-coal lands were added to the list, and 12,379 acres were established as non-coal lands. Part of the U.S. Geological Survey's program
of mapping geological features in the public domain, the study was
not tied to a particular program of economic development but was
informational in nature. Now, a prospective coal operator could lease
land with better knowledge of its potential for actually yielding coal.[38]

It was anticipated that the mining operations would create about
750 jobs for local men and women. Some projections claimed that by
the time the project was fully completed it would generate as many
as 2,300 jobs.[39] At the regional Five-County Association meetings in
March 1965, representatives of the counties took up the issue of coal
mining. Elton Buell, supervisor of scientific research for Resources
Company, reported that forty test holes had been drilled on the
Kaiparowits Plateau by the company to an average depth of 850 feet
at a total cost of some $5 million. Their efforts had resulted in find-
ings of veins of coal ranging from one foot to twenty-five feet thick.
He said that if the company received its requested permission to use
water from the Colorado River it could proceed with confidence in
building the power plant. He told the group that the total project
might create 2,400 jobs with a payroll of $25 million per year, which
was welcome news to those assembled.[40]

Early in 1965, the Utah Water and Power Board approved the
application of the company for the allocation of 102,000 acre-feet of
Colorado River water to permit operation of the proposed power
plant. It was anticipated that the water permit would facilitate

approval of the mining of coal on the Kaiparowits Plateau in eastern Kane County.[41] When U.S. Representative Laurence J. Burton spoke on the issue in August 1965, he said that the next step toward approval was getting a contract with the Ute Indian Tribe through the Bureau of Indian Affairs to use the tribe's rights to Colorado River water. It also needed to be approved by the Bureau of Reclamation and by Secretary of the Interior Stewart Udall. In a letter written to the Kane County Commissioners, Burton emphasized the importance of wise planning of these resources and commended the leaders for their foresight in preliminary planning efforts "for the establishment of the new industry and new community in the county," and in seeking a favorable site for the projected new mining town.[42] The Kane County Commission periodically met with Governor Calvin Rampton and representatives of Resources Company about the development of the Kaiparowits power complex.[43]

The economic benefits of the project were appreciated by local leaders. Besides the millions of dollars that would benefit the Utah economy, the entire capital cost would create a larger tax base in the county. Over the fifteen-year construction phase, the construction payroll would be some $95 million, and another $8 million would be generated in sales and use taxes. When it was completed, the plant and mining enterprises would pay property taxes, and royalty payments would generate some $2.2 million for the federal and state governments.[44]

Not all studies conducted on local coal deposits came up with such favorable conclusions, however. The University of Utah presented results of a study in January 1969, "Utah Coal—Market Potential and Economic Impact," which was submitted to the Kane County Commission. As reported in the *Southern Utah News,* it stated in part,

> The Kaiparowits Coalfield, which covers portions of Central Kane and Southwestern Garfield County, is the largest of those in Southwestern Utah, and it contains the greatest coal reserves. . . . The Bureau of Mines reports that the area is topographically diverse, varying in altitude from 5,000 feet to 7,500 feet. The area is cut by canyons, some of which reach depths of 1,000 feet. Over the

greater part of the Kaiparowits Field, topography on a small scale consists of numerous, intricately trenched, narrow, steep-walled canyons several tens or hundreds of feet in depth. The rugged surface combined with flash floods in the summer makes travel through the area difficult and at times virtually impossible.

These factors combine to make the Kaiparowits Coalfield the most remote and inaccessible of any field in the Southwest part of the State.[45]

Furthermore, the report continued, the coal beds have individual seams that vary from about five feet to twelve feet in thickness, are lenticular, and are often discontinuous and therefore not amenable to highly mechanized mining. Under these particular conditions, the study predicted that the output would likely reach only twenty-eight tons of clean coal per man per day at best.

The coal produced on the plateau is classified as bituminous coal that is low in ash and moderately high in sulfur. The report continued,

Run-of-the-mine coal ranges from 11 to 12 per cent moisture and averages 11,200 BTU/lb. Kaiparowits coal cannot be used for metallurgical purposes because it is noncoking; its geologic location makes it best suited for mine-mouth power generation, or for transportation of coal by pipeline. In summary, the Bureau of Mines reports that "Conditions observed in the Kaiparowits coalfields are not ideal." It is probable that much of the mining will require roof bolting.[46]

The significance of this last element was that it would increase the cost of production of a ton of coal by about one dollar. In conclusion, this report stated that coal mining on the Kaiparowits Plateau would be very difficult and not yield the type or amount of coal anticipated by other reports.

Utah elected officials continued to meet with officials of the Interior Department and other agencies through 1969 to lobby for support of the project. At a meeting with fifteen Democratic party candidates and representatives at the county Democratic convention in June 1968, Governor Rampton said, "The Kaiparowits Project is moving at last, and several concessions regarding the allocation of water have been worked out."[47] The State of Utah and the U.S. Department of the Interior signed an agreement assuring water from Lake Powell for the project in late 1969.[48] Despite this, in April 1970 James G. Watt, Deputy Assistant Secretary of Interior for Water and Power, speaking to a group in Kanab described the project as "still in the study stage." Watt emphasized the importance of further studies about the environmental impact of the project, the economic benefits, and the costs.[49]

It wasn't long before environmentalist groups became part of the dialogue over the Kaiparowits project. In 1971, at hearings before the Senate Interior Committee held in Salt Lake City, a grim picture was painted by opponents of the plan. "Towering smokestacks are joining the towering red cliffs overlooking Lake Powell, and plans of more to come have sparked a conservationist drive and public hearings in the U.S. Senate on what air pollution effects will be experienced in the Glen Canyon National Recreational Area," the *Southern Utah News* reported on 1 April 1971. Mrs. Fred Dinnewies, expressing the view of the Citizens for Best Environment of Page opposing the new power plant for its impact added to that of an existing power plant in the region, said, "The developers can't build their plants in California, because of strict air pollution limits, so they want to have the power in California, but dump their tons of coal smoke on us. . . . With both these plants operating, our blue skies will turn gray pretty fast," she concluded. L.E. Holmes, chief of water and land operations for the Utah and Colorado basins of the Bureau of Reclamation, responded by saying that the pollution could not necessarily be predicted, but maintained that "no one can authoritatively say whether or not they will ever actually form a visible cloud over the lake. . . . We will remove as much of the pollutants as technologically possible from the emissions, and the rest is just part of the price we have to pay for our growing population and its need for electricity."[50]

In June 1973, Republican Secretary of the Interior Rodgers C.B. Morton dealt what the *Salt Lake Tribune* called a "death blow" to the plan by rejecting all applications for right-of-way permits for the project. This news apparently came as a complete surprise to Kane County officials. According to the report in the local paper: "The proposed Kaiparowits plant would impose severe additional adverse environmental impacts upon this major recreation area through the construction of associated facilities, such as transmission lines, roads, pipelines and plant and coal mining facilities, the secretary said. The plant, also would adversely affect air quality in the Lake Powell region."[51]

John C. Whitaker, undersecretary of the Interior Department, speaking to a group of National Park Service rangers, further explained the position taken by the government. "Since Secretary Rodgers C.B. Morton took the position that the plant could not be built on the border of the Glen Canyon National Recreation Area because of its proximity to the Navajo Plant near Page, the companies involved and the department have been working on the problem." He further remarked that it was crucial to protect the five to six mile buffer zone between the plant and the recreation area to protect the lake and its scenic beauty. Acknowledging that it was still important to produce more electrical power for the growing population in the greater Southwest, Whitaker stated that the solution was to find a different site.[52]

Although talk and speculation continued for another two years, the project finally died when the utility companies decided to abandon the project in 1975.

Politics

In the 1960 presidential election, Kane County voters supported Richard Nixon over John F. Kennedy, 876 to 213, continuing their tradition of supporting Republican candidates. The majority also voted for Republican George D. Clyde for governor against his opponent, William A. Barlocker. In 1964, the county cast double the number of votes for conservative Republican presidential nominee and Arizona senator Barry Goldwater against Lyndon B. Johnson, and 714 also voted for archconservative Ernest Wilkinson against 414 who voted for Democrat Frank Moss, showing the county's conservatism, as both Democrats won easily in the state, as did Johnson nationally.

A chair chosen by the county commission presided over all meetings, which had to include at least two members to conduct valid business. Commissioners were required to be residents and voting members of the county. Over time, county commissioners were overwhelmingly Republican, reflecting the political affiliation of most county voters. Kane County officials include the three-member commission, a county sheriff, county recorder, county clerk, and county treasurer. During the twentieth century, the county also has always had a county attorney. Earlier, legal work was handled by local attorneys on a case basis. County departments included management of a wide variety of functions, including engineering and surveying, maintenance of buildings and grounds, elections, planning and zoning, sheriff's office, county jail, fire suppression, building inspection, health services, public welfare, highway maintenance, county fair, county library, and the county's agricultural extension service.

The Kane County Clerk recorded the proceedings of all commission meetings and also performed other traditional duties. Among other duties, the clerk is responsible for the issuing of all marriage licenses in the county, the execution of all real estate transactions approved by the commission, and the administration of oaths to county officials. The county clerk published notices of elections and offices open for election; organized the distribution of ballots, voting booths, and all other supplies; designated the polling places for voting districts; oversaw voter registration; prepared lists of delegates; and certified elected delegates. For almost two decades, the county clerk was D.M. Tietjen.

For the past fifty years, Kane County has had a county auditor. The auditor is the principal budgetary officer of the county and calculates annual property taxes, keeps accounts of receipts and disbursements for all departments of the county, and annually examines all county books. During the Depression years, the devaluation of property became particularly complicated and this became the responsibility of the auditor.

The county assessor determines the taxable valuations of real and personal property. Tax assessments and valuations provide valuable information about local economic conditions.. The county treasurer collects all property taxes levied on property in the county. The county recorder keeps the permanent books and files of deeds, mortgages, maps, plats, judgments and other court orders, military records, and other legal documents up to date, and ensures that they conform to national standards.

Besides coordinating with other county governments, county officials also worked in cooperation with federal agencies. For instance, on 11 March 1963 National Park Service official James Edan again met with the commission to discuss jurisdiction of roads within the Department of the Interior Glen Canyon withdrawal area in Kane County. Commissioner William J. Smirl asked for the cooperation of the park service in opening up the area and developing future roads that he thought would be necessary.[53]

During the 1960s, county officials increasingly appealed to state government leaders to give more support to economic development of southern Utah. On 10 March 1969, Kane County Commissioner H. Bernell Lewis read a resolution drafted by the body to the Utah Senate and House of Representatives "setting forth the lack of economic development in Kane County and the many things that could be done to start and stimulate this development."[54]

Also in 1969, the Kane County Commssion began development of a comprehensive master plan. By April, detailed maps had been made of each of the county's cities and towns. The commissioners were being assisted by Planning Research Associates, Kendell Brinkerhoff of the Farm Home Administration, the Kane County Planning and Zoning Commission, and John C. Willie, a planning consultant who had been hired to review the comprehensive sewer and water plans as part of a $4,500 study funded by the Farm Home Administration.[55]

The county commission held a series of public meetings while developing its plan for the county to promote the value of a master plan, to discuss growth potential in the county, and the value of the plan regarding proposed development. A meeting held 30 April 1970 at the Kanab BLM office included representatives from several local governmental agencies, businessmen, mayors of nearby towns, and state representatives. The meeting was held after the initial introduction of a draft of the Kane County master plan, to see if it matched the objectives of federal agencies involved in the management of county lands. A particular focus was the Kaiparowits Plateau power project, and the minutes of the meeting illustrate how complicated the interactions between the different agencies had become in the planning process. Because the projected coal mines were on BLM land, that agency had the power to decide whether or not the project should go forward. The National Park Service was also involved because of the proximity of the project to Zion National Park and Glen Canyon National Recreation Area, and it was particularly concerned about potential environmental impacts caused by pollutants emitted by the proposed plant. William G. Bruhn of the Utah State Planning Commission spoke of the need for industrialization in the area and for greater utilization of local resources in the production of electrical power. The Utah State Road Commission was concerned about roads that would lead to the project. Also in 1970, the county commission reviewed a study of the Escalante drainage system conducted by the BLM under the direction of Fred Howard.[56]

The master plan was finally adopted on 22 October 1970 after six years of discussion. To meet the objections of those who opposed any regulation, commission chair H. Bernell Lewis stressed, "There may be—there can be—changes made in the Master Plan. This is not a binding situation. This is for orderly growth, development and progress in the county. Zoning is there to be changed. This is just a starting point. Zoning is there to prevent that which you don't want done in the county."[57]

County commission work still basically involved local matters. In September 1970, for example, commissioners approved an appropriation for scholarships awarded to the Kane County queen and her attendants.[58] In February 1971 the commission reviewed the results of a health survey conducted by the Kane County health nurse and a report from the Long Valley Lions Club about the annual county fair.[59]

Although after 1972 Utah counties were given the power to determine the form they would assume, Kane County continued with its three-member board of county commissioners, two of whom were elected for four-year terms and one to a two-year term.[60] In May 1972 the commission voted on school district reapportionment and created six county voting precincts.[61] Members also designated $1,000 for the county fair budget. Commissioners were assigned to specific areas of supervisory responsiblity such as road construction and maintenance and law enforcement. The county hired an advertising agency to help bring Kane County's natural attractions to the attention of potential tourists.

At the November 1972 election, the majority of voters in the county again voted Republican for the presidential candidate, supporting Richard Nixon with 1,146 votes against George McGovern, who received 218 votes. They also supported Republican candidate for the House of Representatives Sherman Lloyd with 950 votes against successful Democrat Wayne Owens. For governor, however, county voters supported popular Democrat Calvin Rampton.[62] In the 1974 senatorial race, the majority of Kane County voters supported Republican candidate Jake Garn, who received 871 votes, against 418 votes for Democrat Wayne Owens.

Transportation and Communication

A significant highway project—Arizona Highway 389/Utah Highway 59—which runs west from Fredonia, opened to traffic in July 1967. This stretch of road facilitated the connection between Fredonia to Hildale, Colorado City, Hurricane, St. George, and Las Vegas.[63]

Traffic volume in Kane County increased by 62 percent between 1962 and 1973 according to the Utah Foundation, a private research organization. The report, commissioned by the Utah State Highway Department, said that highways and roads in the county averaged 143,300 vehicle miles per day in 1972 as compared to 88,400 in 1962.[64] Because the county has been neither a significant destination attraction in itself nor the location of major traffic routes, Kane County's traffic is relatively light compared with that of more populated Iron and Washington counties to the west. There are few, if any, travel agencies, bus companies, airports, or railways in the county. Truck hauling and motor freight companies are found in Kanab, however, as are some automobile dealers, repair and service companies, and parts suppliers.

A new facility was built for the Kanab Post Office in 1960, located near the intersection of Main and Center Streets.[65] It opened on 1 November with 3,175 square feet of floor space, a large parking lot, and two thirty-foot covered loading docks.

During 1965 the Kanab's Lions Club was instrumental in bringing television transmission to Kane County. The area received transmission of the major network channels and the public educational
television channel out of Salt Lake City. Radio station transmissions
coming out of Cedar City, Provo, and Salt Lake City also reached the
county.

In 1960 Bonanza Airlines decided to withdraw airline service at
the Kanab Airport because of limited use.[66] In 1968 Pacific Western
Airways began daily service to Kanab.[67]

County Life and Economic Growth

In 1959, Kane County commissioners began discussions about
building a new fifteen-bed county hospital. They budgeted $500 for
the development of plans, selection of a site, and the exploration of
funding sources, according to Odell J. Watson, chair of the Kane
County Hospital Board. They proposed funding the hospital without
a tax raise, taking advantage of the federal Hill-Burton Act, which
provided funds for local governments for projects that would have a
public benefit. In September a successful bond election was held in
support of the hospital; only forty-six votes were cast against the
idea.[68]

The new hospital was built, and it was dedicated in October
1962. During the ceremonies, Dr. George Aiken spoke about the history of efforts to provide medical care to the county's residents. The
Southern Utah News described the facility as including the latest
equipment and increased space for local patients: "The new 13
patient rooms, with beds for 26, has been several years in the building. Completely air conditioned it has oxygen piped into each room,
a modern all-electric kitchen, and a nurse call that goes throughout
the building. It has a complete laboratory and such new equipment
as a 300 M.A. X-ray and the latest style surgery table and light."[69]

In 1961, California Pacific Utilities began purchasing power from
Garkane Power Association, which would result in a savings because
of the cooperative's hydroelectric plant at Boulder, Utah. A local
reduction in rates of 17 percent was predicted. The Glen Canyon
Dam project promised even greater electrical savings.[70]

In the early 1960s the county had one bank and trust company

and no savings and loan associations. The nearest machine shop was
located eighty miles away. The weekly newspaper was the *Southern
Utah News,* which was published in St. George. In 1961 the *Southern
Utah News* reported on the most recent study conducted by the Utah
Bureau of Economic and Business Research, published by the College
of Business at the University of Utah. It included information that
average non-agricultural employment in Kane County increased by
nearly 10 percent, brought about by increases in the service industries that were formed to satisfy the needs of construction workers in
the area. As well as increased tourism and the opening of the concrete
plant in the county to provide material for Glen Canyon Dam.

For other Kane County workers, the picture was less positive,
however. The average monthly non-agricultural wage was $295, an
increase over that in 1960 but far less than the state average of $369.
Construction had declined to almost half the figure of 1959. There
was no new residental construction at the time of the study. Dun and
Bradstreet studied sixty-four manufacturers, wholesalers, retailers,
and other Kane businesses and reported a dip in business activity.
The report in 1963 listed eight businesses in Orderville; three in
Alton; and forty-nine in Kanab.[71]

Kane County's thirty-eight service establishments total revenue
in 1963 was $662,000, according to a Bureau of the Census report.
Forty individuals were employed in the service sector at miscellaneous businesses—auto repair, the motion picture industry, distribution and recreation businesses, and motels.[72]

Census Bureau figures in 1965 revealed that Kane County's forty-
six retail establishments had decreased by four percent in total sales
from the numbers posted in 1958—to a total of $2.8 million.[73] There
was some new business activity, however. Wesley and Thurma J.
McAllister began a greenhouse business in 1964 selling plants out of
Mac's Green House. Next door to the greenhouse was the Skabelland
Horse Trailer Construction business. The Arizona Fuel Corporation,
four miles south of Kanab, employed numerous Kane County men
and supplied oil to local customers.

The president of California-Pacific Utilities, E.K. Albert,
announced on 29 July 1965 that the company had signed a contract
with the U.S. Bureau of Reclamation to purchase power from the

Colorado River Storage Project. This contract arranged for the delivery of power to the Kanab-Fredonia system that would result in considerable savings to local customers. When the change was effected, the system shifted from diesel-generated power to hydroelectric power from Glen Canyon Dam. The plant at the north end of 100 East Street in Kanab was shut down.

Long-distance telephone service came to Kane County in 1966 through a Mountain States Telephone Company microwave system linking Kanab and Cedar City.[74] Residents felt that they were part of the national communication revolution that was linking Americans almost instantaneously to news sources through telephones, radio, and television. Over time, service expanded and new systems updated antiquated equipment. In 1973, for instance, two hundred new phone lines were added to the Kanab system.[75]

A clothing manufacturing plant out of Barco, California, came to Kanab in the late 1960s, supported by the efforts of the Kanab Chamber of Commerce and other locals. Citizens from local clubs and other civic groups helped paint, clean, and renovate the facility, and the Kane County Commission and Kanab City assisted with sewer lines and beautification of the lot. The Barco plant opened in November 1968 with considerable fanfare. The Kanab High School band played, President Daniel S. Frost of the Kanab LDS Stake offered a dedicatory prayer, and William Smirl of the Utah Industrial Promotion Commission and Kanab Mayor A.D. Findlay welcomed the company to Kane County. Barco specialized in making uniforms for nurses and industrial workers. Kane workers would sew the uniforms at the plant using pre-cut fabric pieces shipped from Gardena, California. The plant manager was Arthur DeBoer, from California. Edna Green and Norma Hamblin traveled to Gardena to be trained in the operation of the company. They then helped train local women in how to use the sewing machines and assisted Barco in setting up the shop. The company employed fifty-two women.[76]

Kanab Wood Products started operations in February 1968, bringing new jobs to the area. Occupying the buildings formerly used by the Dame Molding Mills (which had moved in 1965), company owners Lloyd Chamberlain, Duke Aiken, Emron Robinson, Carol Barnson, and Dell Stalworth of Hurricane brought their own equipment to initiate production. The Kanab Development Corporation assisted them with the structures. The mill purchased low-grade lumber from the Kaibab Lumber Company and produced from it pallets, trailer frames, two-by-four studs, survey stakes, and other products.[77]

Kanab was by far the largest town in the county, with a total population of 1,645 in 1960; but its population dropped to 1,381 by 1970. Orderville had 371 residents in 1950, 398 in 1960, and 399 in 1970. Glendale had 226 people in 1950, shrinking to 223 in 1960 and 200 a decade later. Alton residents numbered 154 in 1950, 116 in 1960, and only 62 by 1970.

Kane County's population dipped in the decade between 1960 and 1970 according to the United States Census. In 1960 the population was 2,667; in 1970 it was 2,421.[78] Fourteen of Utah's twenty-nine counties experienced similar declines during this same decade. The counties that had successfully developed non-agricultural industries generally were those that were able to keep a stable or increasing population base. Despite the general population decline, Kane County's school district population increased from 742 to 770 students.[79]

The county was sparsely populated, and no towns were technically considered urban areas. Ten percent of the total population were over the age of sixty-five and another 10 percent was between the ages of fifty-five and sixty-four. A large group was middle-aged, between thirty-five and fifty-four—514 persons, or 21 percent. Children below the age of eighteen represented 43 percent of the population. There were 722 children and adults between the ages of three and thirty-four enrolled in school. Of the county's adults, 64.4 percent of the men and 69.4 percent of the women had graduated from high school. Of the total population, only 0.8 percent were foreign born, and 4.7 percent were second-generation immigrants. Most people in the county were native-born citizens.[80]

Of the group older than sixteen years in age, 74.1 percent of the men were employed, as were 38 percent of the women. In terms of occupational composition, the county had changed from earlier generations, most markedly in terms of a greater diversification of occupations; 42 percent had white-collar jobs, and 23 percent were government workers. The total work force numbered 1,290. The largest categories of workers were in retail (225 people), non-agricultural common labor (250), and government (250). Others were employed in construction, public utilities, mining, and other types of jobs. Kane County's principal mining production was coal.[81] In the effort to reach out to distant markets as a tourist destination, Kane County businesses, and Kane County itself, began advertising more regularly in statewide publications like the *Salt Lake Tribune* and the *Deseret News* and continued to advertise in the *Southern Utah News.*

The average monthly wage of Kanab's work force was $288 in 1963, $324 in 1967 and $396 in 1973. Although only $45,100 was spent in new residential construction in 1963, the figure was $325,100 in 1973. An increase also was seen in non-residential construction. The largest employers in the county during the period were the Kane County School District, the federal, state, and county government offices in Kanab, Bullfrog Marina, and various motels and cafes. The Maxwell Brothers sawmill, located in Glendale, also employed a number of local men, as did the Kane County Ready Mix Company, located in Kanab and an important producer of concrete. Vaughn Judd also had a sand and gravel business located in Kanab. Arizona Fuels produced oil, gas, and coal. Lewis Meats, near Kanab, was a producer of meat products. In Kanab, the Utah Sportswear Company employed about forty-five workers and the Eddy Manufacturing Company had ten employees.

A study conducted by the Utah Foundation, a private research organization reported that Kane County business activity rose 22.7 percent between 1965 and 1970—to a total volume of $4,492,000. The study also suggested that business activity increased in 1970 by 11.7 percent, although this was largely due to inflation. It increased another 21 percent in 1971, and another 20 percent in 1973, a trend that would continue through the decade due to high rates of inflation.[82] Retail sales for 1974 were $2,800,000.

Kanab

The new Kanab LDS stakehouse, dedicated in February 1960, was built at a cost of $360,000. The 18,905-square-foot addition almost tripled the original square footage and included twenty classrooms, a baptismal font, Sunday School room, library, and full-size basketball court.[83]

In 1964, a third city well was dug at the mouth of Cave Lake Canyon. Mayor H. Bernell Lewis and his city council directed the construction of a 342-foot-deep well. That same year, the Federal Housing and Home Finance Agency installed a chlorination system to the water supply. Expansion of the water system in the 1960s and 1970s was largely driven by fluctuations in weather conditions. A 100-day dry spell in 1972 and other severe droughts in each decade suggested the necessity for developing more efficient ways of storing water and anticipating future needs.[84]

A public swimming pool, new city park, and other recreation facilities were constructed in the 1960s—new amenities that improved the standard of living in Kanab.[85] The city council proposed a mobile-home ordinance to try to maintain the quality of residential areas, as residents looked for government assistance or regulation in some areas while opposing it in others.[86] Kanab Jaycees staged an annual "Wild West Days Rodeo" in late June. Sponsoring semi-professional as well as professional roping, bareback, saddle bronc, and Brahma bull riding, bull dogging, and a team ribbon pull, the communitywide event was a local favorite.[87]

Although it continued through the 1960s on a volunteer basis, Kanab's Volunteer Fire Department had twenty-seven members, a system of inspections and drills, and up-to-date equipment. Each Thursday evening, the department volunteers met for reviews and drills to ensure they kept current on procedures.

By the 1970s, the county hospital in Kanab had thirty-one beds and was staffed by three practicing physicians, two dentists, and six nurses.A group of business leaders and other concerned individuals began a "Doctor's Fund" in 1970 to help attract doctors to the area. The group included prominent local leaders of women's clubs—Joan Wright, president of the Ladies Literary League; Joyce McAllister, president of the Junior Cultural League; and Nellie Jones, president of the Kanab Women's Civic League.[88]

Orderville

Architect Paul Evans designed the Valley Elementary School, which was finished in 1968. Reflecting modern educational philosophy at the time, the school facilitated "individualized instruction" and "team teaching" with its flexible classrooms that could be made large or small with portable partitions, depending on the need.

The economic development of Orderville came to a virtual halt at the end of the united order period. In the 1960s, however, local leaders began discussions about ways to draw manufacturers or other businesses to their town. The Orderville Community Development Committee also sought to find work to carry local workers through the winter months. With the encouragement of county agents Carl Hatch and Wayne Rose, the group organized to bring "some progress to the town." The importance of bringing television reception to town was discussed as was building low-cost, affordable housing for newcomers. Planning and development subcommittees included such things as parks, recreation, community beautification, industrial development, real estate, public relations, publicity and advertising, tourism, and television.[89] Their efforts led to some modest successes, although, for the most part, Orderville today remains a quiet rural community.

Alton

In 1962 additional remodeling to the local Mormon chapel brought a bishop's office, kitchen, recreation rooms, and storage areas. To unify the hall and its several additions, the entire meeting-house was covered with aluminum siding resembling the white, horizontal wood siding found throughout town.[90]

Glendale

A gas station was opened in 1966 and a drive-in was completed in 1968 in time for the Fourth of July. According to one writer, Glendale has proclaimed itself to be "one of the richest towns" in the state for its size.[91] This may have been true in historic times. Certainly the outstanding architecture of the demolished 1890s meetinghouse and social recreation hall and several existing fine dwellings attest to a sophistication and quality one would expect to find in more urban settings.

Tourism and Movie Making

The Utah State Road Commission described the importance of the tourist and movie business to Kane County by the 1960s:

Kane County has been the location for a number of movies during the last several decades. (Utah State Historical Society)

For a number of years it was estimated that the movie companies that made pictures in Kanab grossed $2,000,000 per year. This will probably be a continuing resource for the community. Parry Lodge does between $50,000 and $55,000 business each year. These together with the nearness of Kanab to Bryce Canyon, Glen Canyon Dam, and Zion's National Park are all related to the tourist interest in this part of the country.[92]

Eighteen Kanab businessmen joined together to promote travel and vacation inducements to Kanab at a meeting in January 1962. C.W. Parry led the discussion, which focused on the need for increased and improved advertising and signs, as well as finding ways to pull tourists into the area from nearby sites such as the national parks of the region. Their immediate plan was to put up four large road signs that advertised Kanab's motels and restaurants. They also planned radio commercials for the peak tourist months.[93]

In May 1962 the *Salt Lake Tribune* featured the Glen Canyon area

In 1963 much of the movie *The Greatest Story Ever Told* was filmed in Kane County. Shown in this picture is the front of the walls of Jerusalem during the shooting of a scene depicting Christ's entry into the city on Palm Sunday. (Utah State Historical Society)

in the magazine section of the paper. Raymond Taylor, president of Consumers Agency, Inc., who had business interests in the county, offered to mail out this sixty-four-page publication to several potential "friends" to Kane County businesses. He also planned to leave in June for Europe, where he planned to show to potential investors a film on Glen Canyon Dam produced by the BLM.[94]

A twelve-month travel survey of motor vehicle travel through the state issued by the Utah Travel Council reported that Kane County received $3,970,300 from tourism revenues in 1970, making it one of the top ten tourist destination areas in the state.[95]

On 7 January 1971 the Parry Lodge in Kanab became the property of Golden Circle Tours, a corporation that included a broad base of local businessmen and individuals.[96] The Parry Lodge expanded under its new owners, adding twenty-four new motel units in June

1972. The units were prefabricated structures built by Boise Cascade and transported to Kanab on trucks. Each unit measured approximately 336 square feet and included heating and air conditioning, king-size beds, and interior furnishings. Norman Cram, president of Golden Circle Tours, said that the lodge was interested in catering to people and tours who "wish to stay in the area for a few days while they visit the nearby national parks."[97]

Occasionally, commission minutes of the period mention negotiations with film companies for the rent of equipment, arrangements to use particular sites for filming, or other matters; but the film industry was not nearly the income generator that it had been before the 1960s. In May 1975 the commission supported the idea of rebuilding "Movie Town," the frontier-town movie set in Johnson Canyon, which had become quite worn down. Funds would be available after 1 July 1975 from the five county association (with Beaver, Garfield, Washington, and Iron Counties) of which Kane was a part to rebuild the main street and other parts of the movie set. Several television program producers had inquired about renting the set.[98]

Kane County still benefited from its proximity to national parks and recreation areas—including the new Glen Canyon National Recreation Area—and the Dixie National Forest. Nearby Utah state parks included Coral Pink Sand Dunes State Park and Kodachrome Basin State Park.

At the three-quarter mark of the century, county residents were relieved with other Americans to finally be out of the Vietnam conflict and hoped that the domestic troubles and scandals of the Nixon administration also were now behind them with Nixon's resignation in 1973 after the Watergate scandal became more fully known. Residents looked to celebrate the nation's bicentennial and hoped-for future prosperity, but it was easy to see that conflicts over public lands would continue to occur in coming years.

Endnotes

1. "Reclamation Action Moves Toward Construction of Glen Canyon Dam," *Kane County Standard,* 4 November 1949

2. "River Project Passed, What Can We Expect in Kanab?" *Southern Utah News,* 1 March 1956.

3. "Speculation Runs High Since Passage of River Bill," *Southern Utah News*, 8 March 1956.

4. See "Richfield-Panguitch Groups Make Another Trip to Capitol to Try to Delay Progress on State Route to Dam," *Southern Utah News*, 13 December 1956; and, "Delegation Disregards Southern Utah Rights, Twist Facts and Confuse Issues," *Southern Utah News*, 22 November 1956.

5. "Utah and Arizona highway officials meet with Bureau of Reclamation officials in Phoenix on Glen Canyon," *Southern Utah News*, 19 April 1956.

6. "Arizona Officials Attend Washington Meeting in Interest Glen Canyon," *Southern Utah News*, 17 May 1956, 7 June 1956.

7. "Kanab Area Sees Start of Activity as Projects Get Underway on Dam," *Southern Utah News*, 28 June 1956.

8. "Complete Plans for New Community at Glen Canyon is Released by Bureau of Reclamation Officials," *Southern Utah News*, 18 April 1957.

9. "Bids on Land Go at High Figures," *Southern Utah News*, 13 June 1957.

10. "Glen Canyon City Holds Community Meeting Wednesday," *Southern Utah News*, 26 June 1958.

11. "Glen Canyon City Students Will Enter Page School," *Southern Utah News*, 19 January 1961.

12. "Highway Dedication Ceremony is Big Success," *Southern Utah News*, 25 September 1958.

13. *Southern Utah News*, 11 April 1957.

14. "First Payload Crackles Off at Glen Dam," *Southern Utah News*, 10 September 1964.

15. "First Concrete Pour at Glen Friday," *Southern Utah News*, 16 June 1960.

16. "Early Water Storage in Lake Powell," *Southern Utah News*, 14 March 1963.

17. "Utah Behind In Development at Lake Powell," *Southern Utah News*, 31 December 1964.

18. "Glen Dam Dedication Today," *Southern Utah News*, 22 September 1966.

19. See the following for background on federal programs and land use policies: John B. Wright, *Rocky Mountain Divide: Selling and Saving the West* (Austin: University of Texas Press, 1993); Julia M. Wondolleck, *Public Lands Conflict and Resolution: Managing National Forest Disputes* (New York: Plenum Press, 1988); Wesley Calef, *Private Grazing and Public Lands* (Chicago: University of Chicago Press, 1960); Sally K. Fairfax and Carolyn

E. Yale, *Federal Lands: A Guide to Planning, Management, and State Revenues* (Covelo, CA: Island Press, 1987); and Elizabeth Darby Junkin, *Lands of Brighter Destiny: The Public Lands of the American West* (Golden, CO: Fulcrum Publishing, 1986).

20. *The Principal Laws Relating to Forest Service Activities,* Agriculture Handbook No. 453 (Washington, D.C.: Government Printing Office, 1974), 194.

21. See United States Bureau of the Census, *Census of Agriculture, 1964* (Washington, D.C.: Department of Commerce, 1965).

22. "Big Turn Out of Stockmen, Others, Air Local Dissatisfaction with BLM," *Southern Utah News,* 3 December 1964.

23. "Dept. of Agriculture Census indicates 127 farms in county," *Southern Utah News,* 30 December 1971.

24. "BLM Dedication," *Southern Utah News,* 4 December 1969.

25. "BLM makes sweeping recommendations at Kanab; local stockmen express displeasure," *Southern Utah News,* 12 August 1971.

26. "Local Stockmen and BLM working toward accord," *Southern Utah News,* 13 January 1972.

27. Ibid.

28. "Kane County livestock men give views to Sherman Lloyd," *Southern Utah News,* 2 September 1971.

29. "Kane County sheep industry begins to fade away," *Southern Utah News,* 10 June 1971.

30. "Kaibab Lumber Company Operation Is Real Asset to Southern Utah Area," *Southern Utah News,* 3 March 1960.

31. "Kaibab Lumber Curtailment Releases Sixty Workers at Fredonia Plant, Market Inventories Ahead of Demand," *Southern Utah News,* 11 August 1960.

32. "Company, Union, Solve Problems at Local Sawmill," *Southern Utah News,* 5 October 1961.

33. "Local Lumber Workers Seek Congressional Action to Protect Jobs," *Southern Utah News,* 31 January 1963.

34. "Cutback set by Kaibab," *Southern Utah News,* 19 March 1970.

35. "Land-use planning group to guide local thought," *Southern Utah News,* 20 December 1973.

36. "Kane County Coal Lands Approved for Leasing to Large Arizona Company," *Southern Utah News,* 2 January 1964.

37. "U. Aide hints 'Bonanza' in Kane Coal Deposits," *Southern Utah News,* 16 January 1964.

38. "Large Coal Lands in Garfield and Kane Mapped," *Southern Utah News*, 24 September 1964.

39. "Utility Firms Plan Utah Power Plant," *Southern Utah News*, 12 November 1964.

40. "Development Studied at 5-County Organization Meet Held in Kanab," *Southern Utah News*, 4 March 1965. See also *Southern Utah News*, 25 August 1966.

41. "Fine Boost for South Utah's Economy," *Southern Utah News*, 11 February 1965.

42. "Rep. Burton Says Coal Generator Plant Looks Favorable for County," *Southern Utah News*, 19 August 1965.

43. See, for example, *Southern Utah News*, 14 October 1965, 29 June 1967, 22 February 1968.

44. "Facts and Figures on Kane Coal," *Southern Utah News*, 21 October 1965.

45. "University of Utah Survey Says Kaiparowits Coal Most Difficult," *Southern Utah News*, 16 January 1969.

46. Ibid.

47. "Lake Powell Roads Delayed Governor Tells Democrats," *Southern Utah News*, 20 June 1968.

48. "Kaiparowits water contracts to be signed," *Southern Utah News*, 2 October 1969; "Kaiparowits closer to reality," *Southern Utah News*, 18 December 1969.

49. "Kaiparowits still in study stage says Watt," *Southern Utah News*, 16 April 1970.

50. Quoted in *Southern Utah News*, 1 April 1971.

51. " Kaiparowits project dealt death blow," *Southern Utah News*, 14 June 1973.

52. "Kaiparowtis project still breathing," *Southern Utah News*, 1 November 1973.

53. Kane County Commission, Minutes, 11 March 1963.

54. Ibid., 10 March 1969.

55. "Kane County Master Plan Reviewed at Commission Meeting," *Southern Utah News*, 24 April 1969.

56. See Kane County Commission, Minutes, 9 July 1970, 23 July 1970.

57. "County Commission Report," *Southern Utah News*, 29 October 1970.

58. Kane County Commission, Minutes, 14 September 1970.

59. Ibid., 18 February 1971.

60. The Utah Constitution was amended in 1972 to read: "The Legislature shall, by general law, prescribe optional forms of county government and shall allow each county to select, subject to referendum in the manner provided by law, the prescribed optional form which best serve its needs, and by general laws shall provide for precinct and township organizations." Before 1972 the legislature was given the responsiblity to establish a uniform system of county government throughout the state.

61. Kane County Commission, Minutes, 8 May 1972.

62. Ibid., 7 November 1972.

63. "Fredonia Holds Ribbon Cutting for Highway 389," *Southern Utah News,* 27 July 1967.

64. "Traffic volume in Kane County increases by 62.1 percent since 1962," *Southern Utah News,* 6 September 1973

65. "Kanab to Get New Post Office Building," *Southern Utah News,* 15 September 1960.

66. *Southern Utah News,* 12 March 1959, 1 September 1960.

67. "Pacific Western Airways Sets Daily Service, Kanab," *Southern Utah News,* 25 July 1968.

68. *Southern Utah News,* 2 April 1959, 24 September 1959.

69. "Monday Ceremony Notes Completion Beautiful New Kane County Hospital," *Southern Utah News,* 25 October 1962.

70. *Southern Utah News,* 28 December 1961, 22 February 1962, 9 September 1965.

71. "Dun & Bradstreet Figures Show Decrease in Kane Businesses for Year," *Southern Utah News,* 3 January 1963.

72. "Kane County Grossed $662,000 in 1963 From Thirty-Eight Businesses," *Southern Utah News,* 1 April 1965.

73. "Census Bureau Figures Show Drop," *Southern Utah News,* 7 January 1965.

74. "Kanab and Fredonia will take step forward to go on direct dialing system January 16th," *Southern Utah News,* 13 January 1966.

75. "200 New Phone Lines to Be Added in Kanab," *Southern Utah News,* 1 March 1973.

76. *Southern Utah News,* 29 August 1968, 7 November 1968, 10 August 1972.

77. *Southern Utah News,* 8 February 1968, 18 February 1965.

78. "County Population drops over '60 census," *Southern Utah News,* 28 January 1971.

79. "Kane County Schools increase enrollment by 28," *Southern Utah News,* 19 November 1970.

80. "Average family income was $7,935 in Kane, says census," *Southern Utah News,* 23 March 1972.

81. *Minerals Yearbook 1969* (Washington, D.C.: United States Bureau of Mines, 1969), 3:739.

82. See *Southern Utah News,* 18 June 1970, 8 April 1971, 20 April 1972, 12 April 1973.

83. "Ward House to Be Dedicated Sunday," *Southern Utah News,* 18 February 1960.

84. "Kanab Studies Water Problem," *Southern Utah News,* 6 April 1972.

85. See *Southern Utah News,* 7 September 1961.

86. "Local trailer dwellers oppose Kanab Mobile Home Ordinance," *Southern Utah News,* 24 September 1970.

87. "Imported Livestock Promise Good Show," *Southern Utah News,* 17 May 1962.

88. "Report on 'Doctor Fund' given by civic clubs," *Southern Utah News,* 22 October 1970.

89. "Orderville Community Development Committee Holds First Meeting Under New Officers," *Southern Utah News,* 15 February 1962

90. Allen D. Roberts, "Survey of LDS Architecture in Utah: 1847–1930," LDS Church Historical Department, 1974.

91. Adonis Findlay Robinson, *History of Kane County,* 429.

92. Ibid., 192.

93. "Kanab Business Men Organize to Promote Travel," *Southern Utah News,* 4 January 1962.

94. "Local Developer Tells Plans to Advertise This Area," *Southern Utah News,* 7 June 1962.

95. "Travel Survey lists Kane in top tourist $," *Southern Utah News,* 3 September 1970.

96. "Lodge Has Interesting History," *Southern Utah News,* 21 January 1971.

97. "Spacious New Rooms Increase Parry Lodge facilities in Kanab," *Southern Utah News,* 29 June 1972.

98. Kane County Commission, Minutes, 12 May 1975.

CHAPTER 12

THE BATTLE OVER LAND, 1976 TO THE PRESENT

K̲ane County contains about 2.5 million acres, over 2 million of which are controlled by the federal government, with another 200,000 controlled by the state, so it was doubtless inevitable that other citizens eventually would want some say in the uses and management of the land. Particularly critical in the years of the Sagebrush Rebellion, which swept through the region in the late 1970s and 1980s, and finally towards the end of the century with the creation of the Grand Staircase-Escalante National Monument and the proposed designation of wilderness land in the county and state, the battle between local interests and other citizens became key themes in the county's history.

Life in the County

Many of the key issues faced by the Kane County Commission in the 1970s and later had long demanded attention—county roads, the library, the hospital, health issues, and schools, for example—but others reflected changing times. Civil defense in the post-World War II years was considered an important priority, welfare after the New

Deal years became a responsibility of government, and boosterism and community promotion were increasingly important and focused on tourism and the county's unique canyonland attractions as recreation destinations. Locals also tried to advertise the county as an ideal backdrop for Hollywood productions. On 25 September 1979 a group called the Kane County Little Hollywood, Inc. asked the commissioners' support to take a presentation to the "State of Utah Movie Makers and to producers in California to make a portfolio."[1] In response to this request, the commission planned to host a welcoming party for producers and other filmmakers. Other groups such as the Kane Travel Council and the Kanab Chamber of Commerce had begun doing the same type of work and had some different ideas about how it should be done. Because the travel council received funding from the county commission and was established by the commissioners, it was accountable to them.

In 1979, Kanab officials applied to the BLM to purchase property near the Kanab airport, where they planned to install lagoons for the sewer system and possibly put the landfill.[2] Because of renewed area growth, plans began in 1979 for a new, larger courthouse facility.

Robert Houston joined Robert Russell and Sterling Griffiths on the Kane County Commission after the 1980 election. One of their first matters of business was hiring a director for the county fair and bringing it back under the auspices of the commission. In the next election, a female candidate—Esther Heaton—was successful in her bid for a place on the county commission. Heaton, Russell, and Calvin Johnson were the first commissioners to have offices in the new courthouse, which was opened in 1982. The old courthouse was demolished. Investigations conducted by the sheriff included sexual harassment charges, misconduct regarding commodities, and various other problems previously unfamiliar to the county's history.

Kane County's total budget in 1984 was $1,925,627. Clearly the county's business had become increasingly complex and required a growing number of employees and structures to house county government. In 1985 the county commission was composed of Calvin Johnson, Jay Ramsey, and Vince Underwood. Kirk Heaton was county attorney, Weldon Glover was county clerk and auditor, and Chris Engstrom was the county treasurer. Many responsiblities that

Kanab High School's basketball team in action against Milford. (Kane County News)

earlier had been given to one individual required the attention of a number of people. In 1985 the county established a juvenile court and probation system. The commission declared 10 November through 16 November 1985 Arts and Humanities Week. Besides other duties, the commission considered subdivision proposals and zoning changes, engineering surveys, maintenance of the courthouse grounds and building, and planning for future growth and change. They established committees and a variety of institutional responses over the years to address the area's needs.

The Debate Over the Use of Public Lands

As early as the Depression years, livestock grazing in Kane County was affected by government policies coming out of U.S. Grazing Service District No. 4, which included Iron, Washington, western Kane, and western Garfield counties. Eastern Kane County came under the jurisdiction of Grazing District No. 5. After the creation of the Bureau of Land Management (BLM) following World War II, local BLM grazing district boards made recommendations about the carrying capacity of the public range, issued grazing licenses and permits, established fees, and created rules for fair range practice, interacting in the process with local grazing associations.

The national debate over the uses and management of public land heated up after the 1960s and the nation's citizens became increasingly polarized over the issues as rhetoric intensified and passions were inflamed. Many westerners believed that they were entitled to continue to use the land in traditional ways, as they or their forebears had worked hard to establish a livelihood in the region. Opponents argued that the former users had benefited at the public's expense from lenient public policies and that the land now needed to be better protected for the benefit and use of all Americans, including future generations yet unborn. The National Park Service, the Forest Service, the Bureau of Land Management, the Kane County Commission, environmental groups, and the citizens of the county, state, and nation engaged in a debate during these decades over the best way to balance competing interests on the questions of the use of natural resources and the management and use of public lands.

Although most residents in Kane County, southern Utah, and much of the rest of the state exulted in Glen Canyon Dam and Lake Powell, opposition had existed to the dam since it was first proposed. Environmental groups had reluctantly muted opposition to Glen

Canyon Dam in the 1950s in order to prevent a dam higher on the Colorado River in Colorado, but many increasingly came to regret their decision, particularly due to the loss of the tranquil beauty of Glen Canyon to the rising waters of Lake Powell. David Brower of the Sierra Club was one prominent environmentalist who regretted the trade-off; and in subsequent years others rose, using Glen Canyon Dam as a hated symbol of environmental losses to developers. Edward Abbey was one prominent author who focused attention on the beauties of the Colorado Plateau and inspired thousands of followers while also irritating many officials and longtime residents of the area, including a number in Kane County. Tensions and ideological differences between the two groups characterized much of county life and development in the last years of the twentieth century.

The Kaibab mill was an important local employer but was severely impacted by concerns over wildlife habitat and other environmental issues that developed in the 1960s. Logging also faced increased foreign competition as worldwide economies developed in the late twentieth century. These factors along with changes in U.S. Forest Service policies and increasing restrictions on timber cutting began to cut into the profitability of logging operations in the area. This caused a gradual reduction in timber harvests from the nearby plateaus. Sawmill operations were reduced gradually over time and were closed altogether in early 1995.

The Sagebrush Rebellion

The passage of the Federal Land Policy and Management Act (FLPMA) in 1976 surprised western conservatives. The act was supported by the BLM and promoted multiple-use and sustained-yield policies for public lands as well as land sales at fair market value—a move that hindered private developers of the land who were trying to divest the government of its holdings. A movement informally known as the Sagebrush Rebellion arose to try to reverse public policies and limit government control of lands or at least their restrictions on traditional users. If possible, it sought to assign public land to the respective states, claiming that it should be owned (or at least managed) by those who lived there.

Many longtime residents of the area and traditional users of the land were also angered by increasing restrictions on any development, including the increasing need for environmental impact statements and public hearings for proposed developments. They also were unhappy about lands that were set aside in the late 1970s as wilderness study areas, with the possibility of later becoming fully protected wilderness areas. After the election of Ronald Reagan as president in 1980, the Sagebrush Rebellion movement to "take back the land" for the states was fostered by Secretary of the Interior James Watt.

The Sagebrush Rebellion fanned the flames of opposition too, however, although most residents of Kane County viewed it sympathetically, while seeing most opponents as "outsiders"—"liberal environmentalists," as they were often labeled—from the cities of the Wasatch Front or outside the state. After 1980 most politicians elected to statewide positions were Republicans who supported the idea of federal lands being given to the state, although the accompanying federal funds that would be lost made many of them hesitate to really push the agenda, most being content with its rhetorical value. However, this was not the case with ranchers and timber and mining interests as well as many local politicians who actively battled conservationists over policies that could dramatically affect them.

Environmentalism

A growing environmentalist movement helped create the most serious debate over land use of federally controlled lands in the county as elsewhere in the West during the latter decades of the twentieth century. Beginning to flourish in the 1960s with various wilderness acts, conservation measures, and such laws as the National Environmental Policy Act of 1969, and continuing in subsequent decades with other important measures, including the Federal Land Policy and Management Act of 1976, these laws were intended to develop federal policy in favor of protecting the environment. They had vital impact on the multiple-use debate over federal lands.

The various measures and proposals have encouraged public participation in the decision-making process—a process that it was hoped would help lead to understanding and consensus but that more often led to polarization and hardening of opposed positions. Still, the environmental movement could claim some victories on behalf of endangered species such as the California condor and the Colorado River ecosystem. In the latter case, in the mid-1990s release flows from Glen Canyon Dam have attempted to replicate the spring floods before construction of the dam, helping build and restore beaches and other habitat below the dam.

Big Water, Utah

The debate over local control of land took an interesting twist in the efforts of a polygamous clan to homestead in Kane County. Alex Joseph and his followers first came to southern Utah in the mid-1970s. Joseph led about ten families intending to homestead disputed federal land who filed thirteen applications for 160 acres each as homesteads under the Homestead Act. The families came from Kentucky, Arizona, California, and Idaho as well as from other parts of Utah. Soon after their arrival, they raised wooden shacks and tents and brought with them house trailers and other temporary shelters, as they squatted, claiming a right to the land.[3] The federal government sued the homesteaders who had filed, and in August 1975 a federal court ruled against the homesteaders for settling on land not established for homesteading. The original claims of the group were located along the Paria River in Cottonwood Canyon. Members of the group subsequently filed another 113 claims for 640-acre desert land homesteads. The claims included more than 38,000 acres of land west of Lake Powell, some of it located on National Park Service property, and other land identified as part of the possible Kaiparowits power plant coal fields.

Alex Joseph was a colorful individual who at one time considered running for governor as a Libertarian candidate, appeared in television commercials, married an estimated twenty-seven women, and served as mayor of a town. Excommunicated from the Mormon church, Joseph founded his own church—the Church of Jesus Christ of Solemn Assembly—but made no effort to give it a more formal organizational structure or dogma. Instead, it was composed of what he described as a "lot of friends who agree with us."[4] His actions led him to be called by some the father of the Sagebrush Rebellion. It has also been claimed that these actions helped spur passage of the Federal Land Policy and Management Act to help the government control the land and prevent such challenges.

Joseph's group squatted on the land based on their interpretation of a 1916 provision that allowed homesteaders to settle on public land while waiting for action on their petitions to the Department of the Interior to reclassify desert land for agricultural use. Utah Judge Aldon Anderson disagreed with their interpretation and issued an order directing members of the group to vacate the land within a thirty-day period. It read in part: "The defendant's homesteading efforts are unlawful since the land in question has not been classified by the secretary of the interior for homesteading. . . . The defendants have no right, title or interest in the lands."[5] Anderson also issued an injunction halting further construction or clearing of the land by members of the group.

Joseph's group homesteaded the land with the claim that the BLM program of multiple-use opened the land to homesteaders. Judge Anderson addressed this interpretation: "While it is true the land in question has been given a multiple-use designation, nothing in this designation removes the necessity of the secretary of the interior's prior classification for homestead entry."[6] Also involved in the case were Joseph's common-law wife Elizabeth as well as about ten other couples or individuals. According to Joseph, most of the homesteaders were not practicing polygamists. Reacting to the order, and referring to the 1890 massacre of Indians in North Dakota by federal troops, Joseph told reporter Robert A. Bryson, "If authorities come under the cloak of illegality, there is no question what we will do. If they come down here illegally—we will make Wounded Knee look like a picnic."[7] No blood was shed, however, when the group abandoned the area in November 1975. The homesteaders did accuse federal marshals of using "storm trooper tactics and burying items they could have confiscated."[8]

When the group eventually vacated the land, they tore down their temporary shelters and moved their trailers to a new location they called Bac Bone, a site off U.S. Highway 89 about fifteen miles west of Glen Canyon City.[9] Over the next several months, the group built more houses and laid out streets with names like Joseph Smith

Boulevard, Brigham Young Boulevard, Liberty Avenue and Independence Drive. They had plans to build the "Eliza Snow Elementary School" and the "Heber Cleveland High School." The Red Desert Cafe that was established employed some of Joseph's wives.

In December 1975 Joseph claimed a temporary victory when U.S. District Court Judge Aldon J. Anderson granted Joseph's motion to kill an order sought by the Bureau of Land Management to require the homesteaders to move once again. Kane County officials maintained that Bac Bone land was zoned for recreation and not as a townsite, and they claimed that Joseph, as leader of the group, needed to file for a zoning change if he intended to build a town there. By December some ten trailers as well as tin shacks and plywood buildings had been erected on the site. The buildings included a knife-making shop, a town hall, and a few dwellings. "We won the war," claimed Joseph. "Now, we'll have to think up another battle. We won one for today."[10] Eventually, however, the group was ordered to pay $14,204.67 for their eviction from their homestead claims.[11]

When Joseph's group moved from Bac Bone in early 1976 they located in Glen Canyon City, the town built during the construction of the Glen Canyon Dam during the 1960s. There they built a family compound they called the "Long Haul" and set up a home school for the group's children, including a military academy for their sons, the "Royal Guard."[12] Many of the children attended Page, Arizona, schools. Alex Joseph served as the town's mayor after its incorporation in 1983, and other members of his family played prominent roles in helping the town—now named Big Water—to thrive. Not long after changing their town's name from Glen Canyon City to Big Water and reorganizing local government, Big Water City Attorney Elizabeth Joseph, a wife of Mayor Alex Joseph, asked the county commission to establish a justice of the peace position for the town and to establish a new precinct to handle traffic tickets.

Joseph's critics accused his extended family of dominating local politics and business. For example, Joseph's real estate company received rent from the city for space in his own home for the town offices while the city hall sat vacant. His wife Delinda served as city clerk and wife Elizabeth for a time was city attorney. Jeff Banfill, Joseph's nephew, was the chief deputy sheriff of Kane County and the town's only paid peace officer. Joseph was under contract to do billing for the city water department and his wife Pamela read water meters. Joseph was very proud of the fact that the town of Big Water collected no property taxes and yet was still out of debt. The town had a population of about 450 in 1989. Locally published, the *Big Water Times* newspaper was edited by Elizabeth Joseph; Boudicca Joseph gathered advertising revenue.

In 1982 Elizabeth Joseph ran as a Republican candidate for Kane County Attorney against fellow Republican and long-time resident of the county Kirk Heaton. A 1979 graduate of the University of Utah Law School, Elizabeth Joseph said one question she would like to see addressed was that of growth versus what she described as the status quo. Elizabeth Joseph lost to Heaton by a count of 984 to 438 and said, "It's just too much for them to believe I could live the lifestyle I do and still be a reasonable person, and I can't blame them for that."[13]

Big Water was never far from controversy. The town built a baseball diamond and cemetery on federal land without formal permission in 1987 and enacted a law which made it a misdemeanor in Big Water for federal officials to exert control over the land within the six-square-mile city limits.[14] In 1988, Alex Joseph led an effort supported by about 350 of the town's residents to separate from Kane County to create a new county—provisionally called Dry Powder County—to better promote development of land near Lake Powell, which proponents of the change claimed that Kane County officials had "dragged their feet on."[15] Under the proposal, Big Water would be the only incorporated town in the new county, which initially would have a total population of about 550 inhabitants.

The idea was received with dismay by Kane County officials. County Commission Chair Vincent Underwood said of the proposal: "I can only speak for myself, but I'm sure we would fight it. Almost any county would. One reason is that the county would lose large tracts of federal land, for which the federal government makes large payments in lieu of taxes."[16] Somewhat ironically, it seems, like other rural westerners elsewhere, federal money for the land was welcomed by those who resented federal management of that same land. In December 1990 an effort to disincorporate Big Water was defeated by a vote of 101 to 71.[17]

The issues faced by Alex Joseph and his family and followers in their efforts to create a town that matched their own sense of what composed the good society was nothing new, echoing the historic battle in Utah between the federal government and the Mormon settlers of the nineteenth century. This twentieth century version illustrated the same tension between strong-minded individuals, bolstered by their sense of what was right, and the formidable power of government and outside interests.

The Battle Over Wilderness

One of the major controversies of recent years in Kane County as throughout Utah in general and southern Utah in particular has been the debate over wilderness designation of public lands—in particular, lands managed by the Bureau of Land Management. After passage of the Federal Lands Policy and Management Act in 1976 pressures increased to set aside federal land as wilderness. As part of this process, by the late 1970s the Bureau of Land Management had inventoried its managed lands and recommended that some of it (including land in Kane County) be set aside and protected as wilderness study areas, with the possibility that they would later become fully protected wilderness areas after further review and public comment.

The public soon commented—on both sides of the issue. Rural residents of southern Utah generally complained, as did their elected representatives and county commissioners, while environmentalists generally believed that more land should have been set aside and campaigned actively to raise the acreage that would be protected. By the 1980s a coalition of environment groups was actively pushing for the establishment of 5.7 million acres of BLM land as wilderness, whereas the BLM had originally called for about 3 million acres. Utah's governor and congressional representatives—all of whom were Republicans by the mid-1990s—wanted less than 2 million acres set aside, and there were many in southern Utah who felt that any wilderness would be too much. Battle lines were drawn to the point that compromise seemed impossible. In fact, rather than attempt to compromise, each side talked of making the gap wider— environmentalists conducting their own reinventory of lands in the

Rodeos are important in Kane County. (Kane County News)

late 1990s to establish more than 5.7 million acres; their opponents threatening to ask for less, and feeling that they generally had the upper hand, since they had the political power in Utah and hoped to push their plans through Congress.

Roads that traverse an area are a significant issue, particularly in
the designation of wilderness areas, opposing sides debating what can
legitimately be considered a road in the affected areas, since the presence of legitimate roads could invalidate an area as a wilderness.
Some county commissioners in southern Utah actively encouraged
recreational all-terrain vehicle (ATV) users and others to traverse
contested areas, further provoking conservationists, who already
lamented what they considered the scarring of the landscape.

A public hearing held in Kane County on 24 February 1995 on
the issue of wilderness designation of certain BLM areas was representative of others held throughout the state during the 1980s and
1990s, as many types of opposing viewpoints over land use were presented. More than one hundred governmental representatives and
private citizens gathered to discuss the issue of the designation of
wilderness areas in Kane County and elsewhere in the state. Each person was allowed only three minutes to speak, but many were able in
that brief time to encapsulate their viewpoint. Although proponents
of wilderness were often in the majority in other meetings held in
other areas of the state, that was definitely not the case in Kane
County meetings. The following excerpts from the minutes of the
meeting illustrated the opinion of many locals that wilderness areas
would impact them economically.

> *Bob McKay.* Mr. McKay stated that he is a resident of Johnson
> Canyon. He said that he feels wilderness closes off land. By its
> nature it is already wilderness. WSAs [wilderness study areas] have
> had the effect of already being treated as wilderness. He opposes
> any wilderness in Kane County.
>
> *Calvin Johnson.* Mr. Johnson stated that much of the WSA is
> in grazing area. There are CCC corrals and a house that were built
> in the 1930s located inside this area. Fences, reservoirs, roads that
> were built during that time are still there and they are still useable.
> Due to wilderness he is unable to run water to his private land. He
> opposes wilderness in Kane County.
>
> *Karen Alvey.* Mrs. Alvey said that she does not believe in
> wilderness. Why type off 1 million acres of land. Many natural
> resources that are important to the economy of Kane County will
> become unusable. All motorized vehicles are forbidden. She said

her handicapped son who will not be able to access this land because wilderness discriminates against handicapped people. She is opposed to wilderness in Kane County.

Kenyon Little. Mr. Little stated that water is a big problem in Kane County. There was very little water when the early settlers came to Kanab. There is still very little water due to encroachment of the pygmy forest. Locking land into wilderness will take away the ability to allow water to recharge. He is opposed to wilderness in Kane County.

Brent Robinson. Mr. Robinson stated that he runs cattle in the Wire Pass area of Kane County. Wilderness has been like trying to work with a ball and chain attached to your leg. WSAs have made it impossible to maintain water lines and to take care of the land. He is opposed to any more wilderness in Kane County.

Jeff Johnson. Mr. Johnson said that he is a life-long resident of Kane County. His ancestors were pioneers and early settlers of Kane County. He said that livestock people develop trails, water, etc. Hikers use these trails and drink the water that livestock people develop. Wildlife is there because of what livestock people have done. The cattle are there two or three months out of the year. Water, mineral blocks, etc. are left and benefit wildlife. He is opposed to further wilderness in Kane County.

Viv Adams. Mr. Adams stated that wilderness is supposed to be an area that is not impacted by man. It will be the playground for the rich, the strong, and the young—which leaves most of the people who live in Kane County out. Wilderness will adversely impact Andalex which would be a very good thing economically for Kane County.

Nils Bayles Dr. Bayles said that he was speaking as the super-intendent of the Kane County Schools. Utah is the most under-funded school system in the nation. If we take away school trust lands, Kane County school children will be adversely affected. He is opposed to more wilderness in Kane County.[18]

Ardent supporters of wilderness could also be found, however, although in Kane County they were far outnumbered by those opposed to wilderness designation of public land. Many Kane County residents believed that they should decide how land in the county should be used no matter who owns it, claiming that traditional uses should continue without any outside interference.[19] Cattleman and former county commissioner Calvin Johnson believed that cattlemen respect the land, make an honest living from it, and make a minimal impact on it. They don't seek to destroy the land, he claimed, but use it to support their families and their community.[20]

Opponents argue that cattlemen and others have abused the land in the past, necessitating such protection for the land as national parks, national forests, and other conservation and preservation measures that are supported by the majority of the nation's citizens. Some of those citizens also are now arguing that the time has passed for such cattlemen and others to have special privileges on land that belongs to all Americans. They have argued that the American taxpayer subsidizes Kane County (and other) cattlemen who use the public land as rangeland, since they pay far less to use it than they would have to pay to use private land; and these citizens no longer want that situation to continue. Others want areas protected for recreational uses; some want wilderness protected for its value alone and for benefits that such land brings to the psyche and ultimate welfare of human beings and the welfare of other species on the earth.

The polarization on the issue that is found throughout Utah thus promised to divide citizens in the future, making compromise on the issue something that is desired by many but very difficult to achieve. The extreme positions of both sides have increasingly polarized citizens of the county, the state, the West, and the nation in general. Bureaucratic officials and others who try to compromise or effect solutions have become increasingly attacked by those on either side of the issue, as responsible civic dialogue by mutually civil parties seems to have disappeared here as in much of political society, where the attempt seems more to win at any cost rather than try to understand and accomodate any legitimacy in an opponent's point of view. Such partisanship can lead to a situation where opponents may not even try to further understanding, instead acting where they are able, and effectively surprising opponents who might have thought they had the upper hand. Such a situation happened in Kane County and other parts of southern Utah with the creation of the Grand Staircase-Escalante National Monument.

Since the establishment of the national monument, the issue has not died down, and at the time of this writing promised to be a major source of debate in Kane County as elsewhere in Utah and the West for many years to come, at least until Congress eventually approves one of the plans for Utah wilderness.

Grand Staircase-Escalante National Monument

The issue of increased federal management of public lands came to a head with President Bill Clinton's creation of the Grand Staircase-Escalante National Monument on 17 September 1996, surprising Utah's state, congressional, and county leaders. The Grand Staircase-Escalante National Monument covers approximately 1.7 million acres in Kane and Garfield Counties, including some land that was part of the wilderness study controversy, and its creation shocked many in those counties and in state government. Headlines on the front pages of Utah newspapers marked the day as significant for Utah's history. One read, "It's a Monumental Day for Utah," "Coal vs. Cool! Does Beauty Outweigh Economic Value?"[21] But emotions ran high and reactions varied dramatically as to whether this was good news or if it promised economic decline for the area.

Mike Gorrell, writing for the *Salt Lake Tribune,* wrote of the region's allure and natural value:

> Orange and red plateaus rise out of gray badlands. Arches abound. Petrified wood remains from ancient forests. Rock formations that stir geologists' souls are right there for the viewing, exposed by erosion over the millenniums. Caves and crannies in canyons carved by trickling streams contain the ruins of bygone civilizations—Anasazi and Fremont. A rich array of dinosaur bones are embedded within layers of rock laid down a hundred million years ago or so earlier. There are large, unbroken stretches of wildlife habitat. And with that, there is a silence and solitude not found in the more heavily traveled world all around.[22]

Southern Utah Wilderness Alliance issues coordinator Ken Rait, one of the most vocal foes of the efforts of mining industries to establish large mining operations in the region, voiced the opposition to the use of the land for the extraction of raw materials. "We ought not let the interests of foreign mining firms dictate American public-lands policy," he said, claiming that the greatest value is "the natural quiet, the uncluttered vistas, the complex canyon country" of the surrounding plateau.[23]

Kane County officials took a radically different view and described the designation of the monument as a "loss of rights." They, along with the majority of county residents, Utah's congressional delegation, the governor, and many other state officials felt that the federal government had overstepped its bounds in creating the new national monument.

The meaning of this event varies according to the special-interest groups impacted by the monument designation. Some stress that the area is rich in energy and mineral resources, and claim that there are at least 11.3 billion tons of coal within the monument area and $200 billion of recoverable coal. In January 1997 the Utah Geological Survey (UGS) estimated that the monument area contains between $221 and $312 billion worth of recoverable coal. The same study estimated the value of other materials in the area to include $2 billion to $17.5 billion in coal-bed methane gas, $20 million to $1.1 billion in petroleum, and more than $4.5 million in other minerals.[24] Before the monument designation, many of these mineral deposits were the subject of numerous claims, including mining claims, mineral leases, and oil and gas leases from the state and federal governments. Many believe that these previously existing claims are in jeopardy due to the new designation, which would make it more difficult to gain access to them, among other things. Critics of mining in any part of the monument area argue that the remote location of these deposits would make it prohibitive to any but the most gigantic and disruptive operation to extract and ship them to market. "That a mineral is present means nothing," according to Lawson LeGate, Southwestern Regional Director for the Sierra Club; "the question is whether you can get it out of the ground economically."[25]

The national monument designation was made possible by the Antiquities Act of 1906, which gives the president of the United States the power to declare national monuments to protect objects of historic or scientific interest located on federal lands. The Antiquities Act has been used dozens of times by various presidents to create other national monuments; the Grand Staircase-Escalante National

Monument was unique in many ways, however. It was by far the largest national monument in the lower forty-eight states and was to be run by the Bureau of Land Management. It also was established with very little if any prior consultation with local government leaders.

Land management under the Antiquities Act is shaped by the particular needs of the situation, namely, the resources the president seeks to protect, and the monument is subject to "valid existing rights." However, while the act does respect previously existing contracts, government agencies could deny ancillary permits, such as those that companies would need to build roads on federal lands to get the mined products out of the area. It was almost certain that the monument designation would stop development of a proposed coal mine by the Dutch firm Andalax Resources Inc. in the undeveloped Kaiparowits Plateau region.

The new monument area encompassed 176,000 acres that belonged to the state of Utah and 200,700 acres of mineral rights owned by the state. These are lands managed by the School and Institutional Trust Lands Administration, and revenues from them are used to provide funds for the benefit of Utah schools. The state mineral, oil, and gas leases already established on these trust lands were worth at least $17 billion according to the UGS and could be worth as much as $25 billion. In January 1997 the agency that managed the state school trust lands was considering a lawsuit against the federal government to claim these funds.[26] Other plans were underway, however, to trade these lands for other federal land in the state with equivalent or greater energy resources, and agreements to this effect were reached in late 1998. Water rights established prior to the proclamation were designated according to state law and present another key concern in the minds of local inhabitants of the county.[27]

Many Kane County residents already were frustrated by years of declining economic opportunity as extractive uses of natural resources declined and were angered by what they perceived as governmental interference in local affairs. The national monument's creation further angered them. Numerous residents gathered in the auditorium of the Kanab High School on 18 September 1996 to protest the new national monument designation. Those who attended this "Loss of Rights" rally wore black ribbons of mourning as they came to the microphone to voice their frustration and anger. Most businesses closed down during the rally, and the town of Kanab was decorated with black balloons and posters expressing such sentiments as "Shame on You, Clinton" and "Why Clinton, Why? You're Our President."

Residents protested President Clinton's methods and said that he ignored locals in the process–particularly the process of asking for and attending to public input. In their minds, the environmental-impact statement for the area that the BLM had been working on for several months was discounted altogether. Mayor Brent Mackelprang of Fredonia, Arizona, criticized the president's decision to make the declaration without local consideration. His cousin Roy Mackelprang owned 1,000 acres in the monument area and feared he would not be fairly compensated for his land's value. Verlin Smith, the manager for the BLM's Kanab Resource Area, wondered publicly how his office would implement the monument's management plan with existing resources—the small, fourteen-member staff was already strained. Even Democratic legislator Mike Dmitrich of Price came out in criticism of Clinton saying, "I'm the kind of Democrat that supports jobs, education and health."[28]

The Kane County Commission unanimously opposed the designation, saying: "During a time when we are sending thousands of U.S. soldiers to the Persian Gulf to defend our oil interests, it appears counterproductive for the White House to sign an executive order that virtually eliminates one of the richest coal reserves in North America."[29] They predicted drastic effects on school-trust funds.

Not everyone opposed the monument, however, although much of the support was from outside the state or from its urban areas along the Wasatch Front. Environmentalist groups like the Sierra Club and the Southern Utah Wilderness Alliance had long focused on the wilderness debate and played a role in influencing Clinton's decision, as did the intractability of Utah's congressional delegation, who perceived that they held the upper hand in the matter prior to the announcement of the new monument, pushing for a much lower wilderness area allotment than most citizens in the state seemed to favor according to polls reported in the news media. Environmentalists pointed out with some pleasure that a Democratic president like Clinton was already unpopular in Utah and had little to lose by exercising his own political muscle, particularly in opposition to Republican politicians who felt they could dictate the state's agenda in regard to federally managed lands.

Kathleen A. McGinty testified before the United States House of Representatives Subcommittee on National Parks, Forests, and Lands Committee on Resources on 29 April 1997 and spoke of her belief in the importance of the decision in setting an agenda of wilderness protection and land-use policy. She said,

> I understand that different people have different views of the lands in the monument. For my part, I have never seen a place as beautiful, as wild, as close to the hand of God. The Earth's own history is openly told as nowhere else in the canyons and plateaus, slickrock and sandstone. The history of courageous, resourceful people graces the land. In a continent of rising noise, urbanization, and busy-ness, I think this remote, quiet, often austere federal land deserved protection. But I respect the views of others, including some of those here today, who saw other values in the land.

For my part, I think that establishment of the monument was one of the most profound and appropriate acts of land stewardship ever taken in this Nation. It is an understatement to say the lands contain objects of scientific or historic interest, as the Antiquities Act requires. Conservation of the lands has been hotly debated for decades, and by last year, the lands were in real jeopardy. The President exercised his authority, despite potential political risk, to assure their continued protection. He protected the land and the traditional uses of the land, such as grazing and hunting, that are central to the area's rural values and quality of life. I think the President did exactly the right thing.[30]

University of Utah economist R. Thayne Robson believed the controversy over the monument to be particularly important because it "illustrates that important segments of the Utah community and national interest groups have created an environment in which the democratic tradition of compromise that produces rational decisions is impossible."[31] He continued, "The political and economic incentives reward conflict and extremist positions, preventing decisions based on the democratic traditions of compromise that provide a foundation for moving forward." For the people of Kane County, many of these pressing issues about land use are vital—they already inhabit the land and want to find ways to continue to provide for their families. The result is an incredibly polarized political environment where federal policies often are pitted against rural local interests in a seemingly irreconcilable stalemate.

There are varying explanations about how this situation came about, but it is in part due to changes in markets for agricultural and mining products and timber as well as fluctuating policies of federal land management involving a greater segment of the population. Robson also noted the importance of Utah politics:

> Since the 1960s, Utah politicians in both major political parties have tried to upstage each other in attacks on the federal government and federal land managers. As a consequence, nationally funded environmental groups have been able to raise significant resources to oppose the Utah political tides. These environmental efforts, as valuable as they may be, have only served to prod Utah political rhetoric to new heights of contentiousness."[32]

It is difficult to believe that this situation could easily change, for many of the opponents have differing views on a great many issues, continually frustrating each other. Many residents believe their opponents to be merely wealthy recreationists or idealistic proponents of wilderness and no development, oblivious to their concerns for making a living. For their part, many of the "environmentalists," as the diverse group as been labeled, often see locals as people so concerned with making money from the land that they would destroy it in the process for their short-term economic gain. Valuable conservation projects such as the reintroduction of endangered California condors to the Vermilion Cliffs area in the early 1990s brought general opposition from locals, much to the dismay of many otherwise moderate conservationists. Rural residents of southern Utah were for the most part dismayed in turn at a proposal gaining support in the 1990s for the dismantling of Glen Canyon Dam—a proposal that is not as nonsensical as it might first seem but which is certain to bring mounting opposition from many quarters if it is more seriously advanced in the future.

For many of the long-time inhabitants of the county, the principal issue is one of survival with a respectable standard of living and the maintenance of local communities. In the words of Scott Truman, residents were trying to preserve established practices or even expand them "so our children would not have to leave or so they would have something to which to come home . . . so our communities would not shrivel up and die."[33] International market forces and other changes of the late twentieth century, however, seem to make it inevitable that rural Utahns will have to find new economic arenas other than the traditional ones. Tourism is one of the more promising, as Americans with more leisure time and disposable income look to areas like Kane County for their recreational or scenic opportunities for diversion.

Andalex Resources, the coal company proposing a development on the Kaiparowits Plateau long at the center of controversy, in early 1997 formally withdrew its mine application that had been pending before the Utah Division of Oil, Gas and Mining since 1991. "Creation of the monument has made development of the mine futile," Andalex Project Manager Dave Shaver said, "We will continue our discussions with the U.S. Department of Interior and see what options remain."[34]

Kane County Commissioner Joe Judd made a statement before the Subcommittee on National Parks and Public Lands in April 1997 that characterized the attitude typical of local residents who felt the federal government had interfered unfairly in their local affairs. Judd described his county as one with 7,000 citizens, an annual budget of $2.25 million and limited opportunities for earning a living. "We just went through the closing of the uranium mine not long ago, costing us 150 jobs;" he said, "closing of the Kaibab sawmills, another 700 jobs; and looking forward to the opening of a coal mine which would have provided 900 jobs." County residents believed this coal mine would compensate for the jobs lost and make it easier for families to stay in the county. Judd continued, "But last September 18, all that changed. We now have condors for neighbors and the promise of the increase in tourism. We now have many things that are going to take place. As far as tourism is it going to offer us a benefit? . . . The government does not have to be at war with the local government. Given the right chance, we can work things out for everyone's benefit," he claimed.[35]

It seems both sides should realize that the "war" was created by them both. To end it, and work things out for mutual benefit, cooperation would be desirable, as would an understanding that things cannot be like they were one hundred, fifty, or even ten years ago in the area. Tourism and the development of other non-extractive economies will benefit the area in the long run and need to be examined by all groups and parties. The new monument (and any new wilderness areas) would not end grazing and other traditional uses of the land, but it seems probable that ranching will continue to decline in the area, if only because it faces increased competition in the international marketplace. Any raise in fees or other restrictions placed on the public grazing lands only underscores that basic fact.

Because approximately 68 percent of the Grand Staircase-Escalante National Monument area is in Kane County–49 percent of the total county area—management of the land was a particular concern of local government. According to Judd, tourists moving through the monument area would strain already limited resources—particularly if they get lost or in trouble, as there are no paved roads on the Kaiparowits Plateau. Others traveling through the area will potentially break laws and strain an already overburdened law enforcement and court system. Limited water resources will also be impacted.

Still, despite these concerns, the new national monument was a fact that area residents had to learn to live with and turn to their advantage, if possible. It helped some to realize that there was similar opposition to the establishment of all the other national parks and monuments in the area, and that all of them were now embraced by the great majority of county residents for the economic benefits they provided as well as for the scenic beauty protected for their enjoyment and that of future generations and their fellow citizens across the nation.

Kane County officials entered into a cooperative agreement with the Department of the Interior not long after the proclamation. In this agreement, the county was to receive $200,000 for improvement of economic, cultural, and other resources in the county. The commission was concerned that they had been left out of the deliberations regarding the creation of the monument and did not want to be left out of the planning process. "We believe the Federal Government has an obligation not only to invite us to participate but to provide the resources which will enable us to fully participate. Otherwise, we simply do not have the budget to be involved in any meaningful way. We are a poor county," Commissioner Joe Judd maintained.[36] A main concern was that the county's and the federal government's roles be clearly defined and not shift with each new administration. The county position reflected a concern for resolving the most immediate pressing issues but also sharing in the planning for the future.

A Demographic Picture: Kane County in the 1990s

The Kane County General Plan of 1993 provides an interesting glimpse into the demographic situation of the area in 1990. Of the total population of 5,169 residents (a large increase from the 4,024 in 1980), the majority live in cities or towns. Kanab had the largest population with 3,289, Big Water had 315, and Orderville had 443 inhabitants. Alton had a population of 100 and Glendale 282. Of the total population, some 60 percent were born in the state of Utah; sixty-nine individuals were foreign born, and twenty-three of them immigrated to the United States between 1980 and 1990.

In 1990 there were 1,728 individual households and 389 non-family households. The median family income was $24,904 per year. The average farm self-employment income was $4,004, which indicates that most farm families relied on farming only to supplement their income. Of the population sixteen years or older, 1,961 individuals were employed. Only nine claimed agriculture as their principal source of income (a decrease from seventy-four in 1980); 434 were employed in retail trade, and 425 were employed by federal, state, or local government. This represented 29 percent of the total and an increase from 22 percent in 1980, indicating a greater presence of government in county life—a fact welcomed by some but lamented by many others. About 82 percent of the town's adult population

Kanab High School's football team is a perennial powerhouse among Utah's rural high schools. (Kane County News)

twenty-five years or older had graduated from high school; 11 percent had received bachelor's degrees or higher. Of the total population, 111 had graduate or professional degrees.

The 1993 Kane County General Plan listed several basic services provided by county government including road maintenance, assessing and collection of taxes, recording of land transactions, law enforcement, care of public buildings, and land use management. The county did not provide services traditionally described as "municipal-type" services but did include a number of special service districts to provide for certain areas with special needs. They included the Glen Canyon Special Service District, Church Wells Special Service District, Mt. Carmel Special Service District, Western Kane County Special Service District, Kanab Creek Ranchos Special Service District, Kane County Water Conservancy District, Kane County Human Resources Special Service District, and the Long Valley Sewer

Improvement District. The county also continued to support hospital and school systems.

The county's one public airport is in Kanab, where Kanab Air Service and Aero Craft Aviation offer charter, rental, and leasing services at the present time. The nearest airports serviced by major airlines are in Cedar City and St. George. There are several private landing strips in the county, including ones at Swains Creek, Strawberry Valley, L.B. Ranch, Carmel Mountain Ranch, and Deep Springs. As the county's population increases and tourist visitation grows, it can be expected that the transportation industry will expand to meet new traveling needs.

Kanab

Over the decades, Kanab's business district has changed and expanded beyond Main Street. Nineteenth- and early twentieth-century buildings largely have been replaced by more modern facilities, many of which cater to the tourist industry. Tourism and related service industries became more important in the twentieth century as land-use restrictions and competitive national economic forces helped push many stockmen out of business or into other more lucrative occupations.

Alton

The town of Alton has declined gradually from its population in the 1930s to its present size of fewer than 100 people. No mills remain actively operating locally, but Alton men have been employed in the county's timber-cutting industry. Immense coal reserves are located near the town, and periodically plans have been broached to strip mine up to 10 million tons annually to ship to proposed coal-fired electric plants near Las Vegas or St. George.[37] Thus far, nothing has come of such plans, although some coal mining has been done to a limited extent. The vitality of the community is evident in the new home or outbuilding that is built every few years.

Orderville

Orderville today bears little resemblance to its appearance during the united order years of the 1870s and 1880s. The united order period buildings—the rock school, the church, and the social hall—

so proudly erected are gone. The north and south entries into town are now marked by several newer buildings catering to tourists, some built in modern false-front "vernacular" architecture. Other attractions feature what some call "tourist kitsch," such as a building south of town in the form of a rock, complete with a "mine entry" and fake "ancient" pictographs. Instead of replicating the town's historic fort from the 1870s, an unconvincing "Apache Fort" has been put up along the east side of the highway near the north entry to Orderville.

Glendale

The population of Glendale ranged from about 200 to 290 throughout the twentieth century, although its figure of 282 in 1990 was well above the low of 200 recorded twenty years earlier, indicating that the town is to some extent participating in the general growth of Utah, including Kane County, in the late twentieth century.[38] In recent years, the citizens of Glendale have beautified their Main Street, the old state highway, with attractive clusters of benches, planters, white picket fences and street signs.

Aside from the addition of a few scattered mid-to-late-twentieth-century structures, present-day Glendale is reminiscent of its more historic appearance. The commercial anchor to the west remains the small group of stores, service stations, and lodging places along U.S. Highway 89. The bungalow style Smith Hotel remains, as does the Mill and Orchards Building. The old mercantile has been remodeled, expanded, and sheathed with board and batten siding to give an "Old West" look to the country store complex. At the east end of town is the Glendale LDS Ward meetinghouse. The present brick building was erected in 1968. In its tall tower hangs the bell that once rang in the earlier frame church. The new church and the 1923 school, now the Long Valley Civic Center, are among the few masonry structures in a town still dominated by wood-frame construction.

Mt. Carmel

Farmsteads of modest frame homes and outbuildings remain scattered throughout the town at the present time. A now-abandoned cafe and a motel, both facing U.S. Highway 89, the town's Main Street, remain from earlier, more active, times. Some pioneer homes

A Kane County student examines the ruins of an old mining building at Paria during a field trip to the historic community in 1998. (Allan Kent Powell)

also remain, among them a plastered one-and-one-half story house with three dormers, a typical Mormon design. Also common in Mormon towns were one-story, double-cell houses with symmetrical facades of two doors and four windows. This plan is sometimes associated with polygamous households. During the Depression era, cottages with English architectural influences were popular; concrete block simulating rough stone and a steeply pitched gable roof invoke the picturesque cottage style.

Future Prospects

Popular films have still continued to use Utah backdrops, including such recent movies as the Indiana Jones series, *Thelma and Louise,* and *Independence Day.* Most Kane County residents favor the growth of the movie industry locally, and in this they are joined by many of their conservationist foes on other issues, most of whom see filmmaking as one of the more benign uses of the land.

Many Utah economists see tourism as Kane County's best bet for future economic development. Largely because of general increases in wealth and income in the twentieth century, tourism, travel, and recreation are growing nationally at surprising rates. The county would be "well advised," according to economist Thayne Robson, "to prepare to receive those expenditures by investing in an infrastructure that will accommodate, in an environmentally sound manner, the people who will visit." Robson believed that "The long-run tourism value of preserving the scenic and undeveloped character of the new Monument's 1.7 million acres will most likely exceed the value of all the resources now known to exist in the area many times over. Southern Utah communities will gain more wealth and income from travel, tourism, and recreation than they will ever gain from development of mineral or agricultural resources over a longer period of time."[39]

Others, however, believe that tourism is an insufficient solution to the economic issues facing the county. In his testimony before the House subcommittee on 29 April 1997 Kane County Commissioner Joe Judd lamented the loss of coal mining and the trade-off in terms of tourism:

> The budget increase we counted on from coal mining will be offset to some degree by an increase in tourism. But a *windfall* for the county? No! While tourism is already a large part of our income, it has its down-side also. First, it is very seasonal–from May to October. Second, it provides jobs that pay a minimum wage with no benefits. And right now each tourist dollar brought in costs us $1.25, just to provide the needed services: law enforcement, visitor aid, indigent care, fire protection, and water and sewer services.[40]

This point of view supported a more broad-based approach to economic development including traditional natural resource harvesting and growth of industry to ensure consistent, year-round economic health.

It is a pervasive opinion in Kane County that the federal government's land-management decisions are made with little regard to local land-use plans or desires. Kane County officials are attempting to become part of developing federal land-management plans, and they insist that federal land-use plans which regulate public lands in the county promote multiple-use and sustained-yield concepts, thus assuring a future for more traditional extractive uses of the land. However, such uses as ranching, mining, and logging are now increasingly subject to international marketplace competition, making marginal enterprises endangered without federal interference and subsidies—the very things so bitterly opposed by many in Kane County and also opposed by millions outside the county.

Solutions to the dilemma will not be easy, but concerned citizens on both sides of various issues are trying to work to both protect and live in the land they love. County officials intend to work with federal agencies in the development of new roads, development of other facilities, and the preparation of federal resource management plans. Acquisition or easements across private lands by federal agencies will be reviewed by the county commission. Ideally, in the future all federal land management agencies will make full assessments of the social and economic impacts of management decisions before acting.

Verlin Smith, BLM Kanab District Manager, said there were two extremes today—the extreme environmentalist who wants no use of the land, no development, but protection of the environment as it is, and the other extreme where residents want no protection, full use of the land and almost unrestrained development. Smith can see almost no common ground.[41] Attempting to gain an understanding of opposing points of view can at least be a start, however, and it appears that Kane County residents will have to accept the fact that some things have changed—just as the area's Native Americans did in the 1860s, the polygamous Mormons did in the 1890s, and their own immediate forebears did in the 1930s.

People like Verlin Smith believe it will be possible to create mutually beneficial and appropriate uses of the land that satisfy both parties. A willingness to explore new opportunities rather than see a conspiracy where there is none will also help. A love of the land is a starting point that people on both sides of the issues share. Clearly, the difference between the environmental point of view and that of the long-time resident will be the focal point in future discussions that promise to continue as long as people both need to earn a living and to care about the earth.

ENDNOTES

1. Kane County Commission, Minutes, 25 September 1979.

2. Ibid., 5 June 1979.

3. "South Utah Homesteaders Continue to Defy Authorities," *Salt Lake Tribune,* 26 October 1975.

4. *Salt Lake Tribune,* 27 June 1976.

5. "Court Orders Polygamist Off Utah Homestead," *Salt Lake Tribune,* 5 August 1975.

6. Ibid.

7. "Polygamist Vows to Stay, Fight," *Salt Lake Tribune,* 10 September 1975.

8. "Eviction ruling awaited," *Salt Lake Tribune,* 4 December 1975, C12.

9. "Polygamist Alex Joseph Takes Family Off Kane Homestead," *Salt Lake Tribune,* 15 November 1975, C1.

10. See "Alex Joseph Wins Battle," *Salt Lake Tribune,* 6 December 1975 and "Polygamist claims victory," *Salt Lake Tribune,* 8 December 1975.

11. "Joseph and 9 followers ordered to pay $14,204," *Salt Lake Tribune,* 12 May 1977.

12. "Polygamy–Best of 2 Worlds," *Salt Lake Tribune,* 12 September 1982.

13. See *Deseret News,* 13 September 1982, 27 November 1982.

14. See "Small Town Ready to Face U.S. Government for Land," *Salt Lake Tribune,* 8 November 1987.

15. "Big Water folks want to split Kane, form Dry Powder County," *Deseret News,* 6 June 1988.

16. Ibid.

17. "Big Water decides to remain a town," *Deseret News,* 19 December 1990.

18. Kane County Commission, Minutes, 24 February 1995.

19. Jackie Rife, interview with Martha Bradley, 9 July 1995.

20. Calvin Johnson, interview with Martha Bradley, 13 July 1995.

21. *Salt Lake Tribune,* 18 September 1996, A1.

22. Ibid.

23. Ibid.

24. "Monument Contains Billions in Coal," *Salt Lake Tribune,* 23 January 1997, B1.

25. Ibid.

26. "Agency Adopts Plan for Lost Trust Acreage," *Salt Lake Tribune*, 23 January 1997.

27. For a more extensive discussion of these legal issues see Thomas W. Bachtell and Michael S. Johnson, "Private Industry and Its Access Rights," in Robert B. Keiter, Sarah B. George, and Joro Walker, eds., *Visions of the Grand Staircase–Escalante: Examining Utah's Newest National Monument,* (Salt Lake City: Wallace Stegner Center and Utah Museum of Natural History, 1998), 121–25.

28. "Kane County Holds a Bitter Wake After Monument Decision," *Salt Lake Tribune,* 19 September 1996, A7.

29. "Monumental Day: Clinton Ready to Act," *Salt Lake Tribune,* 18 September 1996, A4.

30. Testimony of Kathleen A. McGinty before the Subcommittee on National Parks, Forests, and Lands Committee on Resources, U.S. House of Representatives, *Congressional Record,* 29 April 1997, 116.

31. R. Thayne Robson, "Monument Planning Through an Economist's Eyes," in Keiter, George, and Walker, *Visions of the Grand Staircase–Escalante,* 115.

32. Ibid., 116.

33. Scott Truman, "Maintaining Local Communities," in Keiter, George, and Walker, *Visions of the Grand Staircase–Escalante,* 151.

34. "Andalex Gives Up on Kaiparowits Mine," *Salt Lake Tribune,* 24 January 1997, B1.

35. Oversight Hearing before the Subcommittee on National Parks and Public Lands of the Committee on Resources, House of Representatives, 105 Congress, 29 April 1997, 74–75.

36. Ibid.

37. See Ward J. Roylance, *Utah: A Guide to the State* (Salt Lake City: Utah Arts Council, 1982), 663.

38. Allan Kent Powell, ed., *Utah History Encyclopedia,* 435.

39. Keiter, George, and Walker, *Visions of the Grand Staircase–Escalante,* 117.

40. Oversight Hearing, 29 April 1997, 74–75.

41. Verlin Smith, interview with Martha Bradley, 13 July 1995, Kanab, Utah.

Selected Bibliography

Allen, James B. "The Evolution of County Boundaries in Utah." *Utah Historical Quarterly* 23 (July 1955): 261–78.

Arrington, Susan, and Leonard Arrington. *Sunbonnet Sisters*. Salt Lake City: Bookcraft, 1984.

Auerbach, Herbert S. "Father Escalante's Route." *Utah Historical Quarterly* 9 (April 1941): 109–128.

Black, William Morley. Autobiography. Utah State Historical Society.

Bleak, James G. "Annals of the Southern Utah Mission." Dixie College Library, St. George, Utah.

Brooks, Juanita. "Journal of Thales H. Haskell." *Utah Historical Quarterly* 12 (1944): 69–98.

———. "Lee's Ferry at Lonely Dell." *Utah Historical Quarterly* 25 (1957): 283–95.

———. *Mountain Meadows Massacre*. Norman: University of Oklahoma Press, 1962.

Brown, Thomas D. "Journal of the Southern Indian Mission." Dixie College, St. George, Utah.

Carroll, Elsie Chamberlain., ed. *History of Kane County*. Salt Lake City: Utah Printing Company, 1970.

Carter, Kate, ed. *Heart Throbs of the West.* Twelve volumes. Salt Lake City: Daughters of Utah Pioneers, 1936–51.

Casey, Edward S. *Remembering: A Phenomenological Study.* Bloomington: University of Indiana Press, 1987.

Chamberlain, Mary E. Woolley. "Edwin Dilworth Woolley, Jr., 1845–1920." Utah State Historical Society.

Christensen, Vera A. "Biography of Ella Stewart Udall." Utah State Historical Society.

Claridge, Samuel. Autobiography. Utah State Historical Society.

Cleland, Robert Glass, and Juanita Brooks. *A Mormon Chronicle: The Diaries of John D. Lee.* San Marino, CA: Huntington Library, 1955.

Congressional Record, 29 April 1997.

Cox, Delaun Mills. "History of Delaun Mills Cox." Utah State Historical Society.

Crampton, C. Gregory. *Land of Living Rock.* New York: Alfred A. Knopf, 1972.

Crampton, C. Gregory, and David E. Miller, eds. "Journal of Two Campaigns by the Utah Territorial Militia Against the Navajo Indians, 1869." *Utah Historical Quarterly* 29 (April 1961): 149–76.

Dellenbaugh, Frederick S. *A Canyon Voyage.* New York: Knickerbocker Press, 1908.

———. *The Romance of the Colorado River.* New York: Knickerbocker Press, 1909.

Dewey, Richard Lloyd, ed. *Jacob Hamblin: His Life in His Own Words.* New York: Paramount Books, 1995.

Dodson, Wilbur E. "Historical Sketch of Kane County." (1937). Utah State Historical Society Library.

Dutton, Clarence E. *Geology of the High Plateaus of Utah.* Washington, D.C.: Government Printiong Office, 1880.

———. *Tertiary History of the Grand Canyon District.* Reprint. Salt Lake City: Peregrine Smith, Inc., 1977.

Ellsworth, S. George. *Samuel Claridge: Pioneering the Outposts of Zion.* Logan: Utah State University Press, 1987.

Esplin, Hattie. Life Sketch. Utah State Historical Society.

Fowler, Fred M. "Mary Fowler: A Child of Pioneers." Utah State Historical Society.

Gardini, Carlo. *Gli Stati Uniti Ricordi di Carlo Gardini.* Bologna: Nicola Zanichelli, 1887.

"The Glen Canyon Survey in 1957," University of Utah, Anthropological Papers, No. 30.1, March 1958.

Glover, Arthur. "A Brief History of the Life of Arthur Glover." Utah State Historical Society.

Gregory, Herbert E. "Scientific Exploration in Southern Utah." *American Journal of Science* 248 (October 1945): 535.

Hepworth, June Cox. "The Oak Grove Farm: History of William M. Cox and His Family." Utah State Historical Society.

Howard, Mary W. "An Example of Women in Politics," *Improvement Era* 17, pt. 2, no. 9 (July 1914): 865–68.

Journal History of the Church of Jesus Christ of Latter-day Saints. Archives of the Church of Jesus Christ of Latter-day Saints, Salt Lake City; hereafter cited as LDS Archives.

Judd, Esther Brown. "Biography of Zadok Knapp Judd, Jr. and His Wife, Ada Marie Howell Judd." Utah State Historical Society.

Junkin, Elizabeth Darby. *Lands of Brighter Destiny: The Public Lands of the American West.* Golden, CO: Fulcrum Publishing, 1986.

Kane County Basic Data of Economic Activities and Resources, Utah State Planning Board.

Kane County Commission, Minutes, Kane County Offices, Kanab, Utah.

Keiter, Robert B., Sarah B. George, and Joro Walker, eds. *Visions of the Grand Staircase–Escalante: Examining Utah's Newest National Monument.* Salt Lake City: Wallace Stegner Center and Utah Museum of Natural History, 1998.

Knowlton, Ezra C. *History of Highway Development in Utah.* Salt Lake City: Utah State Department of Highways, n.d.

Kolb, Ellsworth L., and Emery Kolb. *Through the Grand Canyon from Wyoming to Mexico.* Reprint. New York: Macmillan, 1946.

Larsen. Wesley P. "The 'Letter' Or Were the Powell Men Really Killed by Indians?" *Canyon Legacy* (Moab, Utah) 17 (1993): 12–19.

Lister, Robert H., and Florence C. Lister. *Those Who Came Before.* Globe, AZ: Southwest Parks and Monuments Association, 1983.

Mace, Blanche H. "Public Library from Scratch." Utah State Historical Society.

Mace, Rebecca Howell. Journal. LDS Church Archives.

"Manuscript History of Kanab Stake." LDS Church Archives.

May, Dean L. "People on the Mormon Frontier: Kanab's Families of 1874." *Journal of Family History* 1 (Winter 1976): 177–79.

May, Dean L., Lee L. Bean, Mark H. Skolnick, and John Metcalf. "Once I

Lived in Cottonwood: Population Stability in Utah Mormon Towns, 1850–1910." Paper given at meeting of Social Science History Association, Rochester, New York, November 6–9, 1980.

McAllister, William James Frazier. Autobiography. Utah State Historical Society.

Mendenhall, Sibyl Frost. "Biographical Sketch of Allen Frost." Utah State Historical Society.

Minerals Yearbook 1969. Washington, D.C.: United States Bureau of Mines, 1969.

Neff, Andrew L. *History of Utah.* Salt Lake City: Deseret News Press, 1940.

Newell, Linda King, and Vivian Linford Talbot. *A History of Garfield County.* Salt Lake City: Utah Historical Society and Garfield County Commission, 1998.

Nuttall, L. John. Diary. Utah State Historical Society.

Pendleton, Mark A. "The Orderville United Order of Zion." *Utah Historical Quarterly* 7 (October 1939): 141–59.

Perry, John, and Jane Greverus Perry. *The Sierra Club Guide to the Natural Areas of Colorado and Utah.* San Francisco: Sierra Club Books, 1985.

Poll, Richard D., Thomas G. Alexander, Eugene E. Campbell, and David E. Miller, eds. *Utah's History.* Provo, Utah: Brigham Young University Press, 1978.

Powell, Allan Kent. *The Utah Guide.* Golden, CO: Fulcrum Publishing, 1995.

Powell, Allan Kent, ed. *Utah History Encyclopedia.* Salt Lake City: University of Utah Press, 1994.

Powell, John Wesley. *Exploration of the Colorado River and its Canyons.* Reprint. New York: Dover Publications, 1961.

The Principal Laws Relating to Forest Service Activities. Agriculture Handbook No. 453. Washington, D.C.: Government Printing Office, 1974.

Reeder, Ray M. "The Mormon Trail: A History of the Salt Lake to Los Angeles Route." Ph.D. diss., Brigham Young University, 1966.

Ricks, Joel E. "Forms and Methods of Early Settlement in Utah and the Surrounding Regions, 1847–77." Ph.D. diss., University of Chicago, 1930.

Roberts, Allen D. "More of Utah's Unknown Architects: Their Lives and Works." *Sunstone Magazine* 1, no. 3:54–56.

———. "Survey of LDS Architecture in Utah: 1847–1930." LDS Church Historical Department, 1974.

Robinson, Adonis Findlay. *History of Kane County*. Salt Lake City: Utah Printing Company, 1970.

Roylance, Ward J. *Utah: A Guide to the State*. Salt Lake City: Utah Arts Council, 1982.

Seegmiller, Emma Carroll. "Personal Memories of the United Order of Orderville, Utah." *Utah Historical Quarterly* 7 (1939): 160–200.

Smith, Melvin T. "Colorado River Exploration and the Mormon War." *Utah Historical Quarterly* 38 (Summer 1970): 207–23.

"South Central Utah," U.S. Bureau of Land Management, 1967.

Statistics of the Wealth and Industry of the United States, Ninth Census. Washington, D.C.: U.S. Department of the Interior, 1872.

Stegner, Wallace. *Mormon Country*. New York: Hawthorne Books, 1942.

Subcommittee on National Parks and Public Lands of the Committee on Resources, House of Representatives, 105 Congress, 29 April 1997.

Thomas, George. *The Development of Institutions Under Irrigation*. New York: Macmillan, 1920.

Tissandier, Albert. *Six Mois Aus Etats-Unis Voyage D-un Touriste Dans L'Amerique du Nord Suivi D'une Excursion a Panama*. Paris, Libraire de L'Academie de Medecine, 1886.

Turner, Frederick Jackson. "The Significance of History." In *Early Writings of Frederick Jackson Turner*, edited by Everett E. Edwards. Madison: University of Wisconsin Press, 1938.

U.S. Bureau of the Census, *Census of Agriculture, 1964*. Washington, D.C.: Department of Commerce, 1965.

———. *Historical Statistics of the United States: Colonial Times to 1957*. Washington, D.C.: Government Printing Office, 1960.

U.S. Department of the Interior, *Compendium of the Tenth Census* (1880). (Washington, D.C.: Government Printing Office, 1883.

Van Cott, John W. *Utah Place Names*. Salt Lake City: University of Utah Press, 1990.

Warner, Ted J., ed. *The Domínguez-Escalante Journal*. Provo: Brigham Young University Press, 1976.

Woodbury, Angus M. "A History of Southern Utah and Its National Parks." *Utah Historical Quarterly* 12 (July–Oct. 1944): 111–223.

Wright, John B. *Rocky Mountain Divide: Selling and Saving the West*. Austin: University of Texas Press, 1993.

Young, John R. Journal. Utah State Historical Society.

———. "Memoirs of John R. Young." Utah State Historical Society.

Index